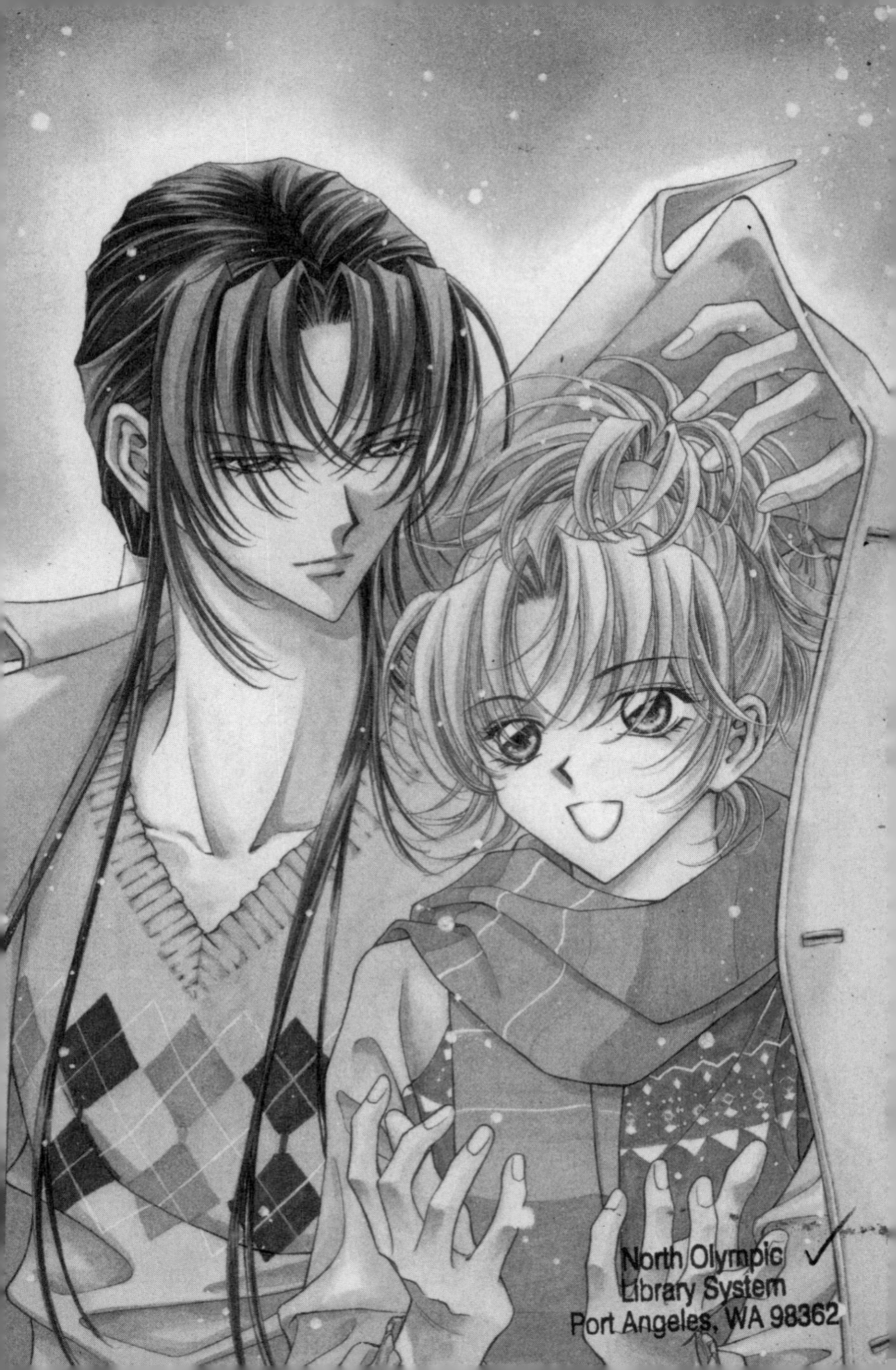

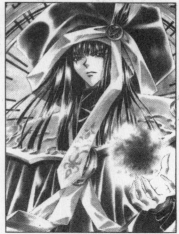

kara

DEMON DIARY

Translator - Lauren Na
English Adaptation - Kelly Sue DeConnick
Retouch and Lettering - Christina R. Siri
Cover Layout - Aaron Suhr
Graphic Designer - Deron Bennett

Editor - Rob Tokar
Managing Editor - Jill Freshney
Production Coordinator - Antonio DePietro
Production Manager - Jennifer Miller, Mutsumi Miyazaki
Art Director - Matt Alford
Editorial Director - Jeremy Ross
VP of Production - Ron Klamert
President & C.O.O. - John Parker
Publisher & C.E.O. - Stuart Levy

Email: editor@TOKYOPOP.com
Come visit us online at www.TOKYOPOP.com

A  Manga

TOKYOPOP Inc.
5900 Wilshire Blvd. Suite 2000
Los Angeles, CA 90036

Demon Diary Vol. 6

MAWAN-IGLI 1 ©2000 by KARA. All rights reserved.
First published in KOREA in 2000 by SIGONGSA Co., Ltd.
English translation rights arranged by SIGONGSA Co., Ltd.

English text copyright ©2004 TOKYOPOP Inc.

ISBN: 1-59182-431-1

First TOKYOPOP printing: March 2004

10 9 8 7 6 5 4 3 2 1
Printed in the USA

DEMON DIARY

Art by Kara
Story by Lee Yun Hee

VOLUME 6

Los Angeles • Tokyo • London

Who's Who In Demon Diary

An orphan, Raenef had to join thieves at an early age in order to survive. Among the thieves, Raenef's kind, gentle, and somewhat ditzy nature made him stand out. Approached by Eclipse, Raenef was eager for a change from his life of stealing just to eat. Unfortunately, Raenef's cheerful and kind-hearted qualities are even less desirable in a demon lord than they are in a thief. Though a poor student and a regular source of embarrassment for Eclipse, Raenef desperately wants to become the greatest demon lord ever. Recently, it was revealed that Raenef is actually the time-displaced future son of Raenef IV.

RAENEF

ECLIPSE

Tall, dark and mysterious, Eclipse is a wise and noble demon assigned by the gods to mentor Raenef. His new pupil's ineptitude is a blow to Eclipse's prestige in the courts. Despite their differences, Eclipse finds himself strangely drawn to Raenef.

Sensing powerful magic coming from Raenef's Castle, the human knight Erutis intended to build her reputation by slaying the demon lord within. At first, she found it hard to take Raenef seriously but, after breaking her sword on the demon-lord-in-training's head, Erutis soon found herself outmatched. To save her life, she convinced Raenef to take her on as his henchman rather than killing her. Since then, she has become Raenef's close friend...and Chris's daily tormentor.

Erutis

Five years ago, a force of demons descended on a town and utterly destroyed it. During the attack, only Chris' heart called out for the god Rased and, thus, Rased spared Chris's young life. The sole survivor of the attack, Chris was rescued by Heiem, High Cleric of the nearby Temple of Rased. Sensing that Chris was brimming with the power of the great god Rased, Heiem took the youngster as his disciple and designated Chris to be the temple's next High Cleric. As an act of mercy, Rased suppressed Chris's traumatic memories, telling Heiem that they would one day resurface. Rased also indicated that the world of the demon lords is soon to change and, at that time, Chris will lead Rased's people. Unaware of Rased's prophesies, Chris has grown into a headstrong, egotistical, demon-hating, bratty young man. Against Heiem's wishes, Chris created a Demon Summoning sign and captured Raenef. The scuffle between the demon lord-in-training and the future High Cleric was brief and, as an apology (and to teach Chris humility), Heiem sent Chris to live with Raenef for a short time. Despite himself, Chris has developed a friendship with Raenef.

Chris

A beautiful female demon seer with an unrequited crush on Eclipse. When Eclipse was assigned to locate Raenef the Fifth, it was Meruhesae who pointed the demon in the right direction. When Raenef the Fourth returned from the dead, he warned Meruhesae--and the rest of demonkind--not to interfere with events at Castle Raenef.

Meruhesae

THE DEMON LORD RAENEF THE FOURTH WAS A POWERFUL AND RESPECTED DEMO LORD WHO, THROUGH THE MASTERY OF INCANTATIONS, BECAME THE MOST POWE FUL OF HIS KIND. 150 YEARS AGO, DURINC THE HANGMA WAR, RAENEF WAS EXTER MINATING THE CREATURES OF HEAVEN WITH IMPUNITY. REALIZING THAT RAENEF COULD NOT BE STOPPED BY ANY CONVEN- TIONAL MEANS, MANY OF THE CREATURES OF HEAVEN SACRIFICED THEIR LIVES TO CURSE RAENEF WITH THE ANNIHILATION OF THE NAME, A CURSE DESIGNED TO SHORTEN A DEMON LORD'S LIFE...AND TO DESTROY HIS HEIRS. RAENEF WITHDREW I AN ATTEMPT TO STUDY AND COUNTER THE CURSE AND, TWO DAYS AFTER HE CLAIME TO HAVE SUCCEEDED, THE DEMON LORD RAENEF THE FOURTH DIED...UNTIL NOW.

RAENEF IV

THE DEMON LORD OF EGAE, KRAYON IS ONE OF THE FIVE OLDEST DEMONS IN EXISTENCE (THOUGH HE CERTAINLY DOESN'T LOOK IT.) DURING KRAYON'S FAILED ATTEMPT TO LURE ECLIPSE AWAY FROM SERVING RAENEF, KRAYON MET--AND, APPARENTLY, FELL FOR--THE KNIGHT KNOWN AS ERUTIS.

KRAYON

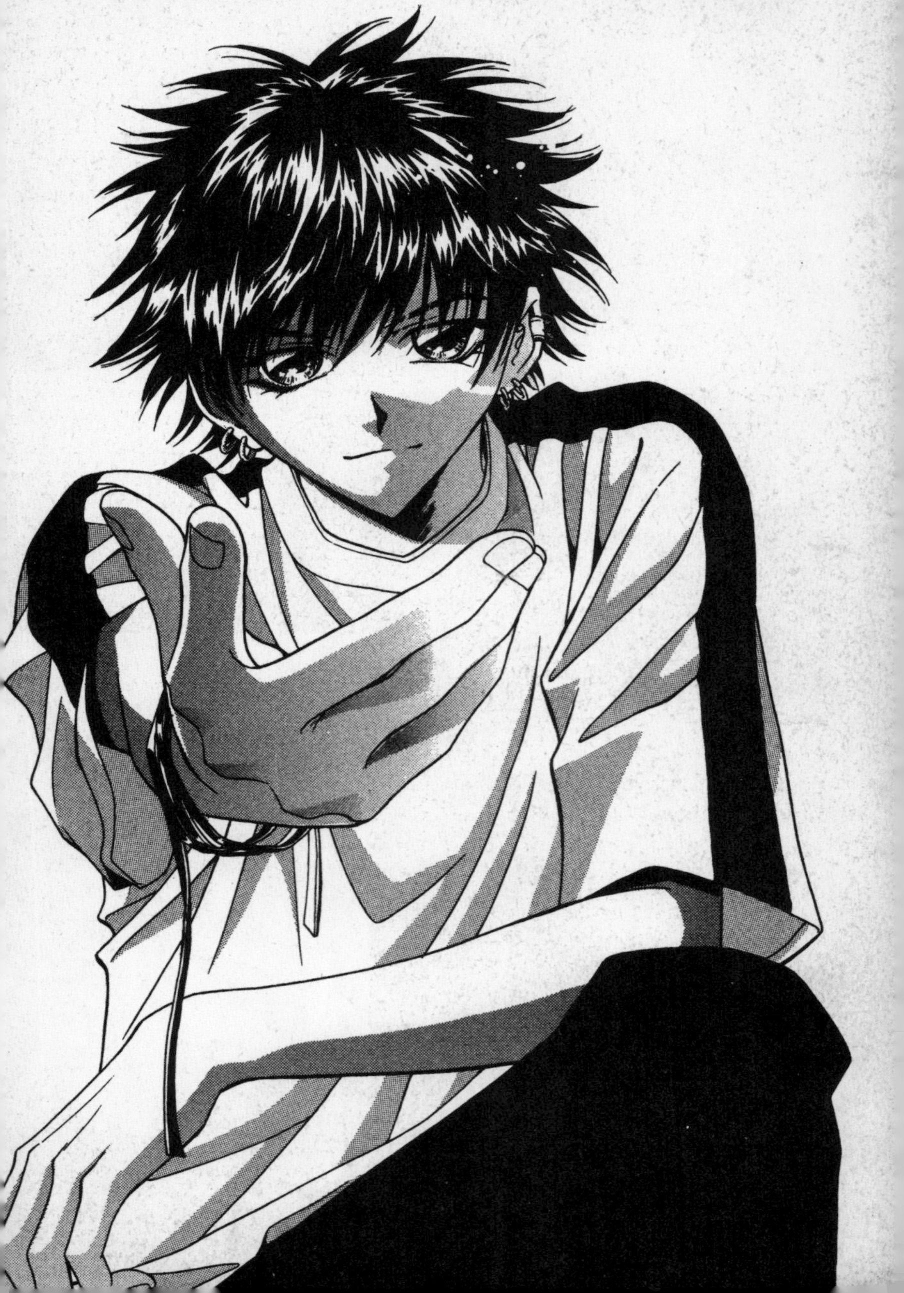

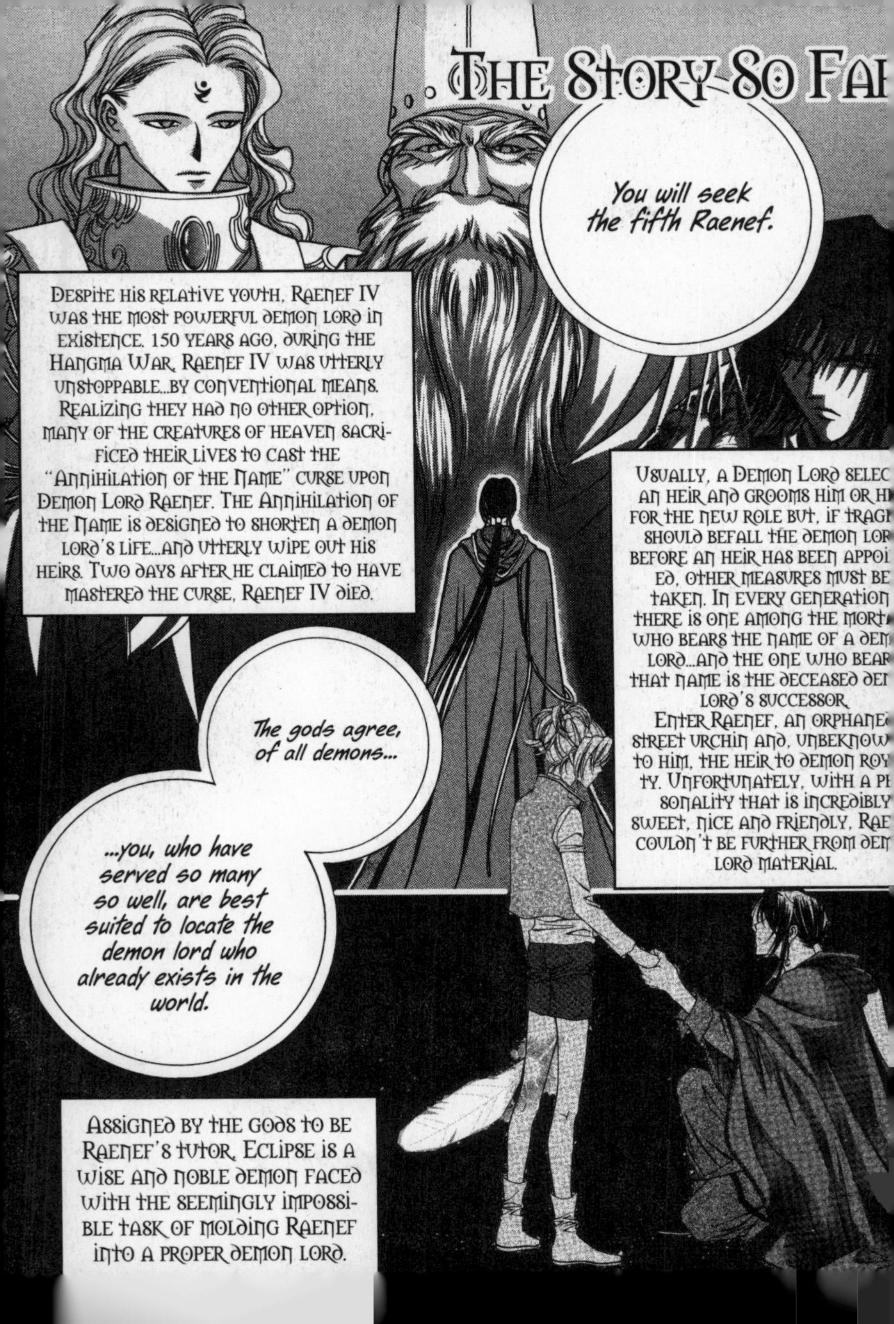
The Story So Fa
You will seek the fifth Raenef.
Despite his relative youth, Raenef IV was the most powerful demon lord in existence. 150 years ago, during the Hangma War, Raenef IV was utterly unstoppable...by conventional means. Realizing they had no other option, many of the creatures of heaven sacrificed their lives to cast the "Annihilation of the Name" curse upon Demon Lord Raenef. The Annihilation of the Name is designed to shorten a demon lord's life...and utterly wipe out his heirs. Two days after he claimed to have mastered the curse, Raenef IV died.
Usually, a Demon Lord selec an heir and grooms him or h for the new role but, if trag should befall the demon lor before an heir has been appoi ed, other measures must be taken. In every generation there is one among the mort who bears the name of a dem lord...and the one who bear that name is the deceased de lord's successor.
Enter Raenef, an orphane street urchin and, unbeknow to him, the heir to demon roy ty. Unfortunately, with a p sonality that is incredibly sweet, nice and friendly, Rae couldn't be further from de lord material.
The gods agree, of all demons...
...you, who have served so many so well, are best suited to locate the demon lord who already exists in the world.
Assigned by the gods to be Raenef's tutor, Eclipse is a wise and noble demon faced with the seemingly impossible task of molding Raenef into a proper demon lord.

What?!

You? You're the demon lord?!

A DEMON LORD'S LIFE IS NOT WITHOUT PERIL, HOWEVER, AND RAENEF HAS ALREADY FACED SEVERAL ATTACKS BY THOSE BENT ON DESTROYING HIS KIND. HOWEVER, DUE TO RAENEF'S LOVABLE NATURE, TWO OF HIS ATTACKERS (A HUMAN KNIGHT KNOWN AS ERUTIS AND THE FUTURE HIGH CLERIC TO THE TEMPLE OF RASED NAMED CHRIS) NOW LIVE IN RAENEF'S CASTLE AS HIS COMPANIONS.

JUST WHEN IT SEEMED THAT LIFE IN CASTLE RAENEF COULDN'T GET ANY CRA-ZIER, A FLOCK OF HEAVEN'S CREATURES DESCENDED TO CARRY OUT THE REST OF THE ANNIHILATION OF THE NAME. AS THE CREATURES OF HEAVEN BROUGHT RAENEF V'S "EVIL" PERSONALITY TO THE FORE, ALL WERE SHOCKED BY THE SUDDEN APPEARANCE OF RAENEF IV. THE FORMERLY DECEASED DEMON LORD THEN ORDERED CHRIS TO SUMMON THE POWER OF THE GOD RASED AND USE IT TO ATTACK RAENEF V!

Game over, kid...

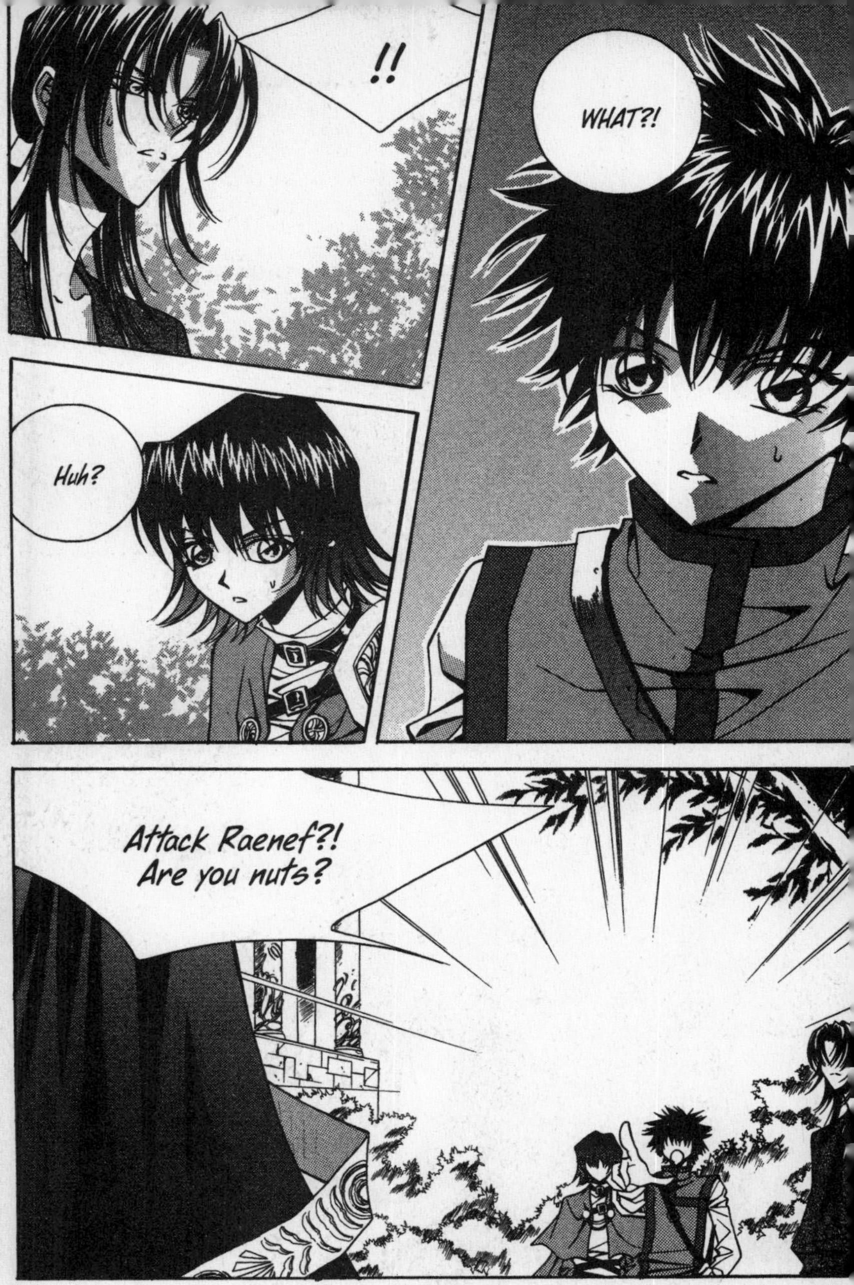
!!
WHAT?!
Huh?
Attack Raenef?!
Are you nuts?

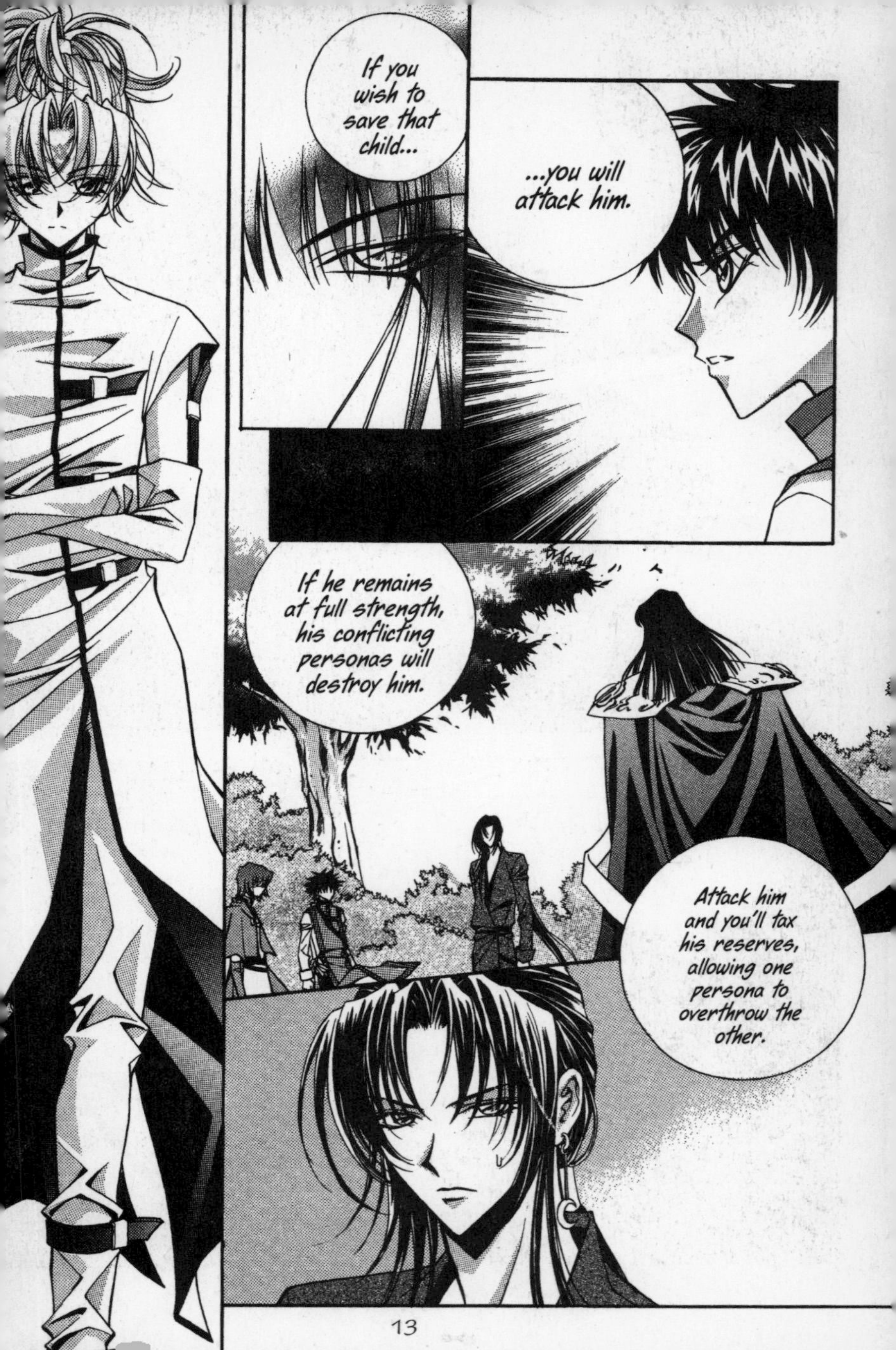

If you wish to save that child...
...you will attack him.
If he remains at full strength, his conflicting personas will destroy him.
Attack him and you'll tax his reserves, allowing one persona to overthrow the other.

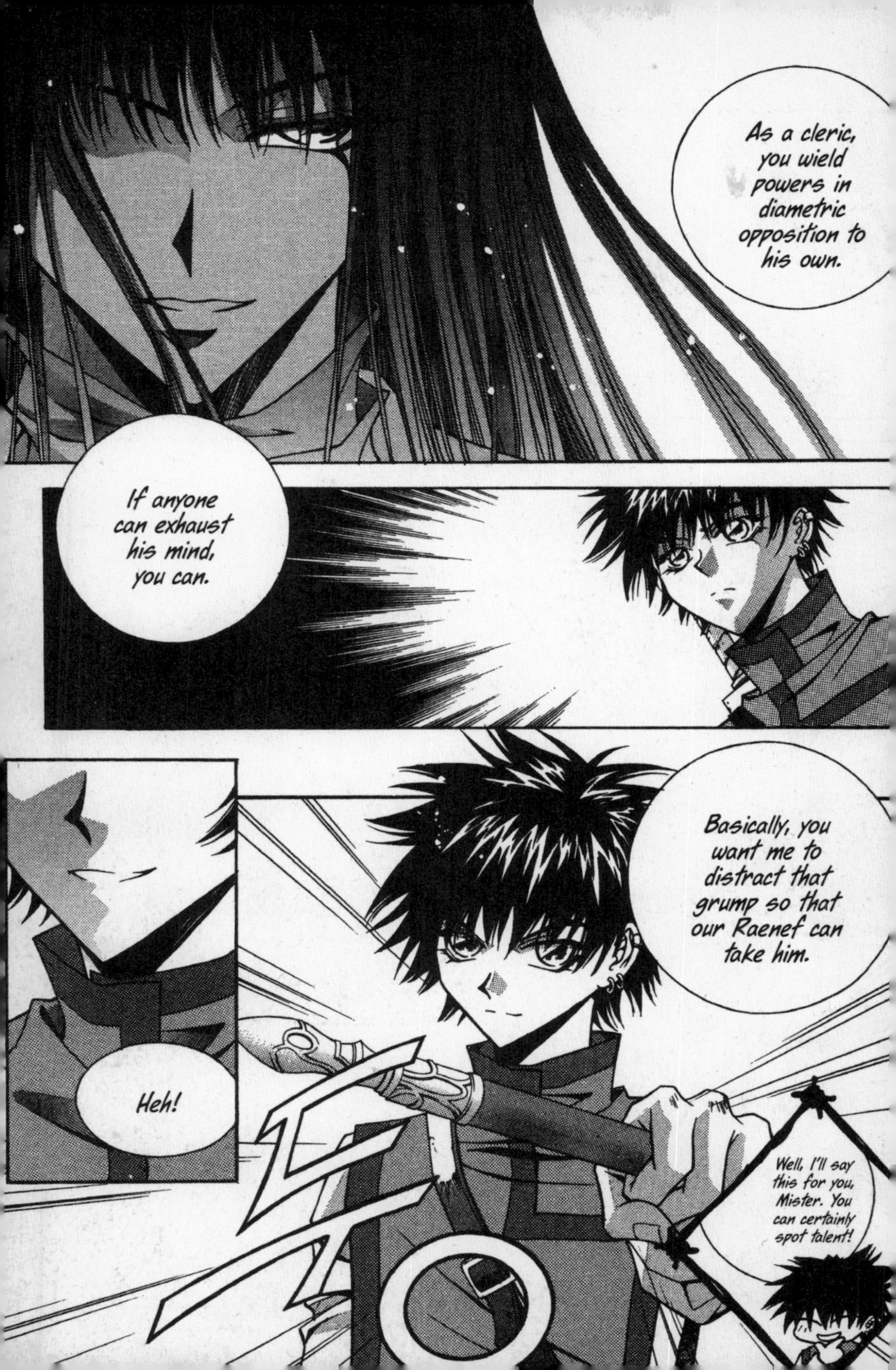
As a cleric, you wield powers in diametric opposition to his own.
If anyone can exhaust his mind, you can.
Heh!
Basically, you want me to distract that grump so that our Raenef can take him.
Well, I'll say this for you, Mister. You can certainly spot talent!

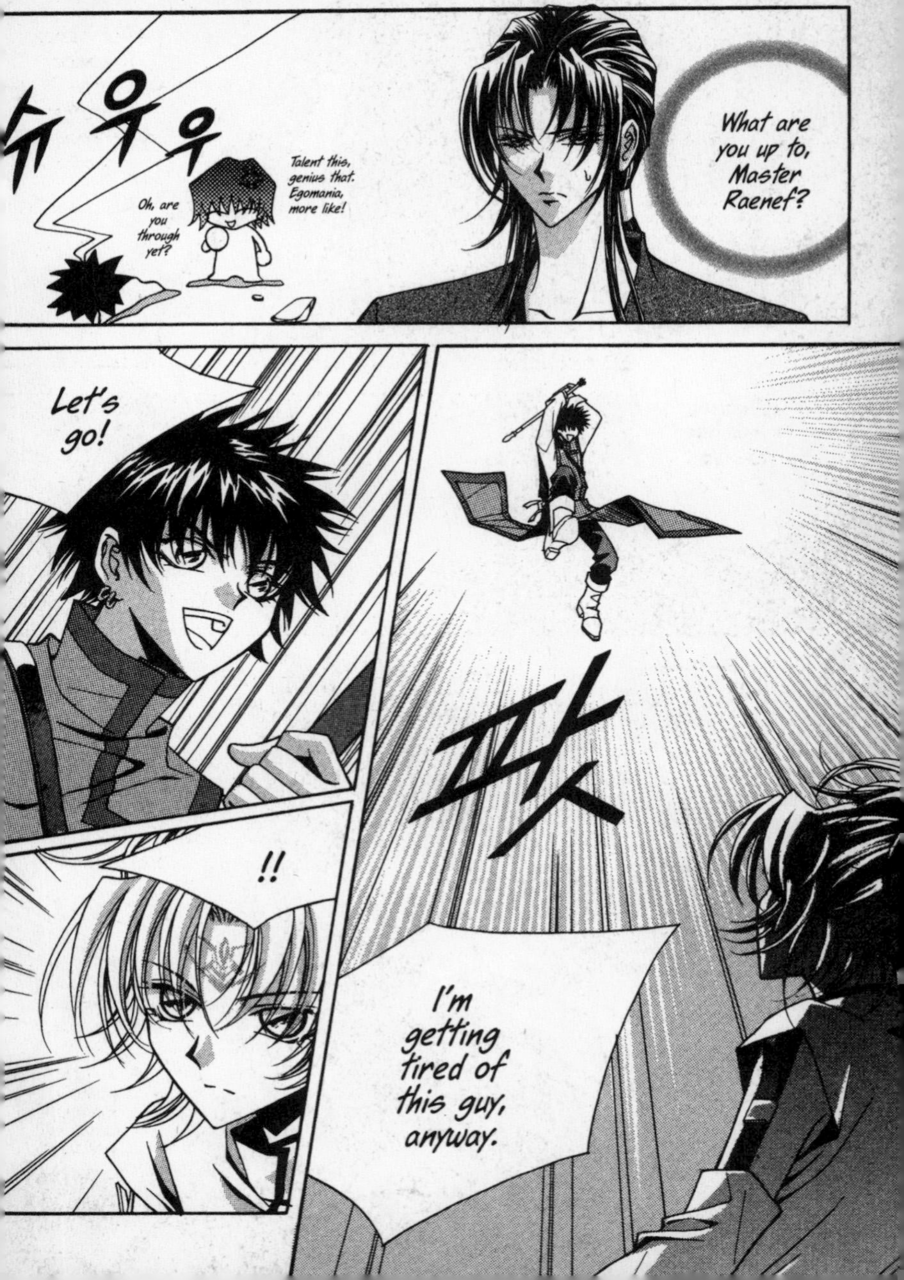

슈우우
Oh, are you through yet?
Talent this, genius that. Egomania, more like!
What are you up to, Master Raenef?
Let's go!
!!
팟
I'm getting tired of this guy, anyway.

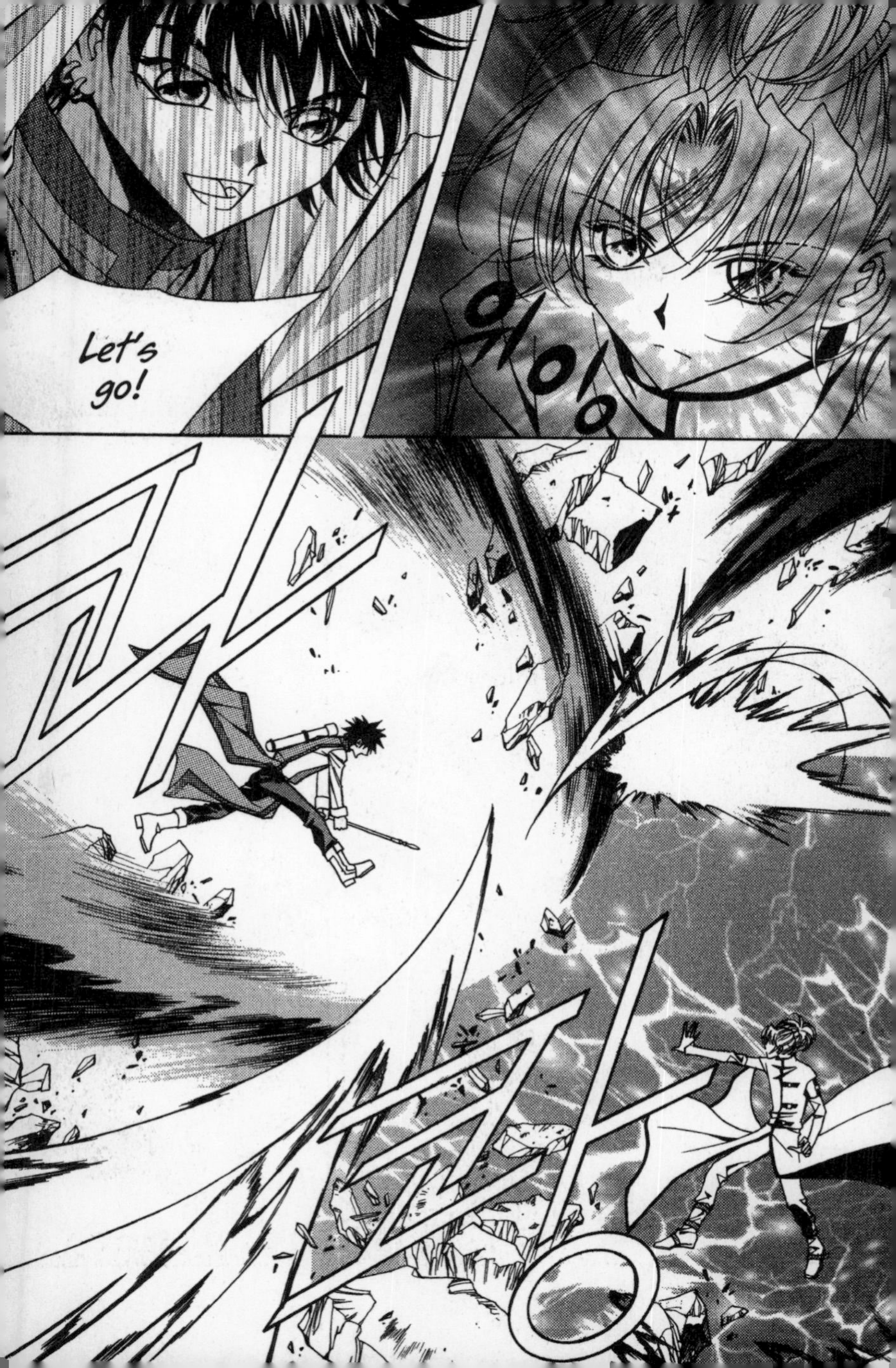
Let's go!

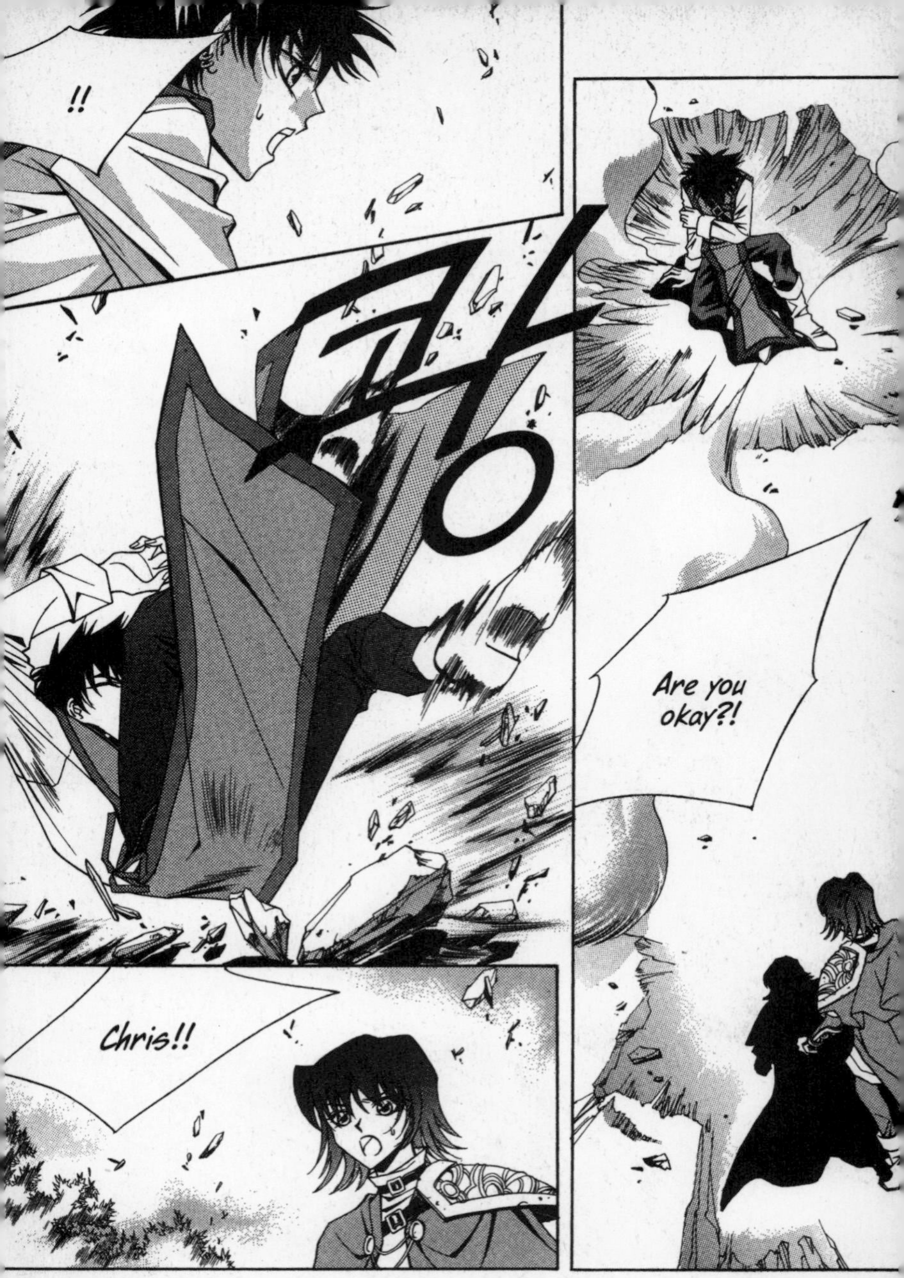
!!
Chris!!
Are you okay?!

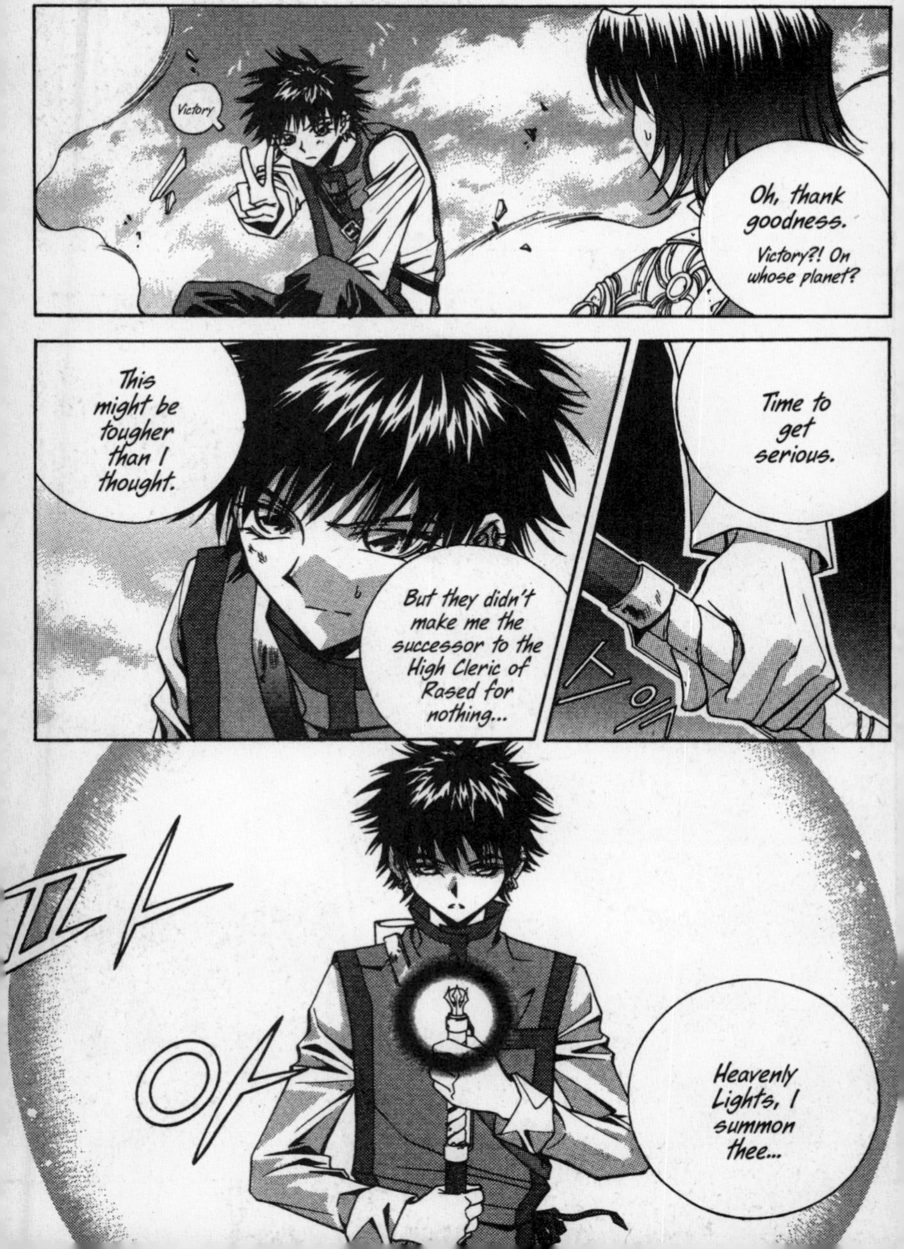
Victory
Oh, thank goodness.
Victory?! On whose planet?
This might be tougher than I thought.
But they didn't make me the successor to the High Cleric of Rased for nothing...
Time to get serious.
Heavenly Lights, I summon thee...

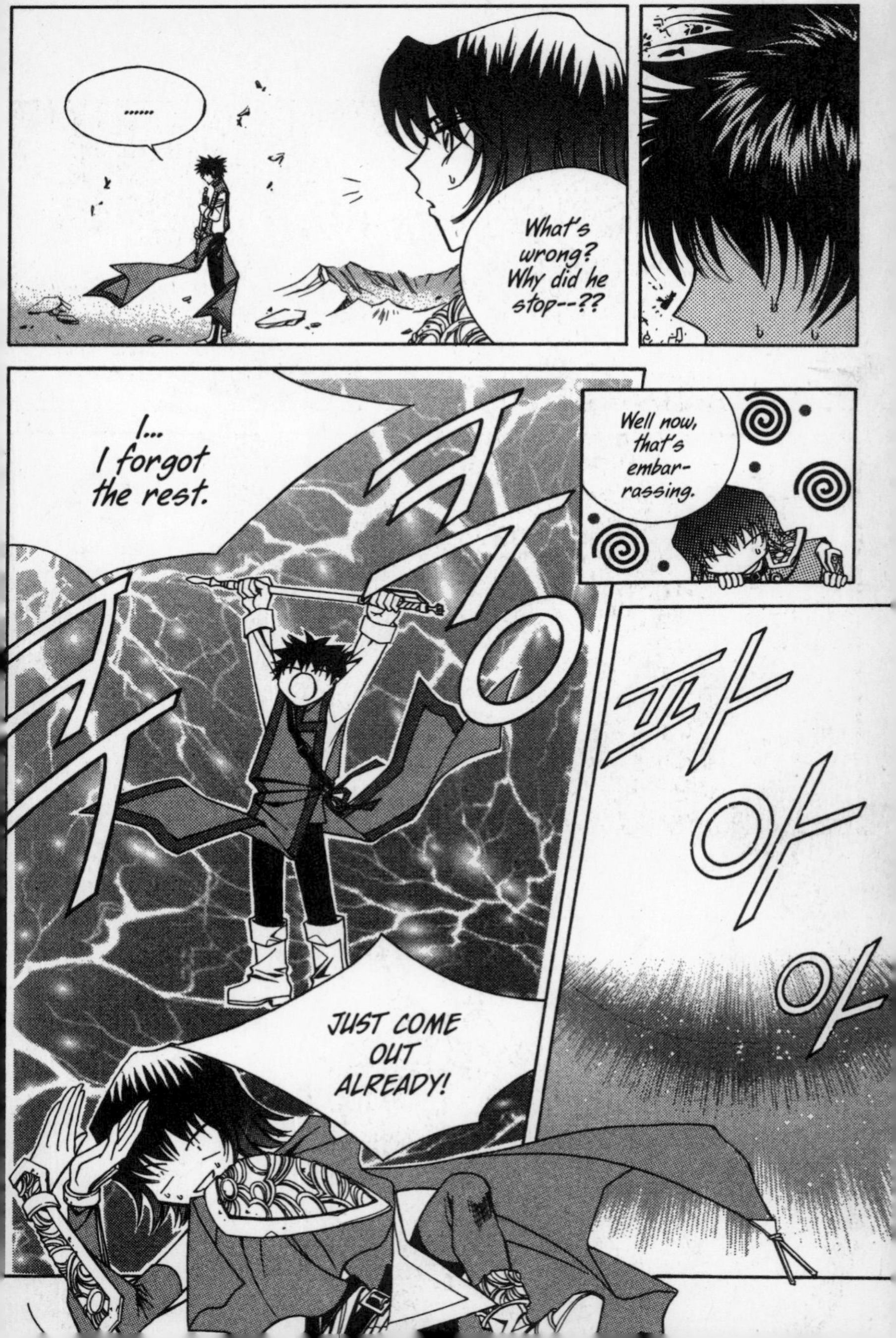
......
What's wrong? Why did he stop--??
I... I forgot the rest.
Well now, that's embarrassing.
JUST COME OUT ALREADY!

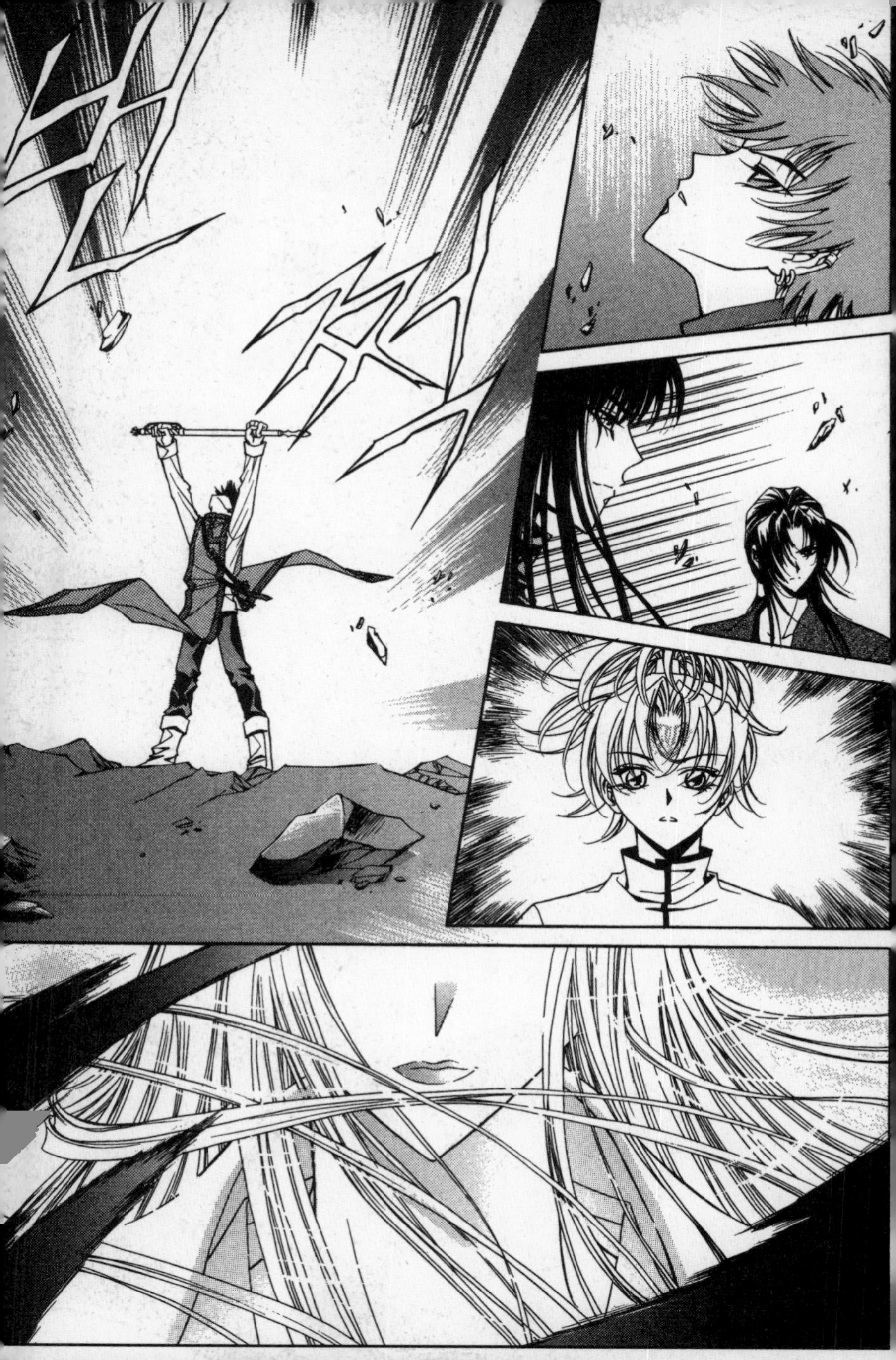

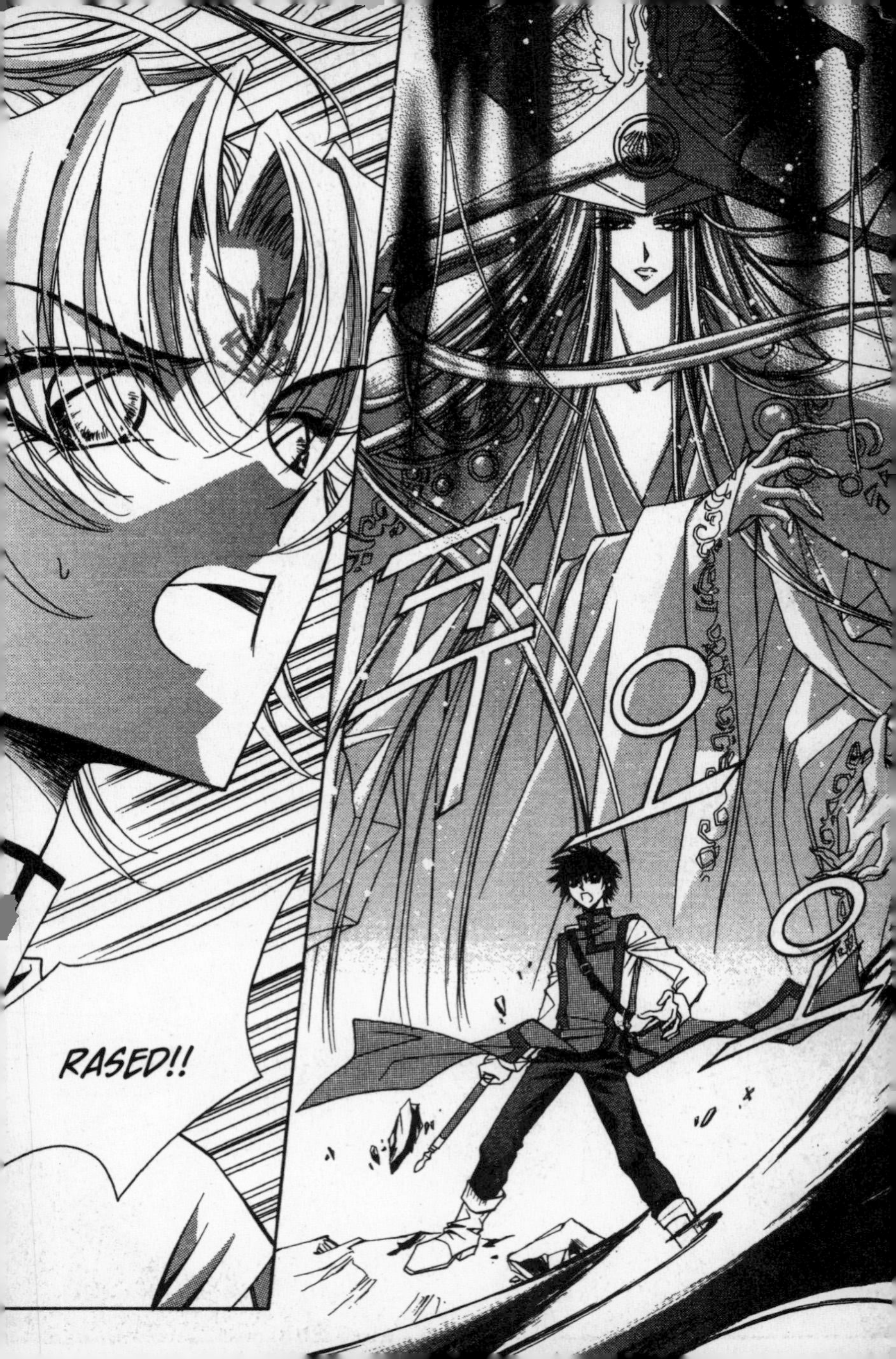
RASED!!

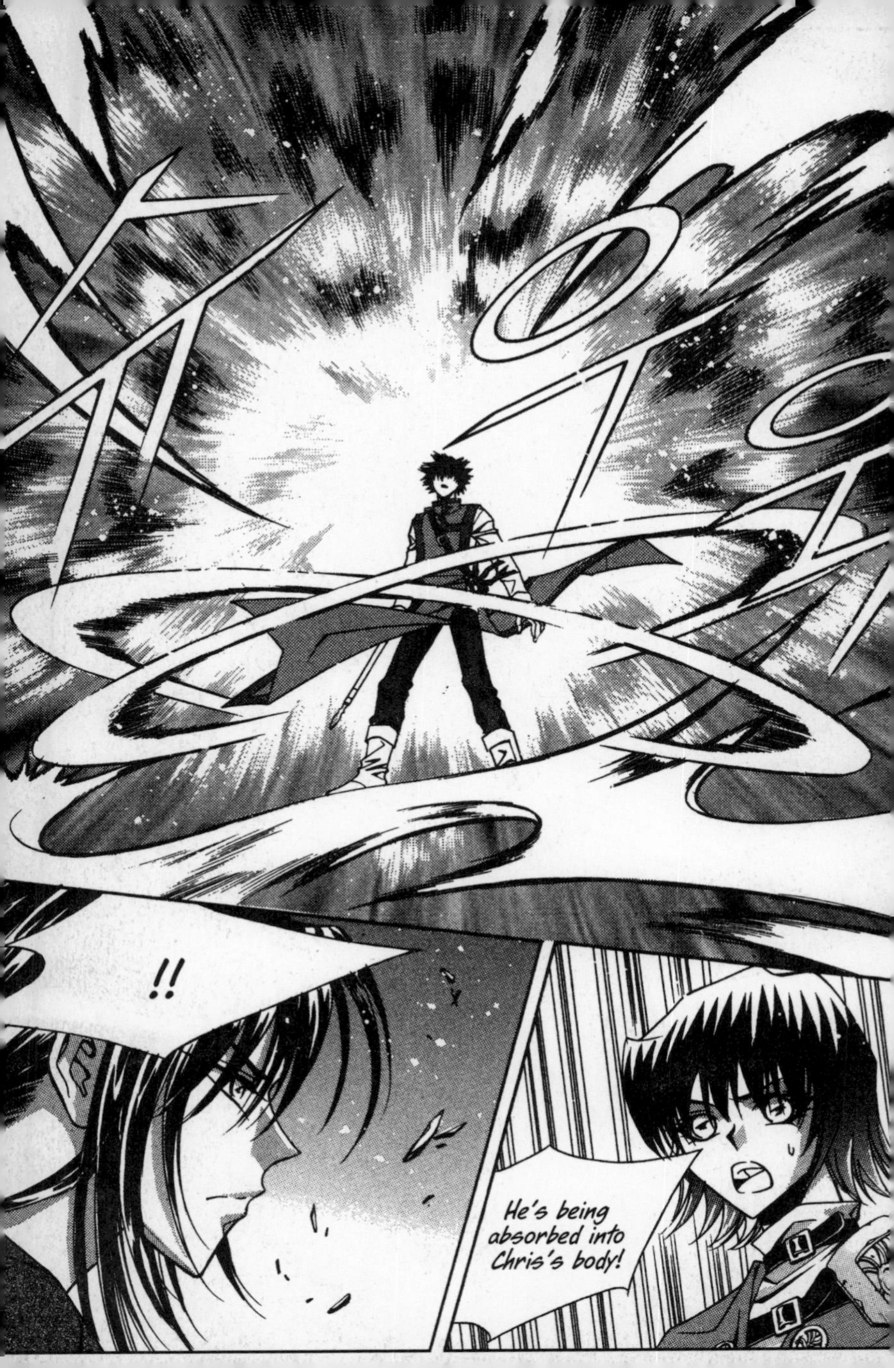
!!
He's being absorbed into Chris's body!

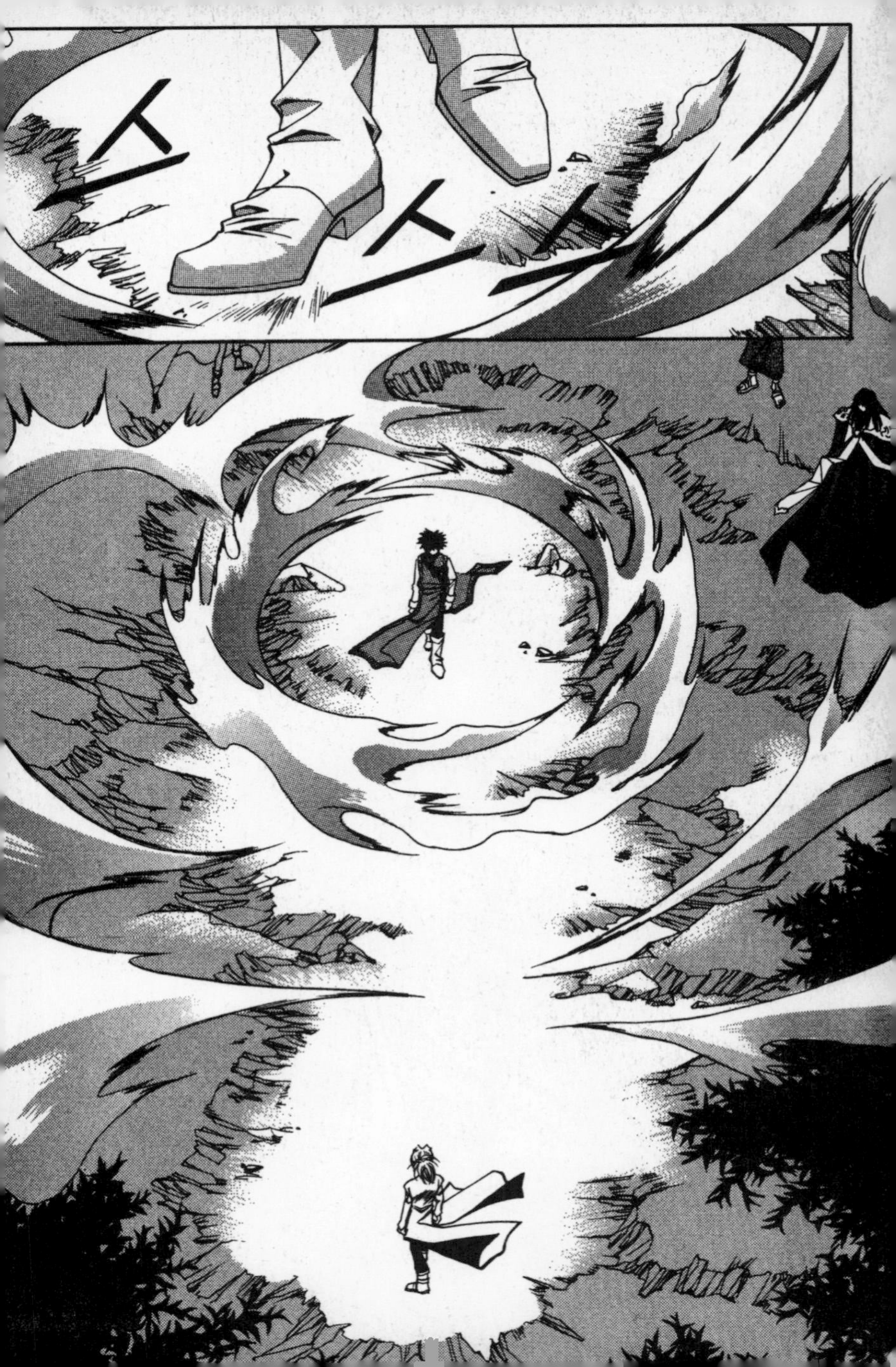

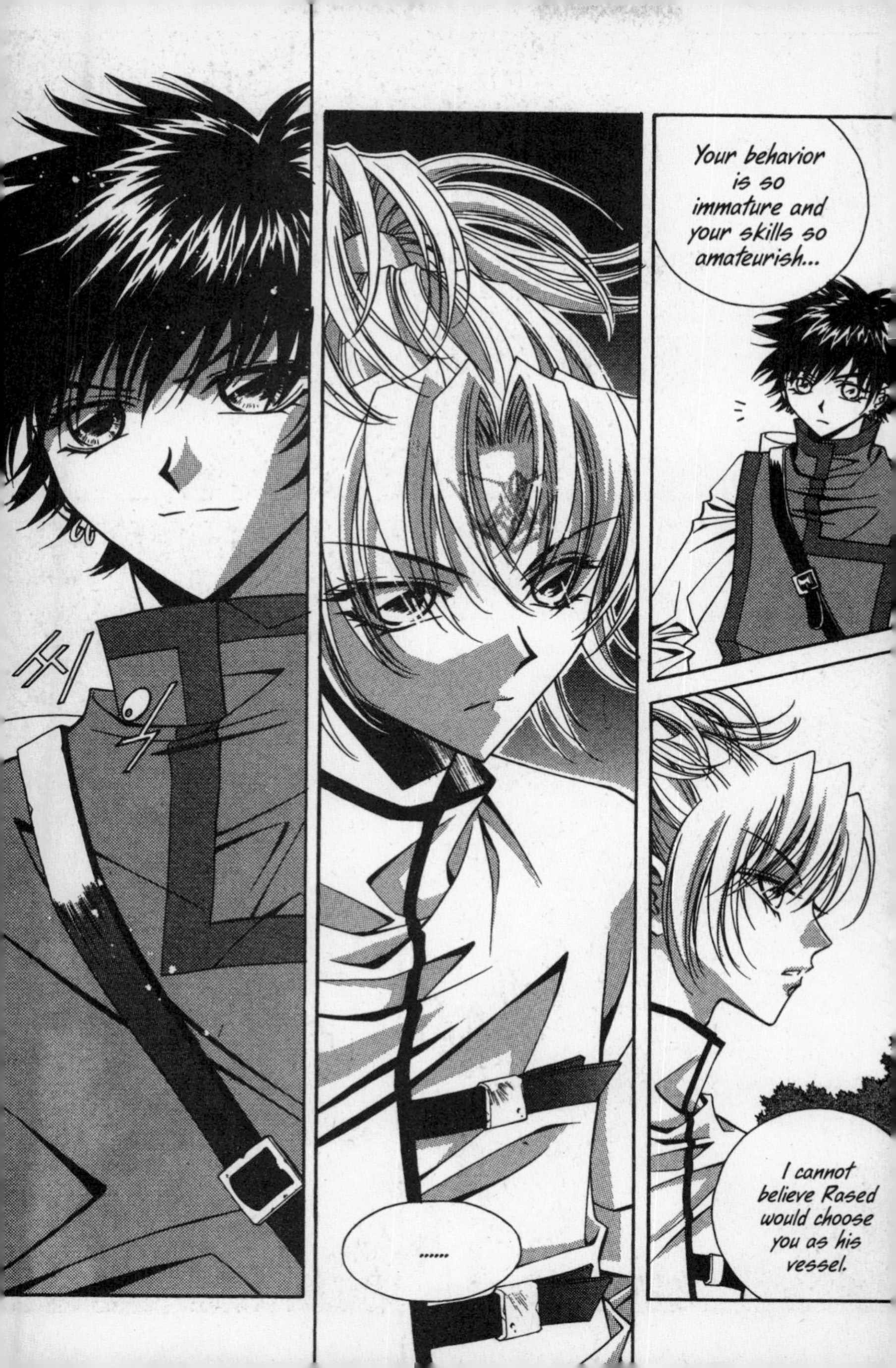
......
Your behavior is so immature and your skills so amateurish...
I cannot believe Rased would choose you as his vessel.

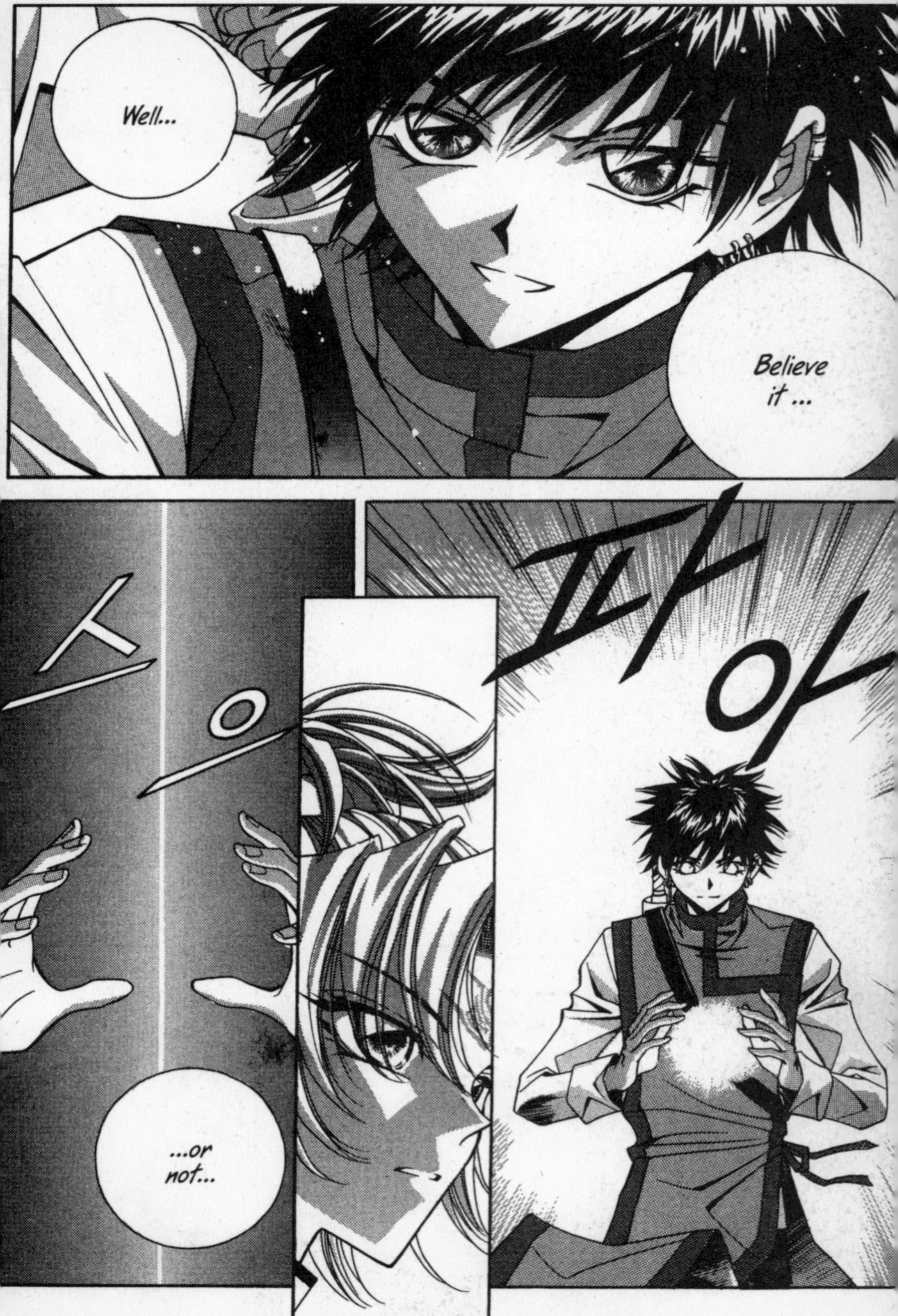
Well...
Believe it ...
스으
...or not...
파아

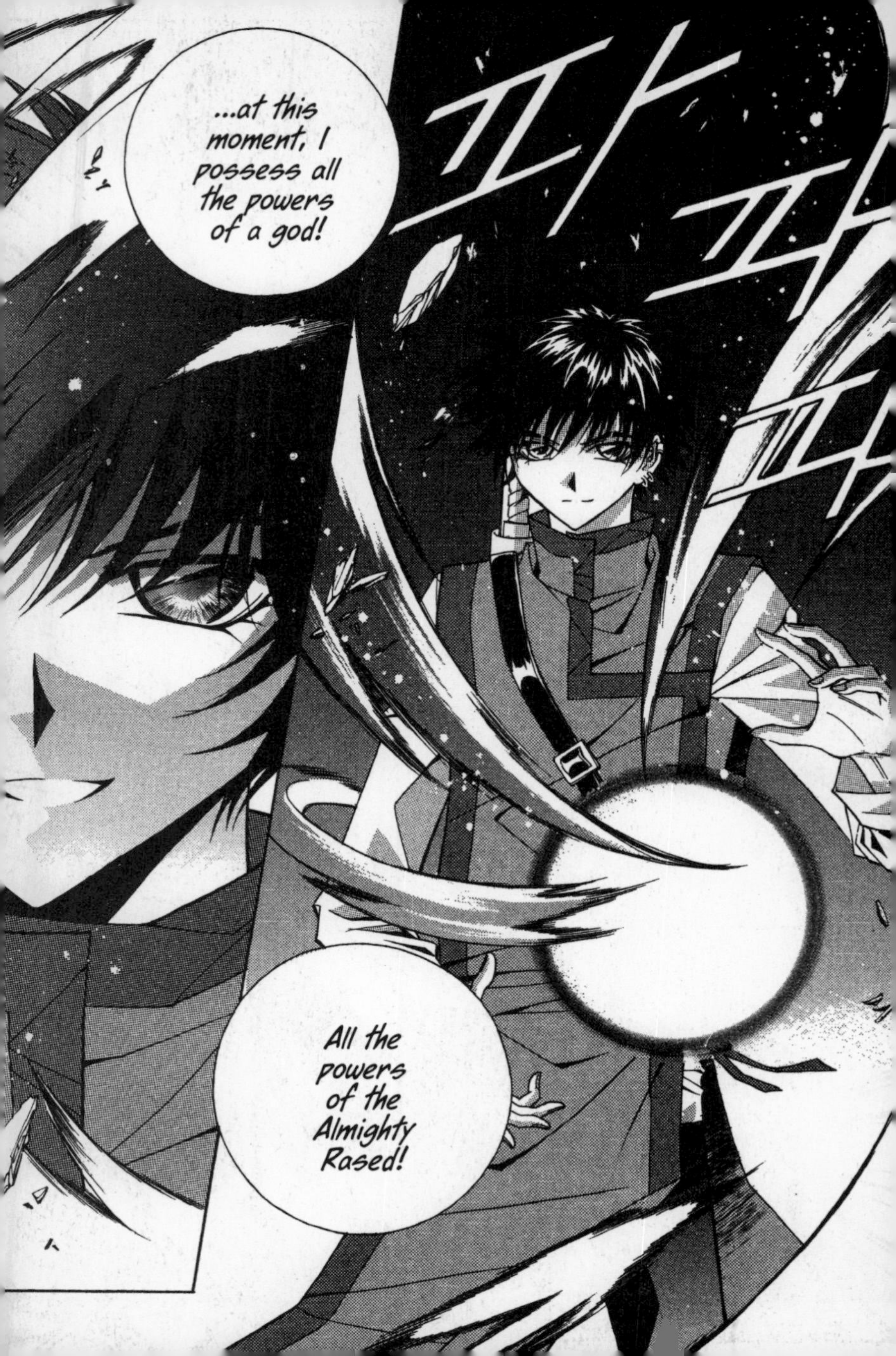
...at this moment, I possess all the powers of a god!
All the powers of the Almighty Rased!

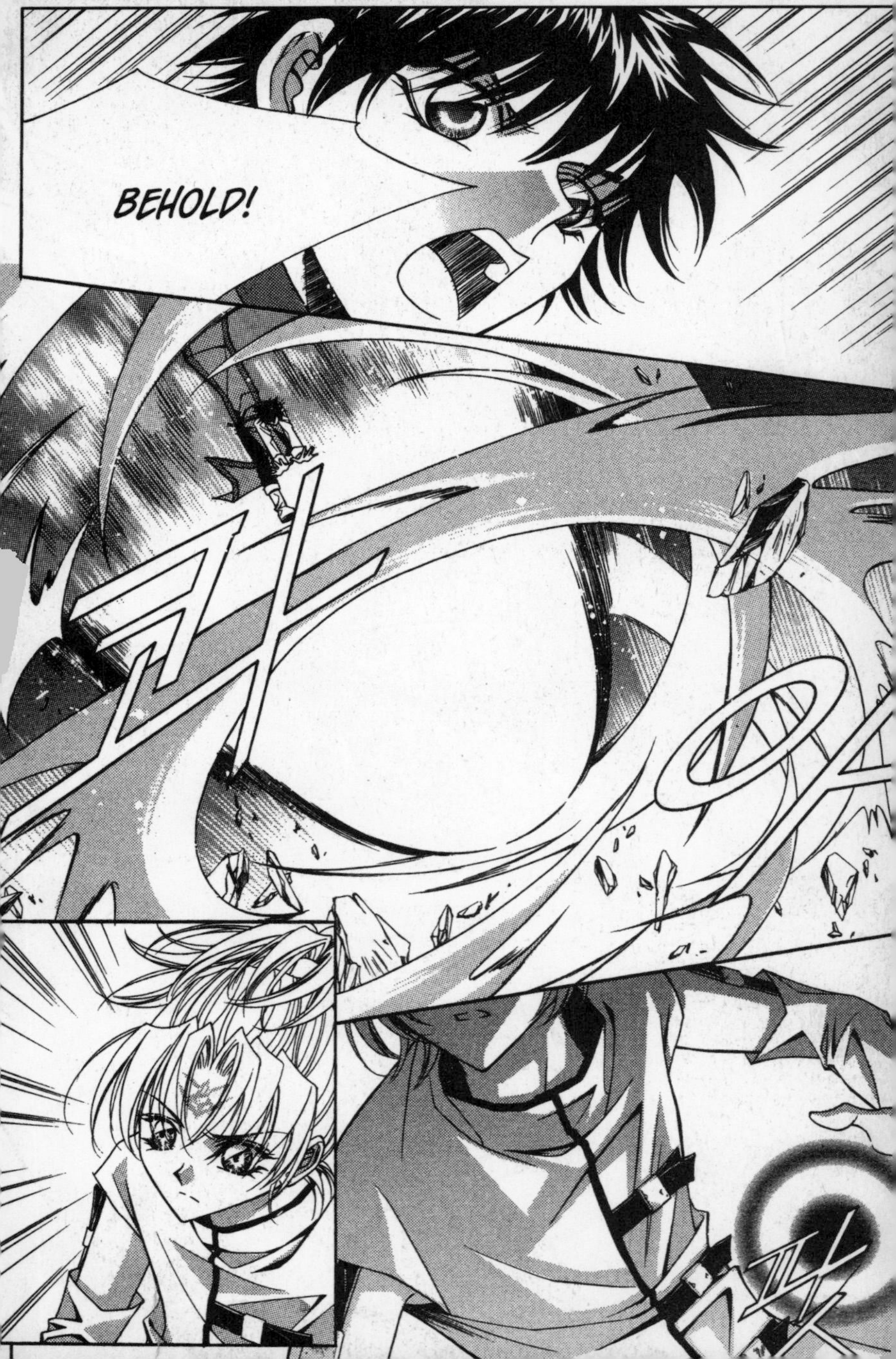
BEHOLD!

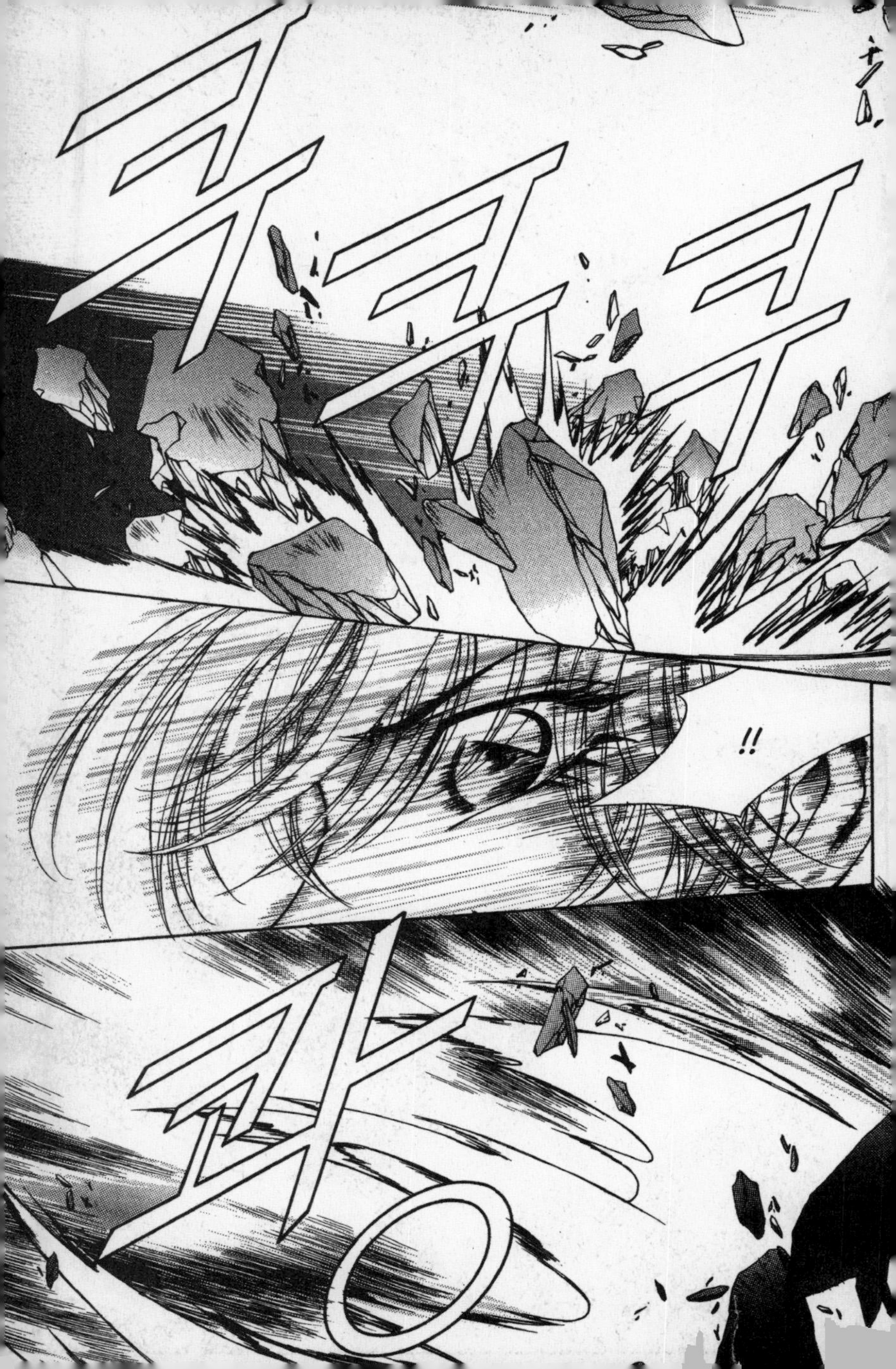
!!

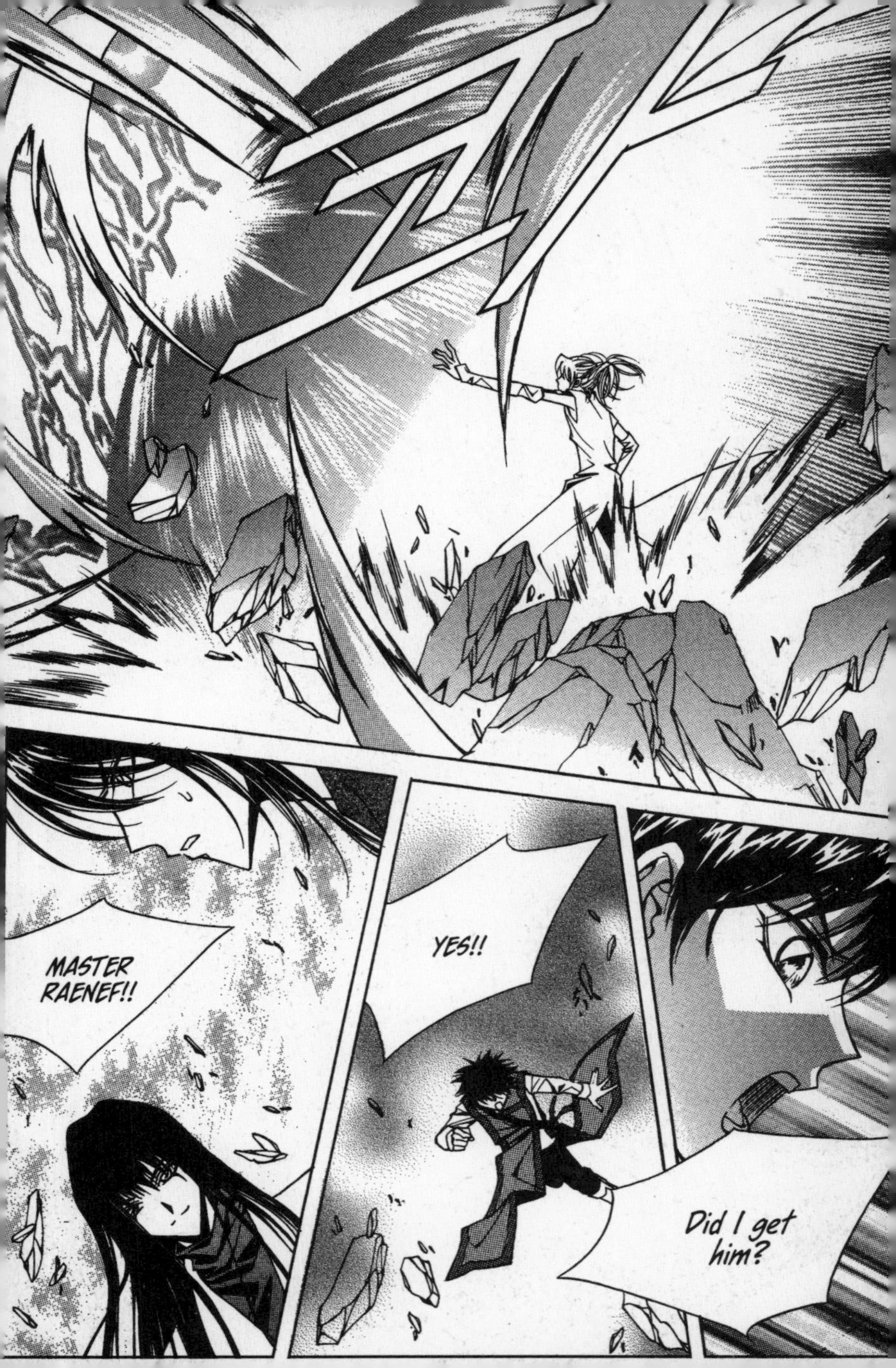
MASTER RAENEF!!
YES!!
Did I get him?

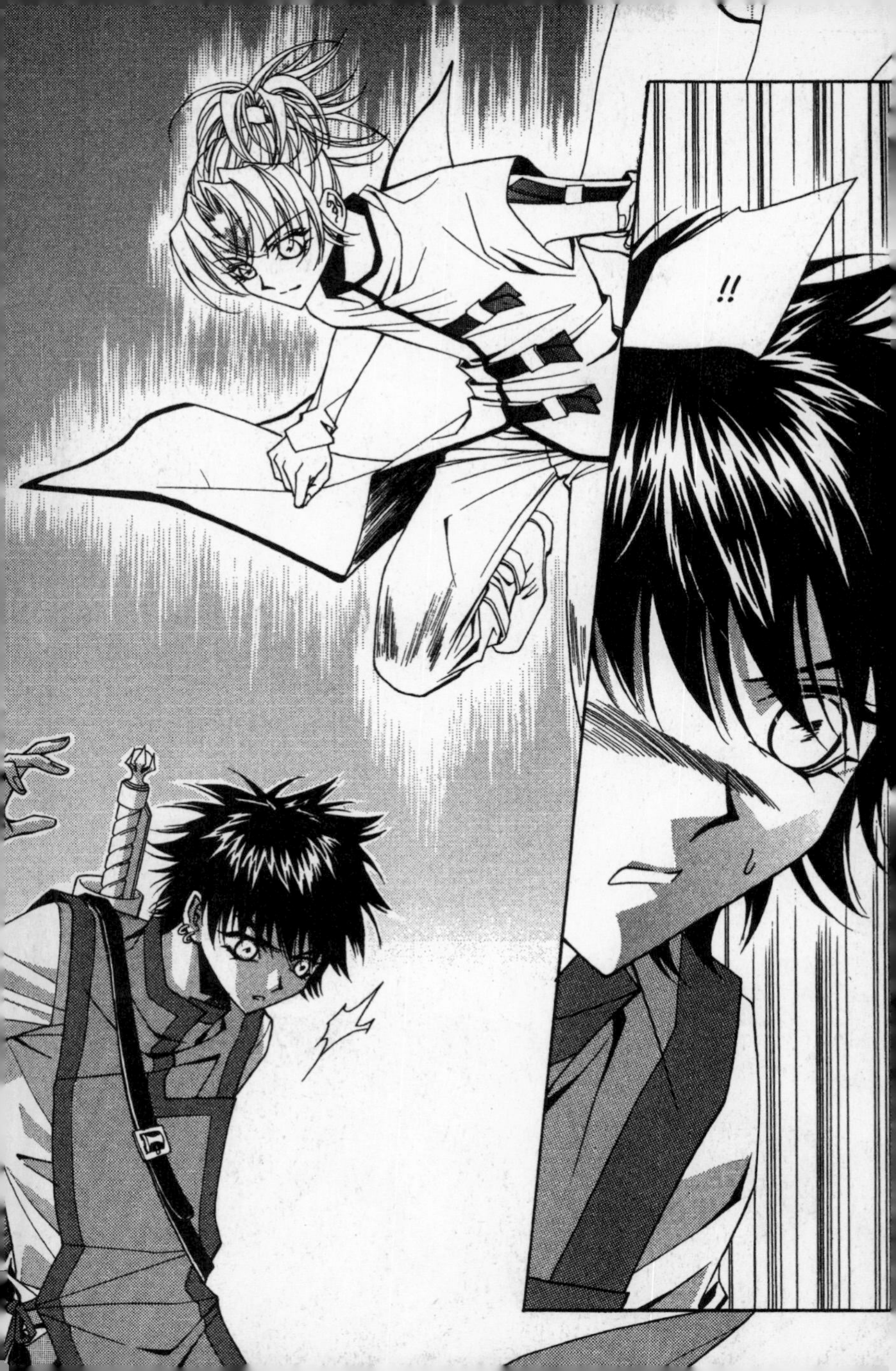
!!

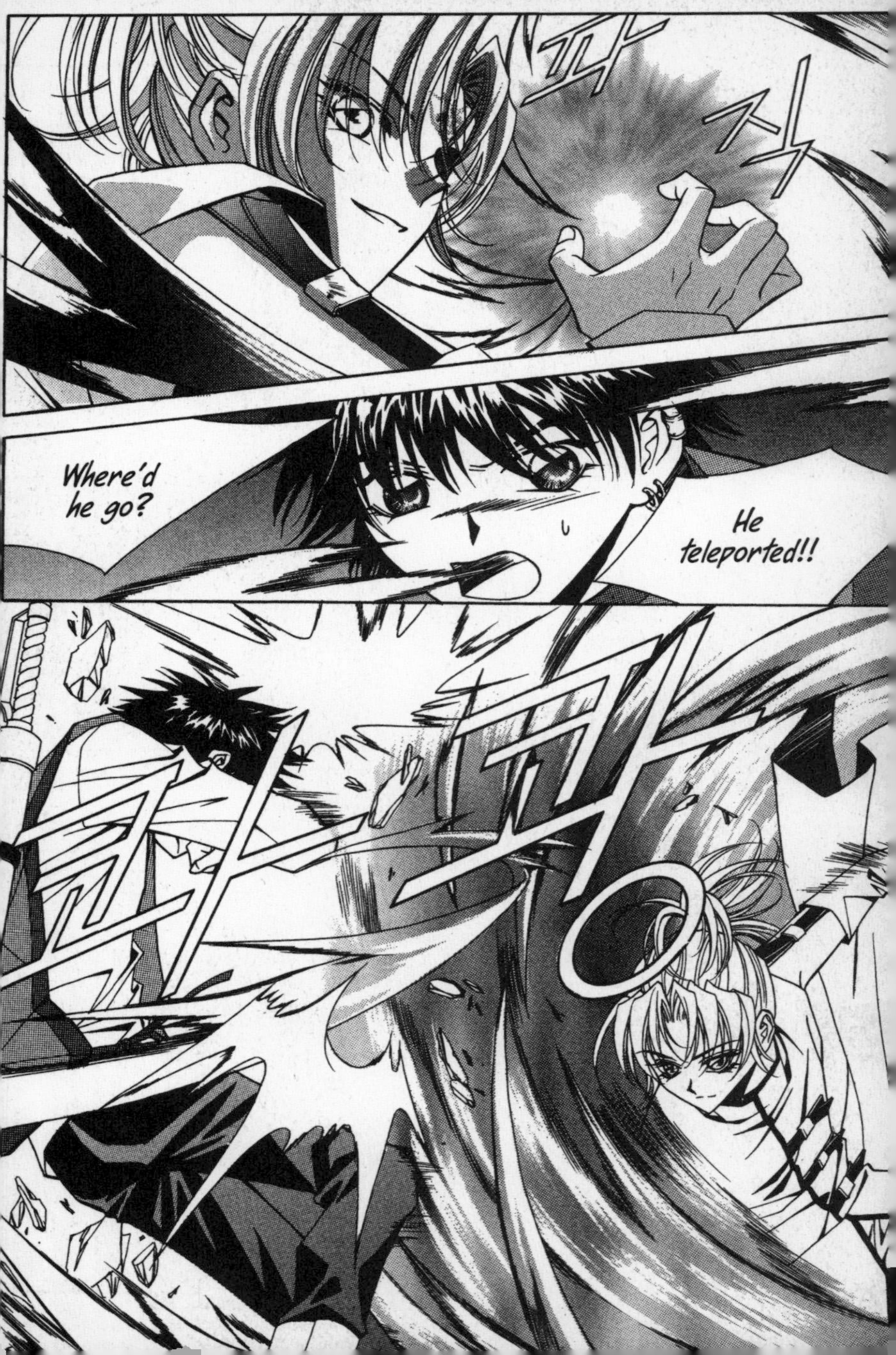
Where'd he go?
He teleported!!

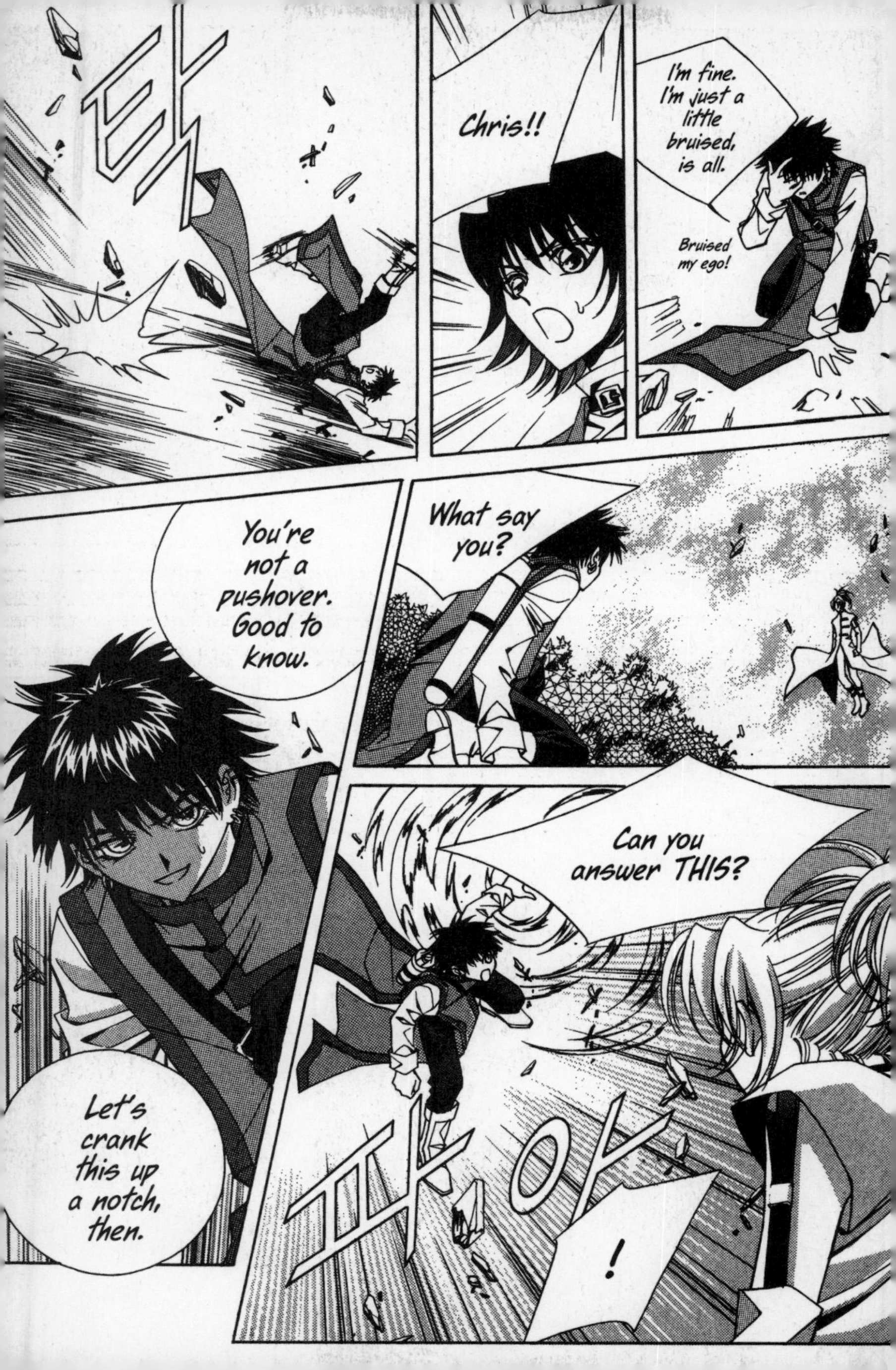
Chris!!
I'm fine. I'm just a little bruised, is all.
Bruised my ego!
You're not a pushover. Good to know.
Let's crank this up a notch, then.
What say you?
Can you answer THIS?
!

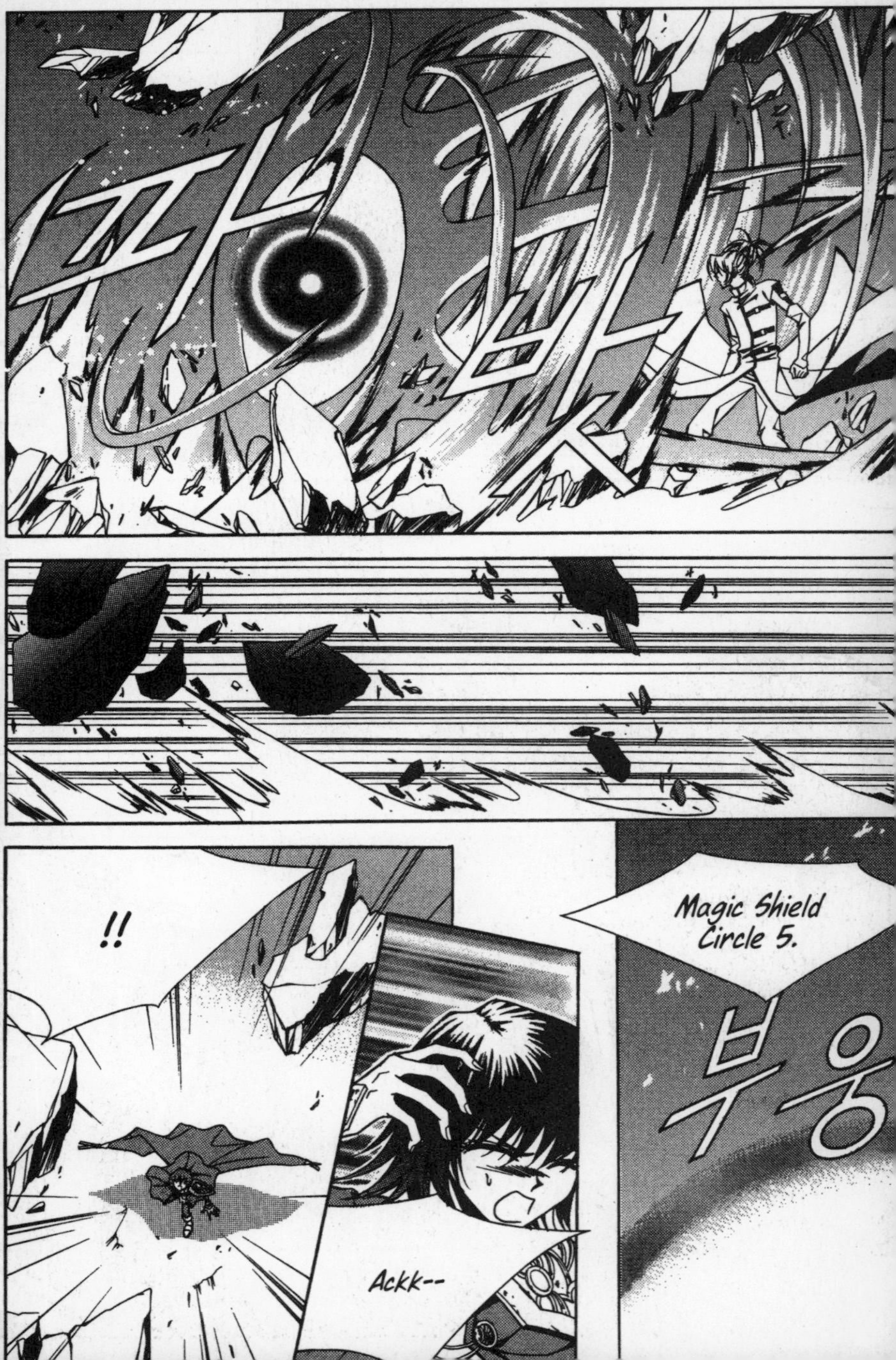
!!
Ackk--
Magic Shield
Circle 5.
부웅

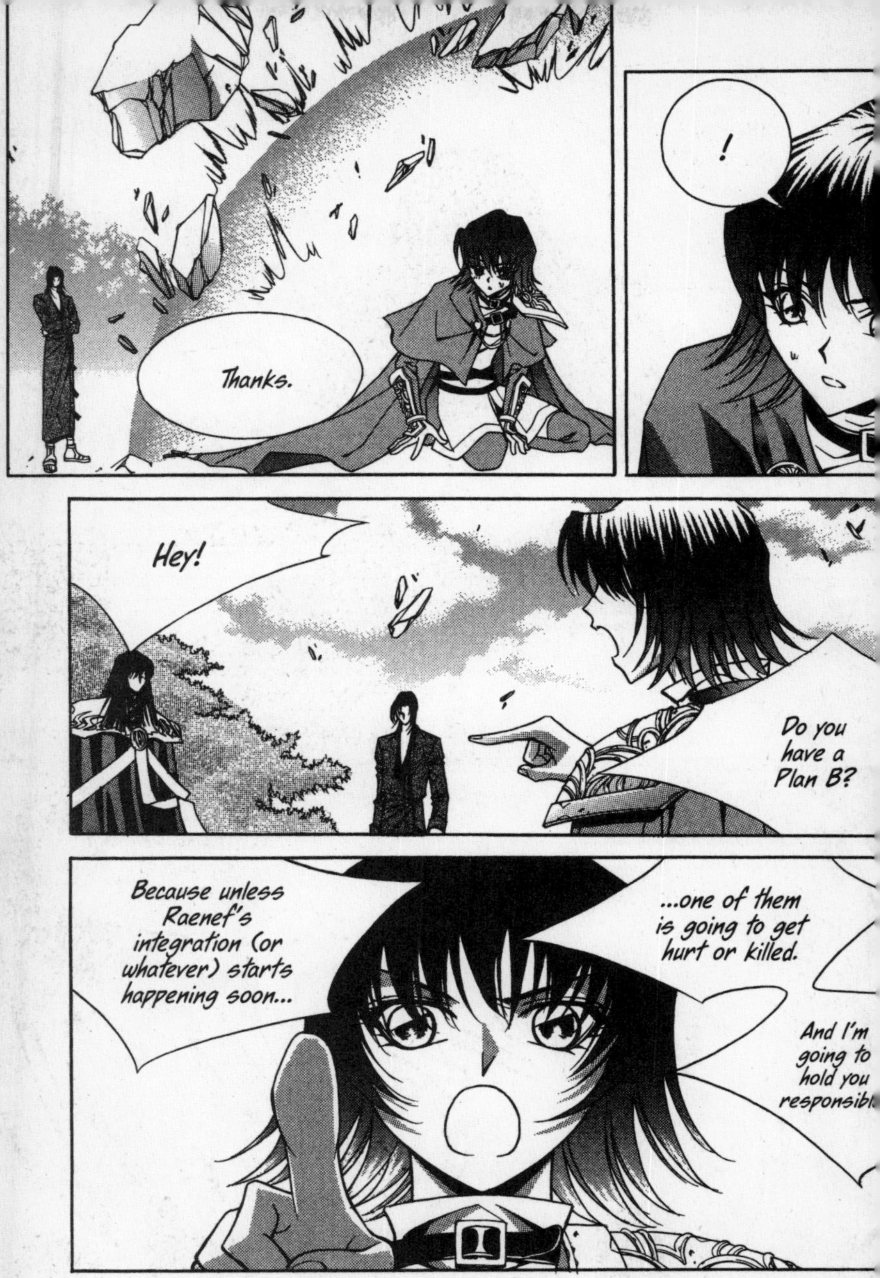
Thanks.
!
Hey!
Do you have a Plan B?
Because unless Raenef's integration (or whatever) starts happening soon...
...one of them is going to get hurt or killed.
And I'm going to hold you responsibl

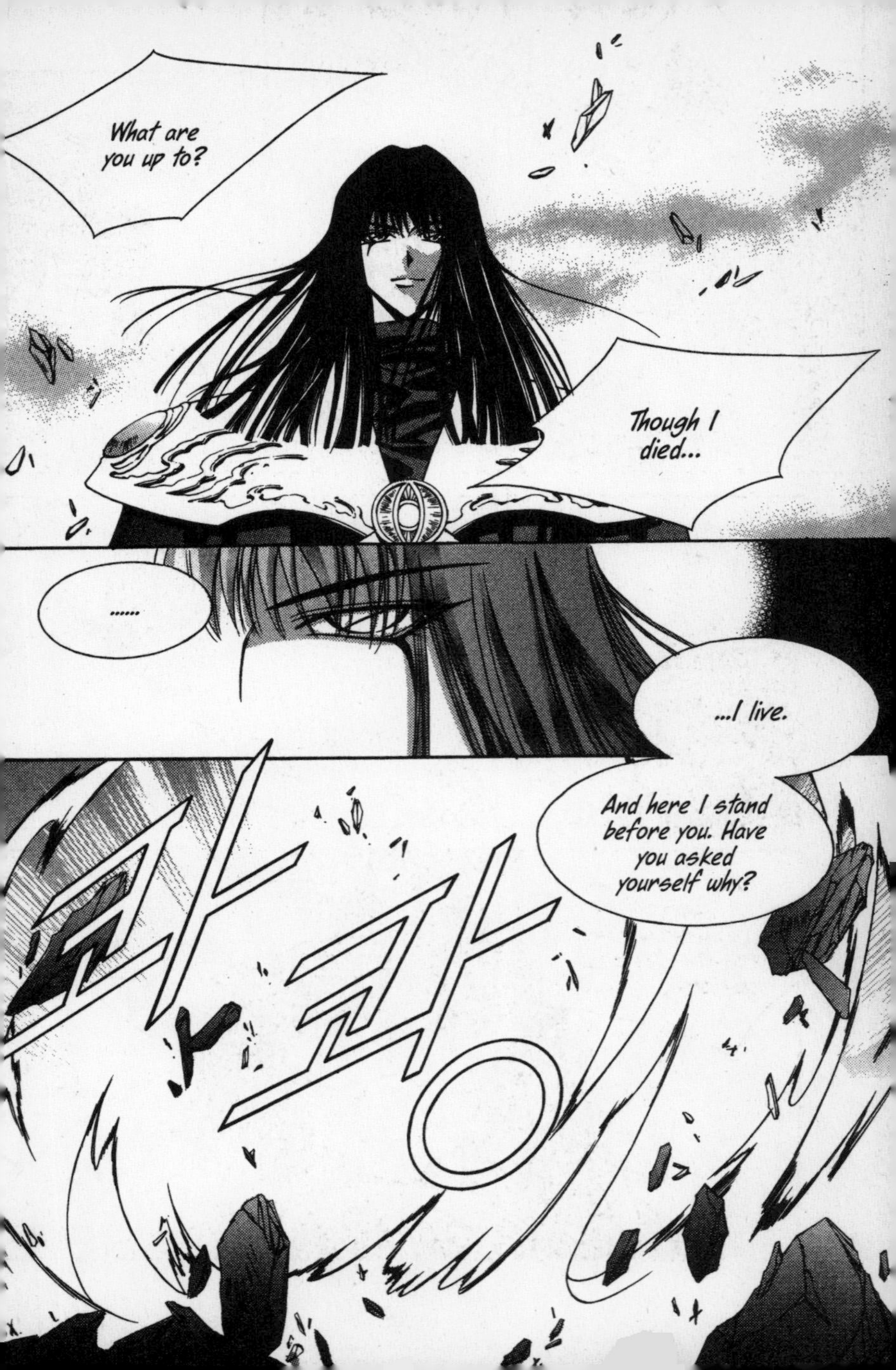
What are you up to?
Though I died...
......
...I live.
And here I stand before you. Have you asked yourself why?

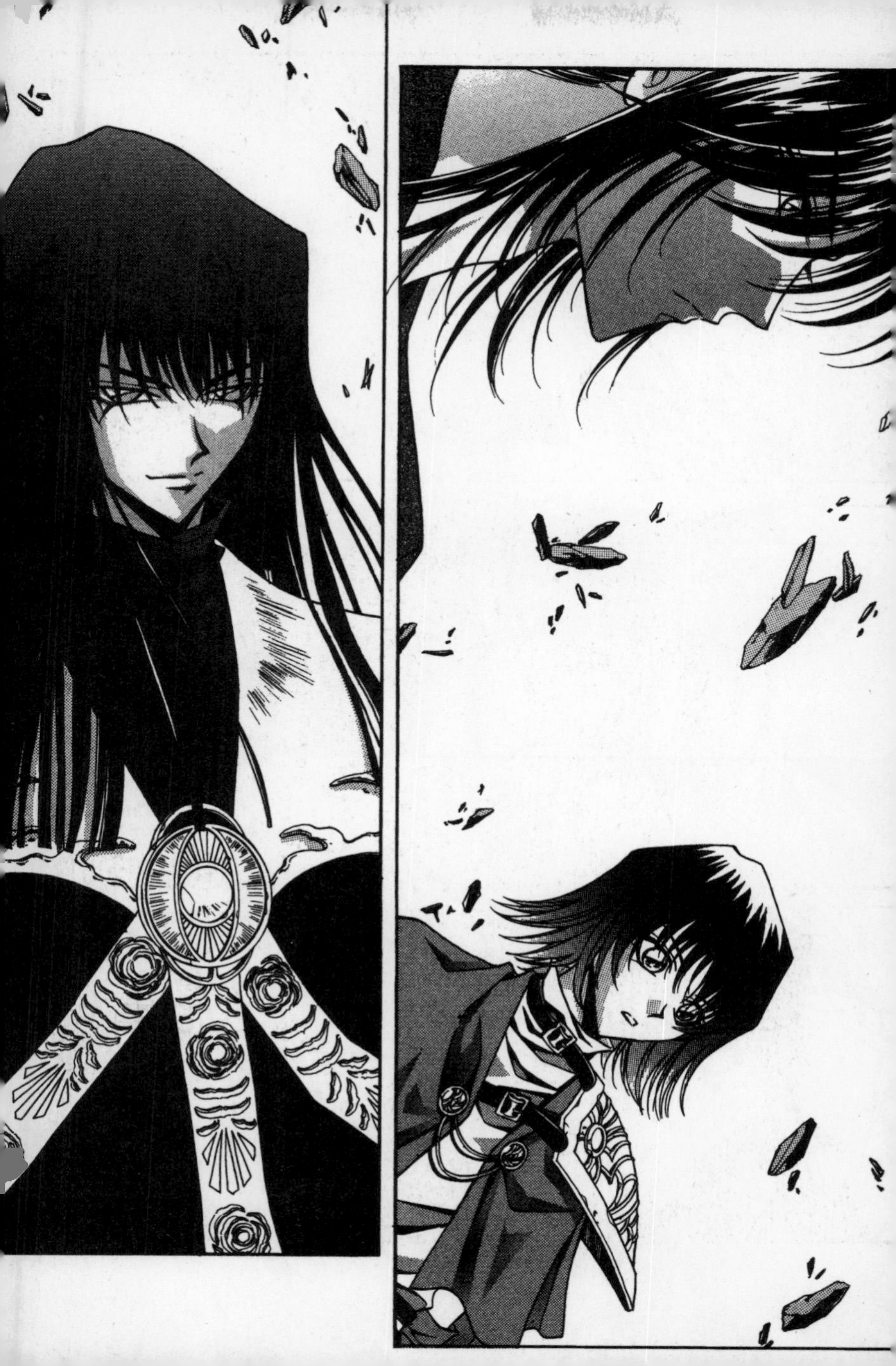

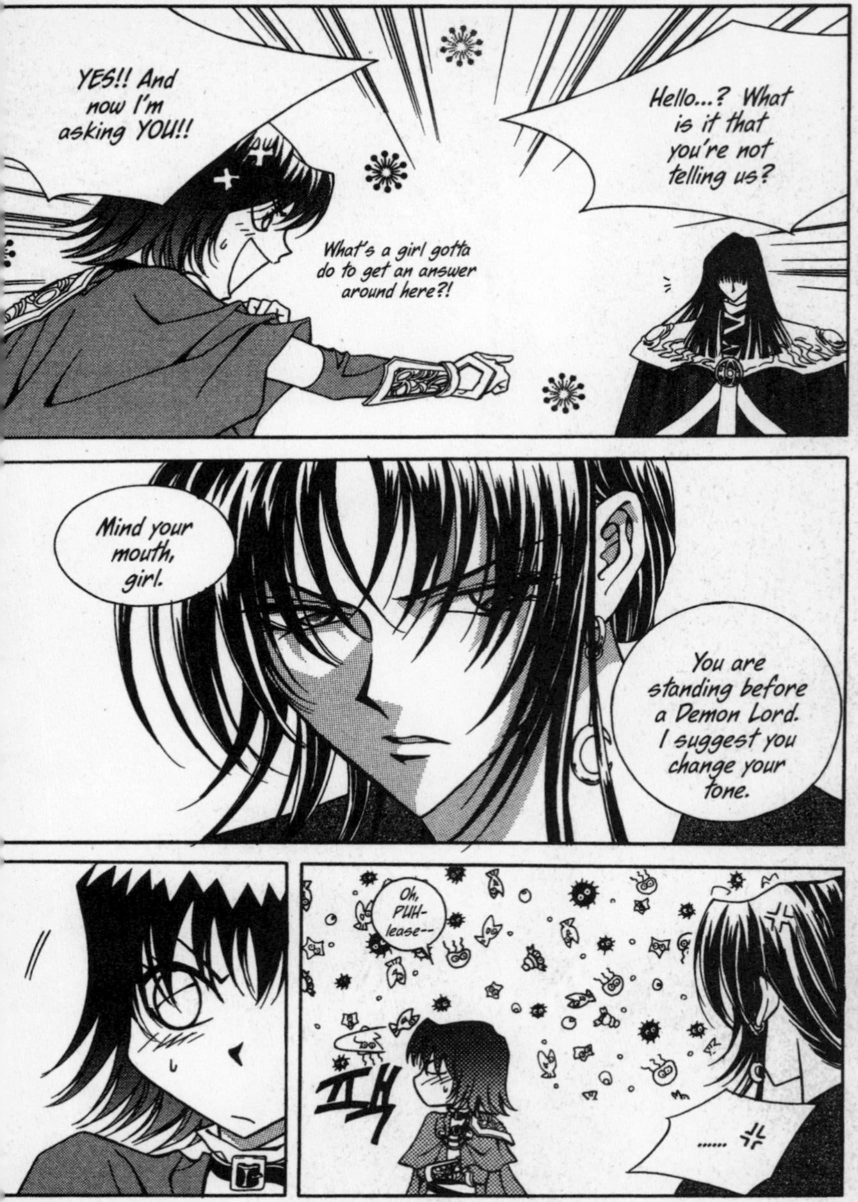
YES!! And now I'm asking YOU!!
What's a girl gotta do to get an answer around here?!
Hello...? What is it that you're not telling us?
Mind your mouth, girl.
You are standing before a Demon Lord. I suggest you change your tone.
Oh, PUH-lease--
......

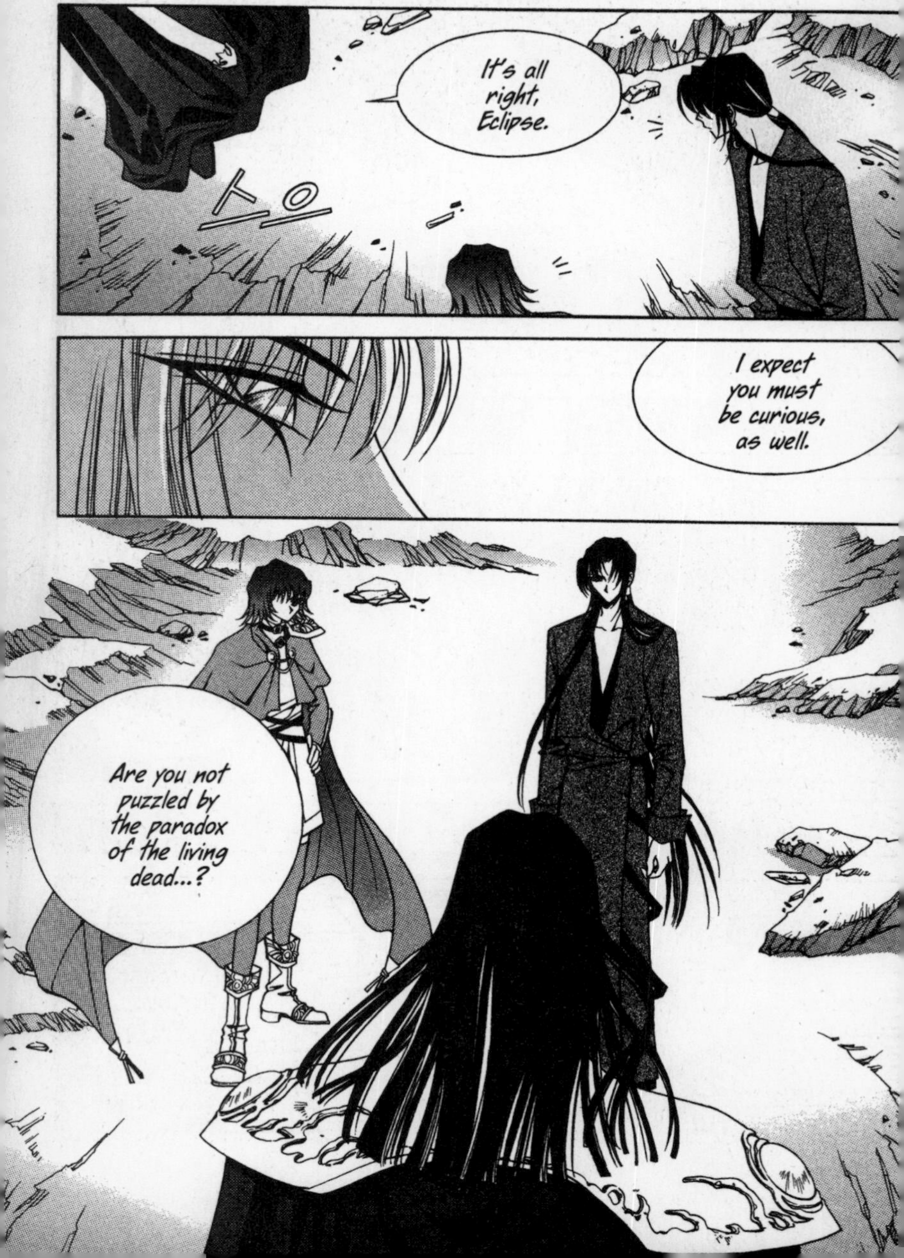
It's all right, Eclipse.
I expect you must be curious, as well.
Are you not puzzled by the paradox of the living dead...?

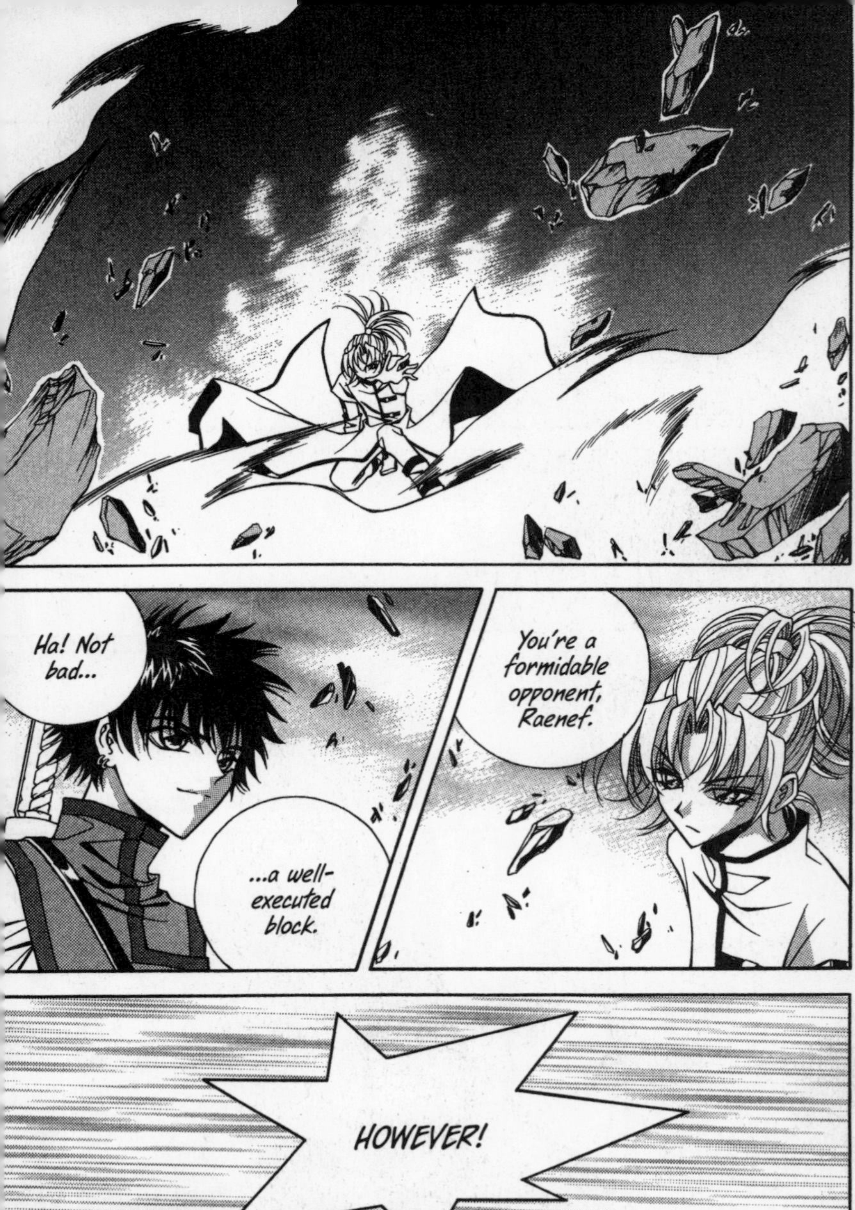
Ha! Not bad...
...a well-executed block.
You're a formidable opponent, Raenef.
HOWEVER!

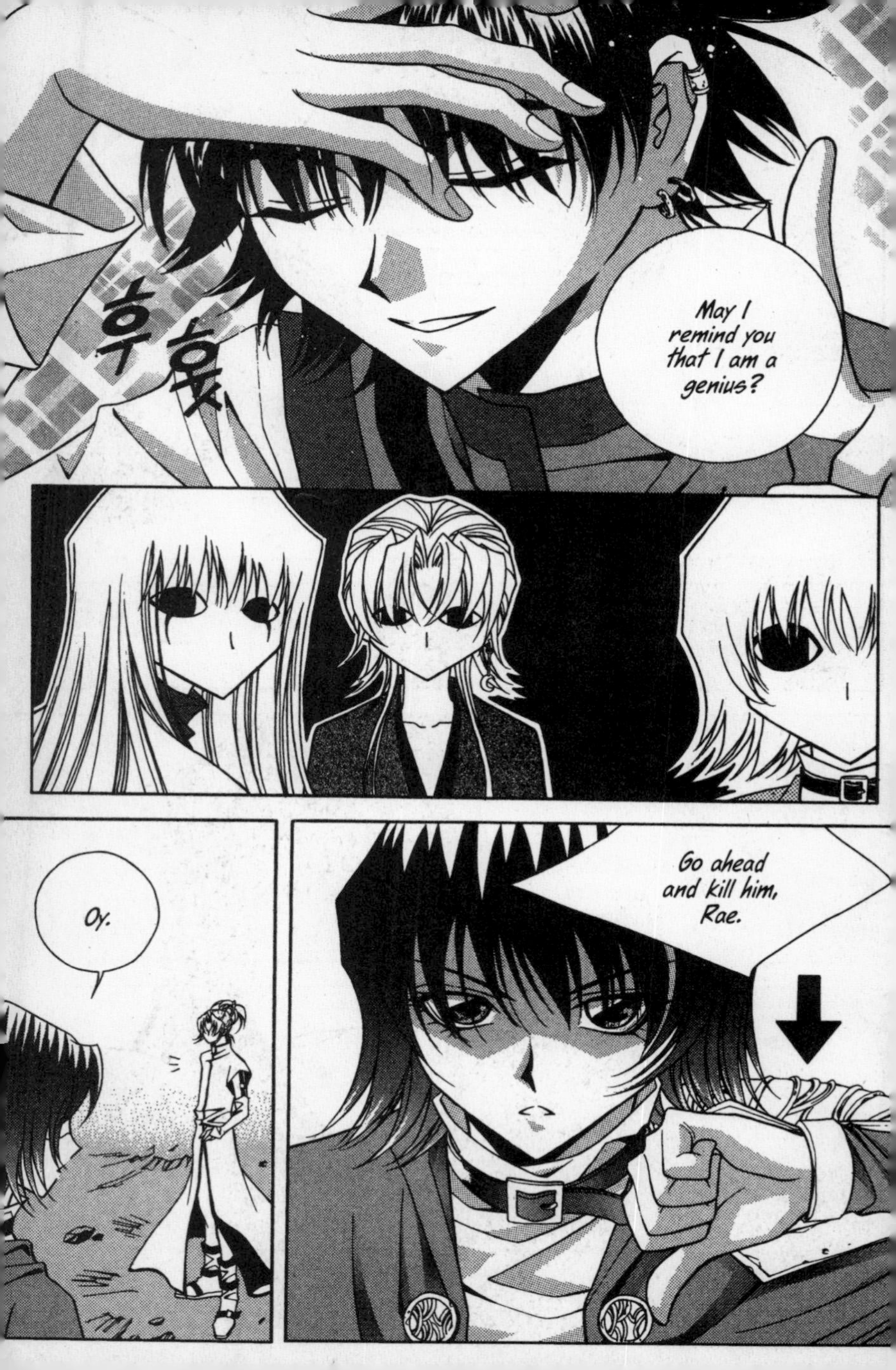
후훗
May I remind you that I am a genius?
Oy.
Go ahead and kill him, Rae.

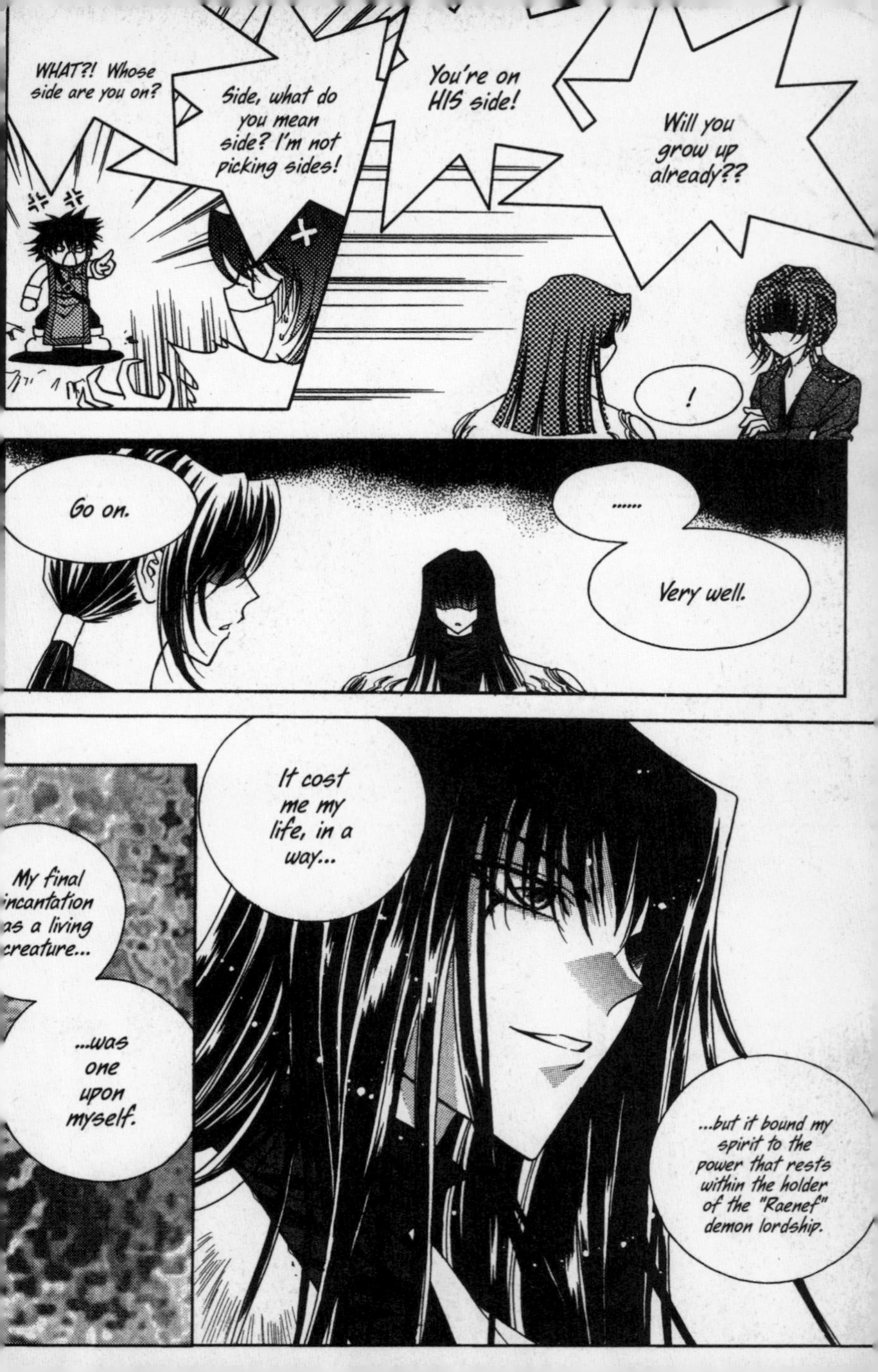
WHAT?! Whose side are you on?
Side, what do you mean side? I'm not picking sides!
You're on HIS side!
Will you grow up already??
!
Go on.
......
Very well.
My final incantation as a living creature...
...was one upon myself.
It cost me my life, in a way...
...but it bound my spirit to the power that rests within the holder of the "Raenef" demon lordship.

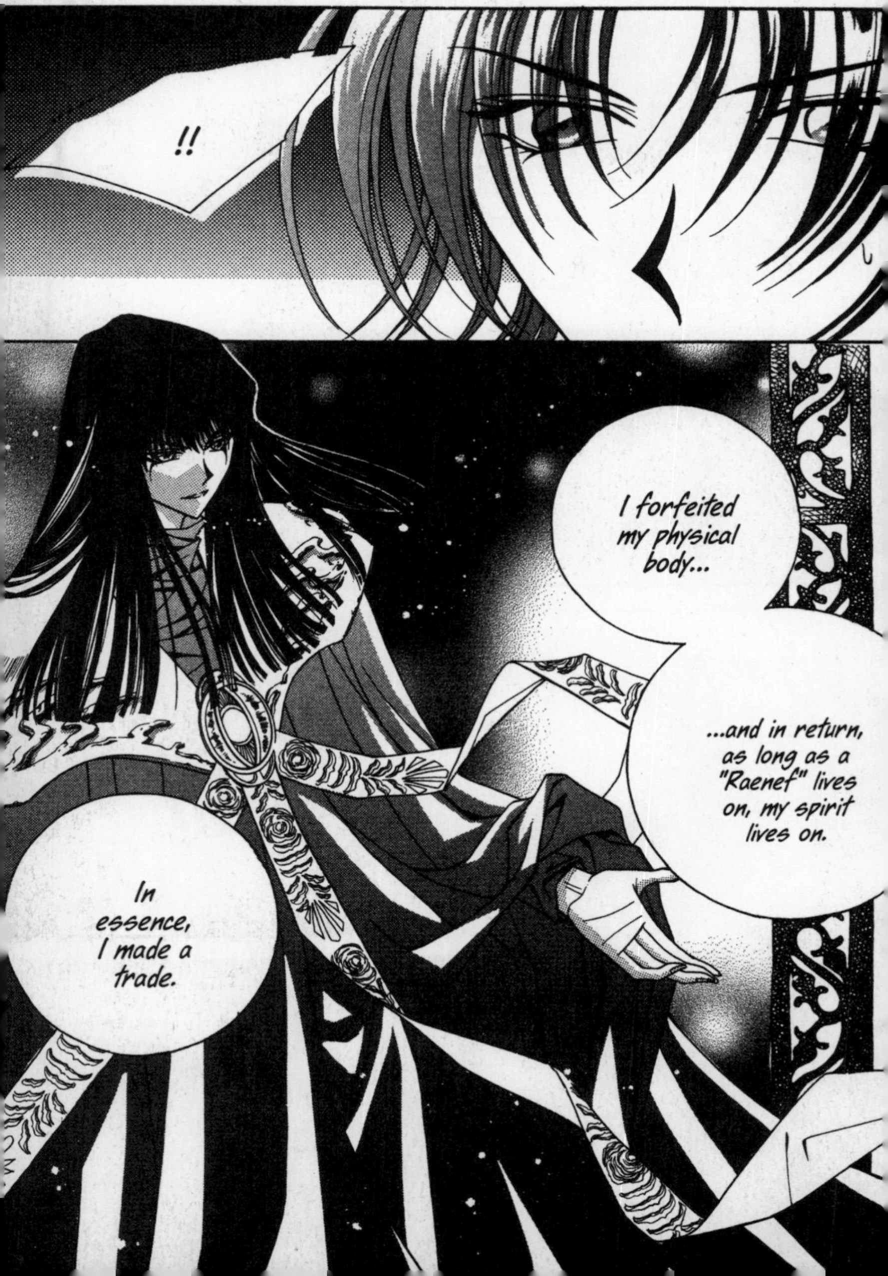
!!
I forfeited my physical body...
...and in return, as long as a "Raenef" lives on, my spirit lives on.
In essence, I made a trade.

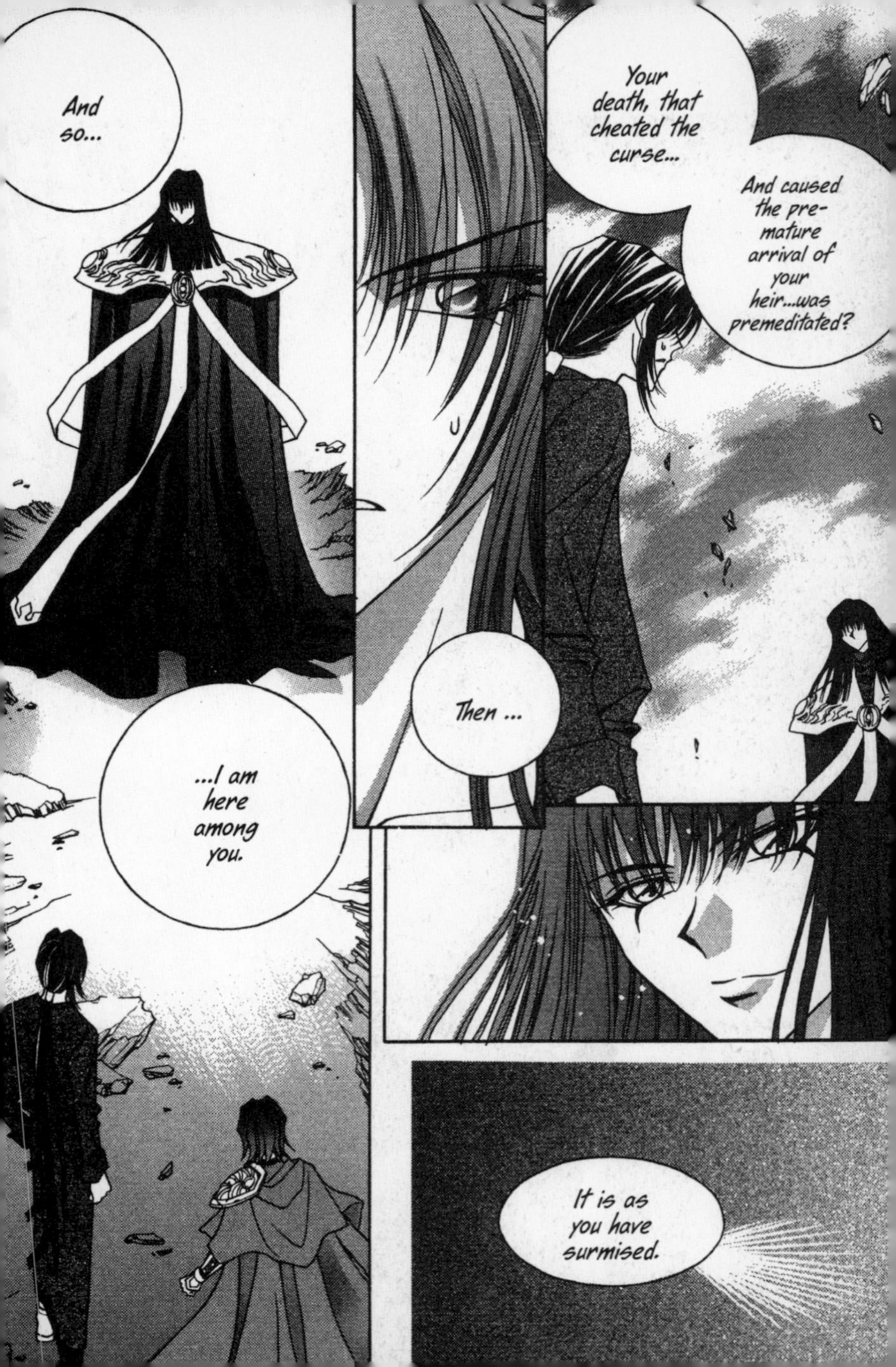

And so...
...I am here among you.
Then ...
Your death, that cheated the curse...
And caused the premature arrival of your heir...was premeditated?
It is as you have surmised.

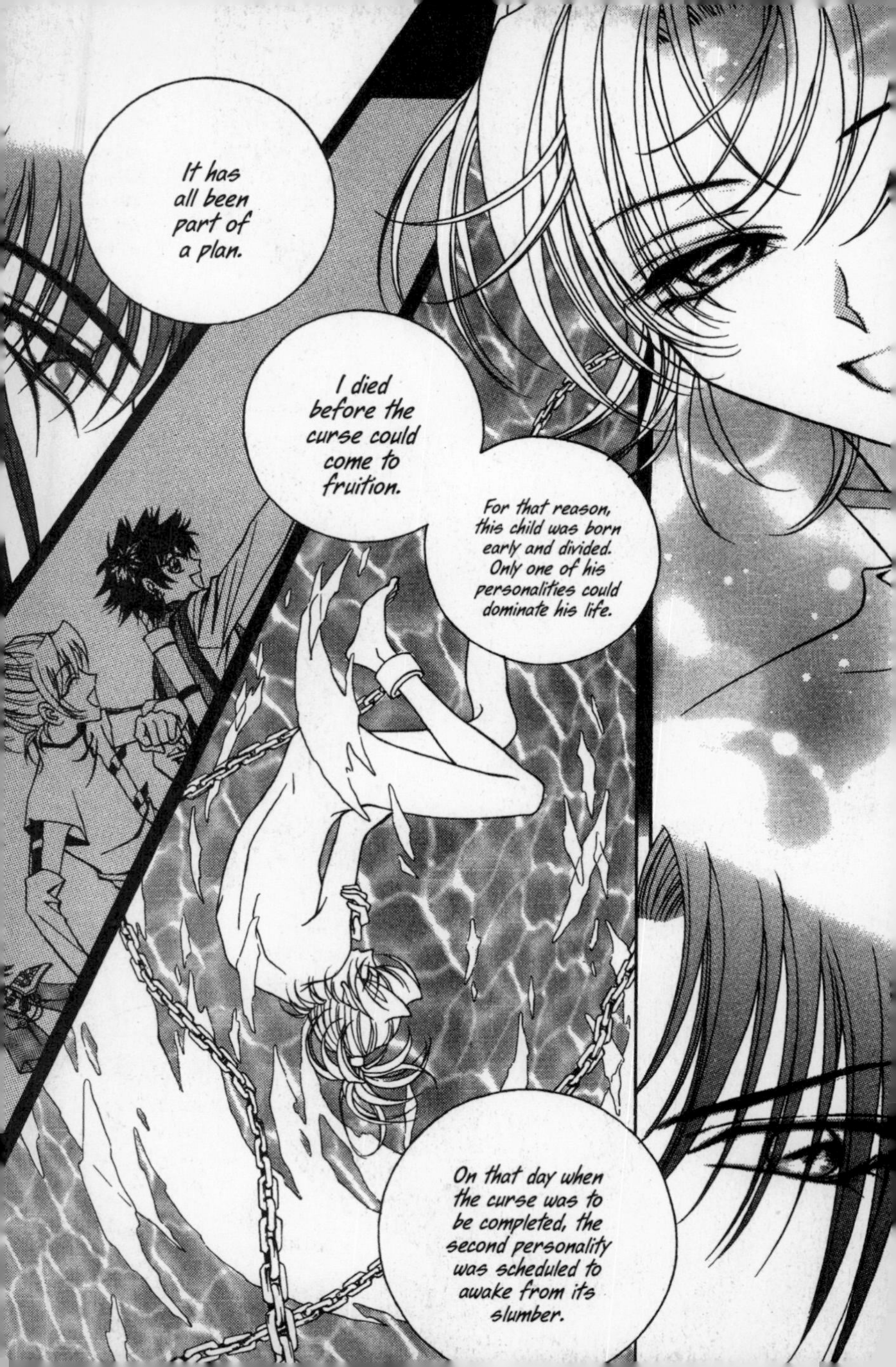
It has all been part of a plan.
I died before the curse could come to fruition.
For that reason, this child was born early and divided. Only one of his personalities could dominate his life.
On that day when the curse was to be completed, the second personality was scheduled to awake from its slumber.

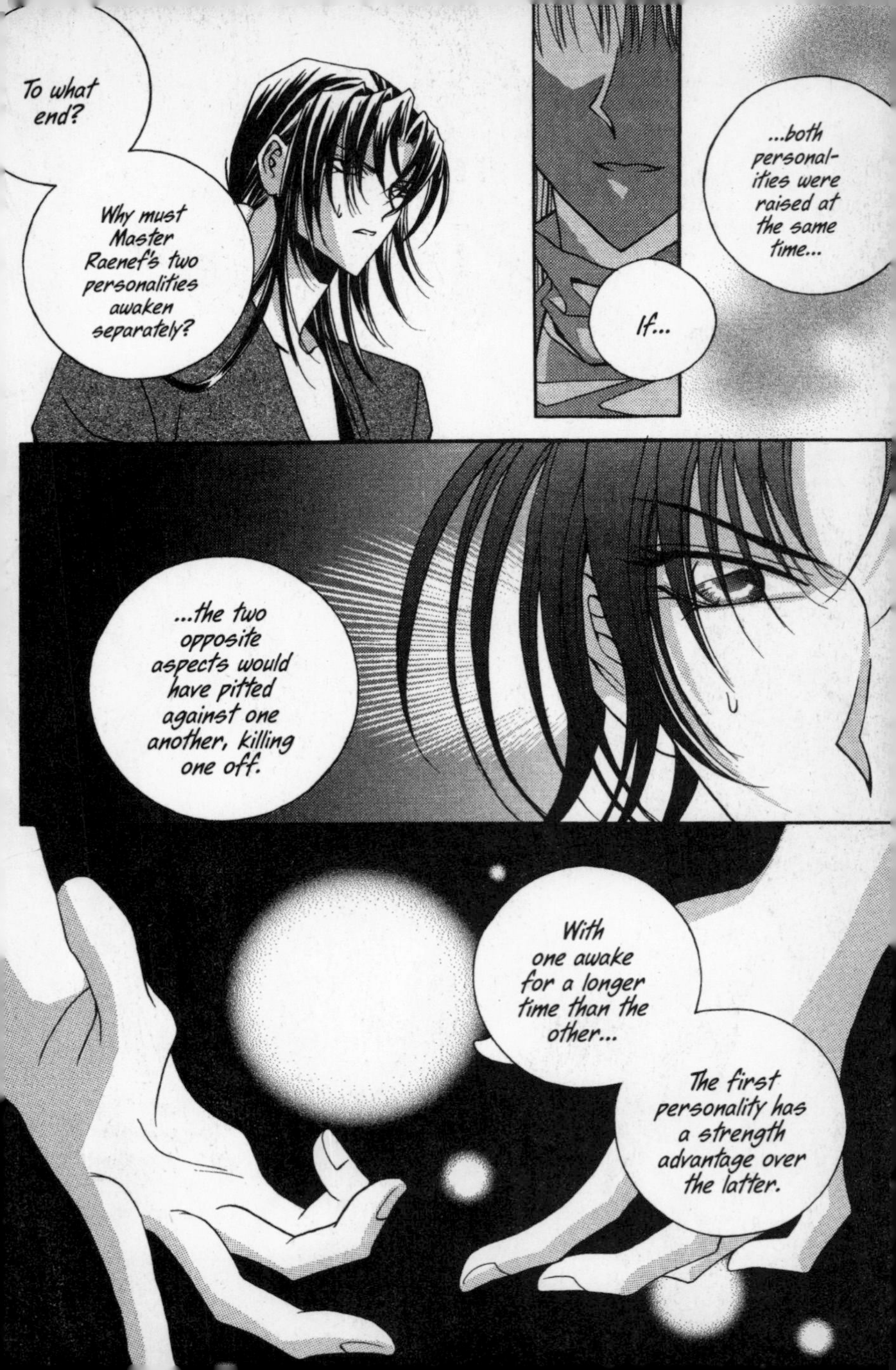
To what end?
Why must Master Raenef's two personalities awaken separately?
If...
...both personalities were raised at the same time...
...the two opposite aspects would have pitted against one another, killing one off.
With one awake for a longer time than the other...
The first personality has a strength advantage over the latter.

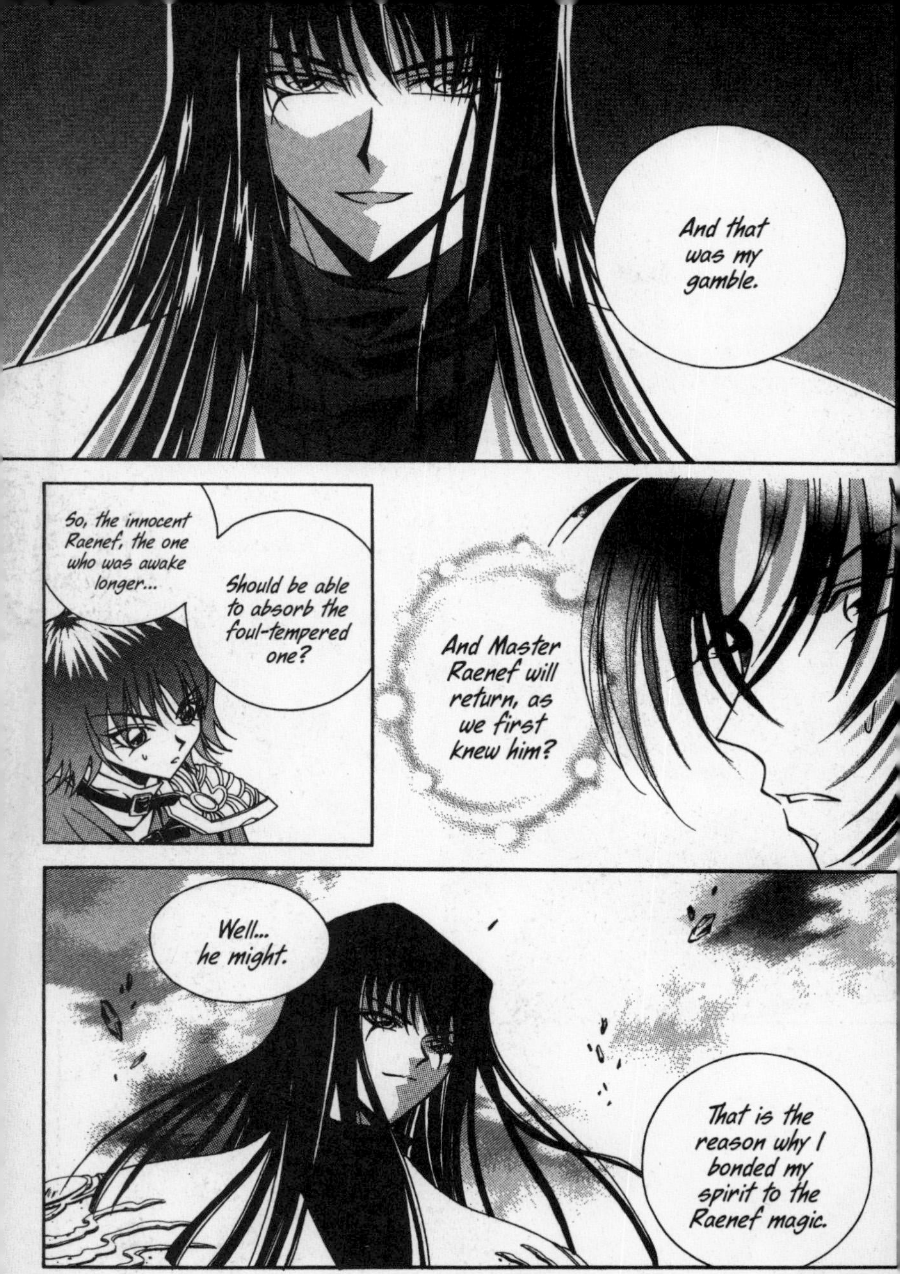
And that was my gamble.
So, the innocent Raenef, the one who was awake longer...
Should be able to absorb the foul-tempered one?
And Master Raenef will return, as we first knew him?
Well... he might.
That is the reason why I bonded my spirit to the Raenef magic.

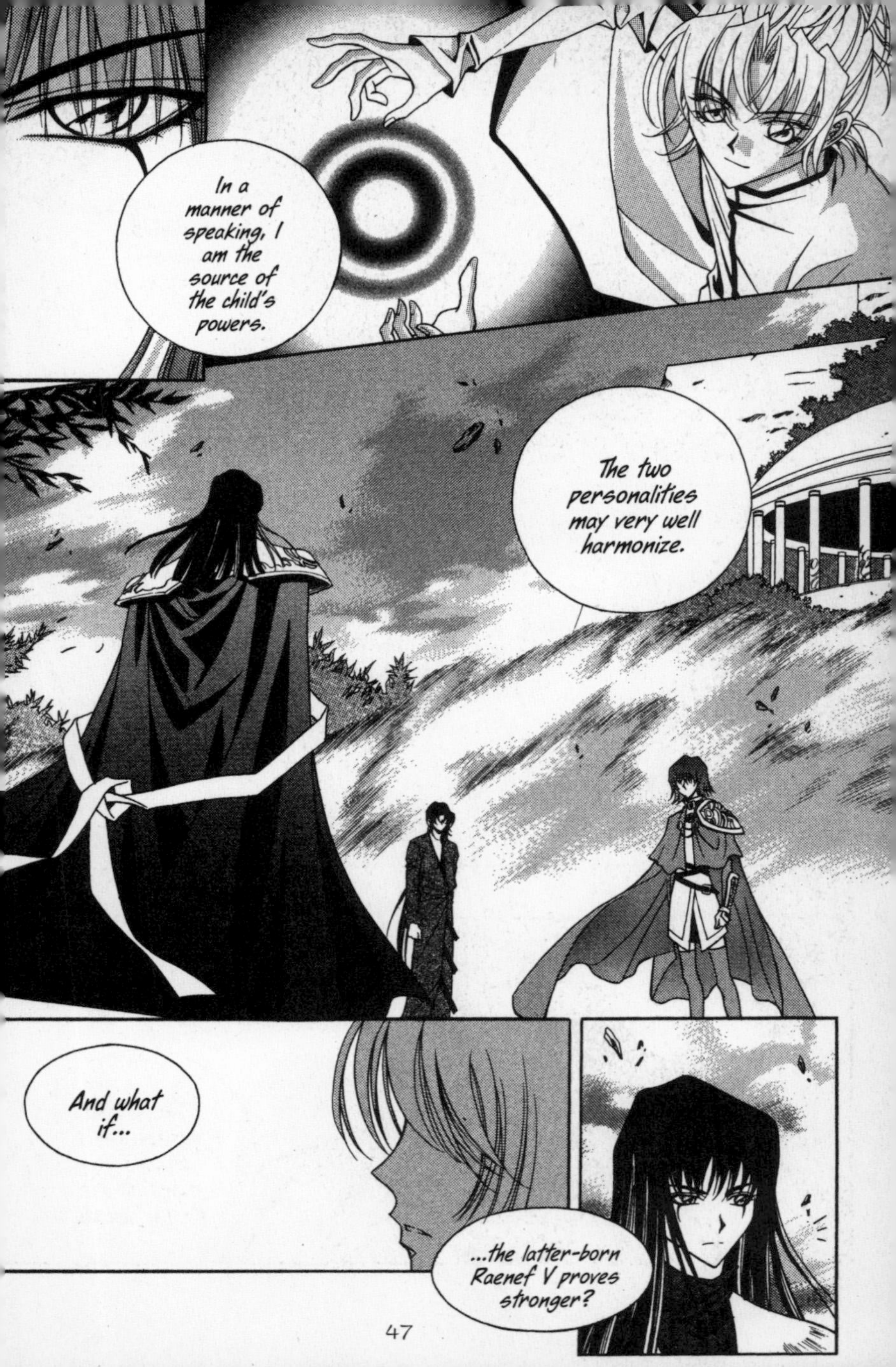
In a manner of speaking, I am the source of the child's powers.
The two personalities may very well harmonize.
And what if...
...the latter-born Raenef V proves stronger?

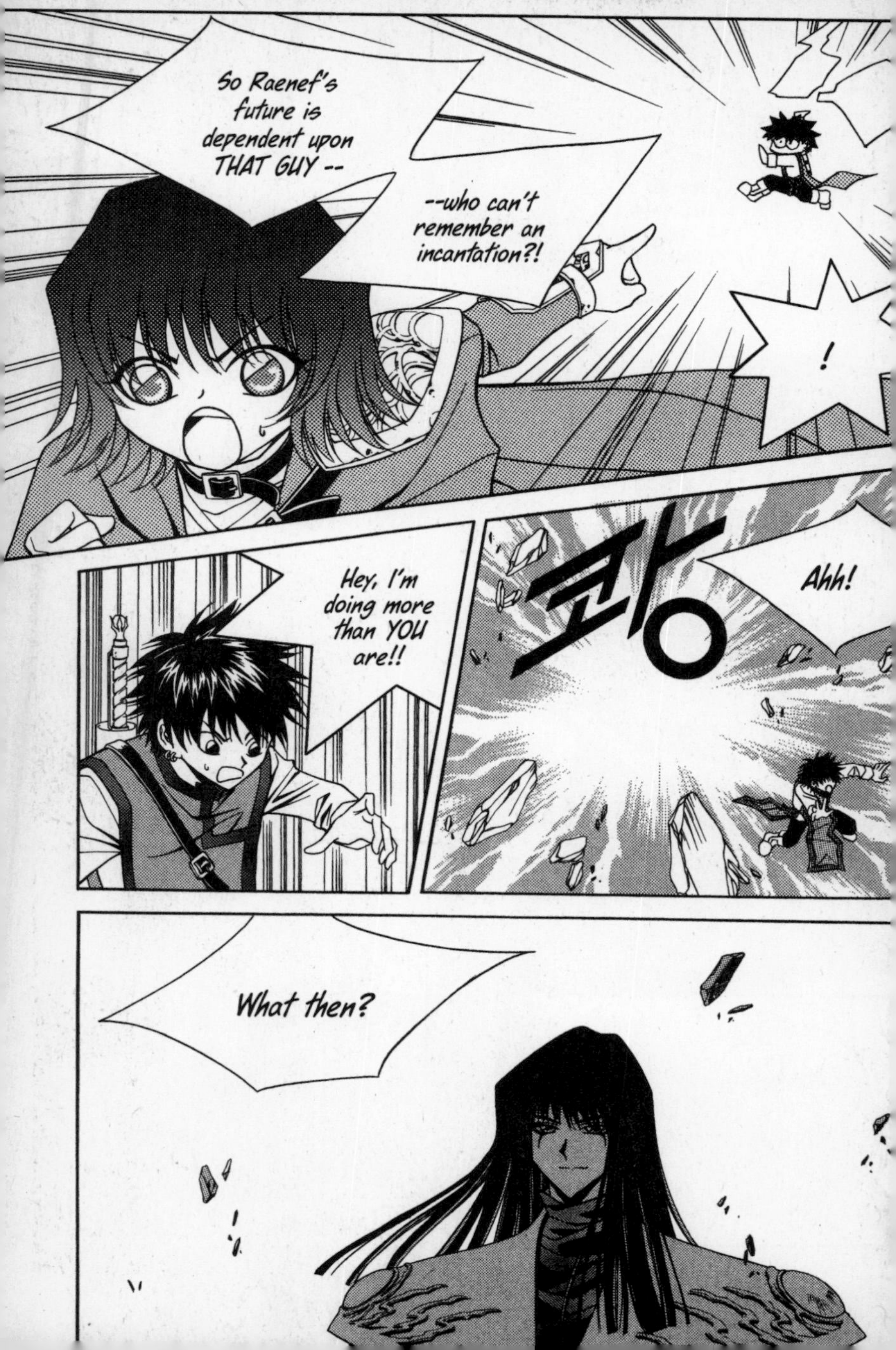

So Raenef's future is dependent upon THAT GUY --
--who can't remember an incantation?!
!
Hey, I'm doing more than YOU are!!
쾅
Ahh!
What then?

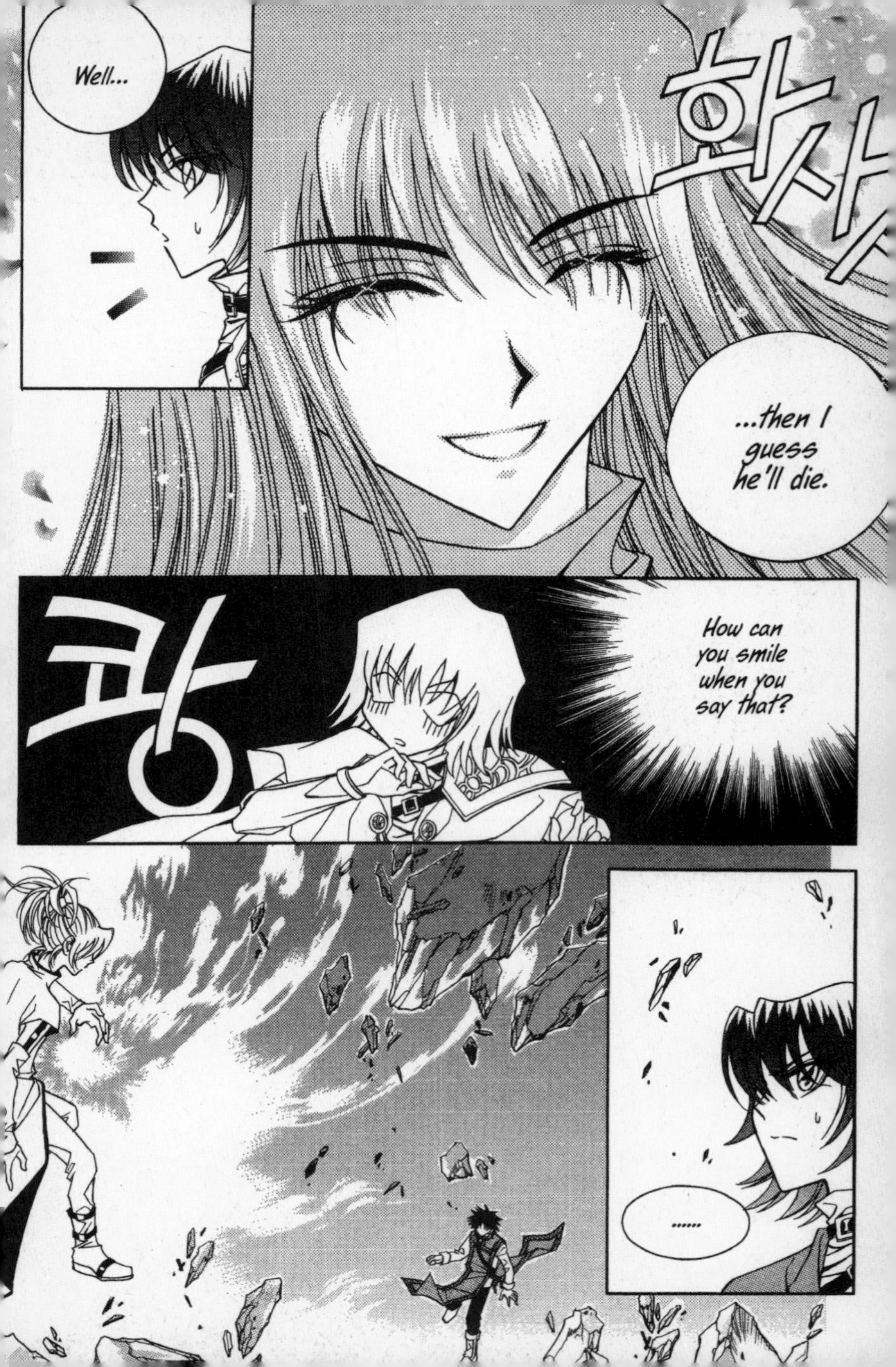
Well...
화사
...then I guess he'll die.
쾅
How can you smile when you say that?
......

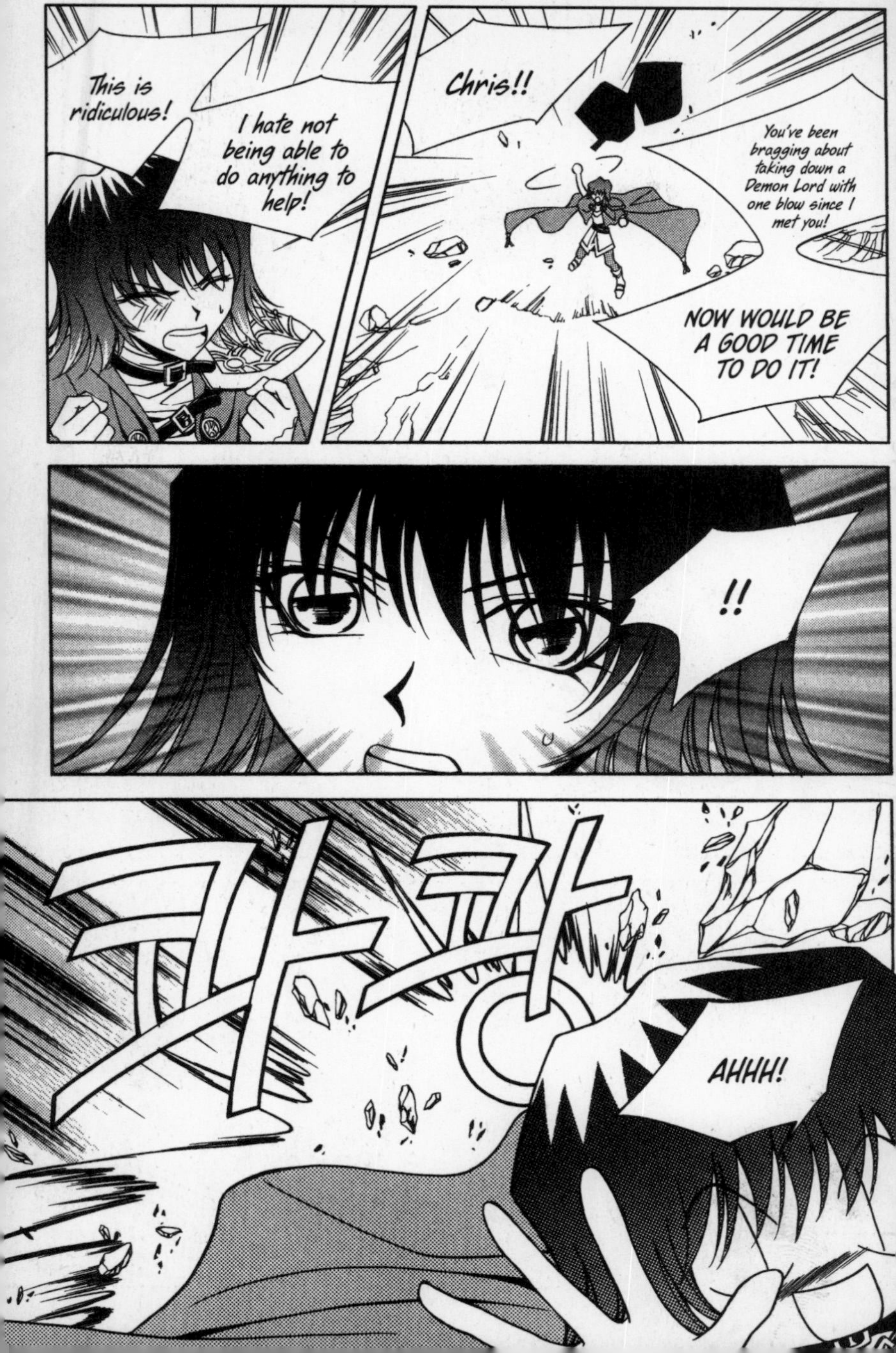
This is ridiculous!
I hate not being able to do anything to help!
Chris!!
You've been bragging about taking down a Demon Lord with one blow since I met you!
NOW WOULD BE A GOOD TIME TO DO IT!
!!
AHHH!

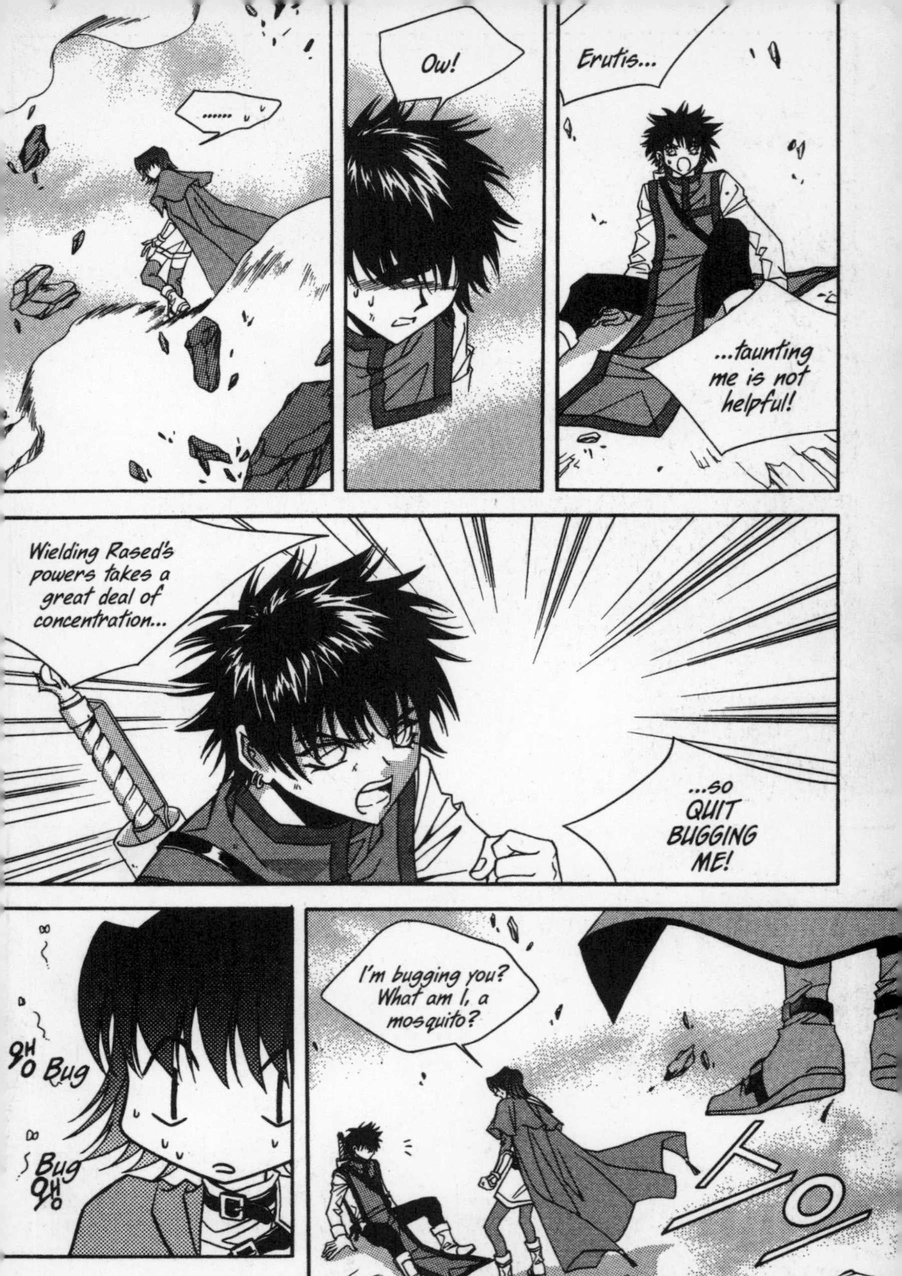
......
Ow!
Erutis...
...taunting me is not helpful!
Wielding Rased's powers takes a great deal of concentration...
...so QUIT BUGGING ME!
Bug
Bug
I'm bugging you? What am I, a mosquito?

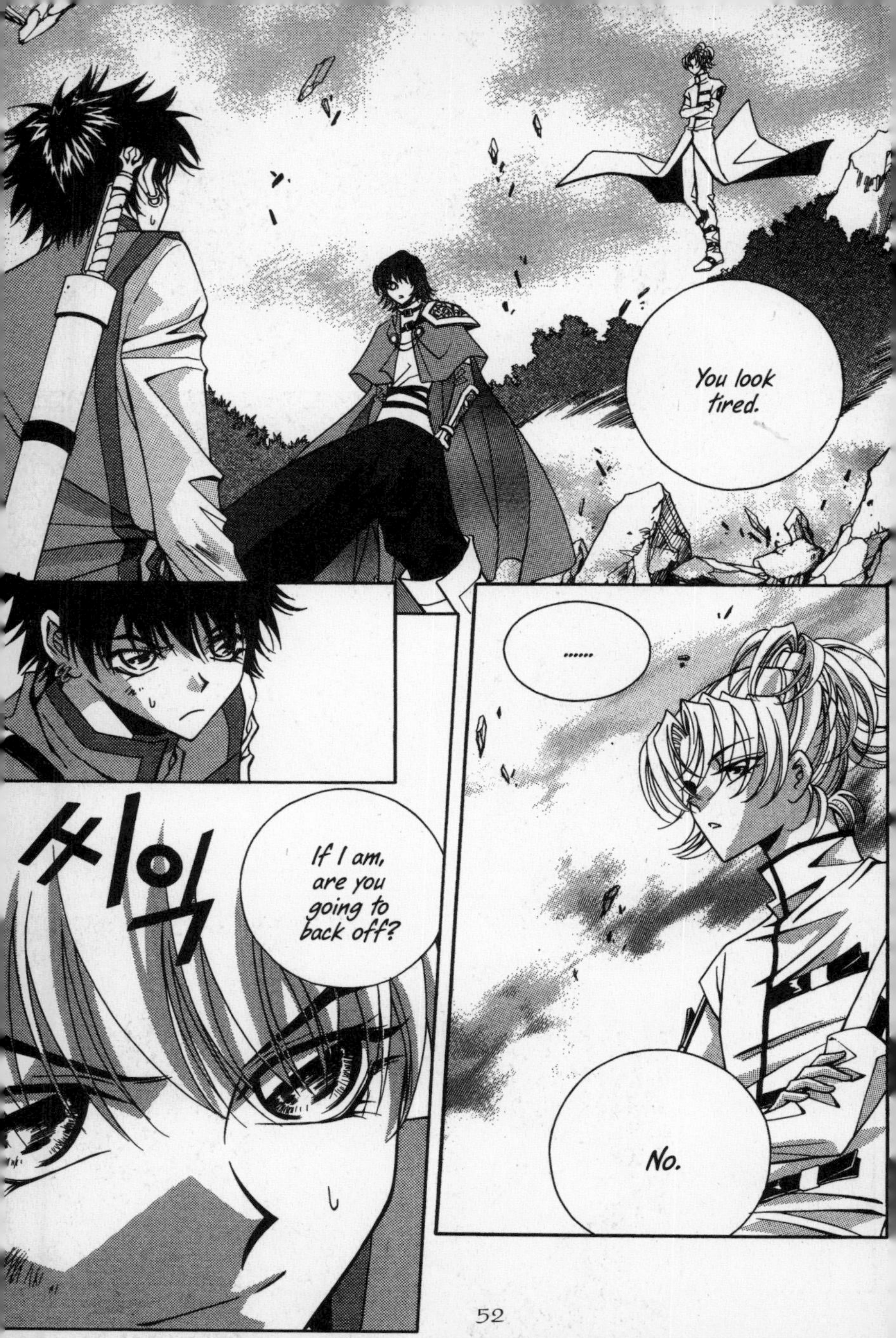
You look tired.
If I am, are you going to back off?
......
No.

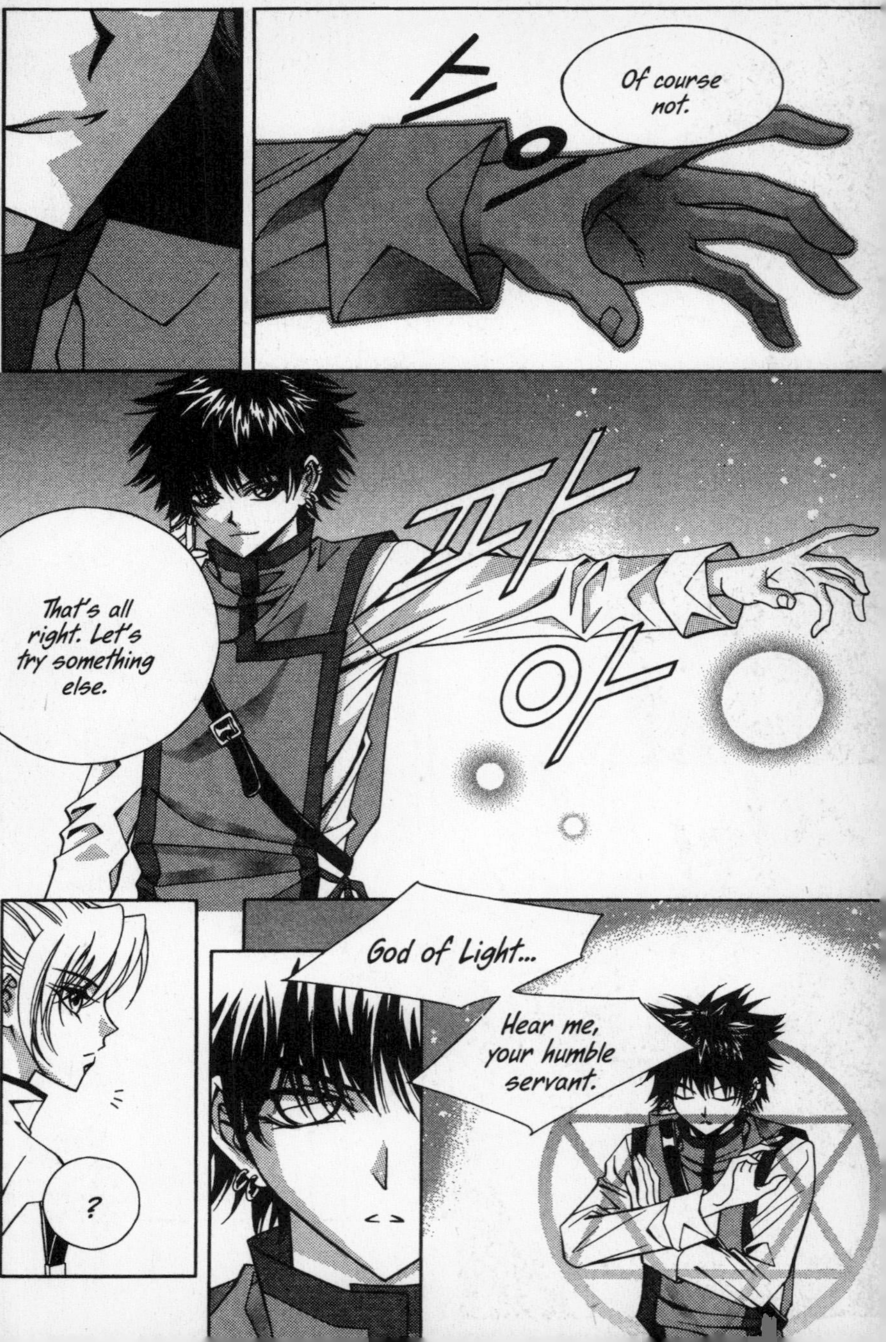
Of course not.
That's all right. Let's try something else.
?
God of Light...
Hear me, your humble servant.

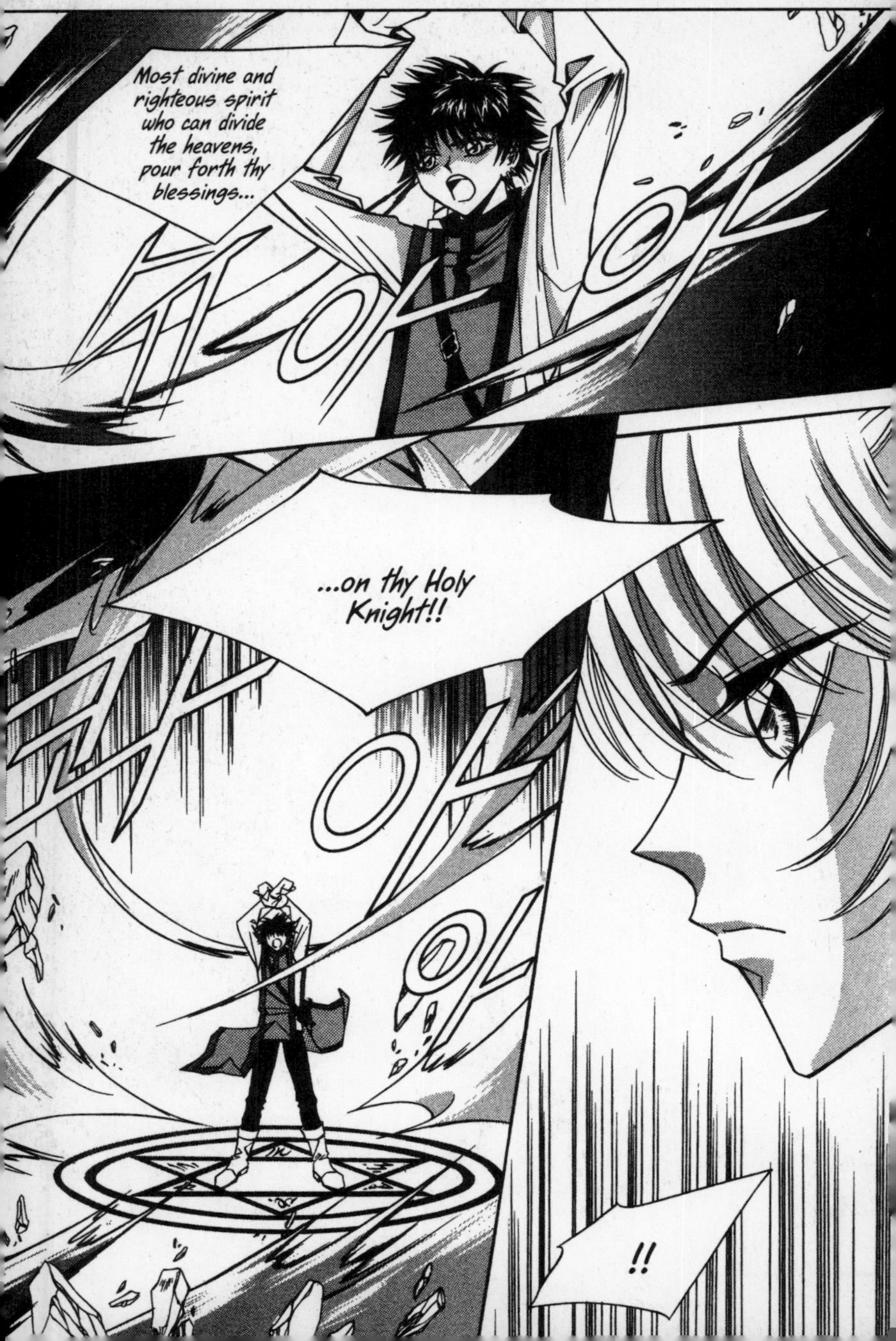
Most divine and righteous spirit who can divide the heavens, pour forth thy blessings...
KA-DOOK
...on thy Holy Knight!!
DOOM
!!

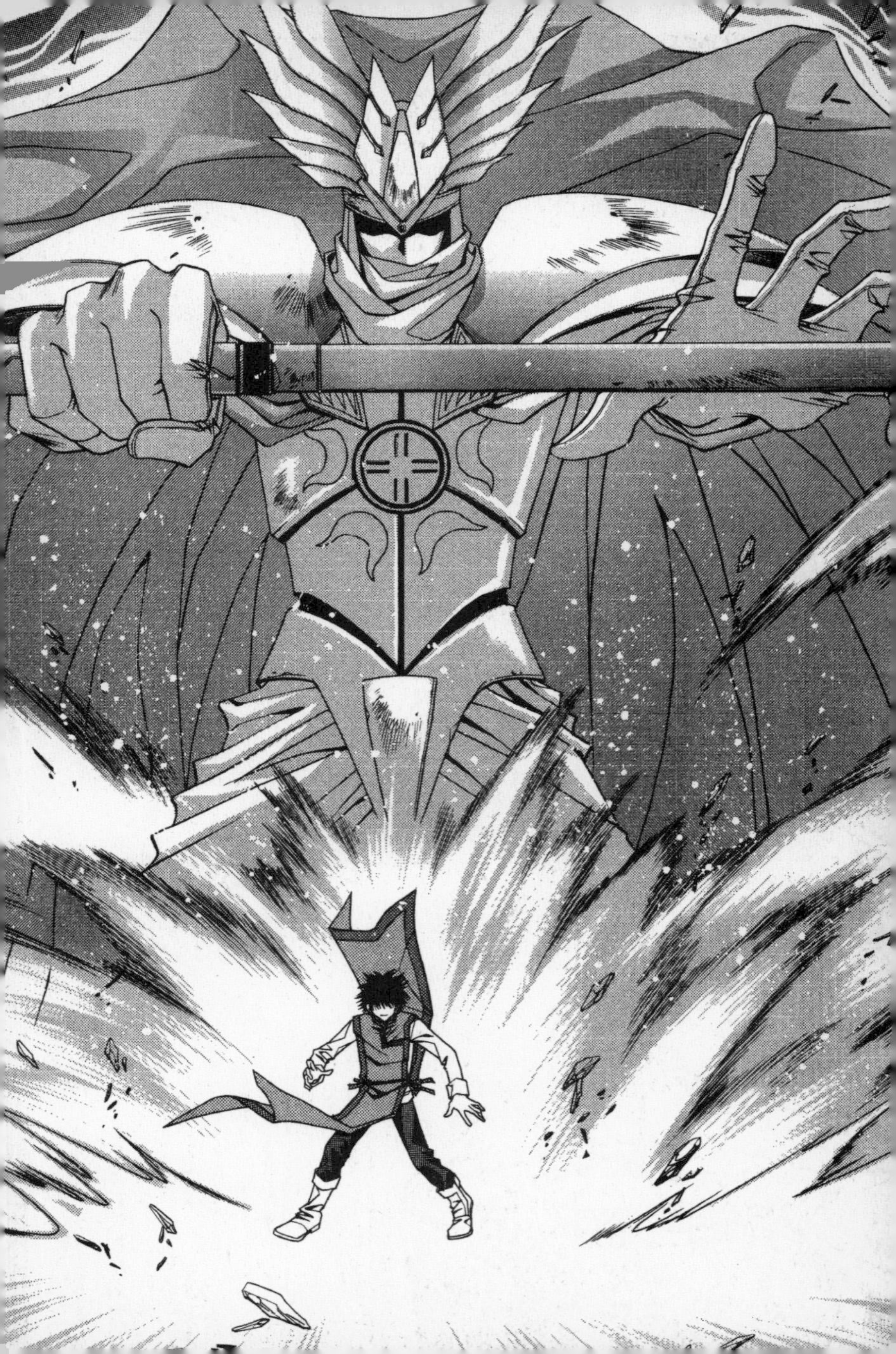

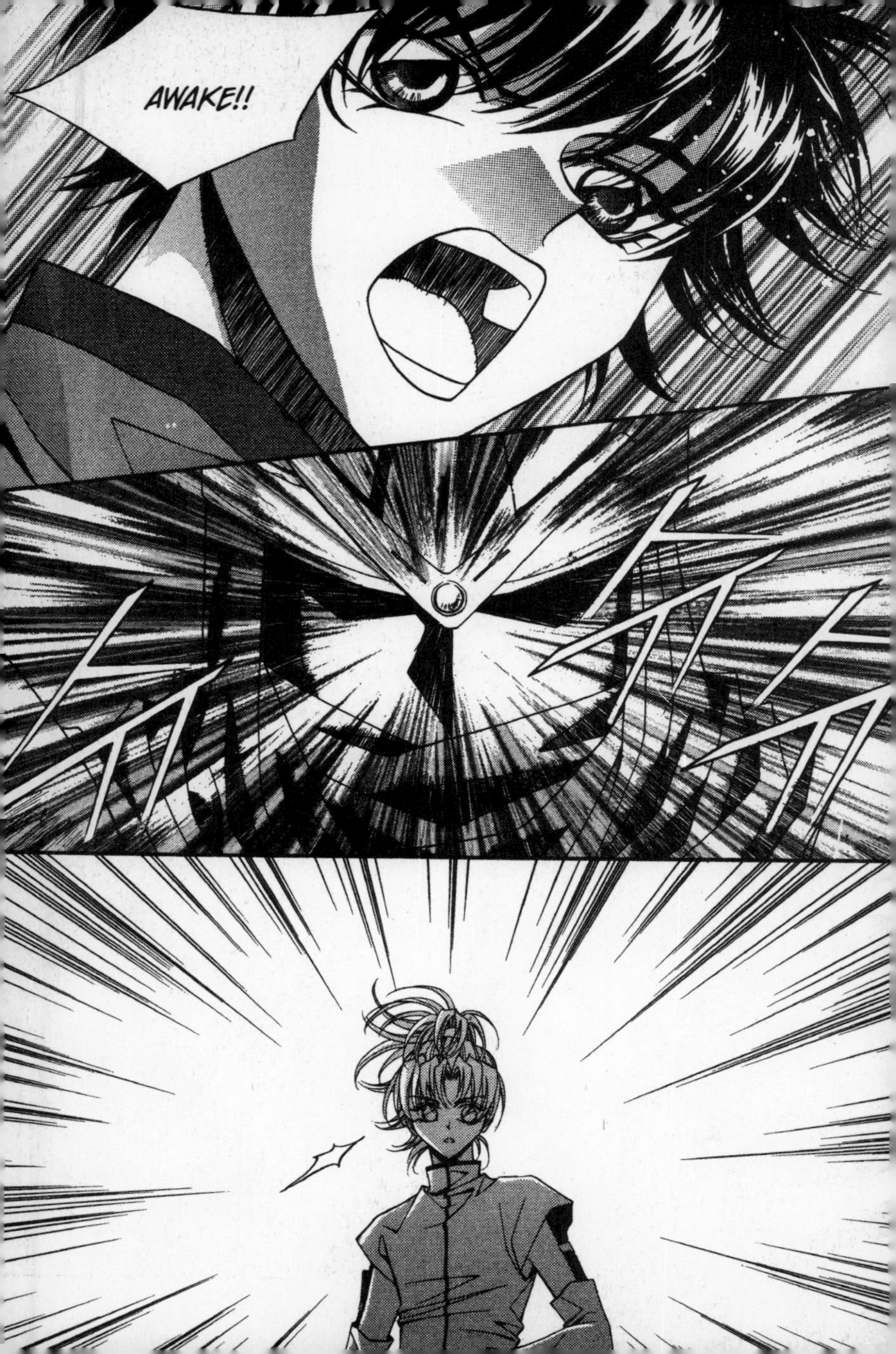
AWAKE!!

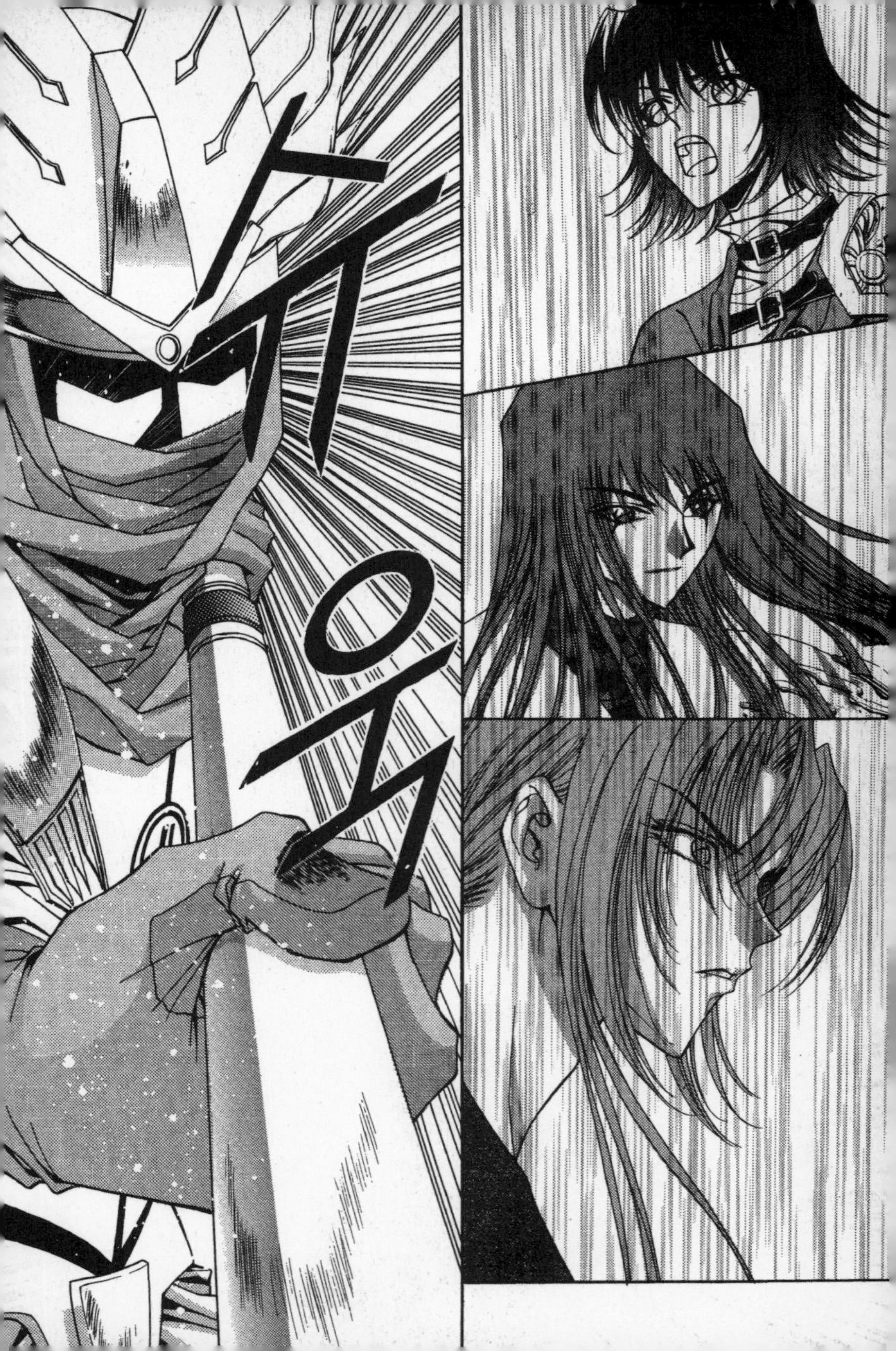

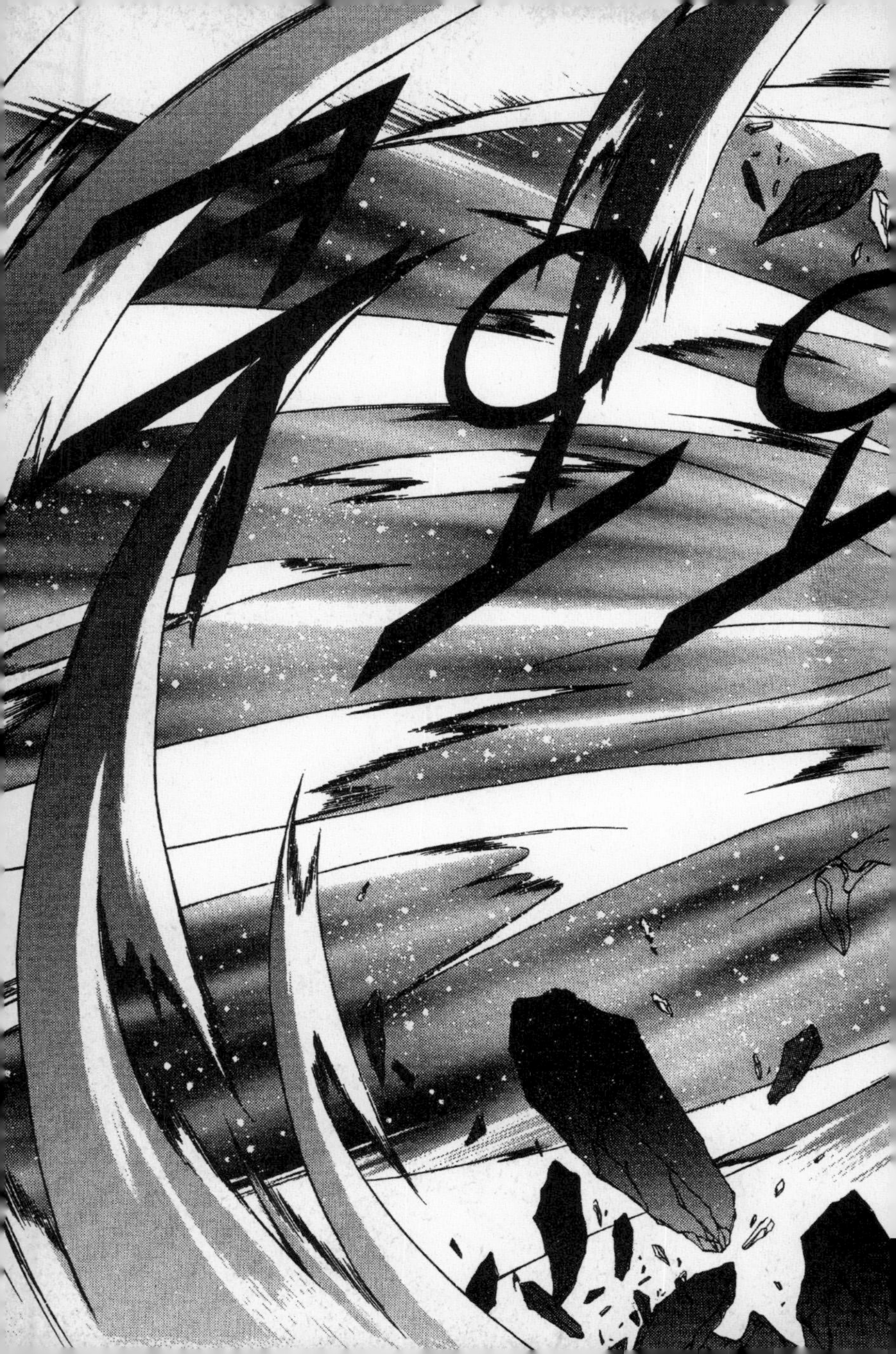

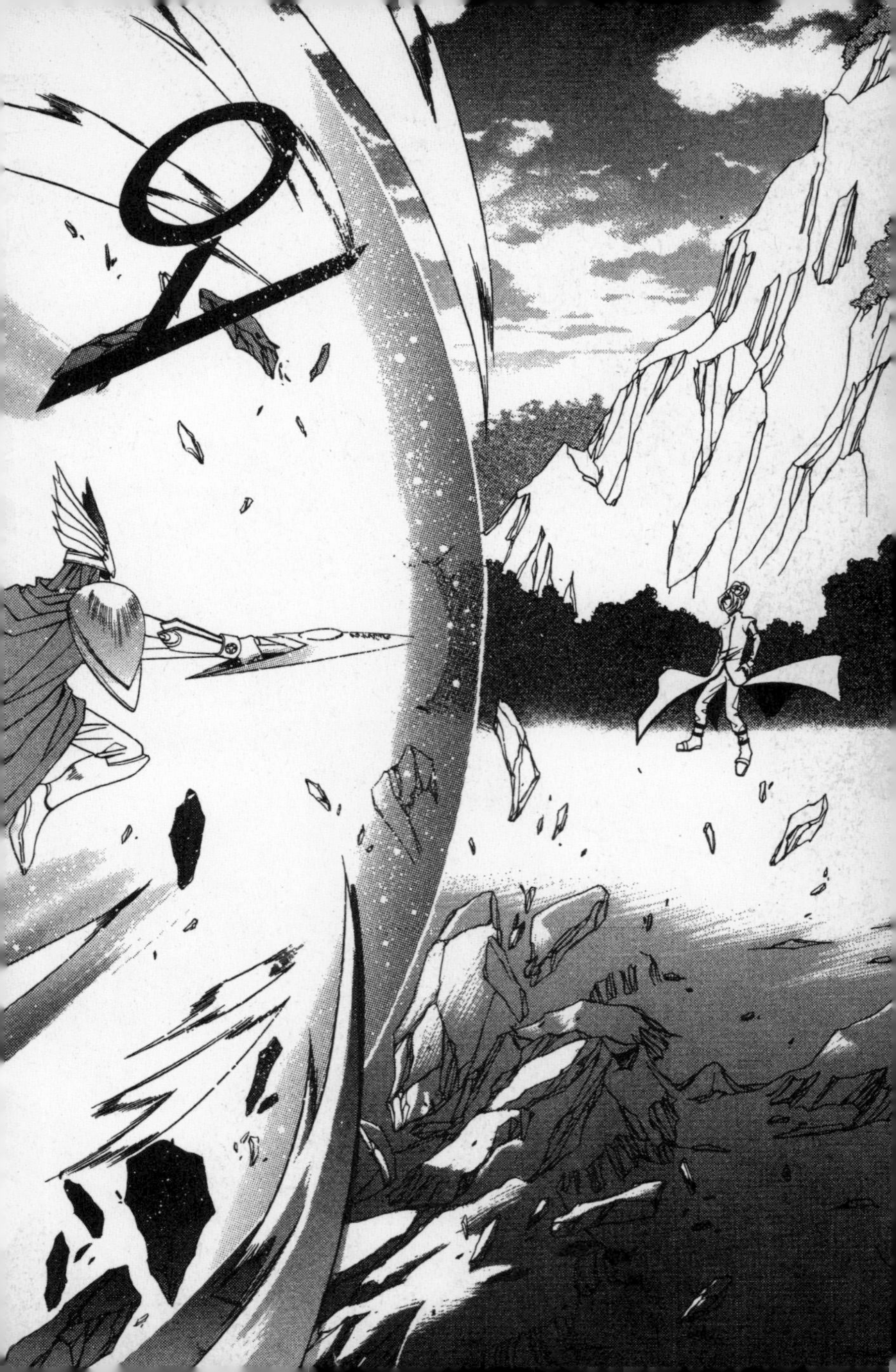

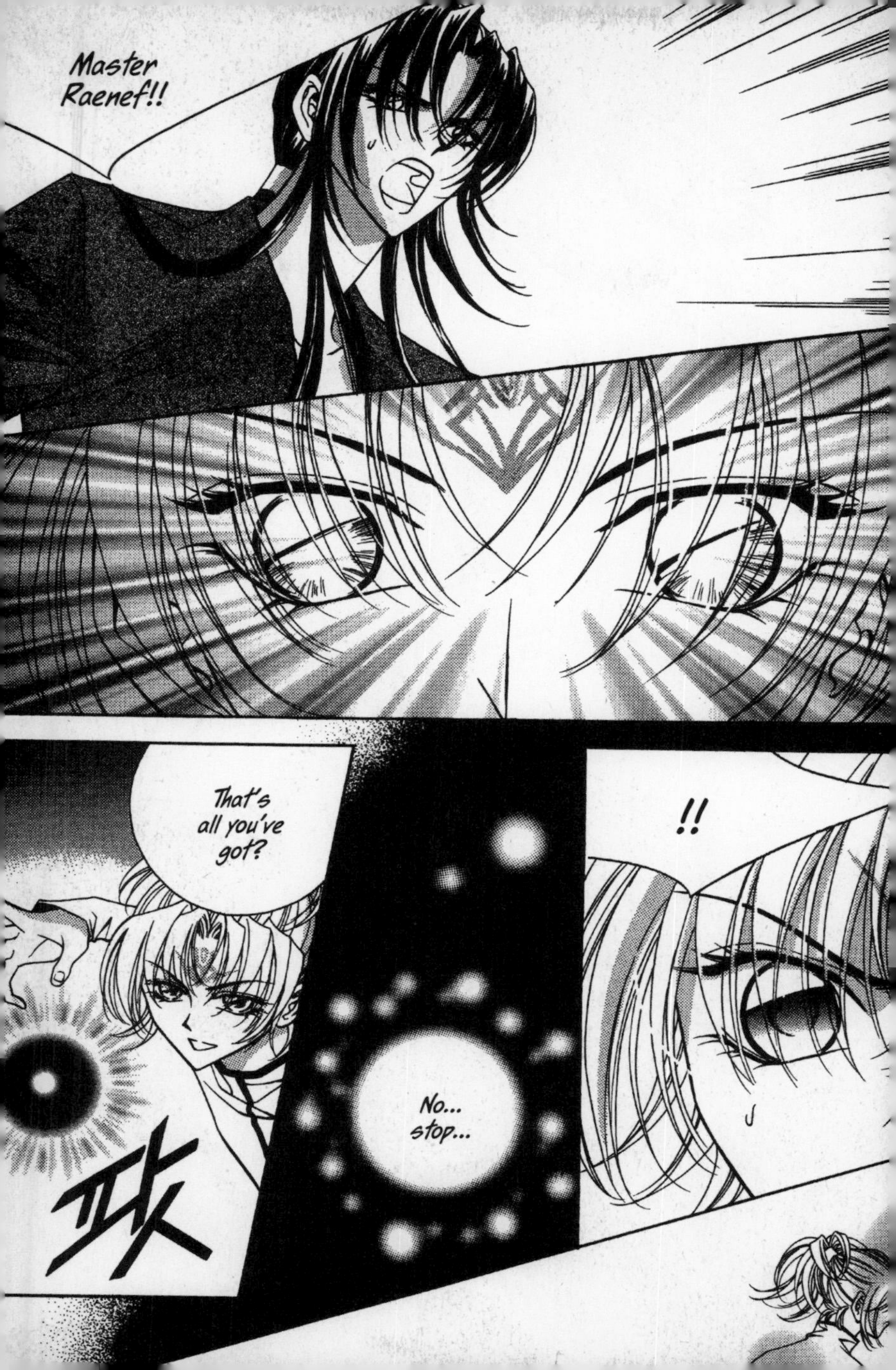
Master Raenef!!
That's all you've got?
No... stop...
!!

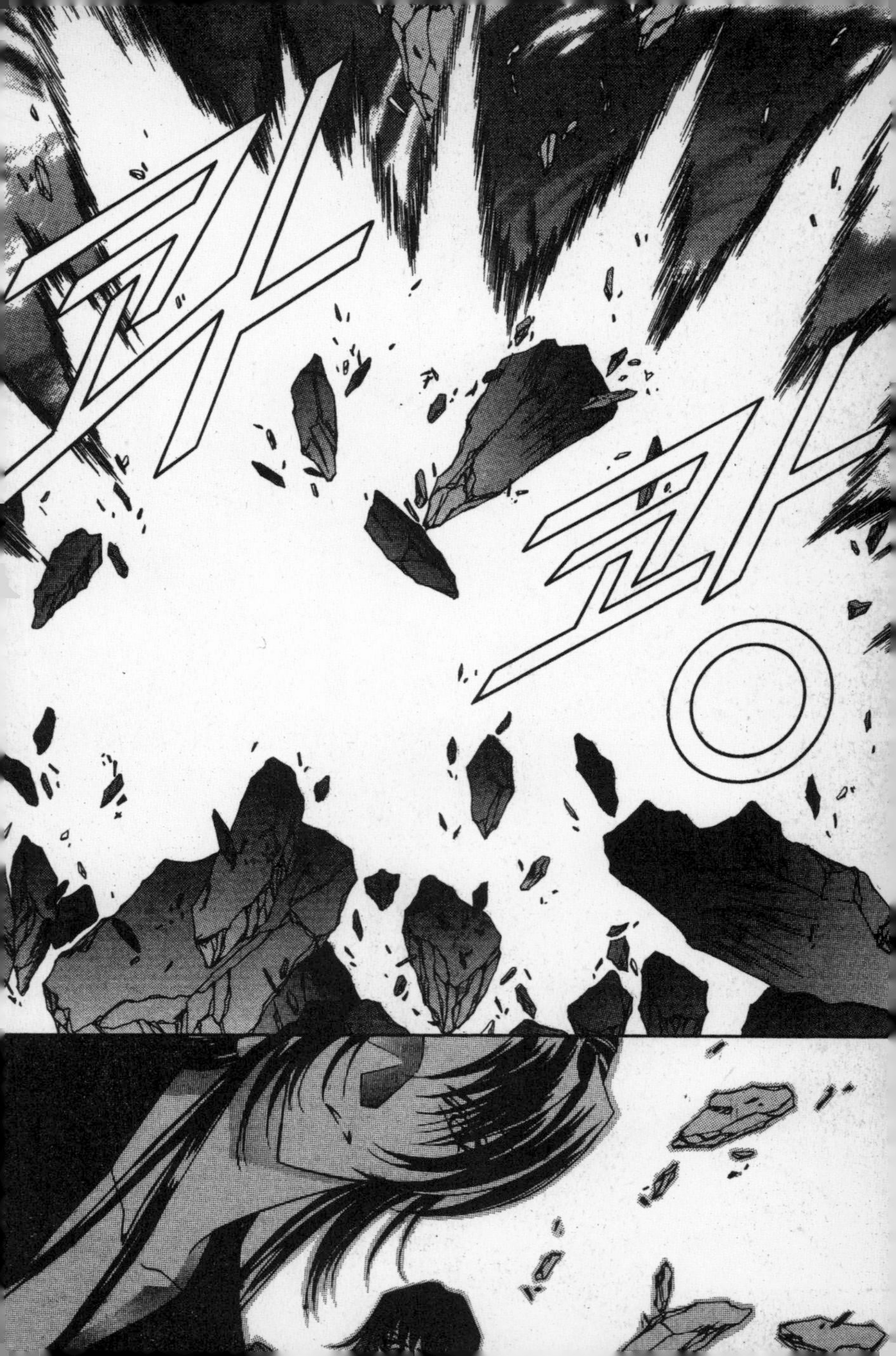
콰광

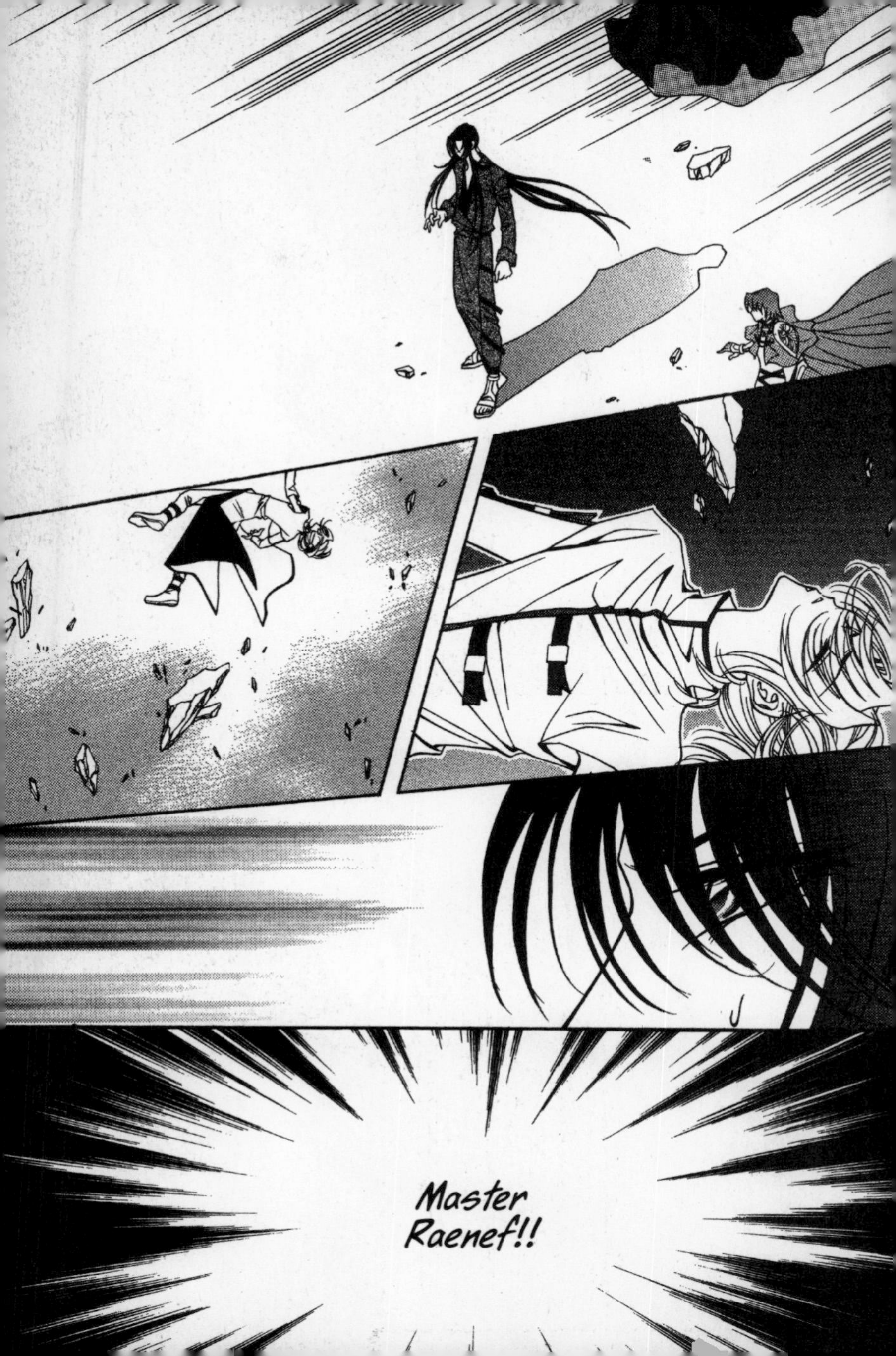
Master Raenef!!

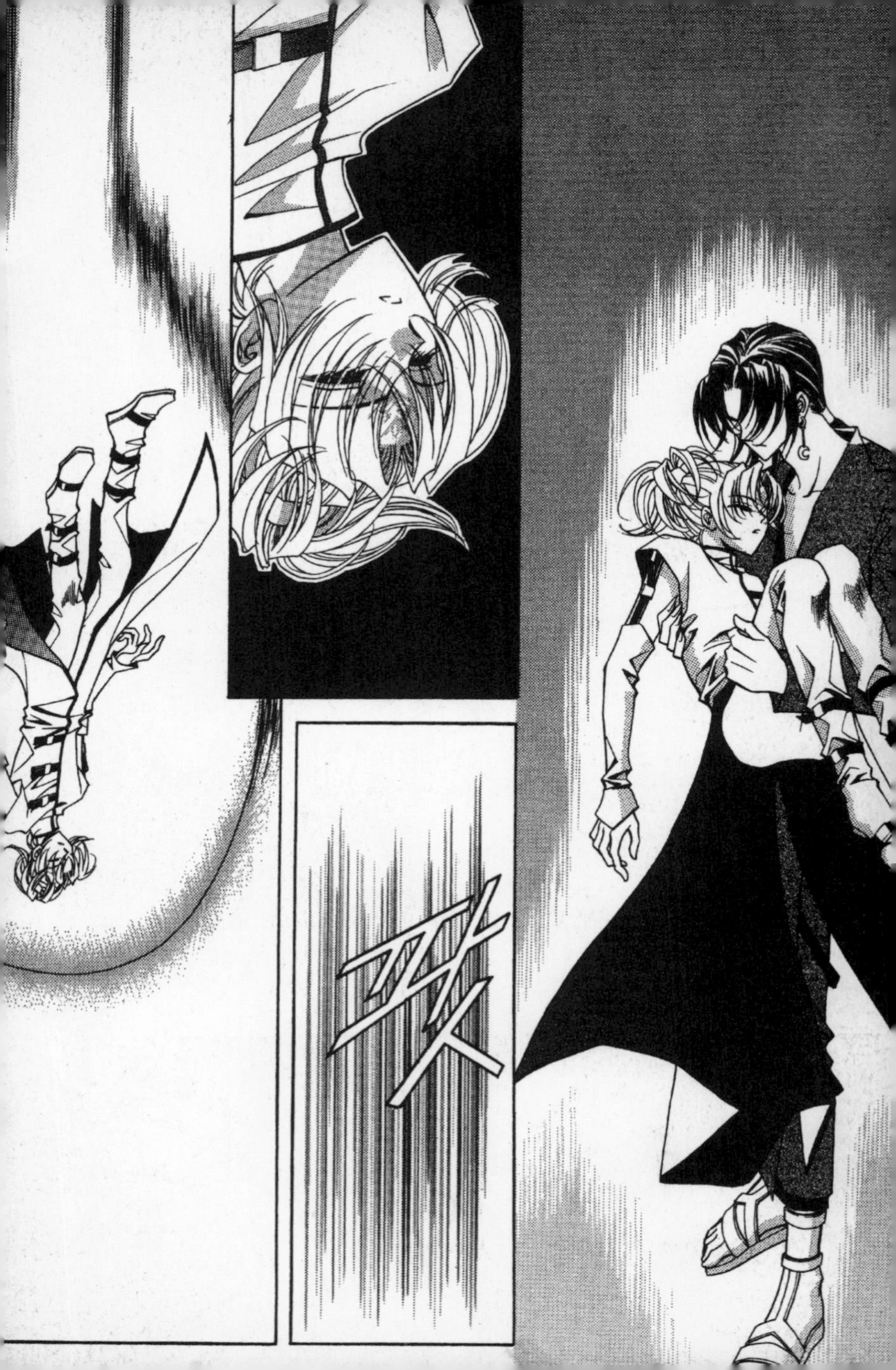

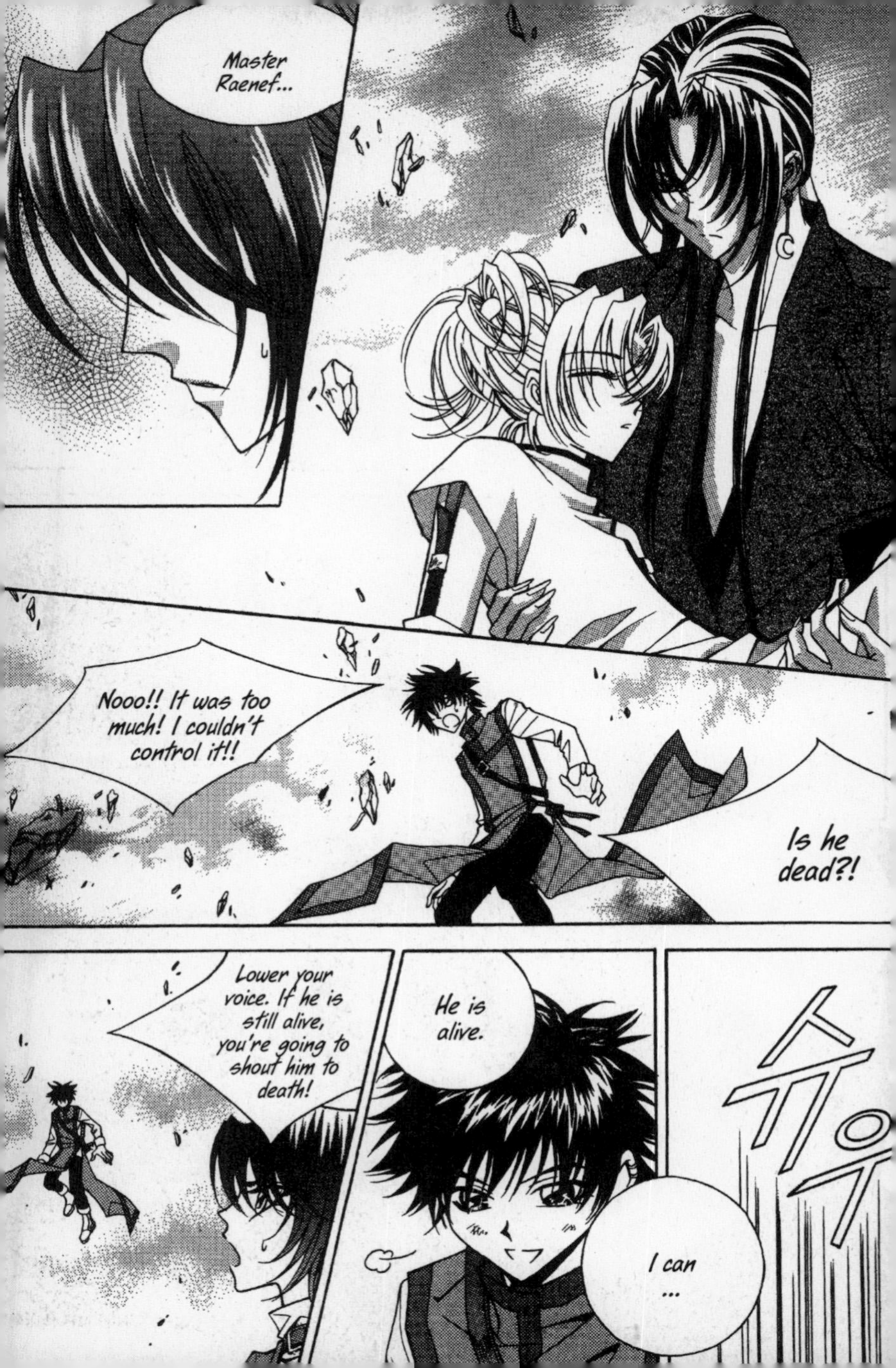
Master Raenef...
Nooo!! It was too much! I couldn't control it!!
Is he dead?!
Lower your voice. If he is still alive, you're going to shout him to death!
He is alive.
I can ...

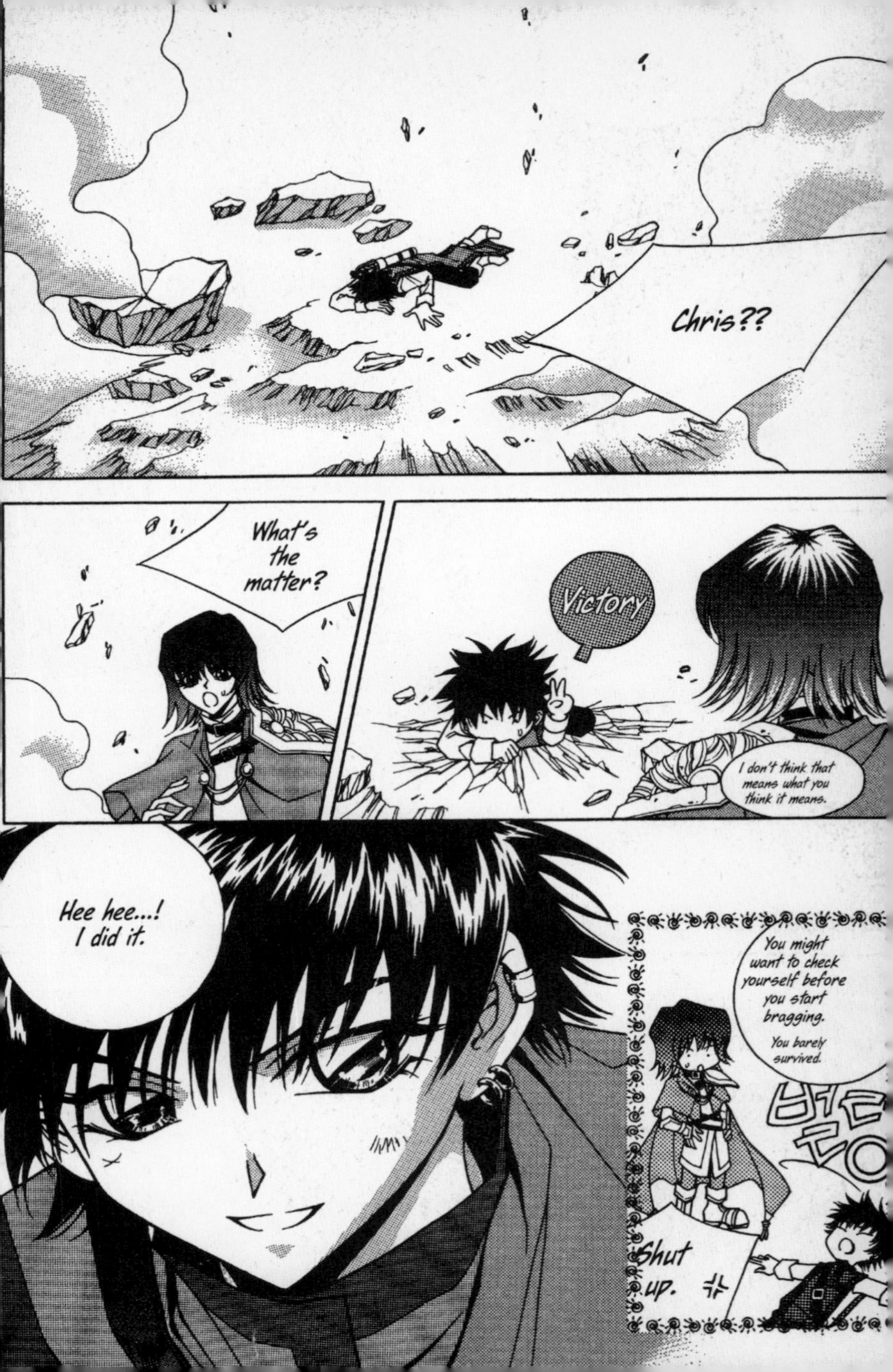
Chris??
What's the matter?
Victory
I don't think that means what you think it means.
Hee hee...! I did it.
You might want to check yourself before you start bragging.
You barely survived.
Shut up.

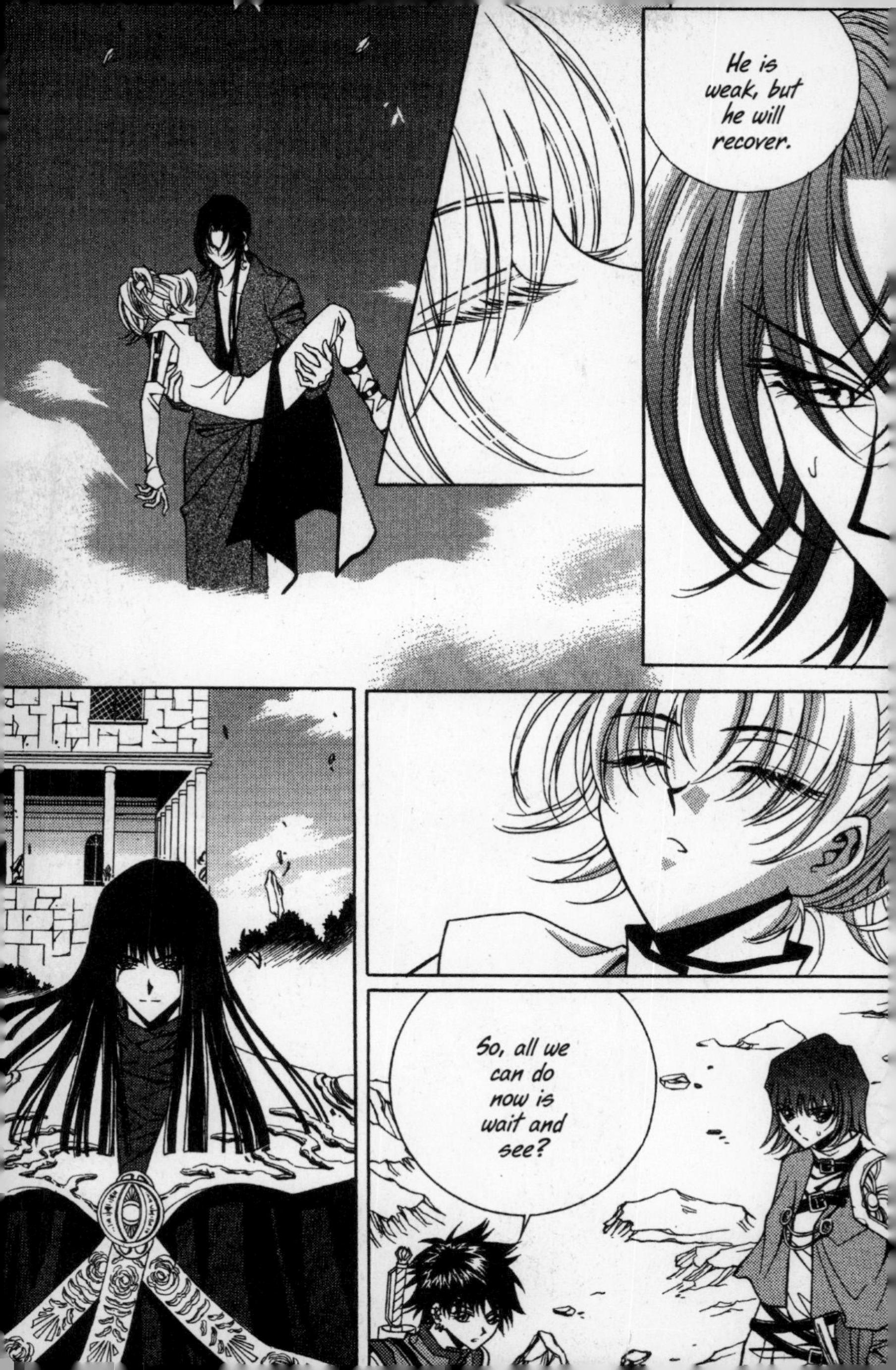
He is weak, but he will recover.
So, all we can do now is wait and see?

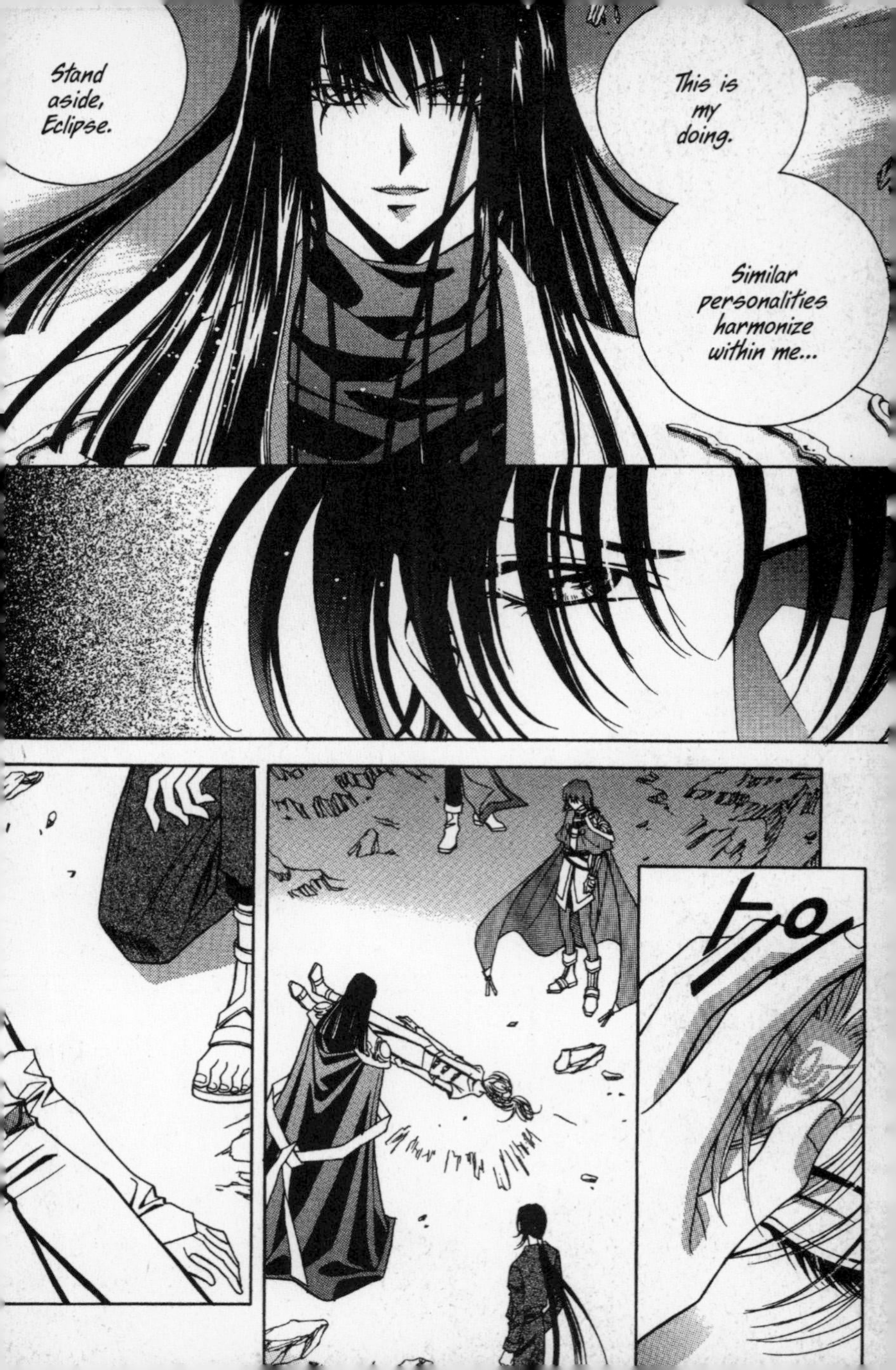
Stand aside, Eclipse.
This is my doing.
Similar personalities harmonize within me...

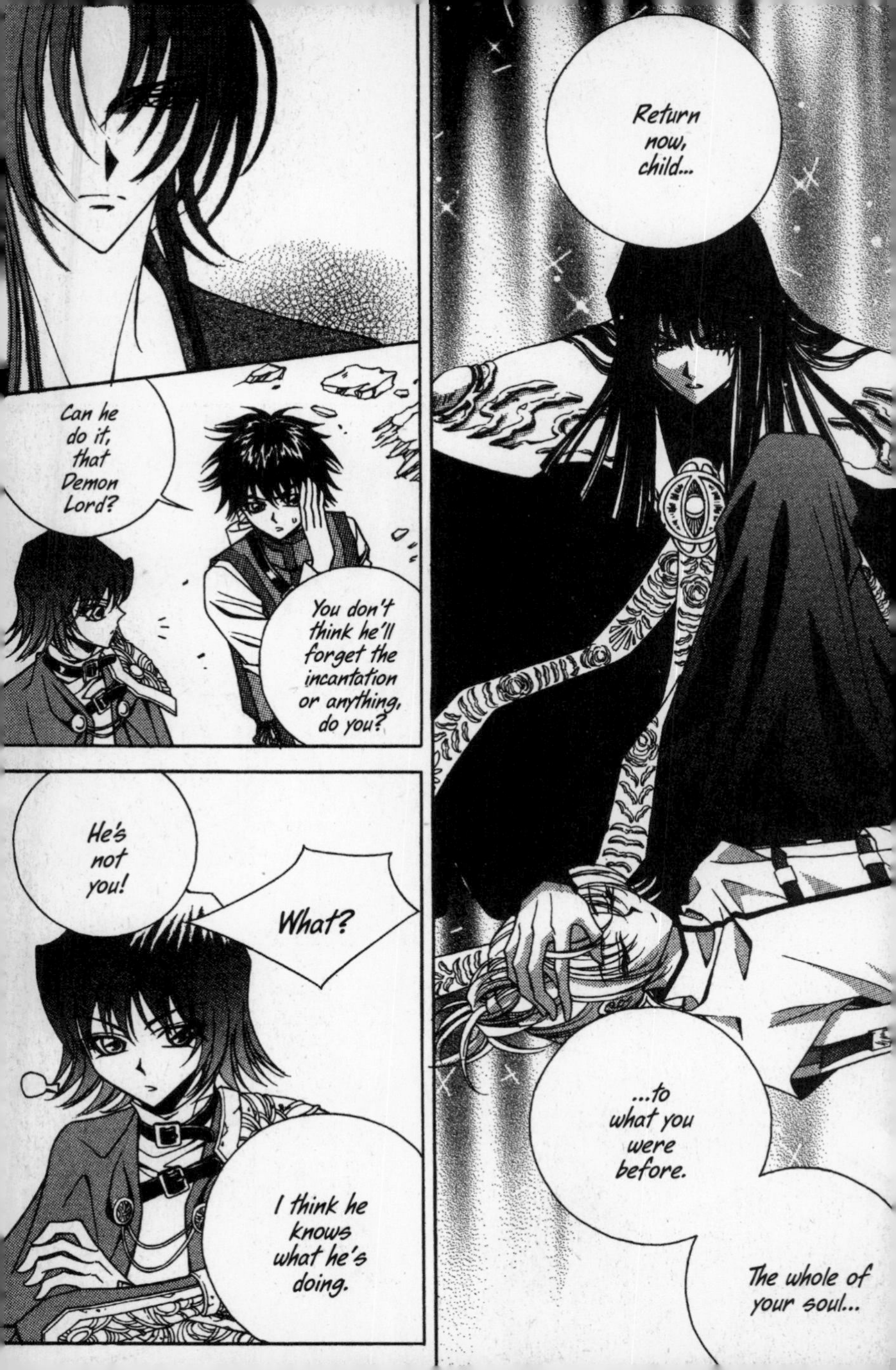

Can he do it, that Demon Lord?
You don't think he'll forget the incantation or anything, do you?
He's not you!
What?
I think he knows what he's doing.
Return now, child...
...to what you were before.
The whole of your soul...

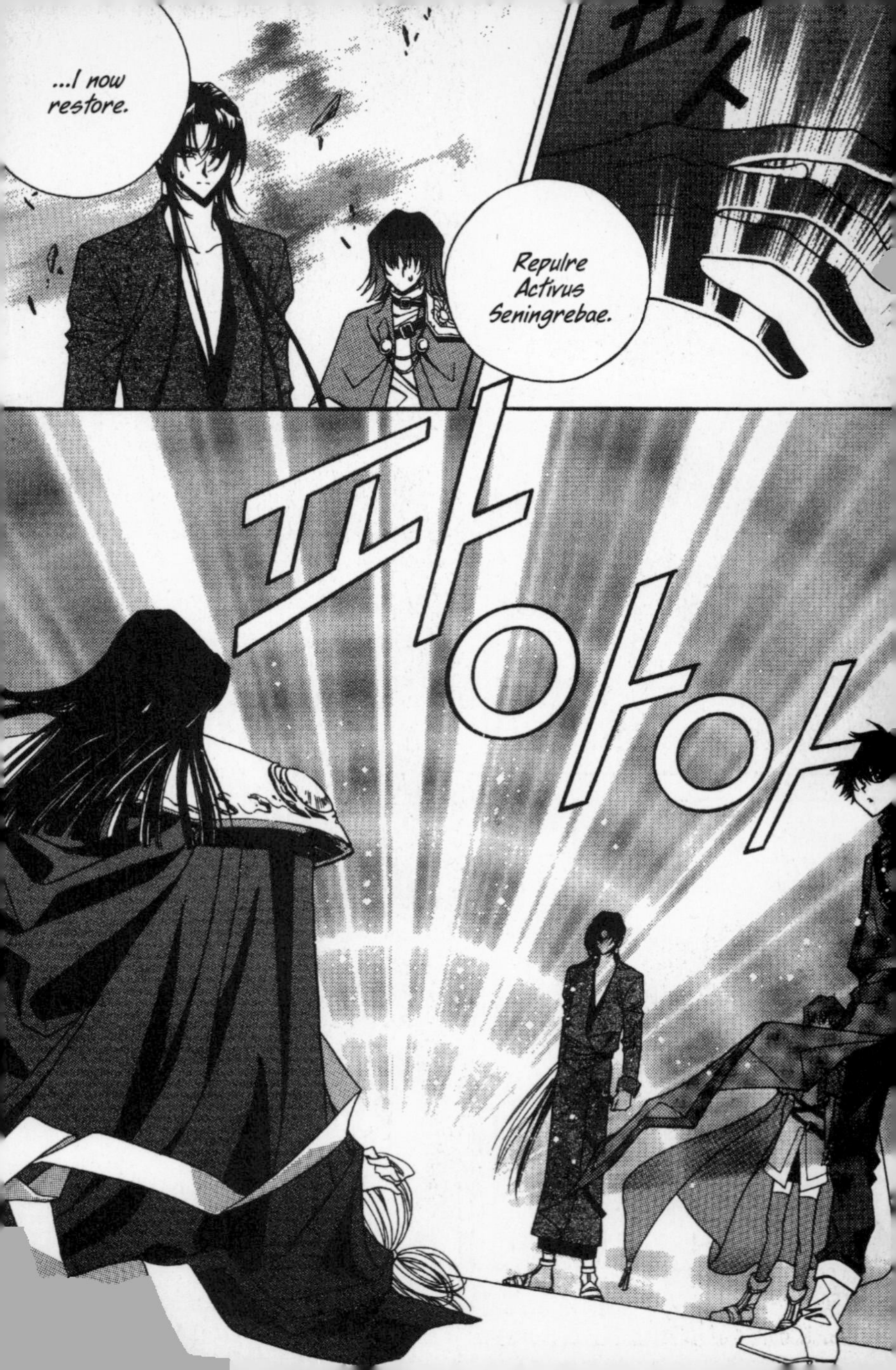
...I now restore.
Repulre Activus Seningrebae.

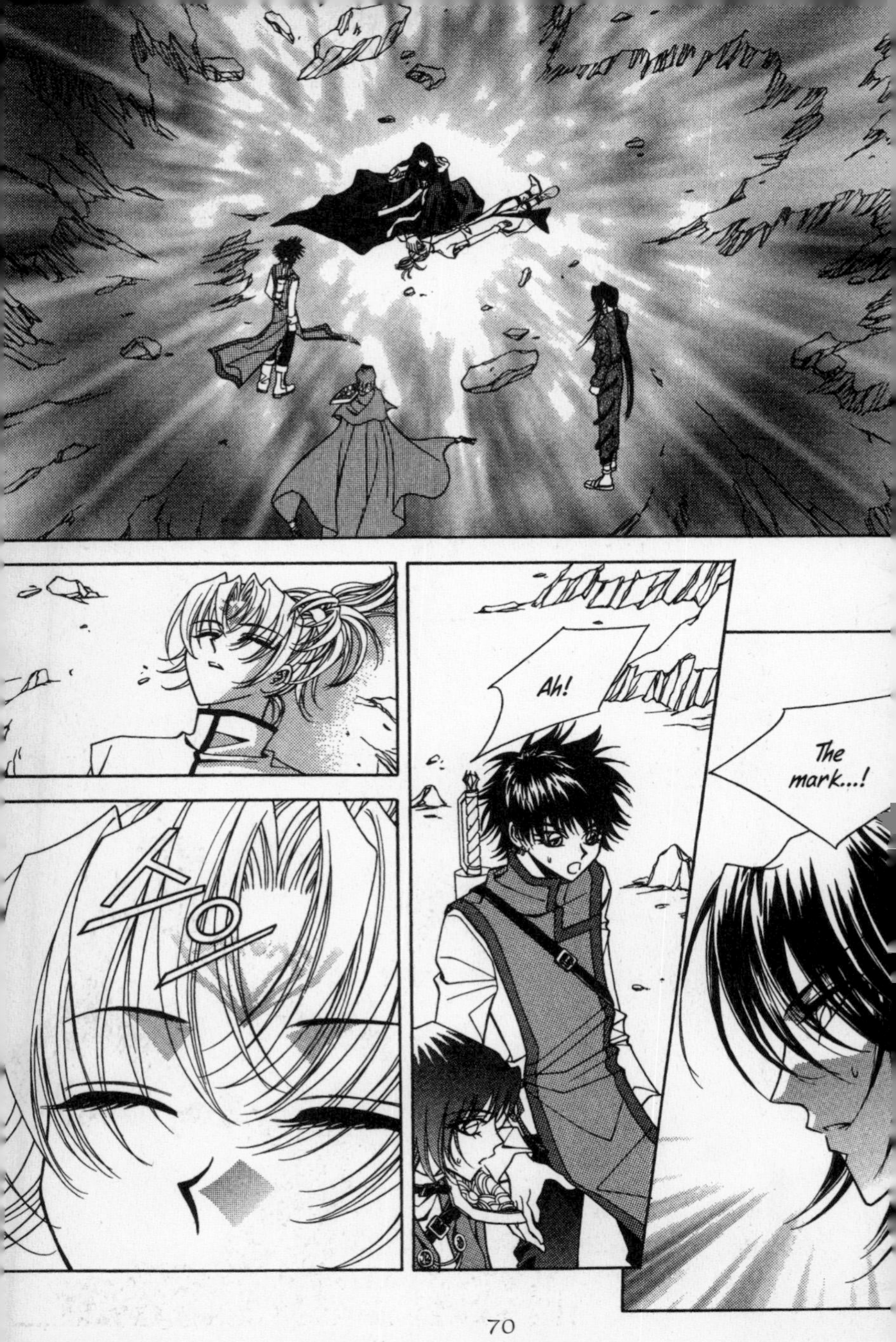
Ah!
The mark...!

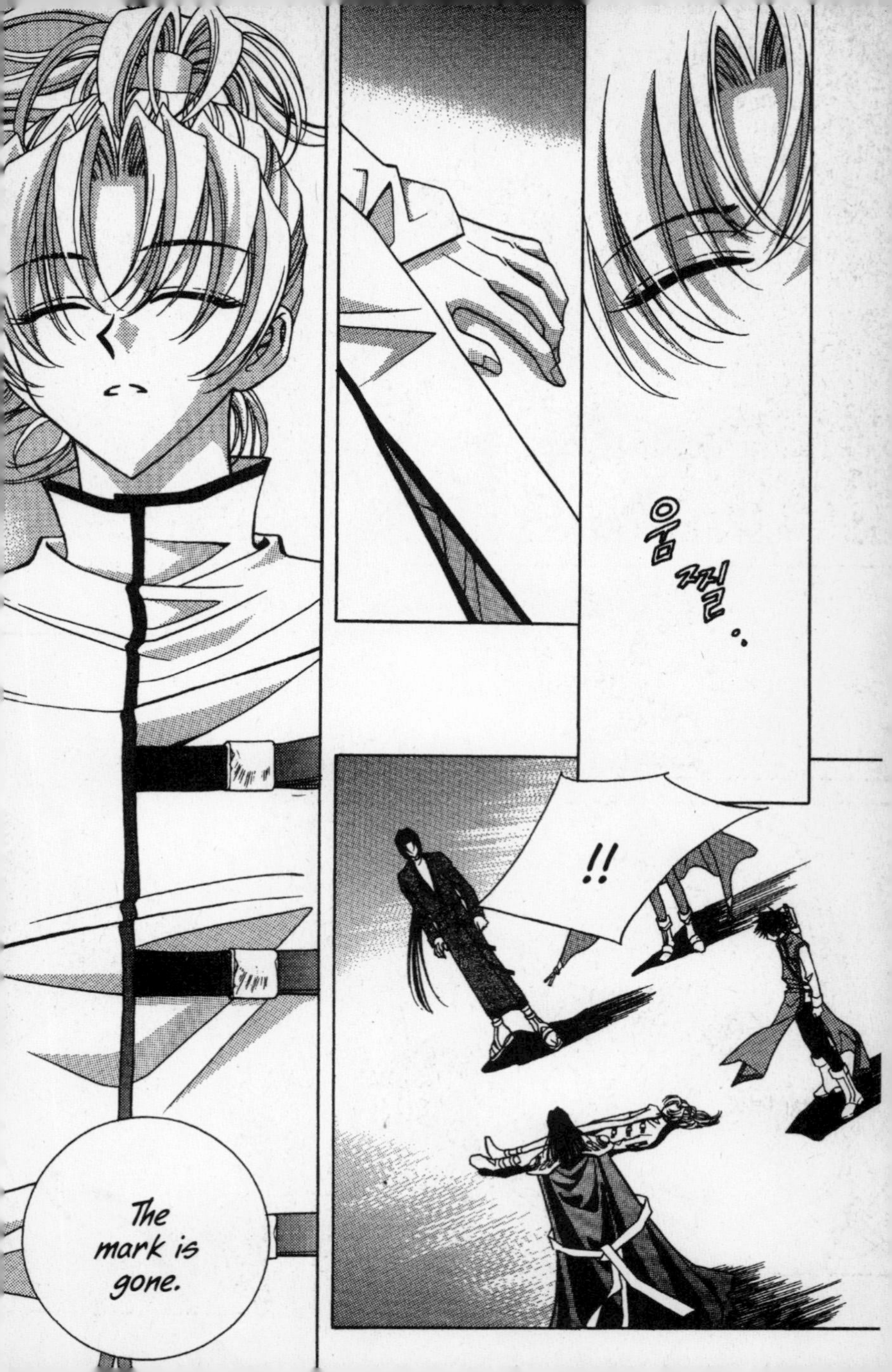
The mark is gone.
움찔..
!!

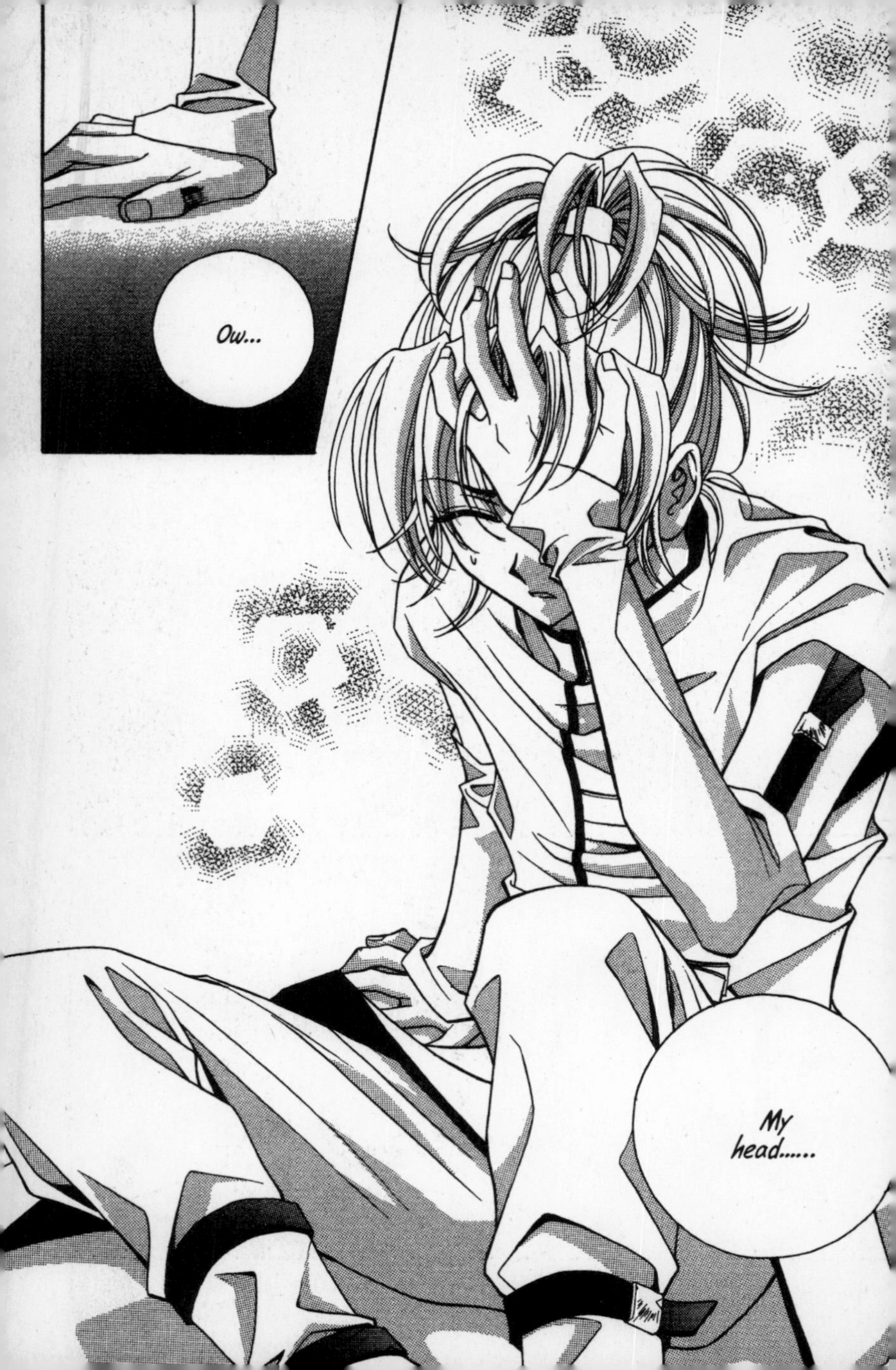
Ow...
My head......

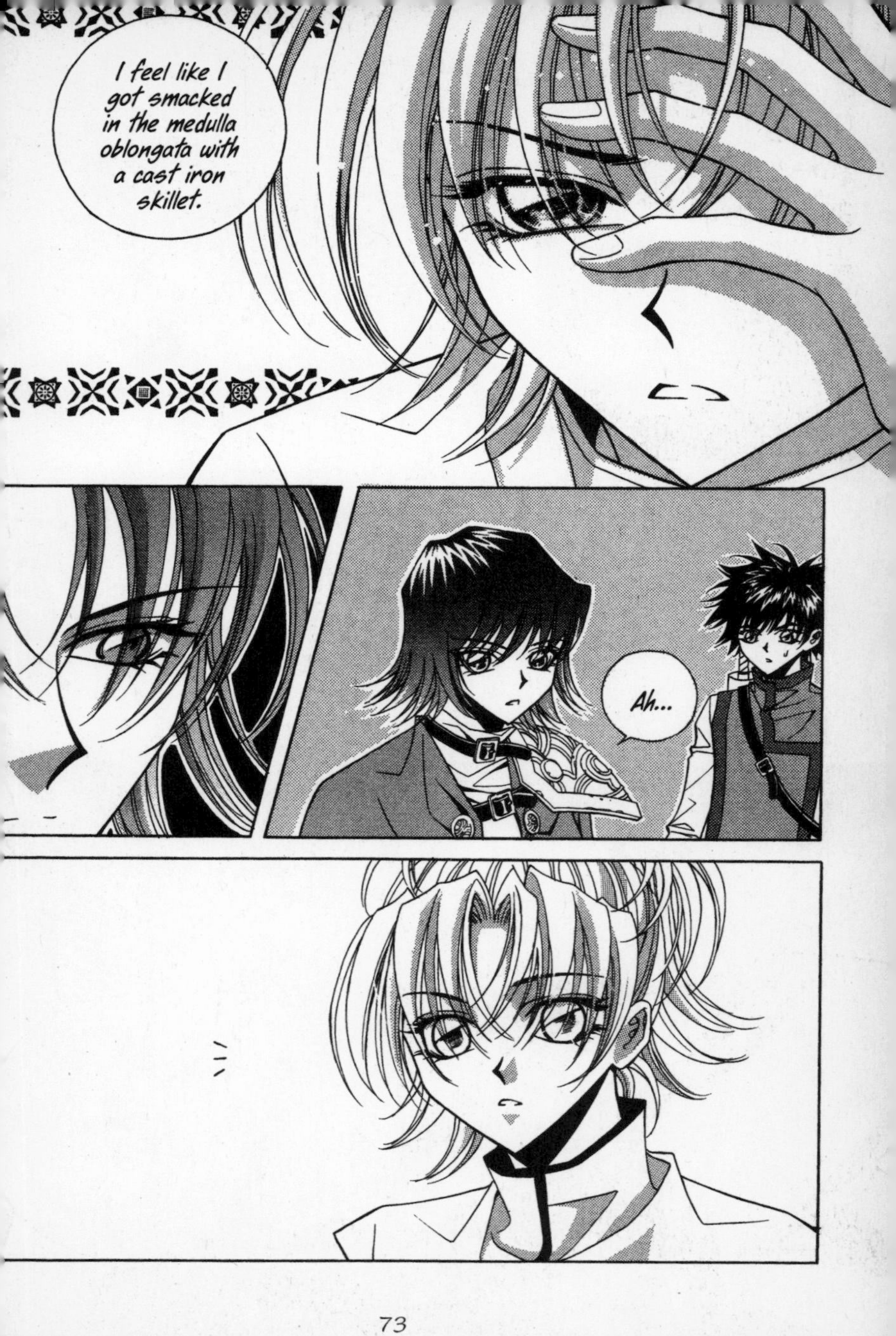
I feel like I got smacked in the medulla oblongata with a cast iron skillet.
Ah...

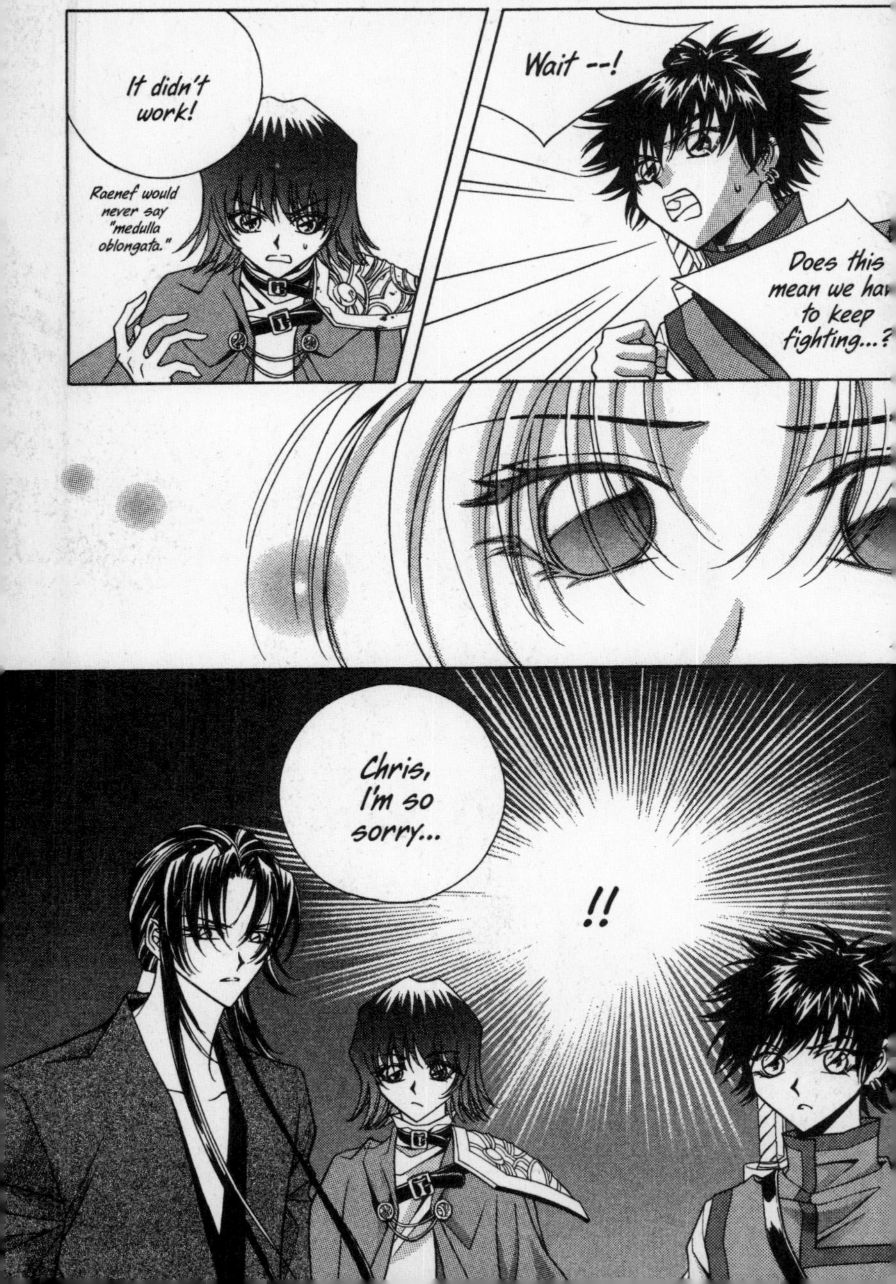
It didn't work!
Raenef would never say "medulla oblongata."
Wait --!
Does this mean we hav
to keep fighting...?
Chris, I'm so sorry...
!!

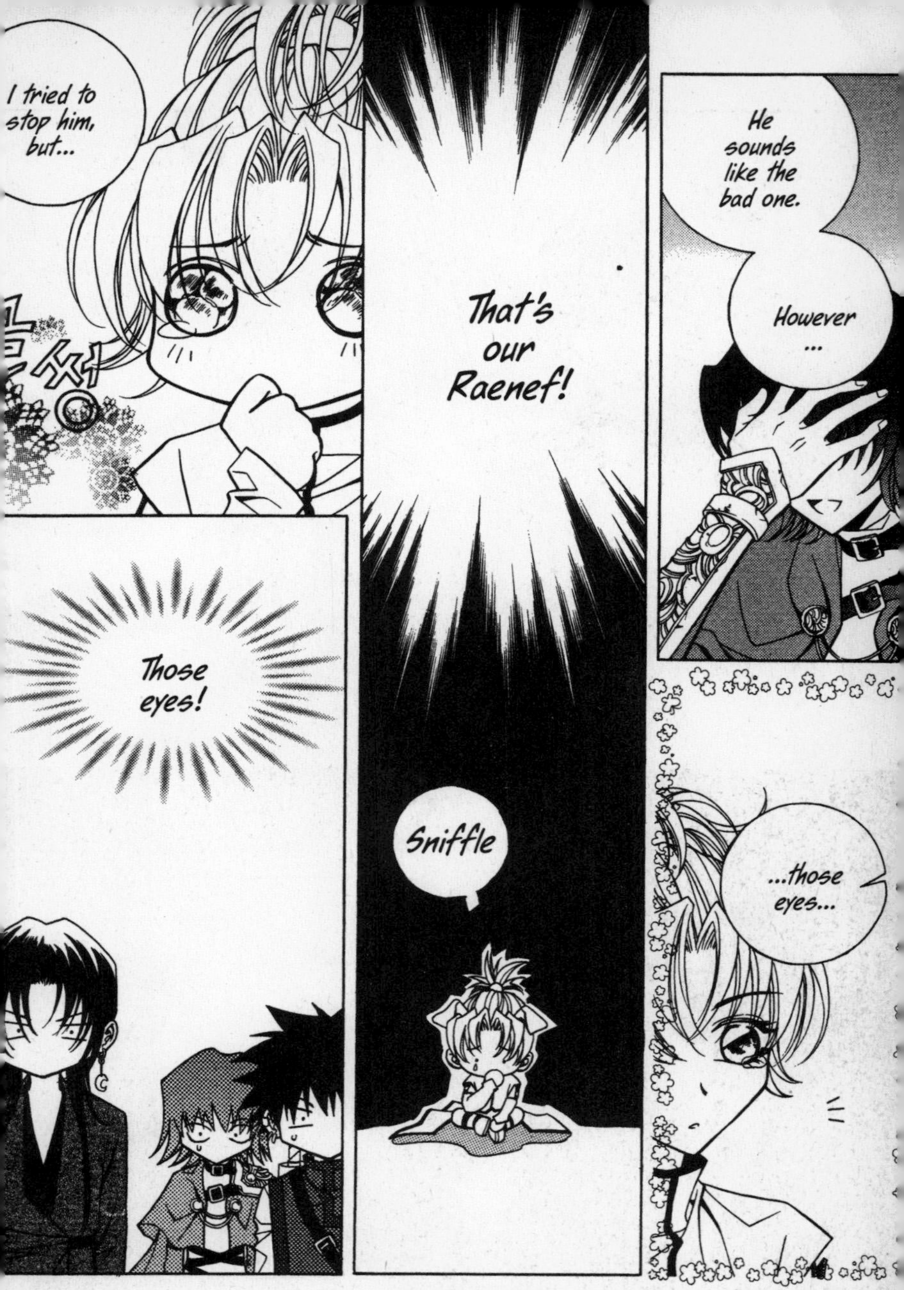
I tried to stop him, but...
Those eyes!
That's our Raenef!
Sniffle
He sounds like the bad one.
However ...
...those eyes...

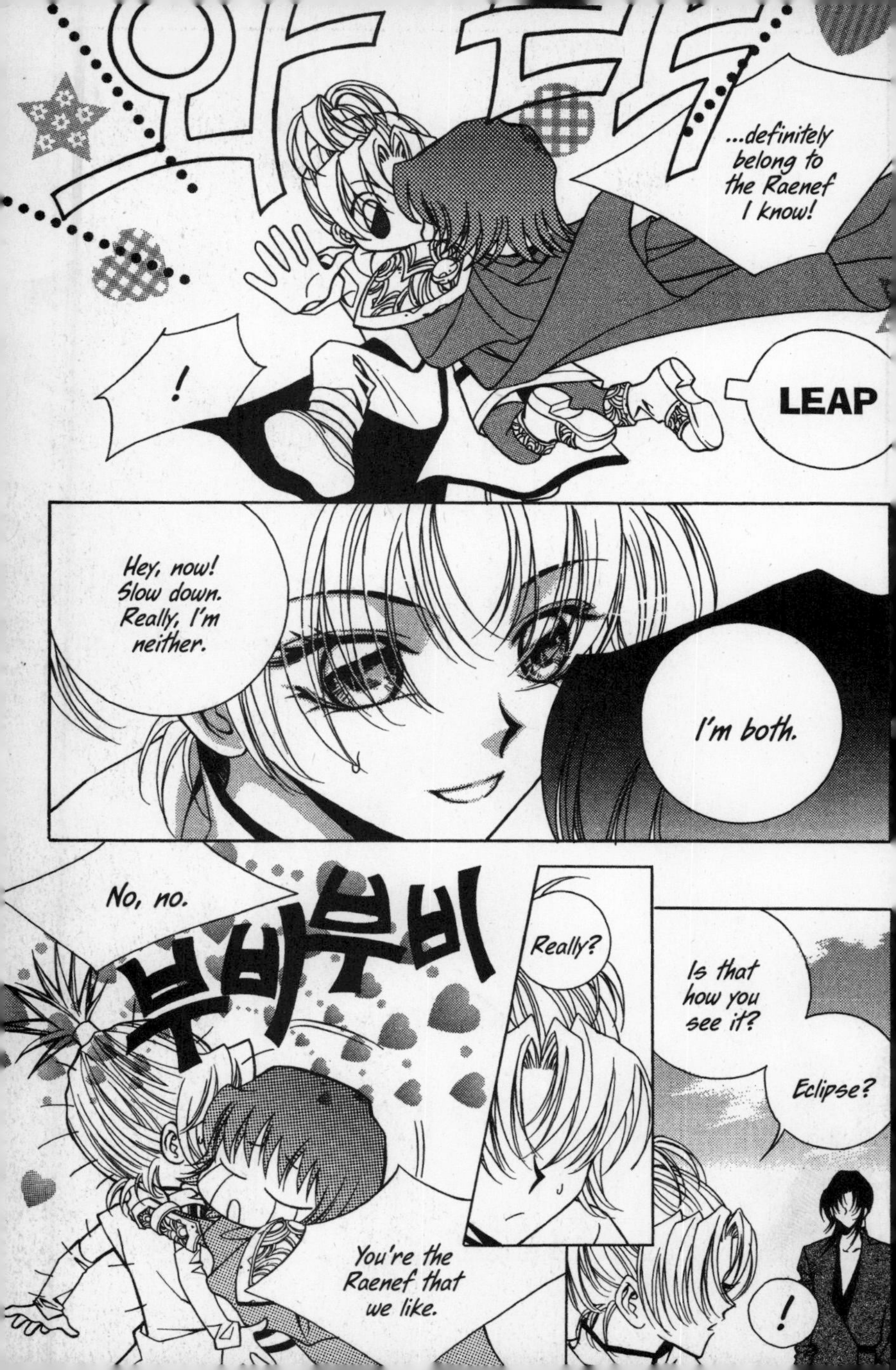
...definitely belong to the Raenef I know!
!
LEAP
Hey, now! Slow down. Really, I'm neither.
I'm both.
No, no.
부비부비
You're the Raenef that we like.
Really?
Is that how you see it?
Eclipse?
!

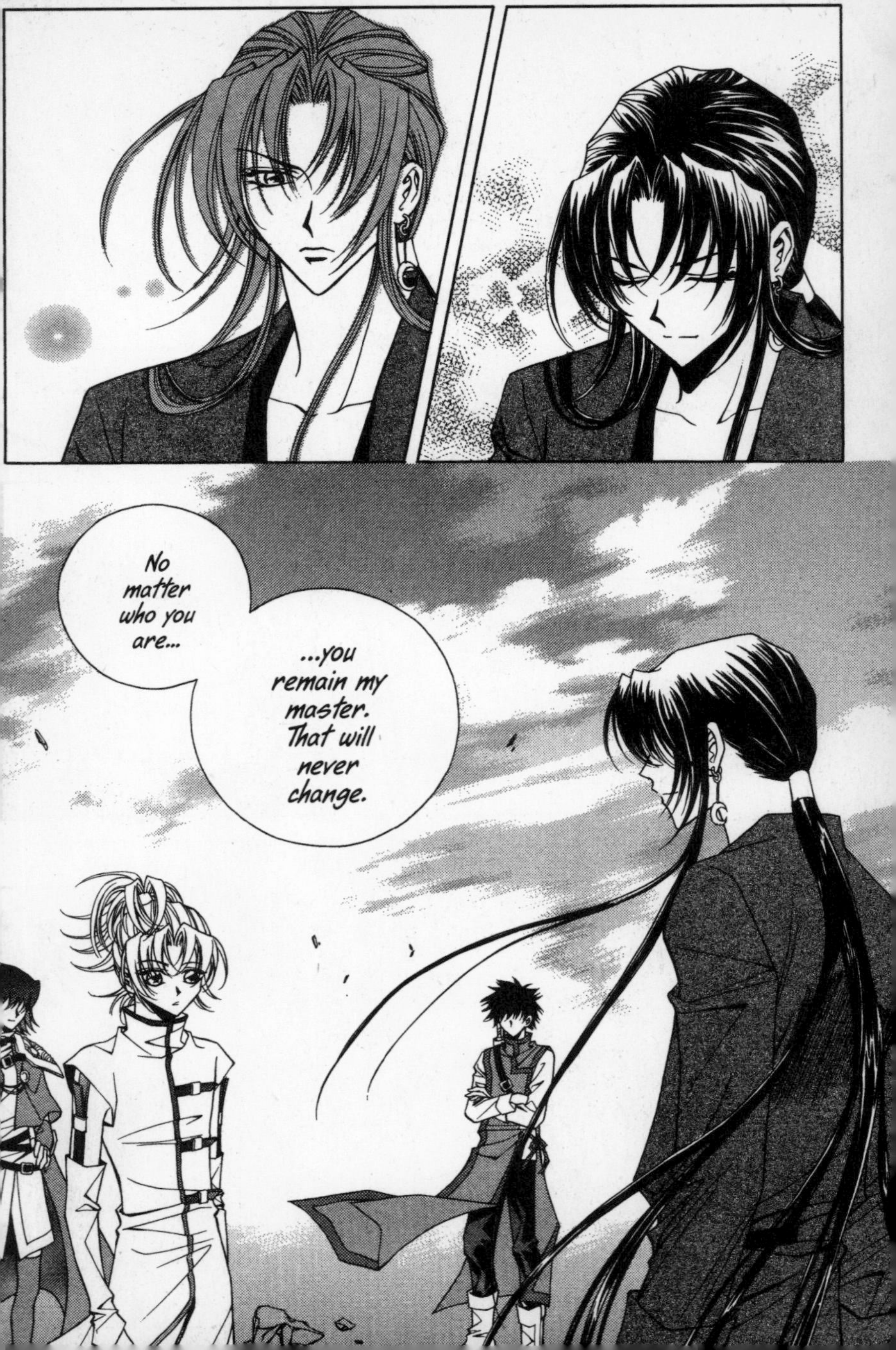
No matter who you are...
...you remain my master. That will never change.

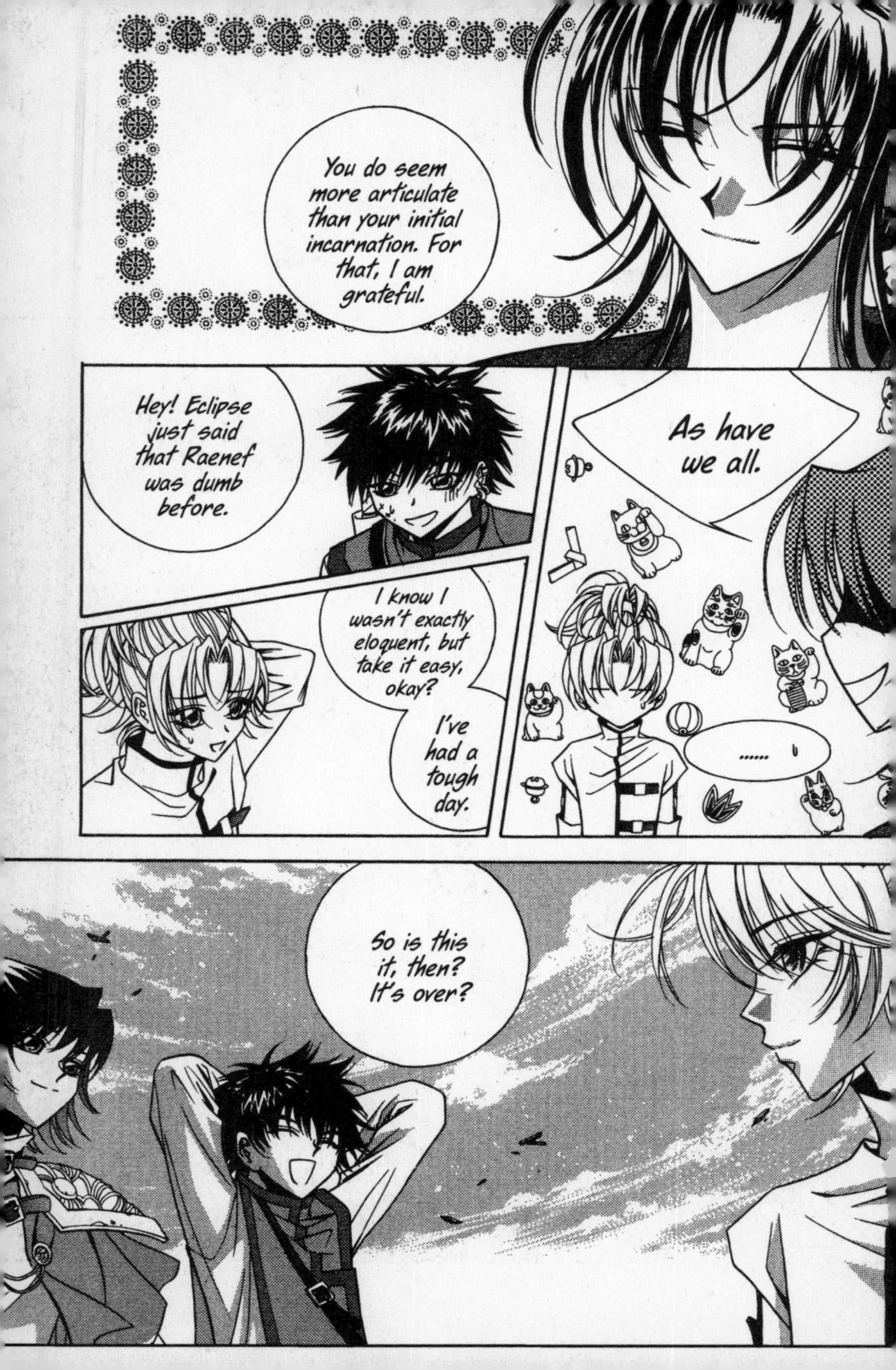
You do seem more articulate than your initial incarnation. For that, I am grateful.
Hey! Eclipse just said that Raenef was dumb before.
As have we all.
I know I wasn't exactly eloquent, but take it easy, okay?
I've had a tough day.
......
So is this it, then? It's over?

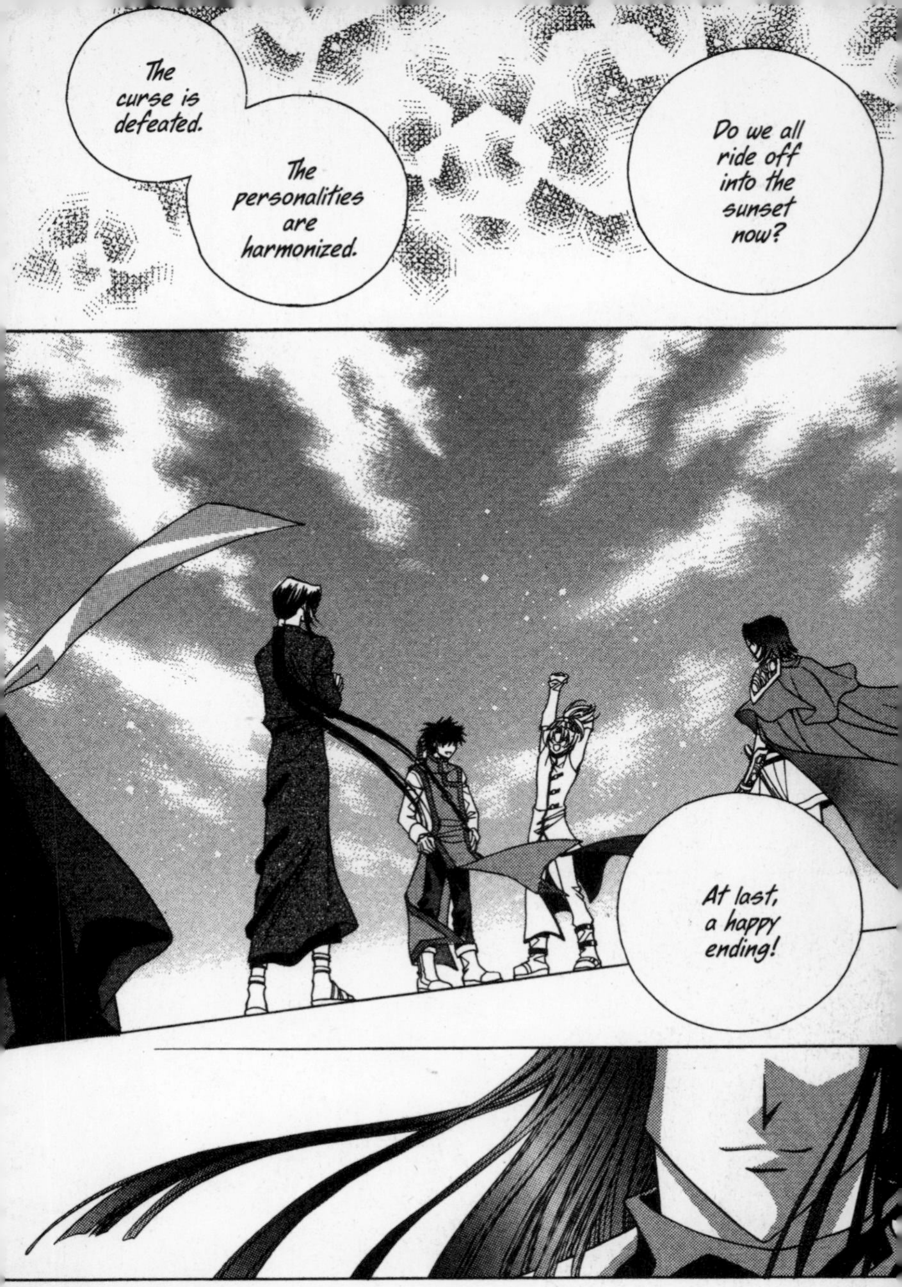

The curse is defeated.
The personalities are harmonized.
Do we all ride off into the sunset now?
At last, a happy ending!

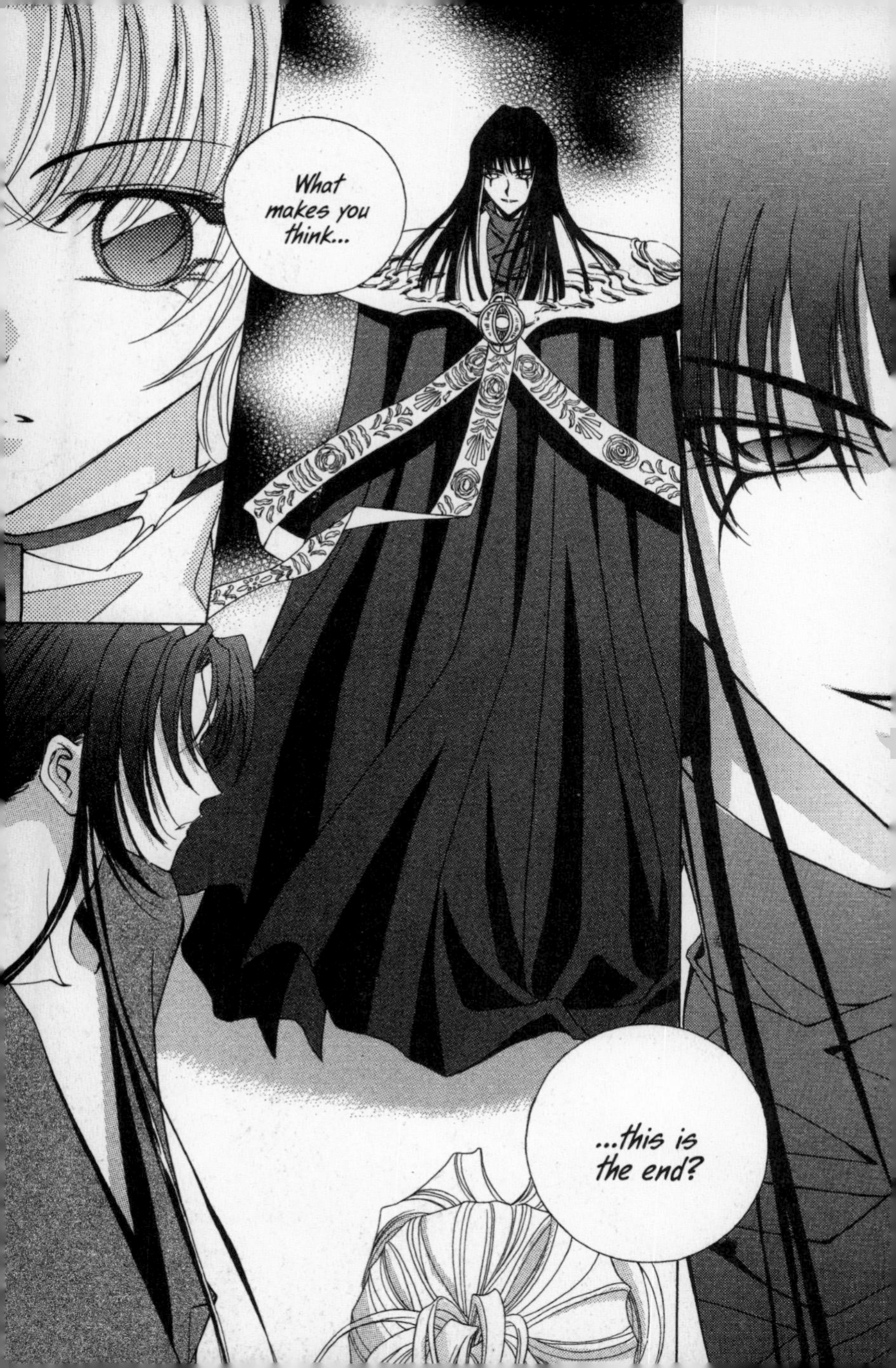
What makes you think...
...this is the end?

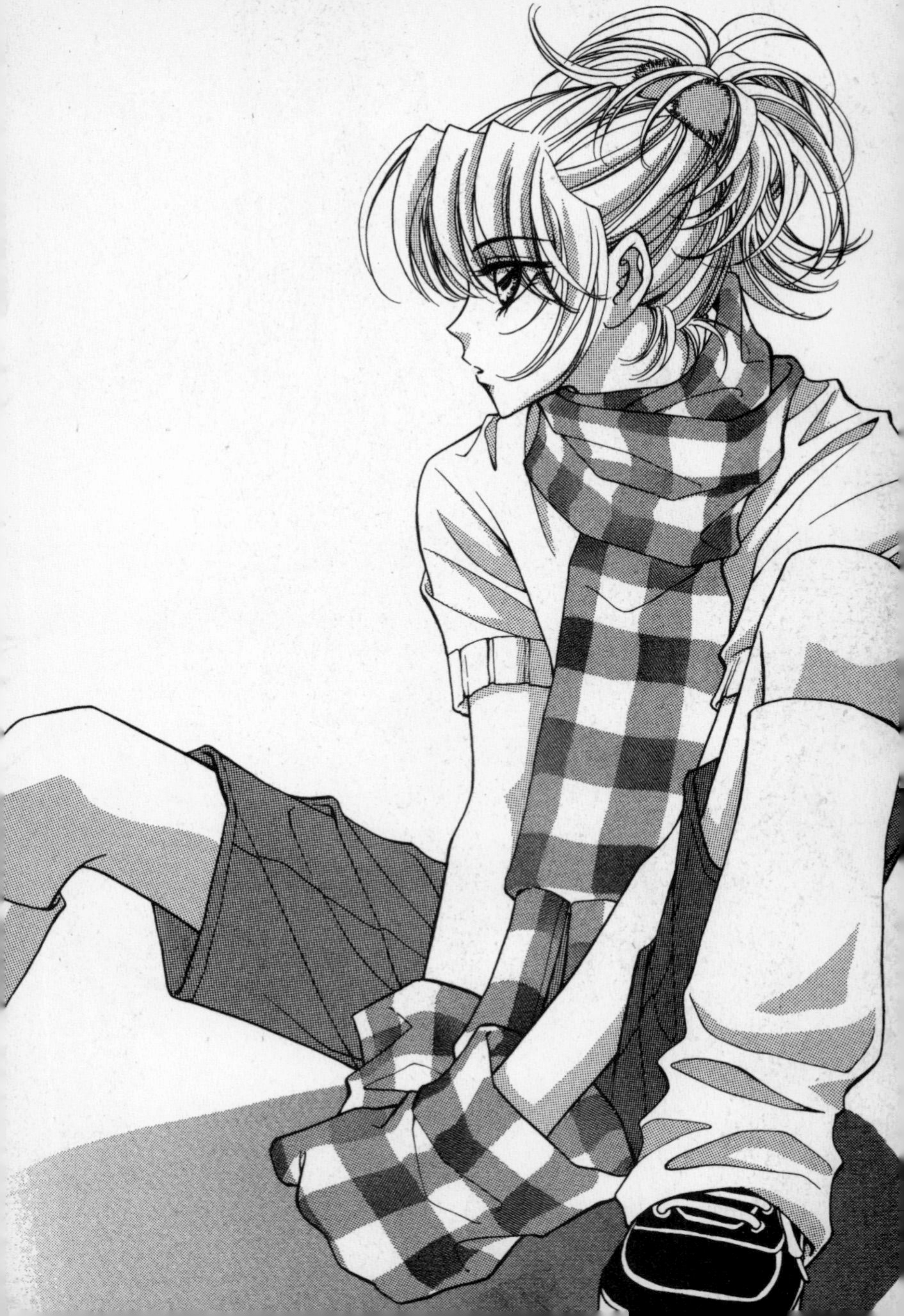

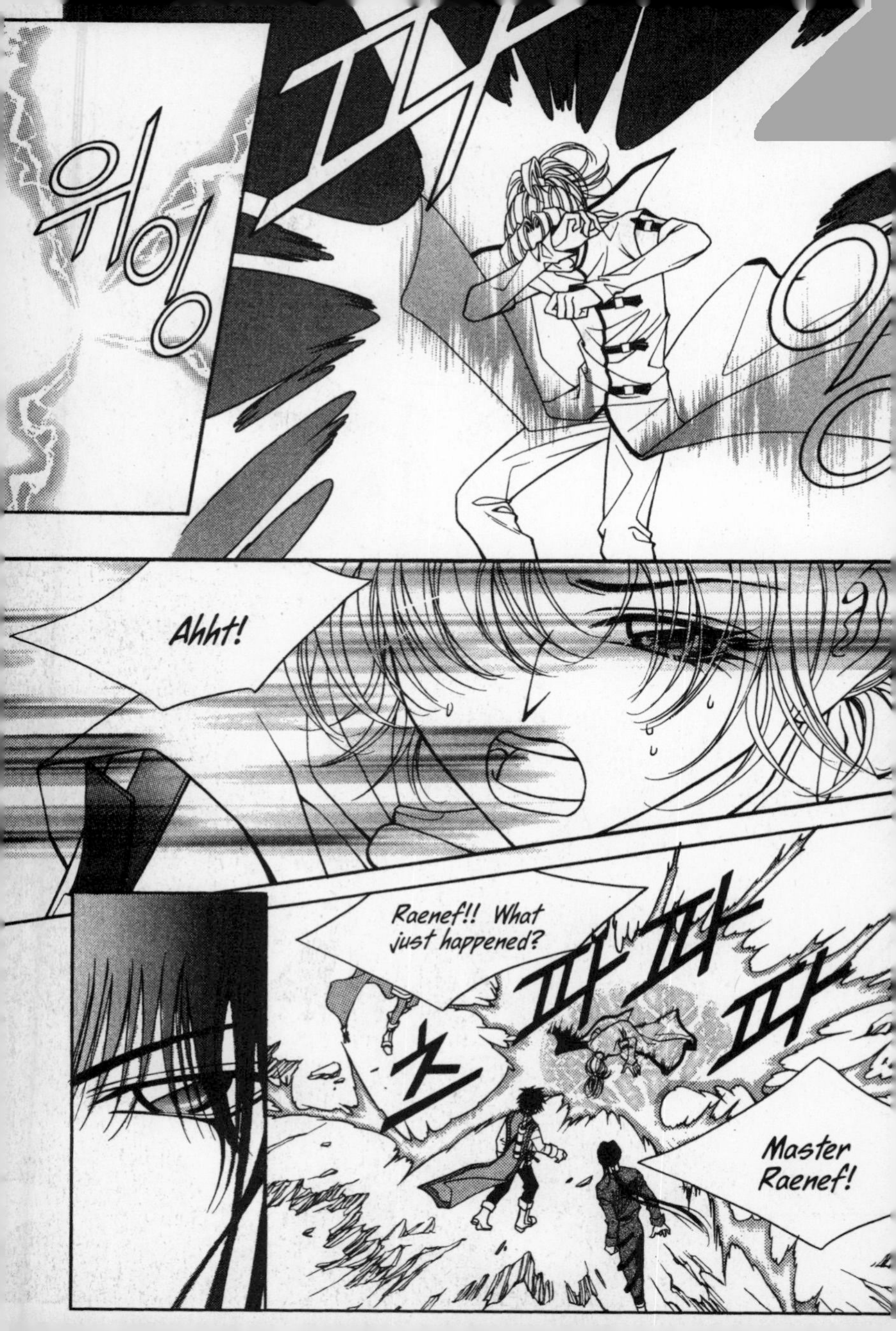
Ahht!
Raenef!! What just happened?
Master Raenef!

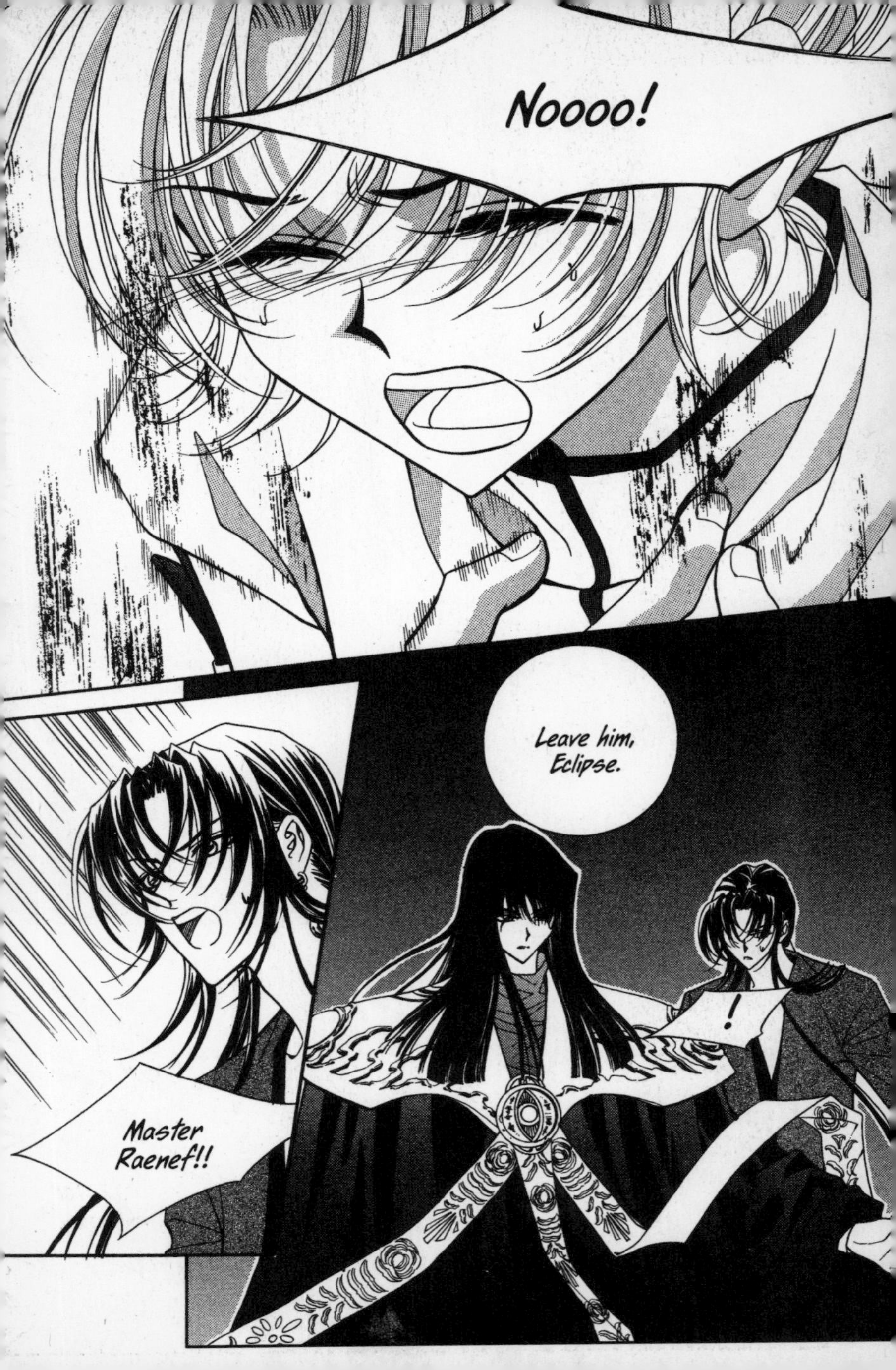
Noooo!
Master Raenef!!
Leave him, Eclipse.
!

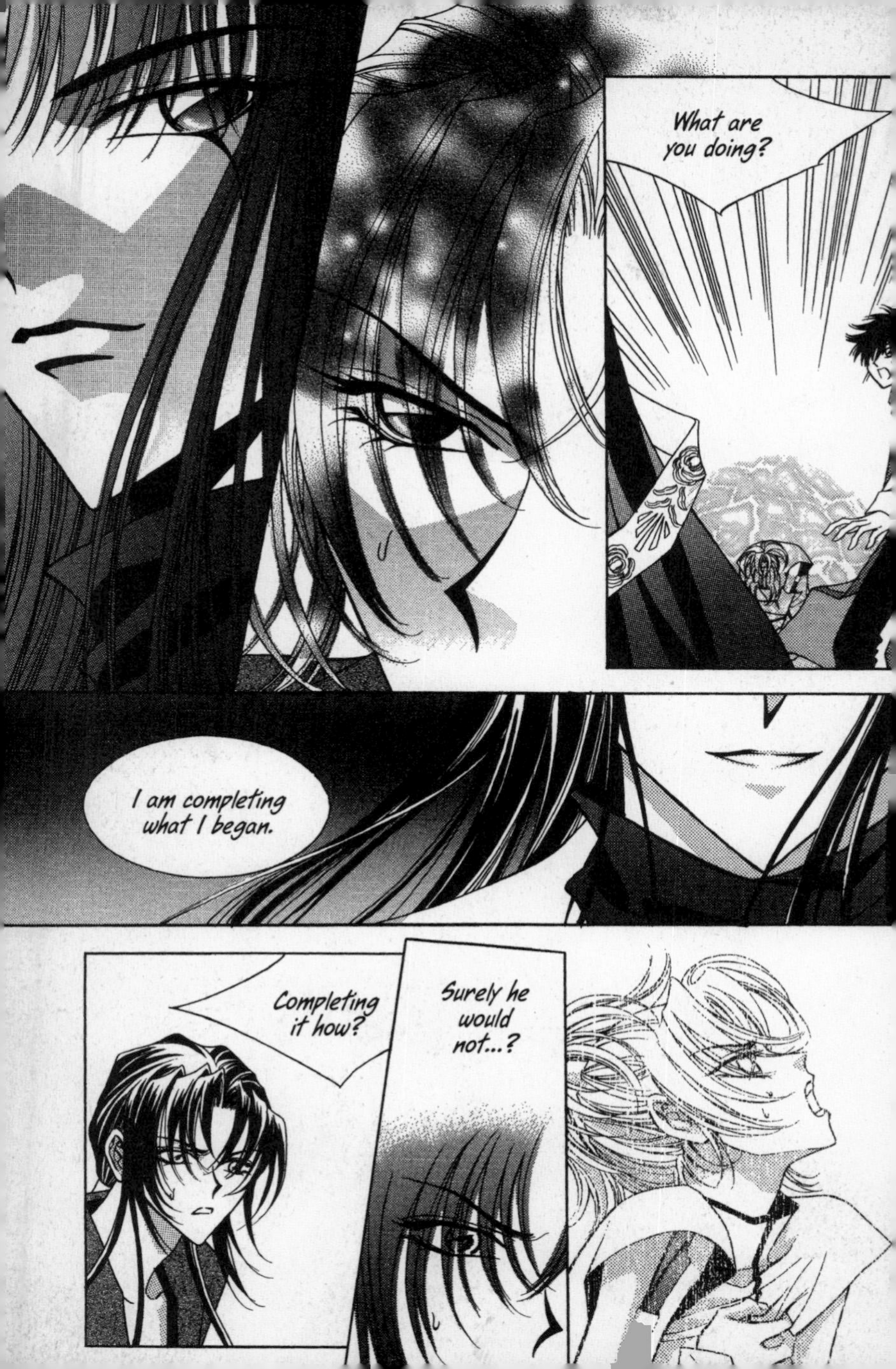
What are you doing?
I am completing what I began.
Completing it how?
Surely he would not...?

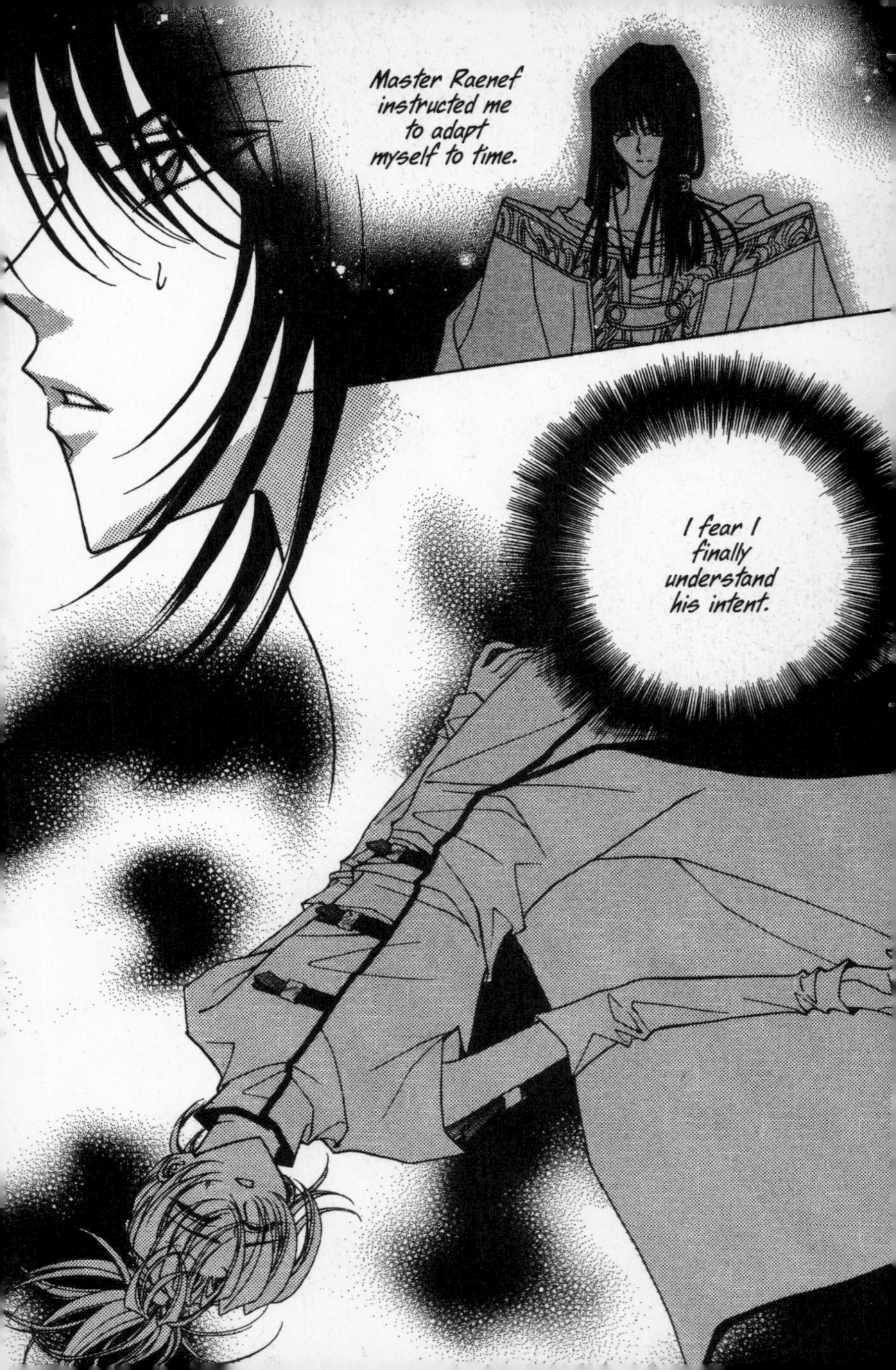
Master Raenef instructed me to adapt myself to time.
I fear I finally understand his intent.

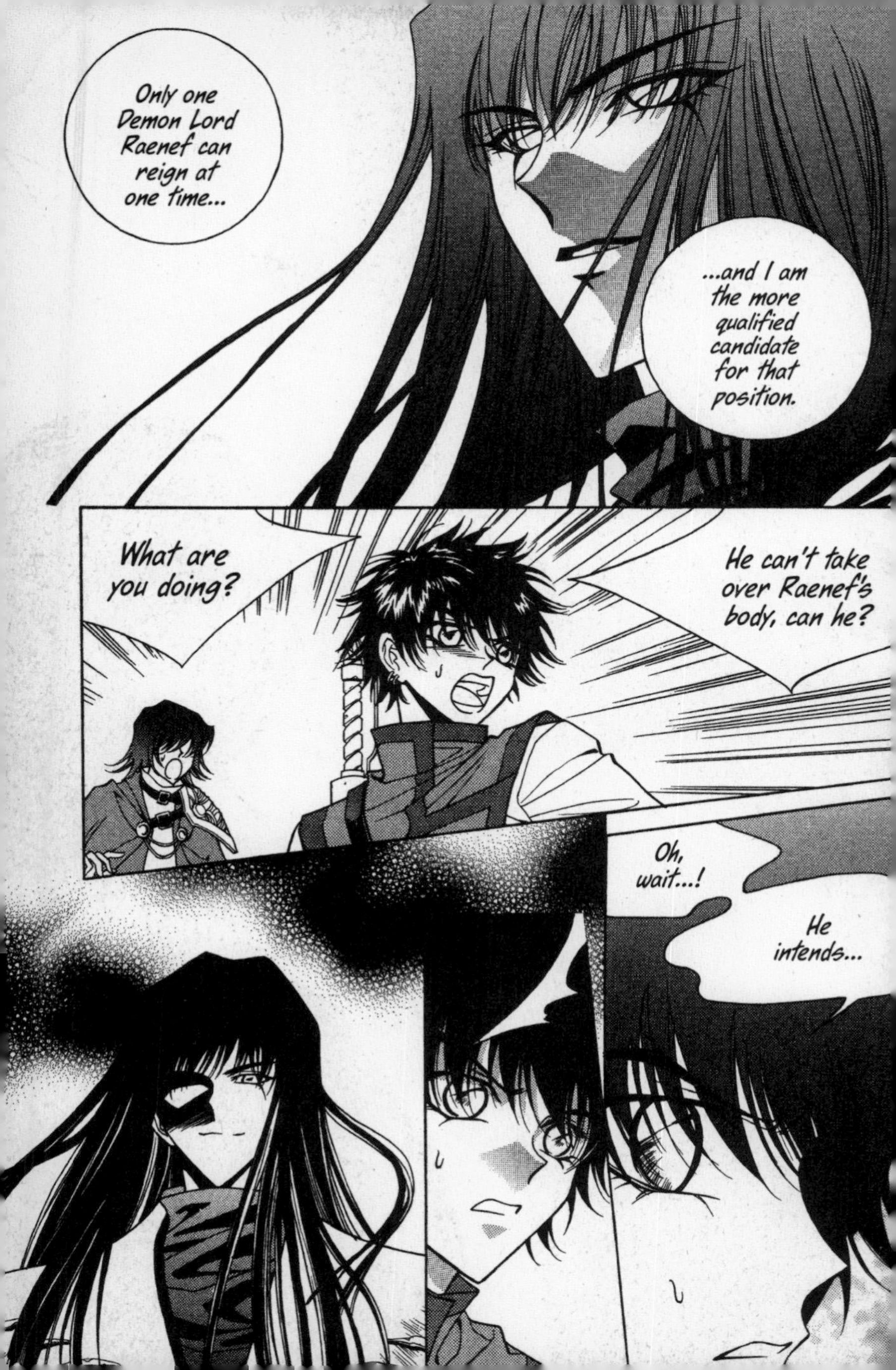
Only one Demon Lord Raenef can reign at one time...
...and I am the more qualified candidate for that position.
What are you doing?
He can't take over Raenef's body, can he?
Oh, wait...!
He intends...

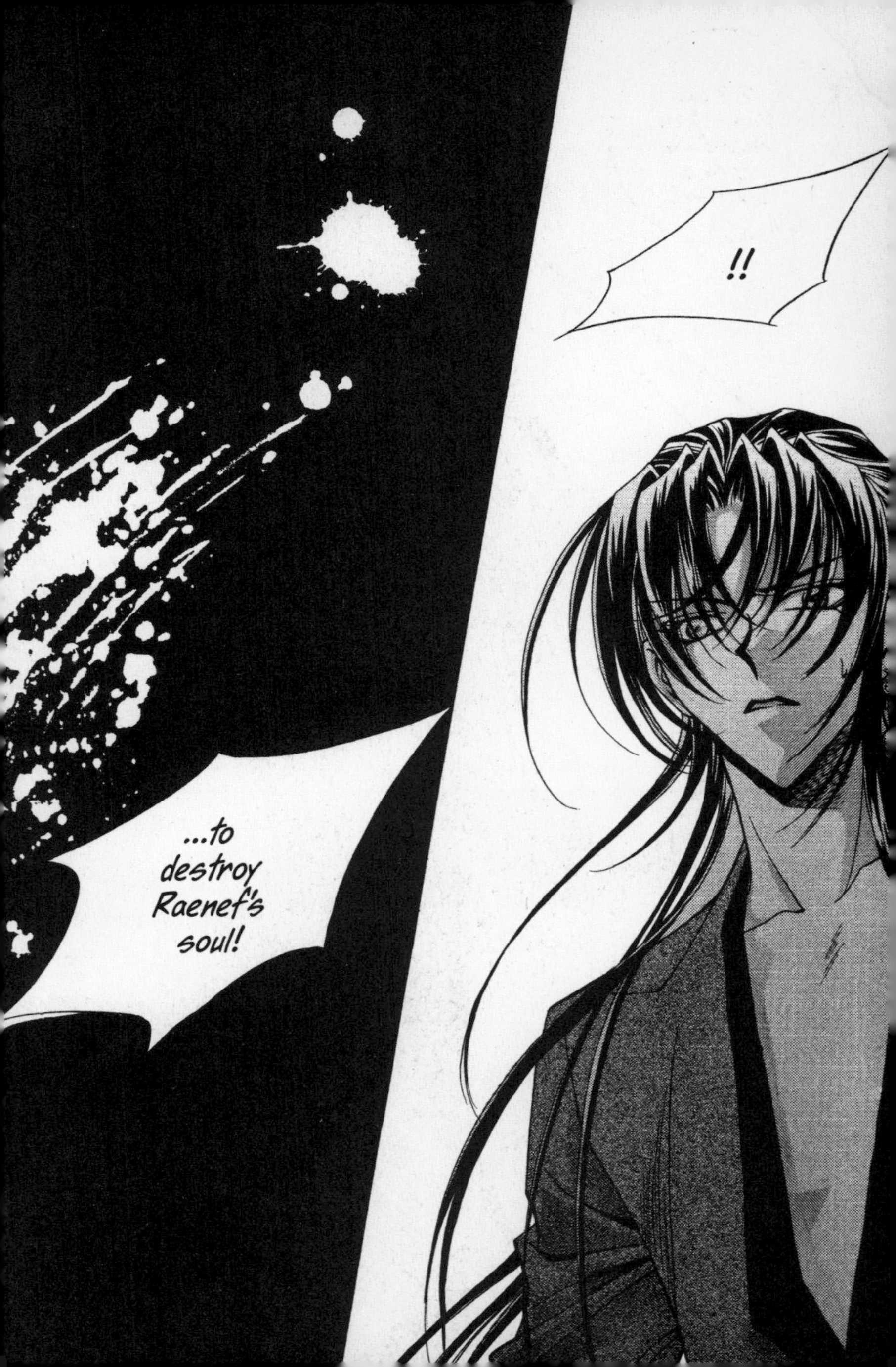
...to destroy Raenef's soul!
!!

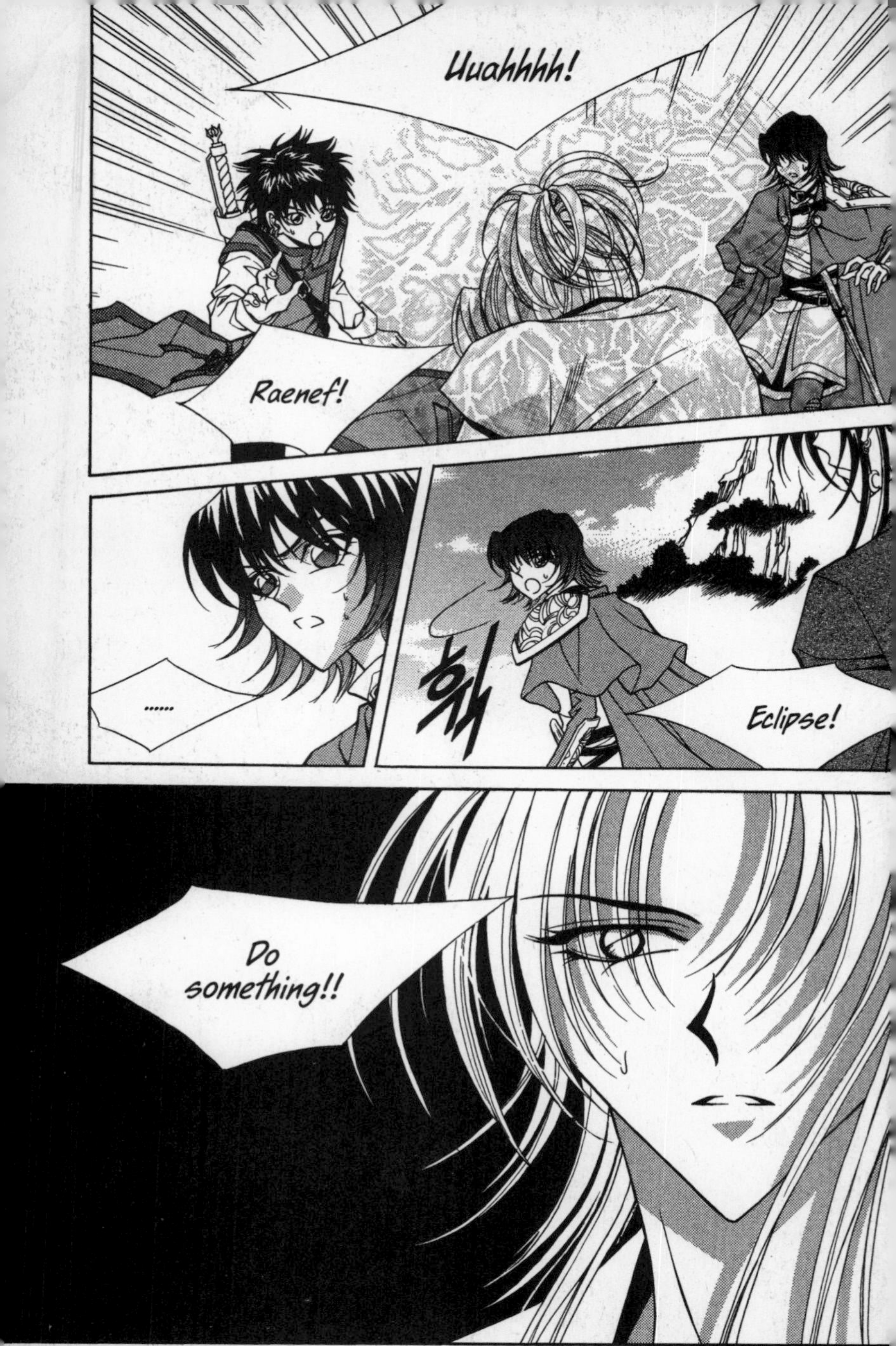
Uuahhhh!
Raenef!
......
Eclipse!
Do something!!

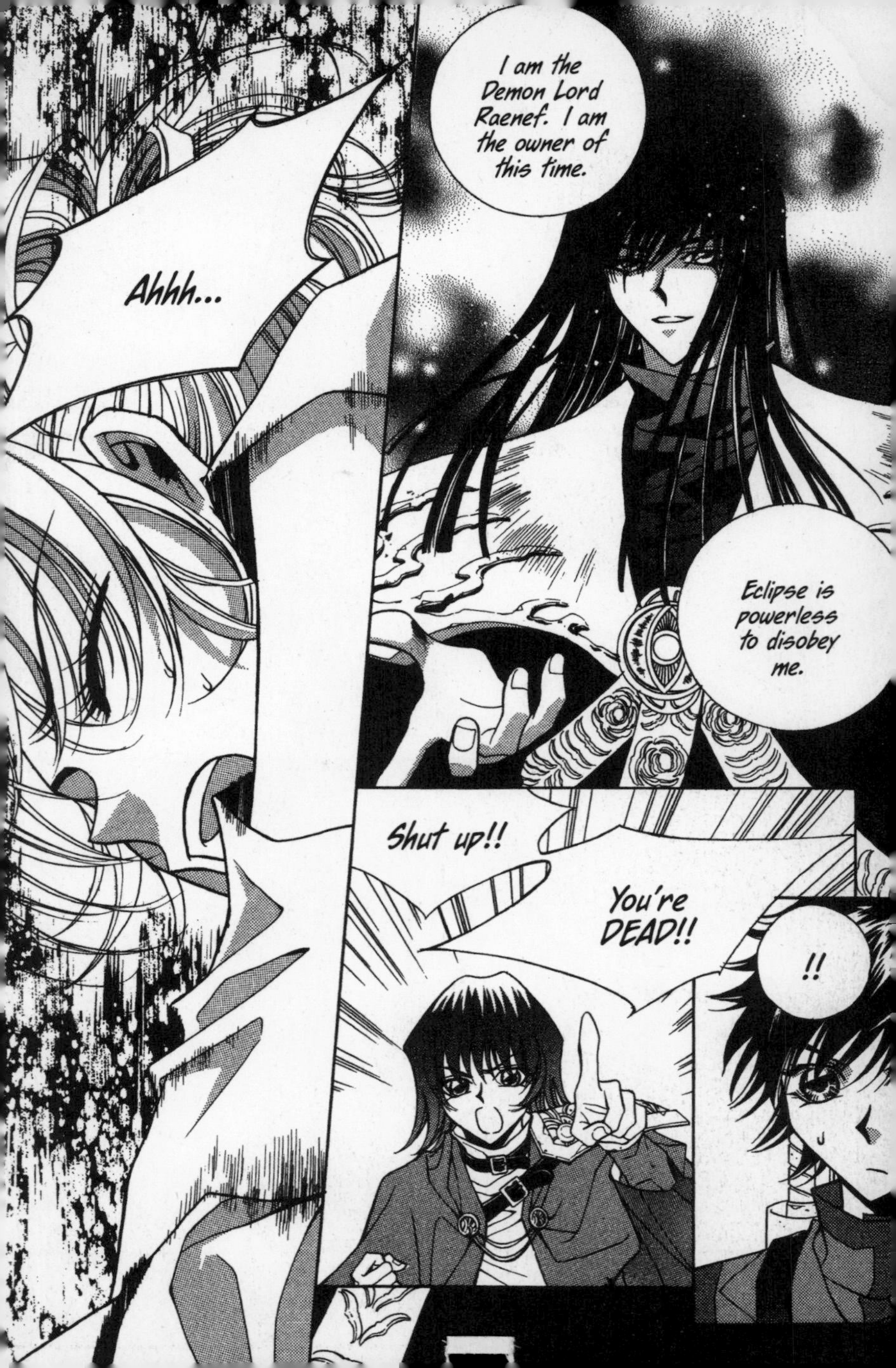
Ahhh...
I am the Demon Lord Raenef. I am the owner of this time.
Eclipse is powerless to disobey me.
Shut up!!
You're DEAD!!
!!

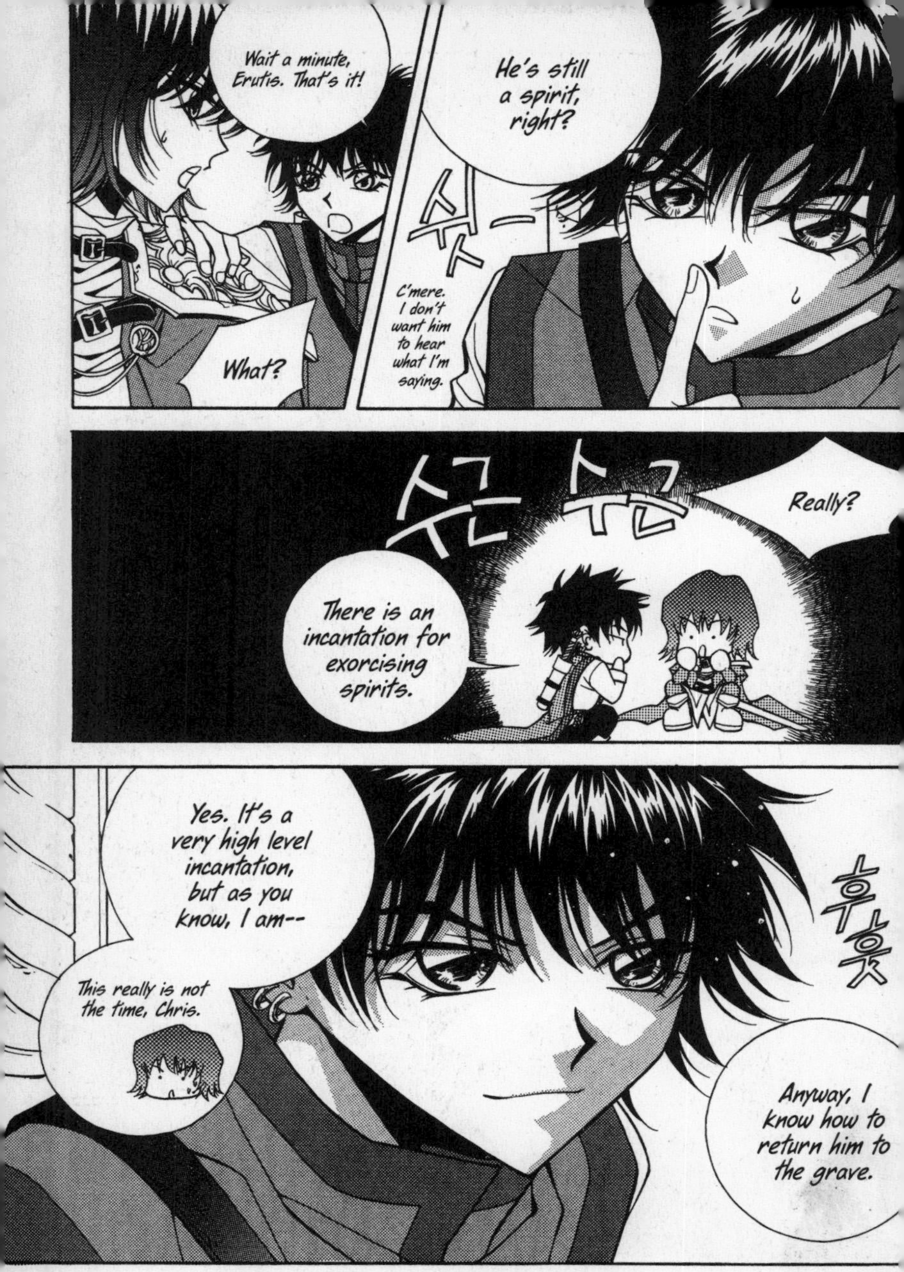

Wait a minute, Erutis. That's it!
What?
He's still a spirit, right?
C'mere. I don't want him to hear what I'm saying.
Really?
There is an incantation for exorcising spirits.
Yes. It's a very high level incantation, but as you know, I am--
This really is not the time, Chris.
Anyway, I know how to return him to the grave.

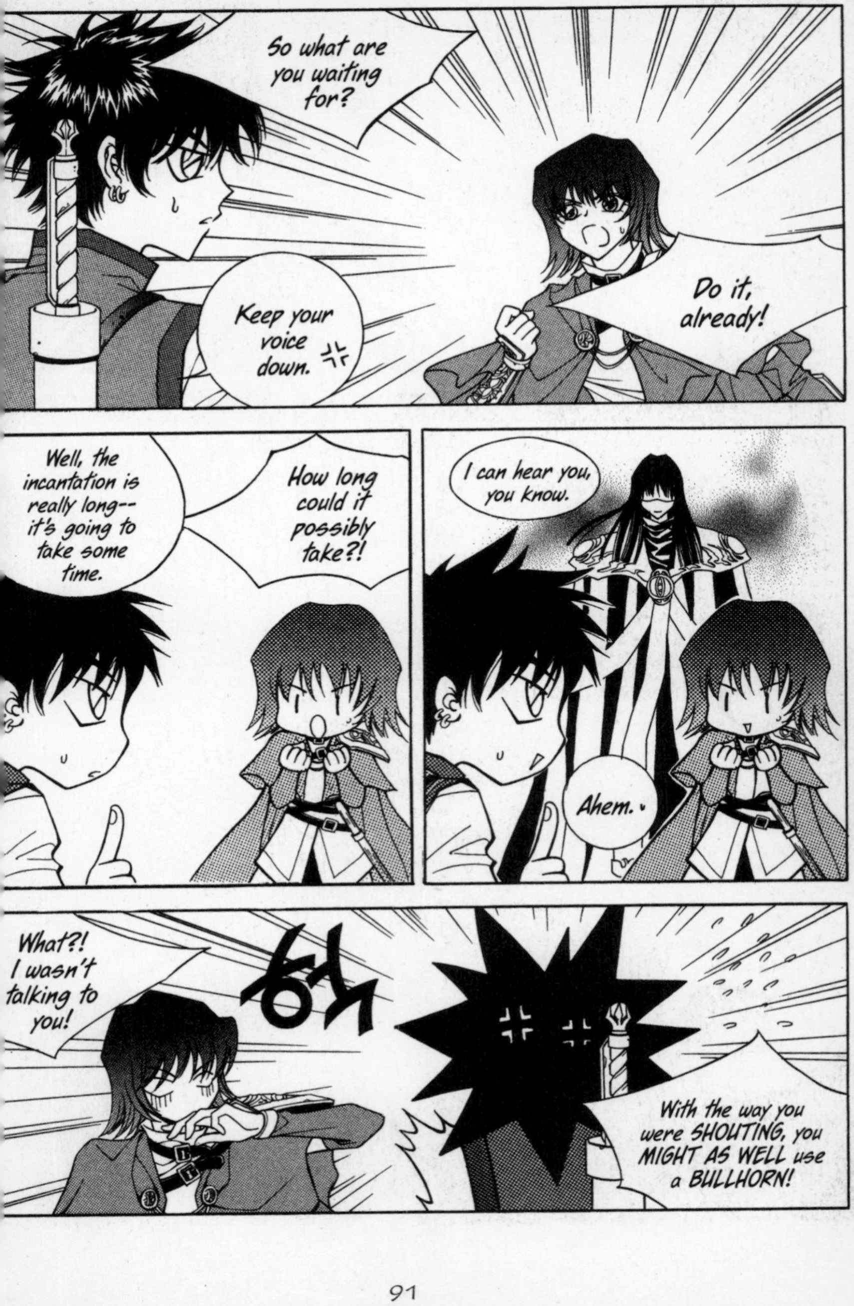
So what are you waiting for?
Keep your voice down.
Do it, already!
Well, the incantation is really long-- it's going to take some time.
How long could it possibly take?!
I can hear you, you know.
Ahem.
What?! I wasn't talking to you!
With the way you were SHOUTING, you MIGHT AS WELL use a BULLHORN!

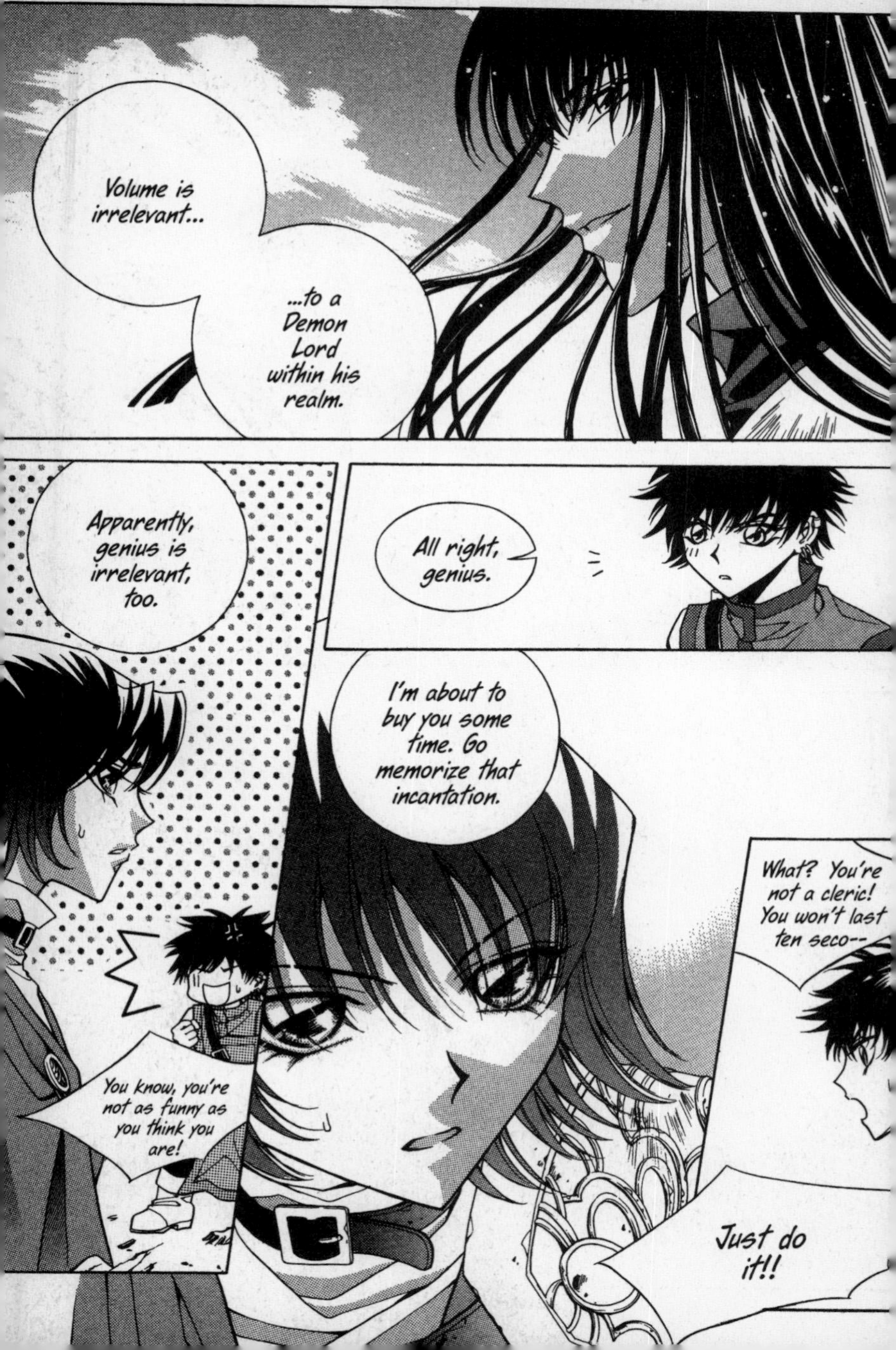
Volume is irrelevant...
...to a Demon Lord within his realm.
Apparently, genius is irrelevant, too.
All right, genius.
You know, you're not as funny as you think you are!
I'm about to buy you some time. Go memorize that incantation.
What? You're not a cleric! You won't last ten seco--
Just do it!!

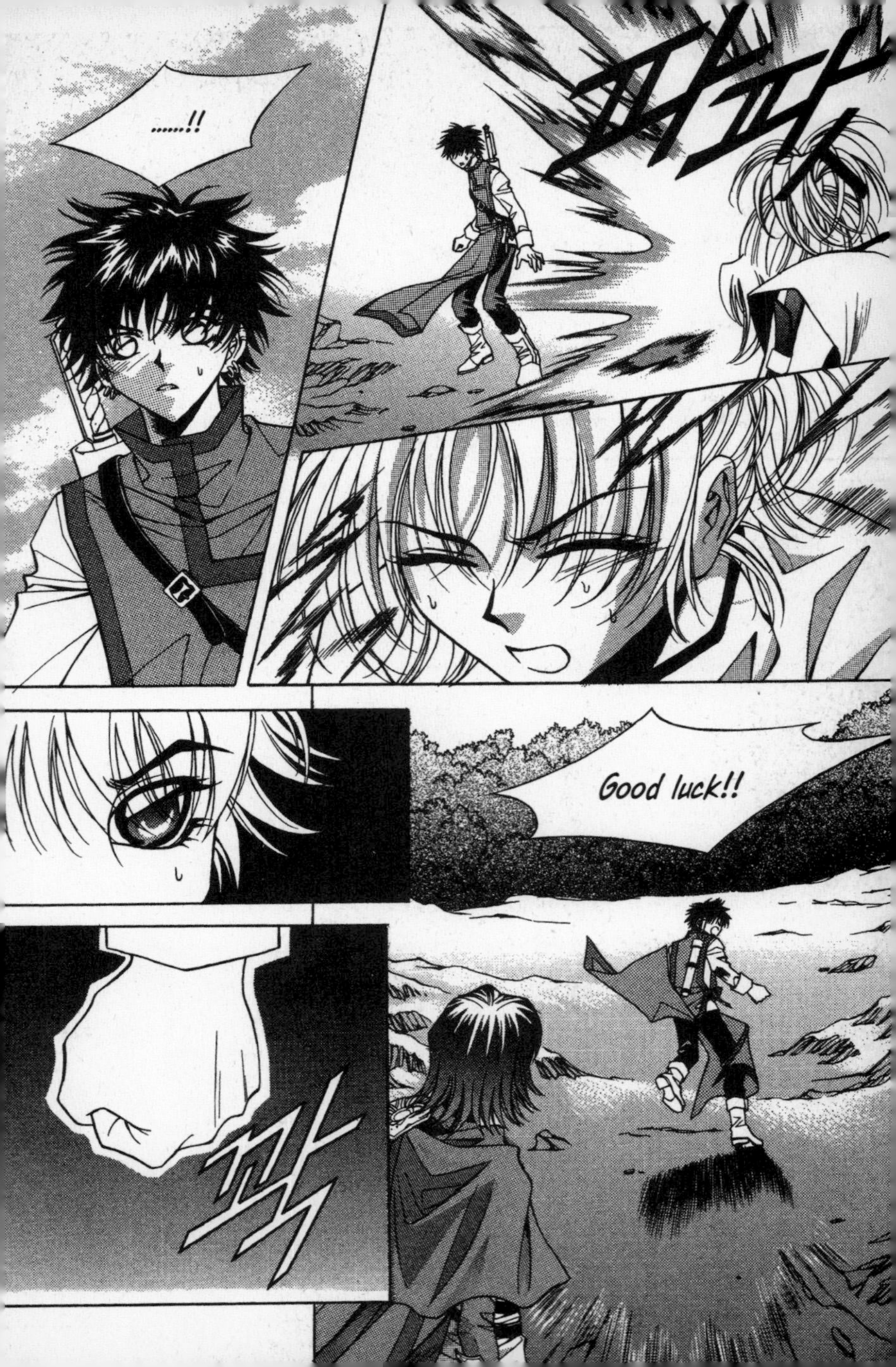
......!!
Good luck!!

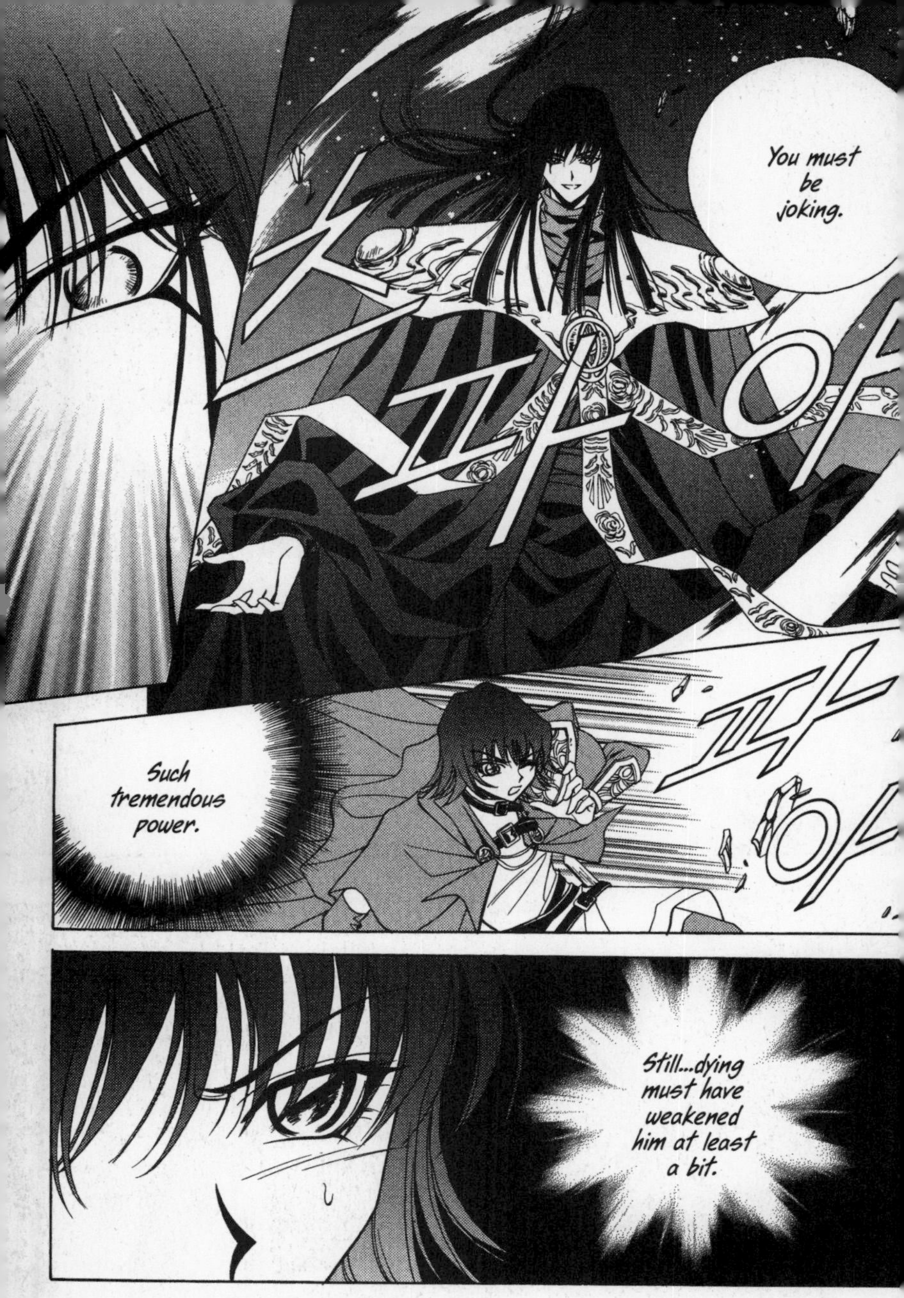
You must be joking.
Such tremendous power.
Still...dying must have weakened him at least a bit.

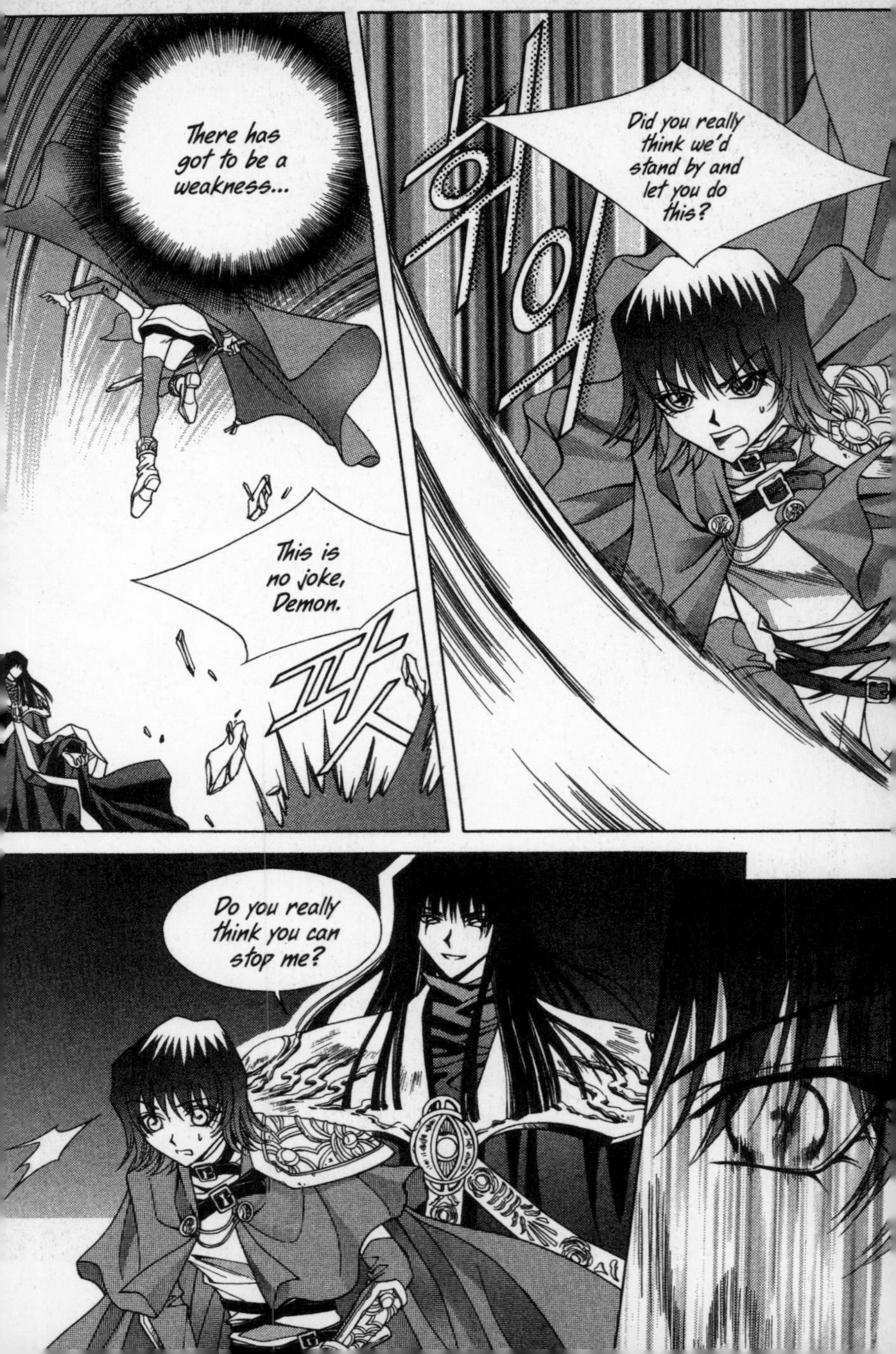
There has got to be a weakness...
This is no joke, Demon.
Did you really think we'd stand by and let you do this?
Do you really think you can stop me?

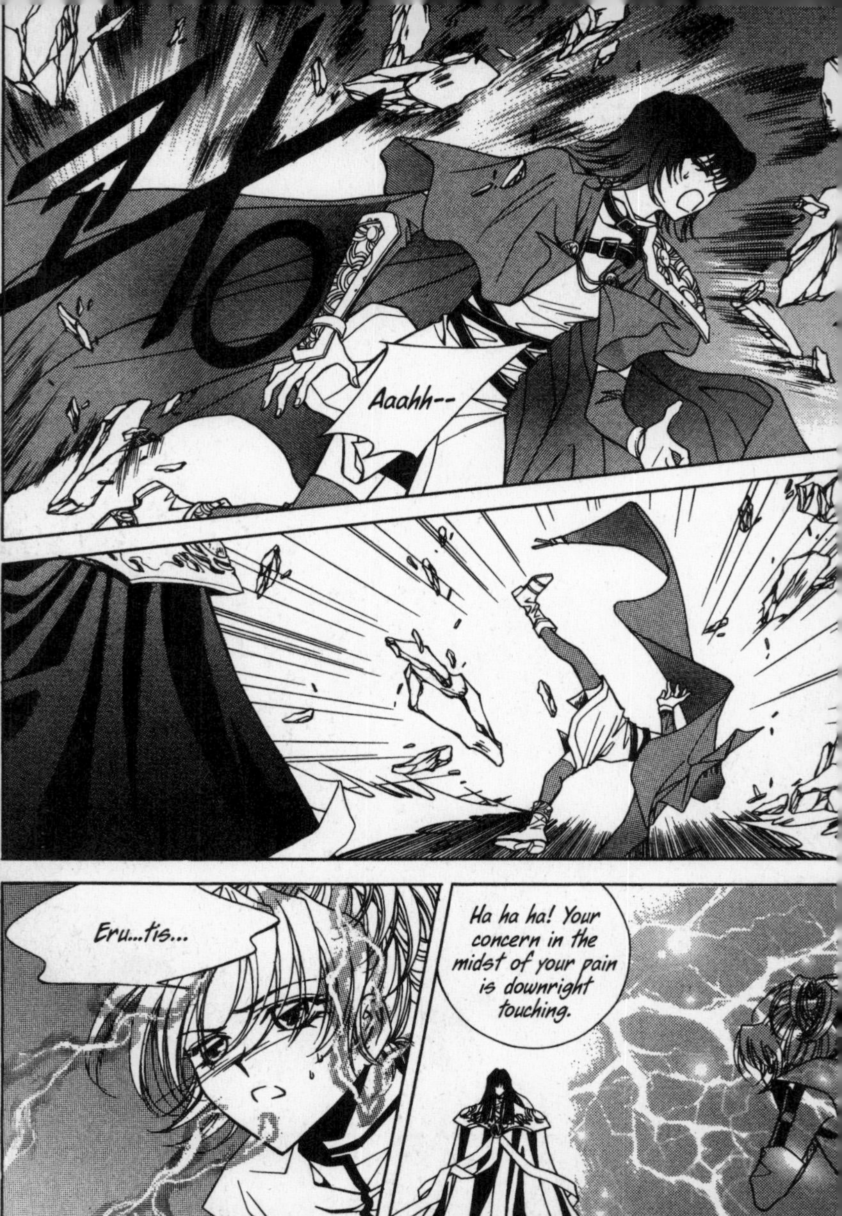
Aaahh--
Eru...tis...
Ha ha ha! Your concern in the midst of your pain is downright touching.

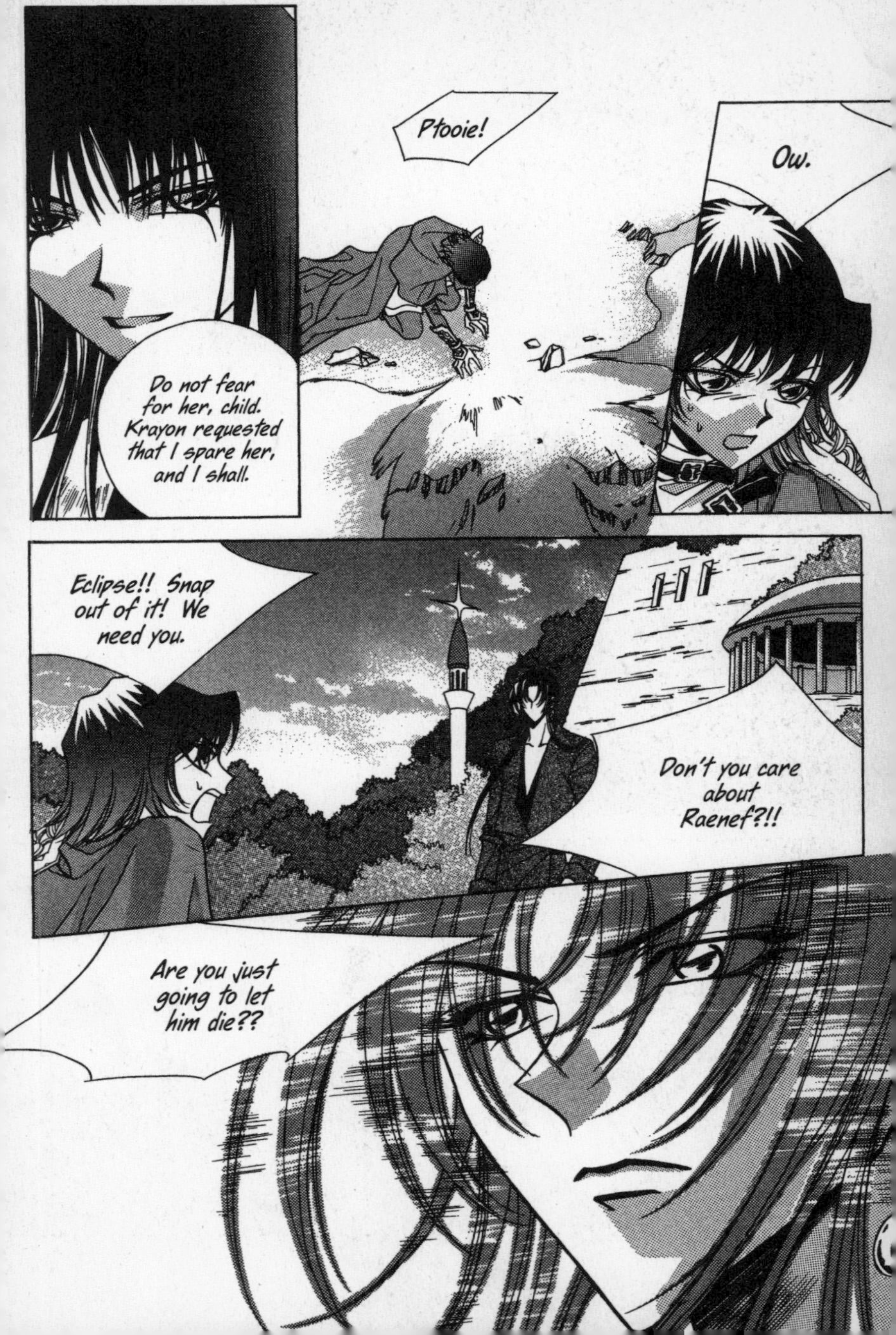
Do not fear for her, child. Krayon requested that I spare her, and I shall.
Ptooie!
Ow.
Eclipse!! Snap out of it! We need you.
Don't you care about Raenef?!!
Are you just going to let him die??

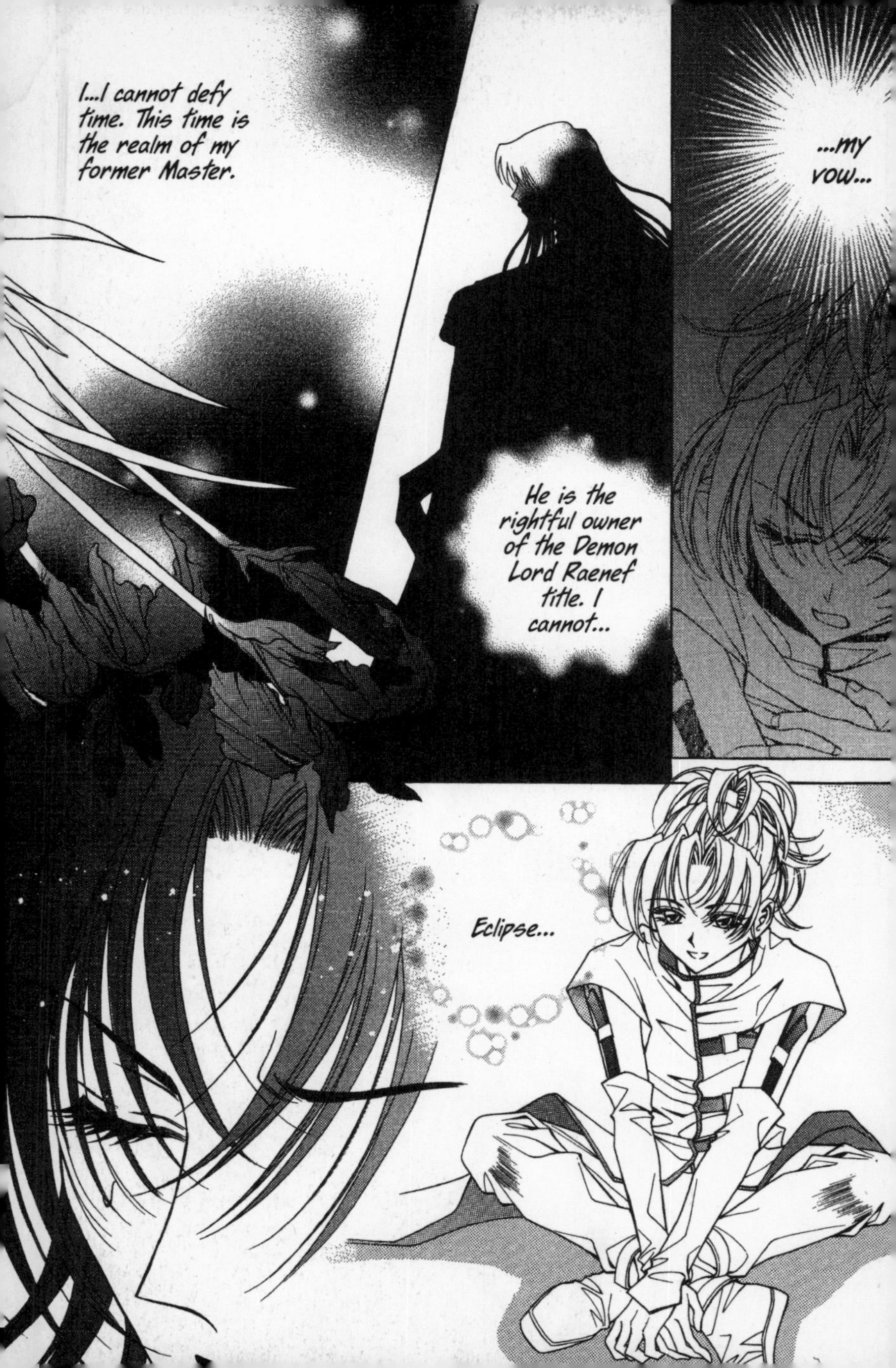
I...I cannot defy time. This time is the realm of my former Master.
He is the rightful owner of the Demon Lord Raenef title. I cannot...
...my vow...
Eclipse...

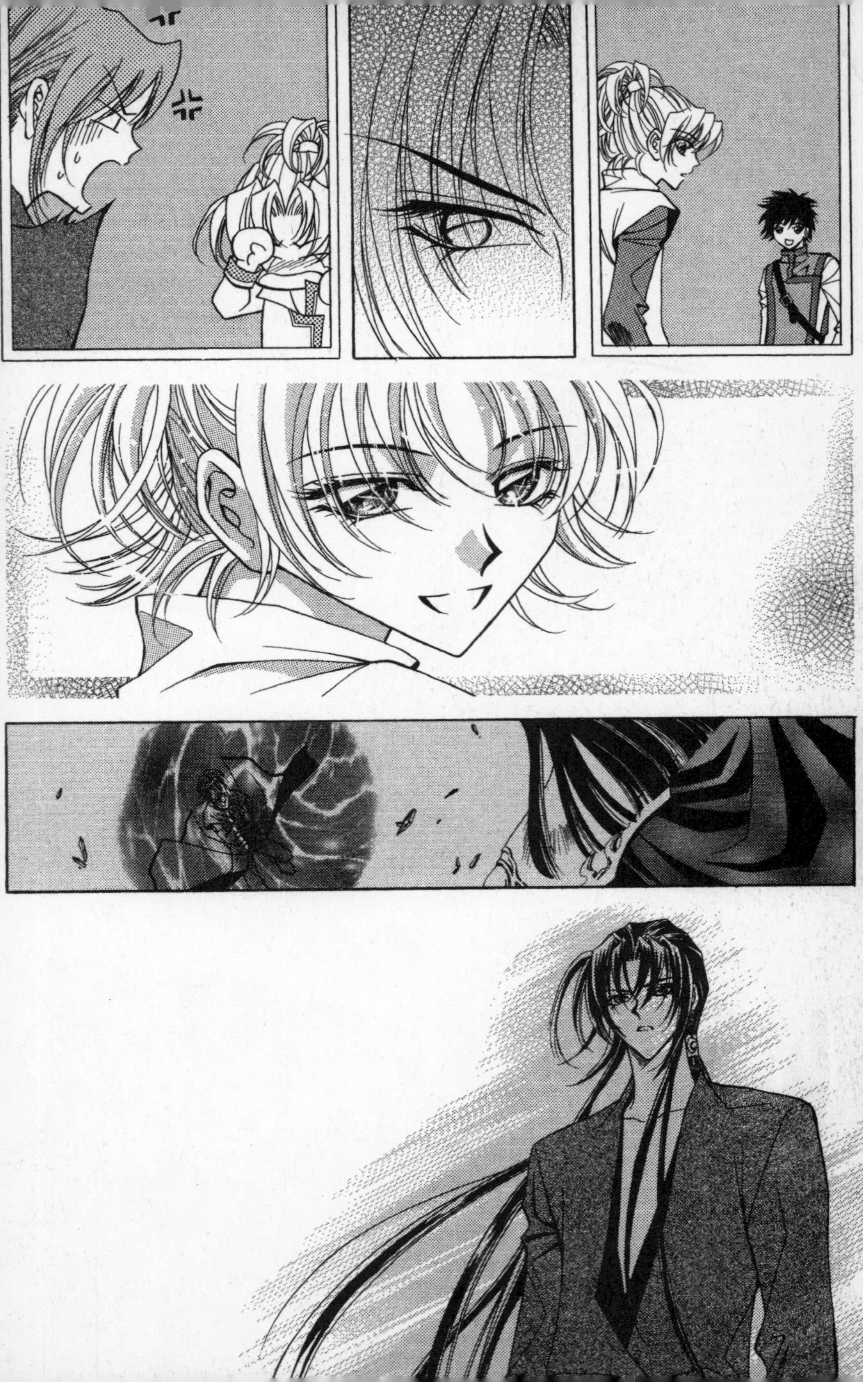

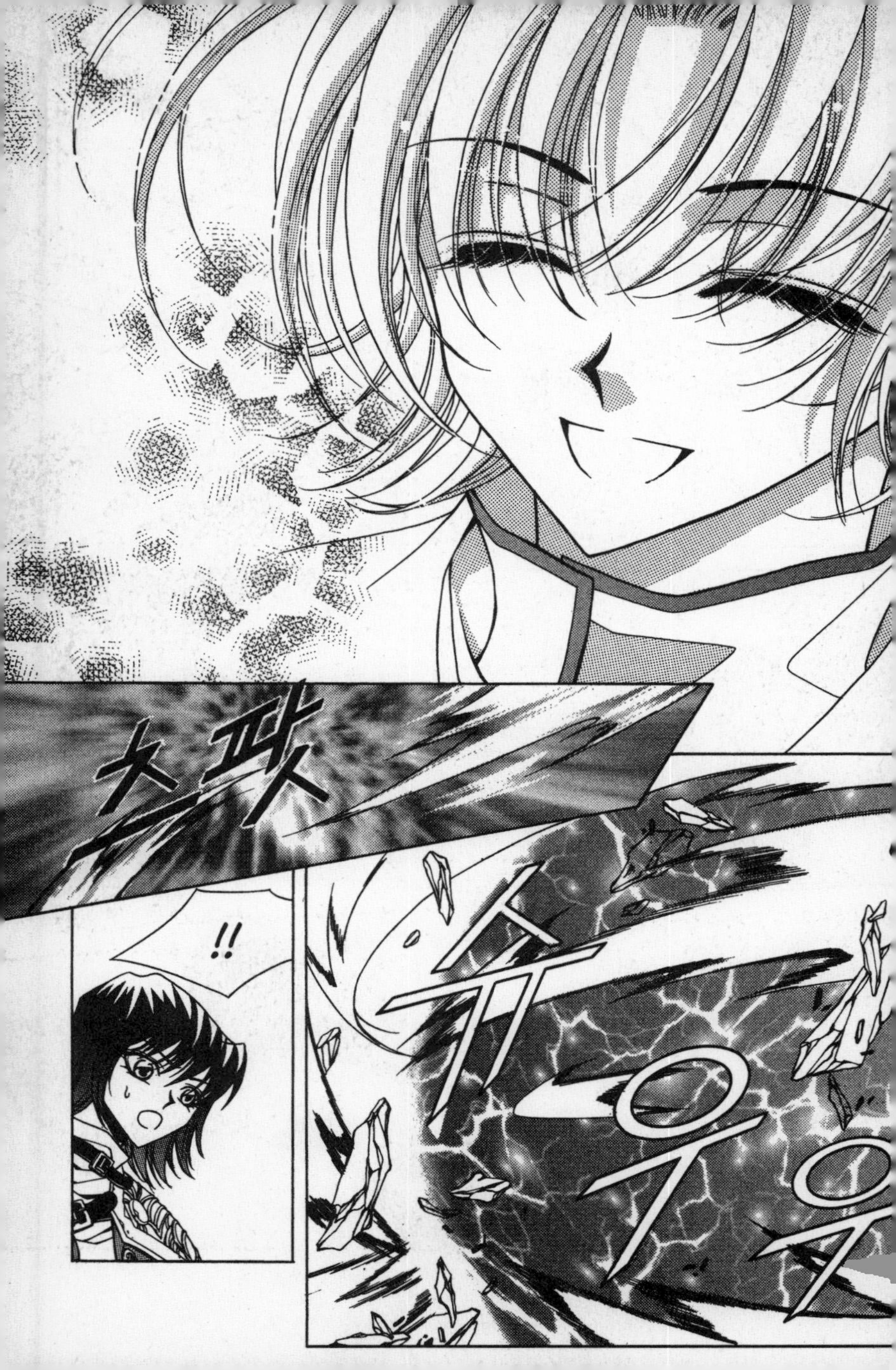
츠팍
!!
슈우우

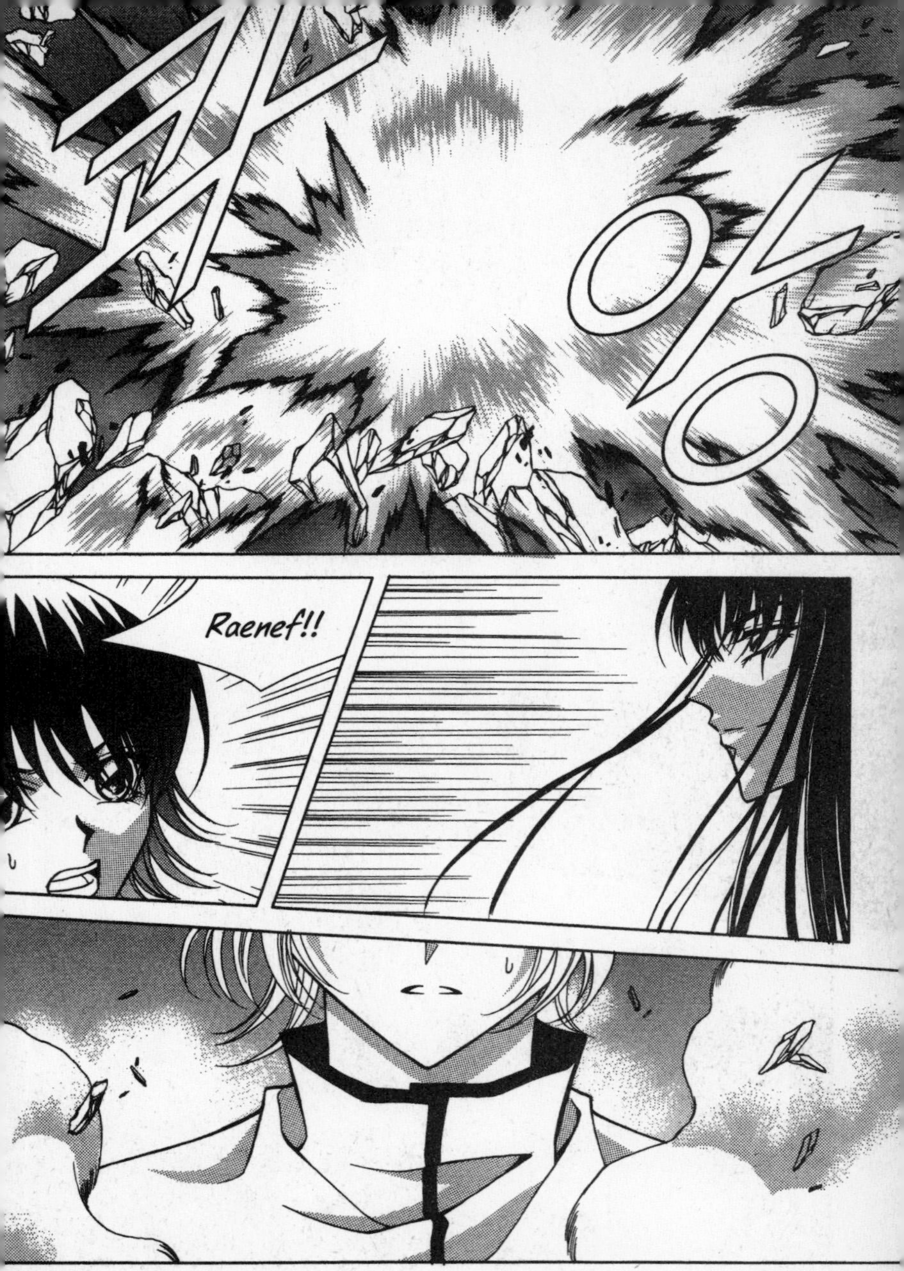
Raenef!!

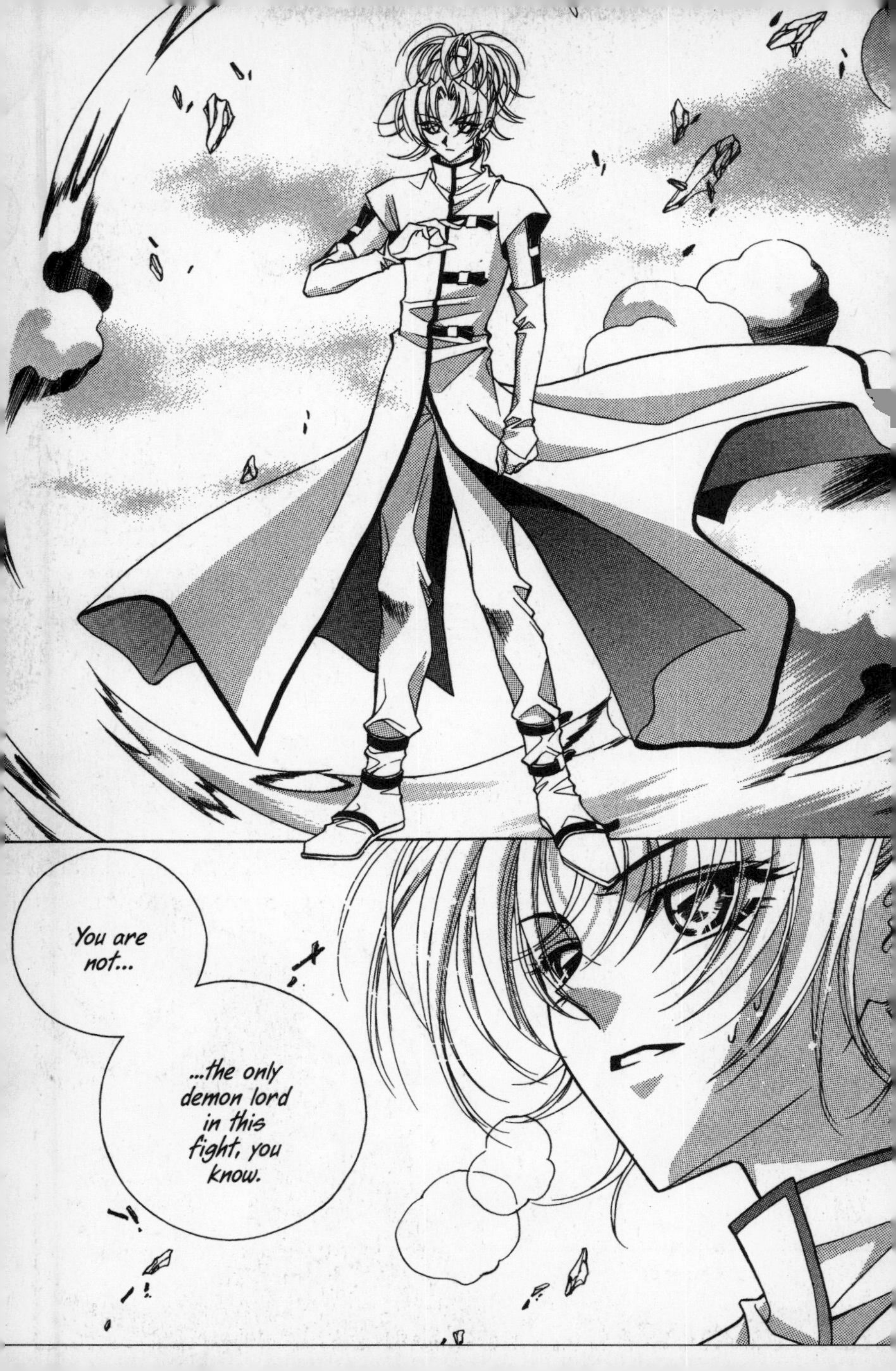
You are not...
...the only demon lord in this fight, you know.

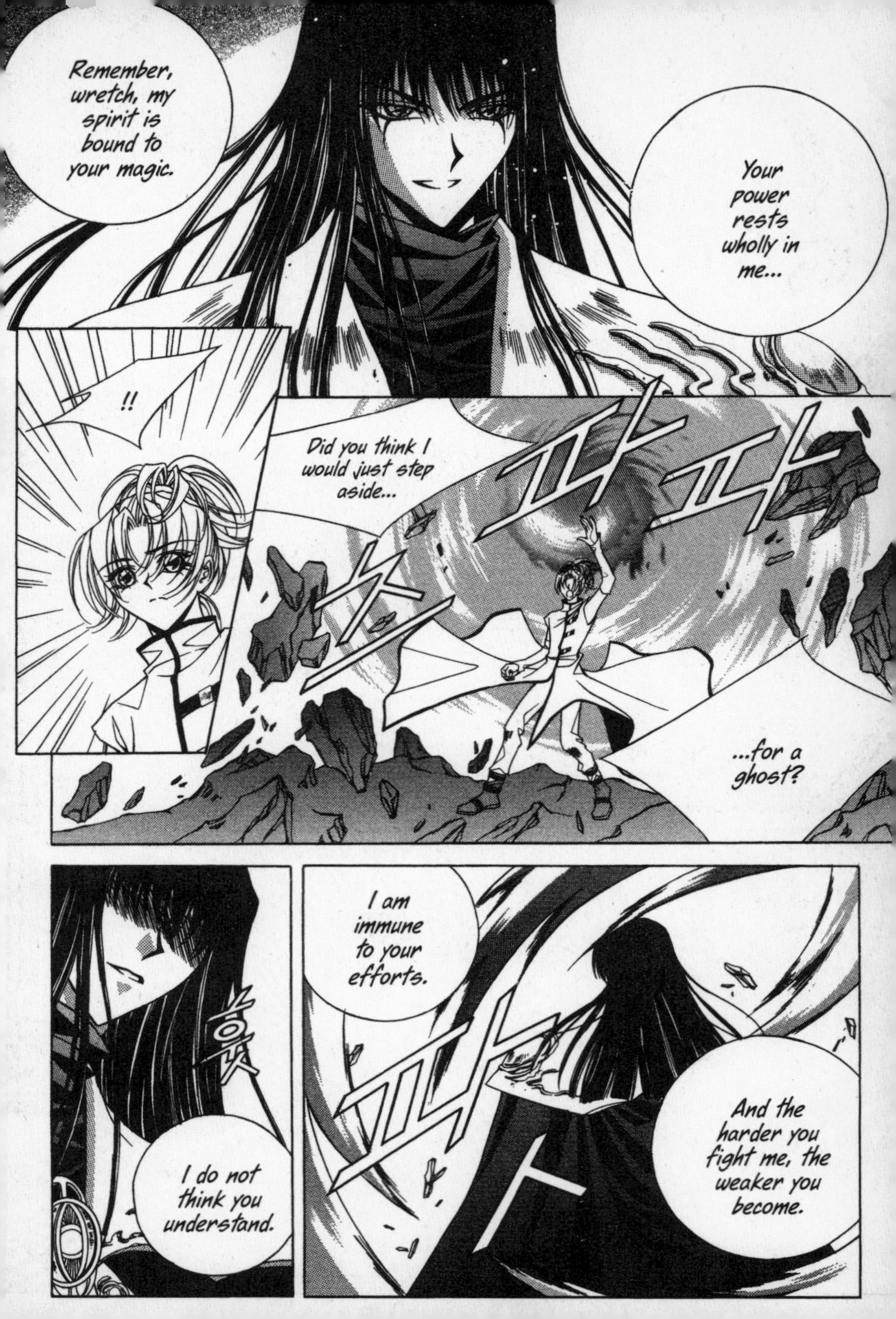
Remember, wretch, my spirit is bound to your magic.
Your power rests wholly in me...
!!
Did you think I would just step aside...
...for a ghost?
I do not think you understand.
I am immune to your efforts.
And the harder you fight me, the weaker you become.

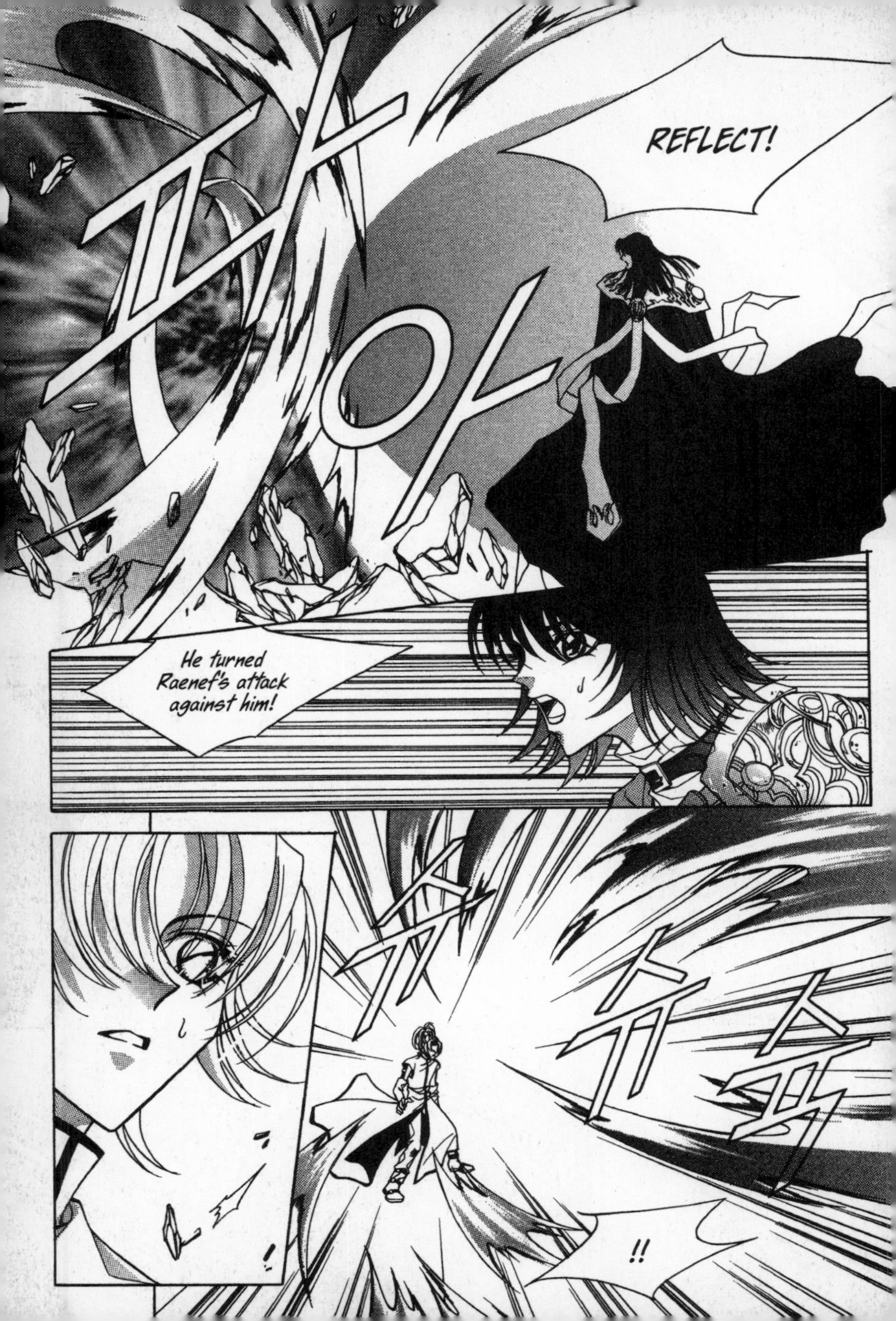
REFLECT!
He turned Raenef's attack against him!
!!

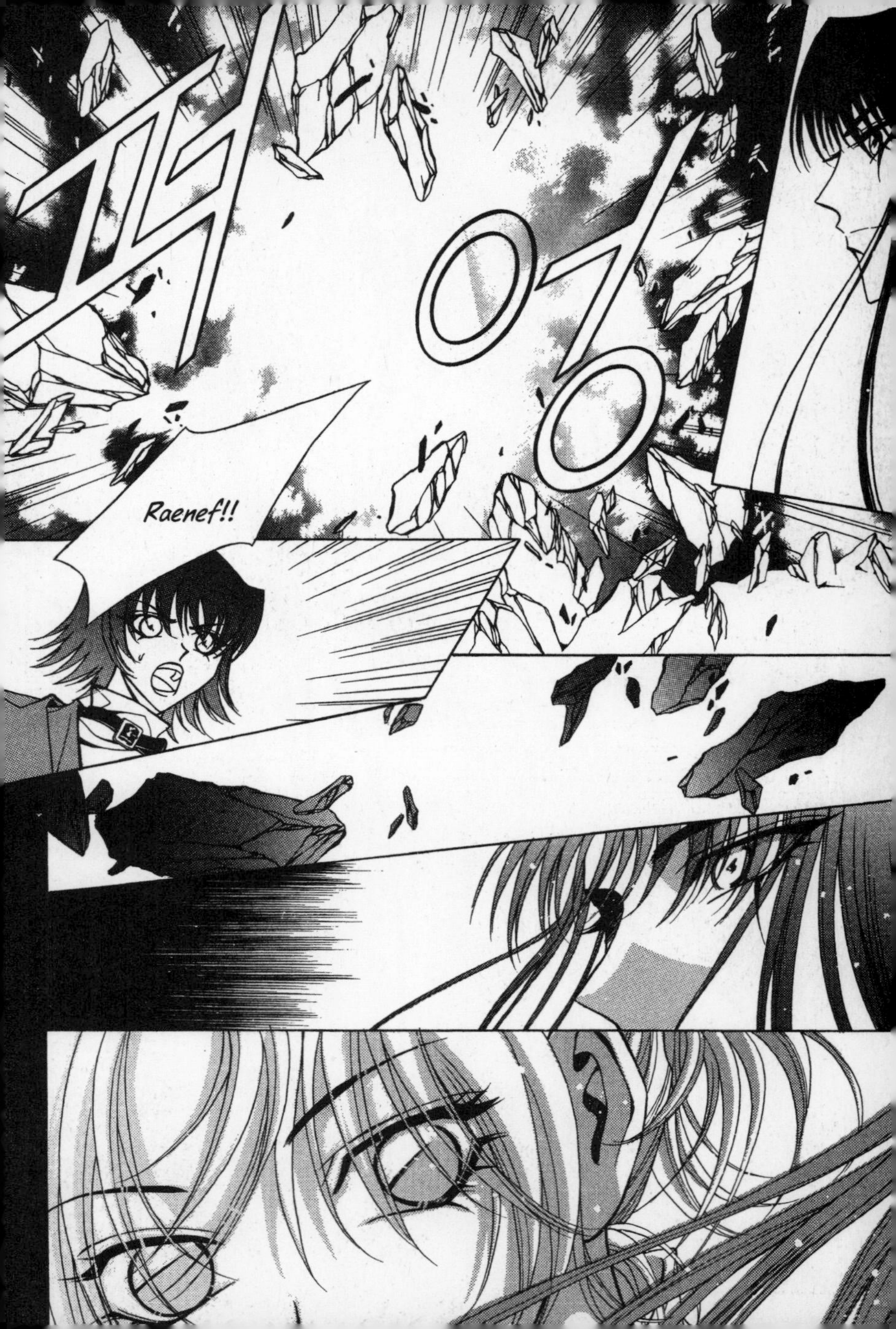

Raenef!!

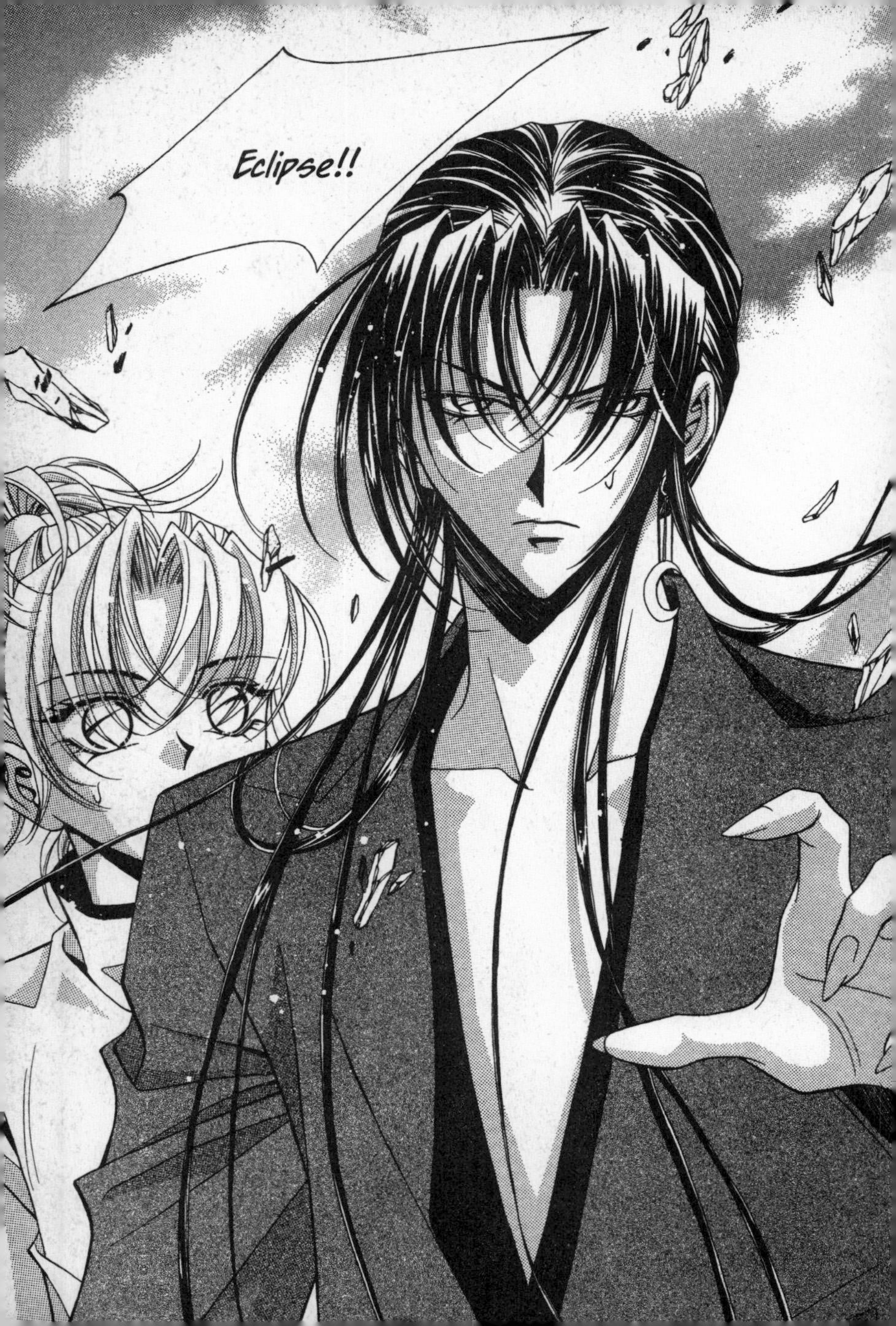
Eclipse!!

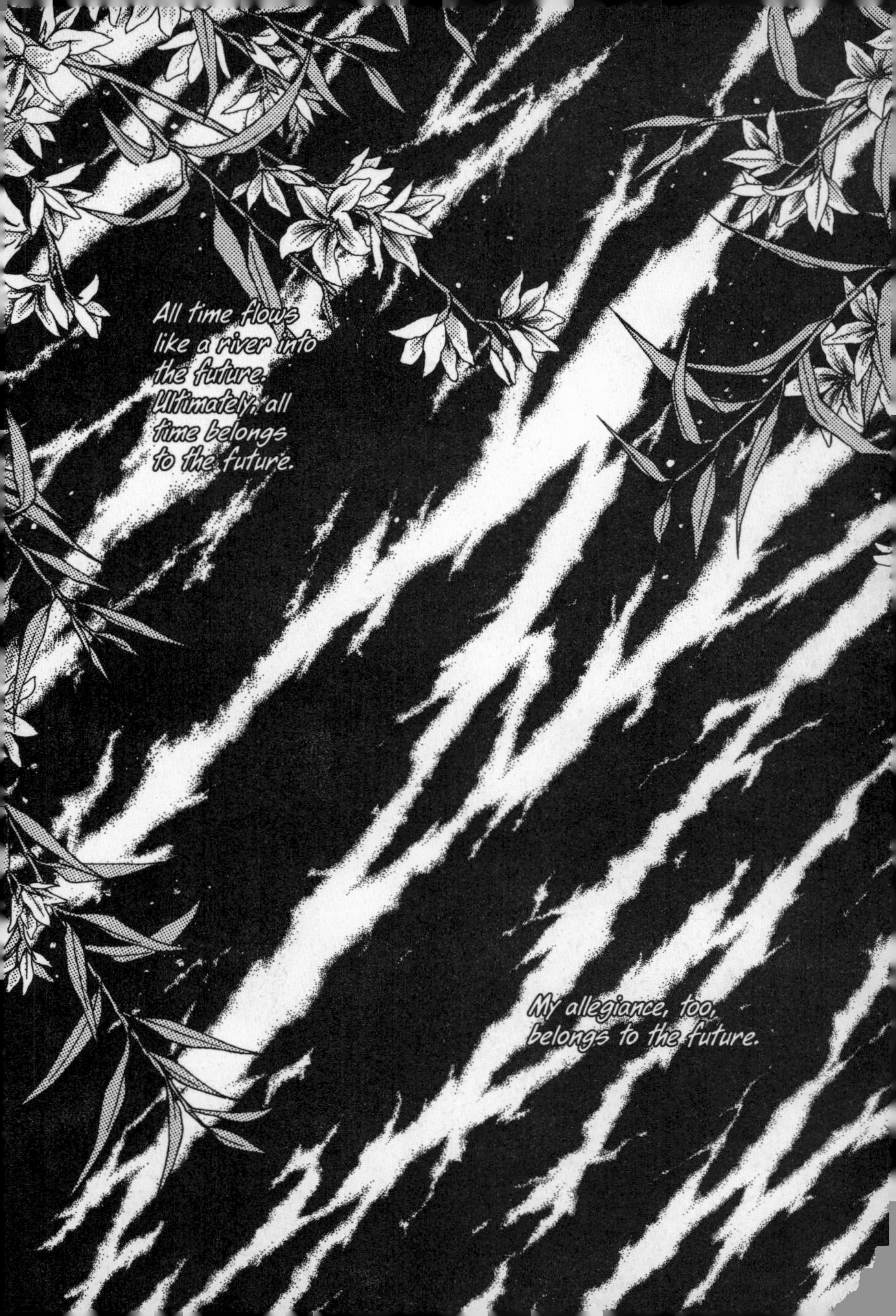
All time flows like a river into the future. Ultimately, all time belongs to the future.
My allegiance, too, belongs to the future.

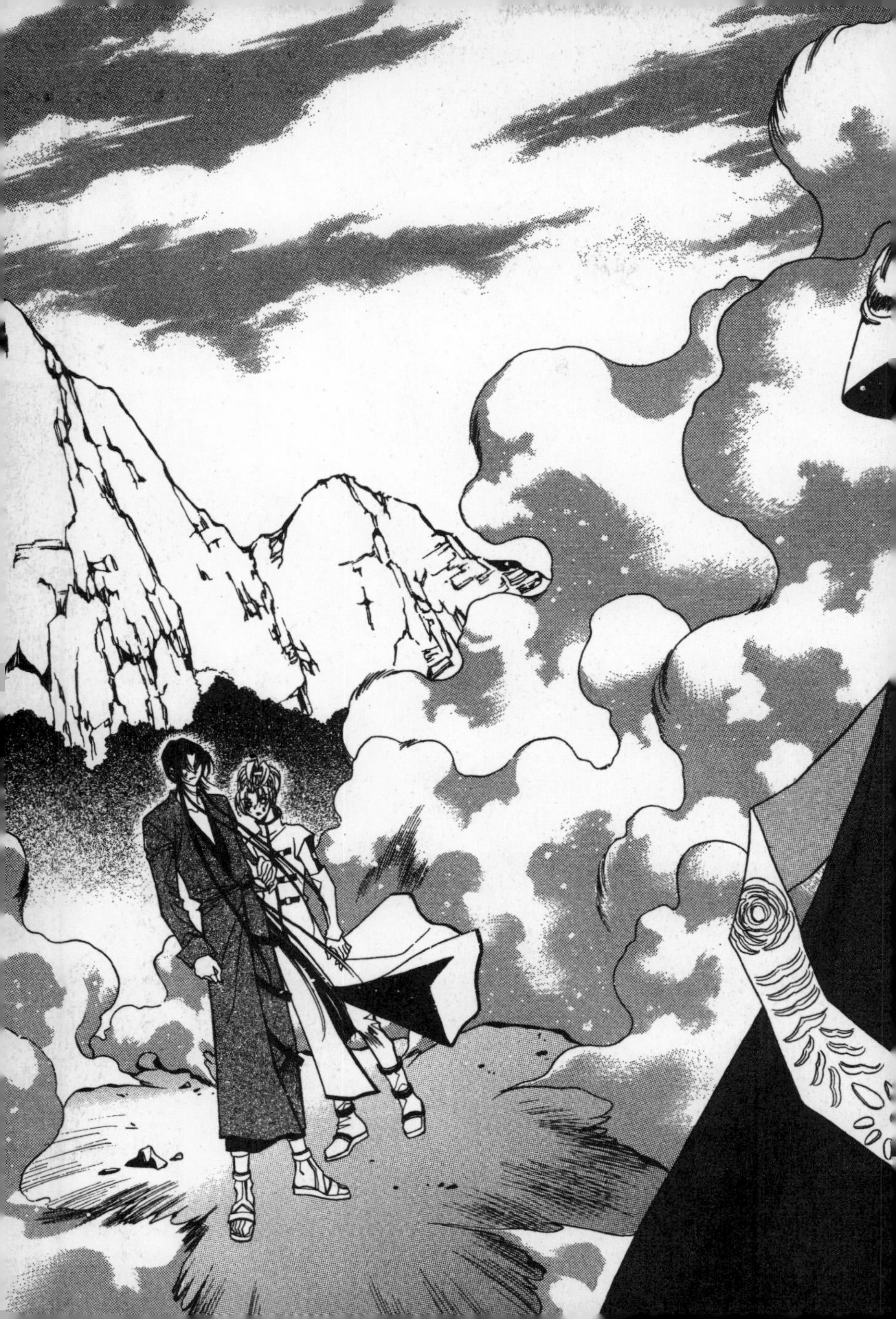

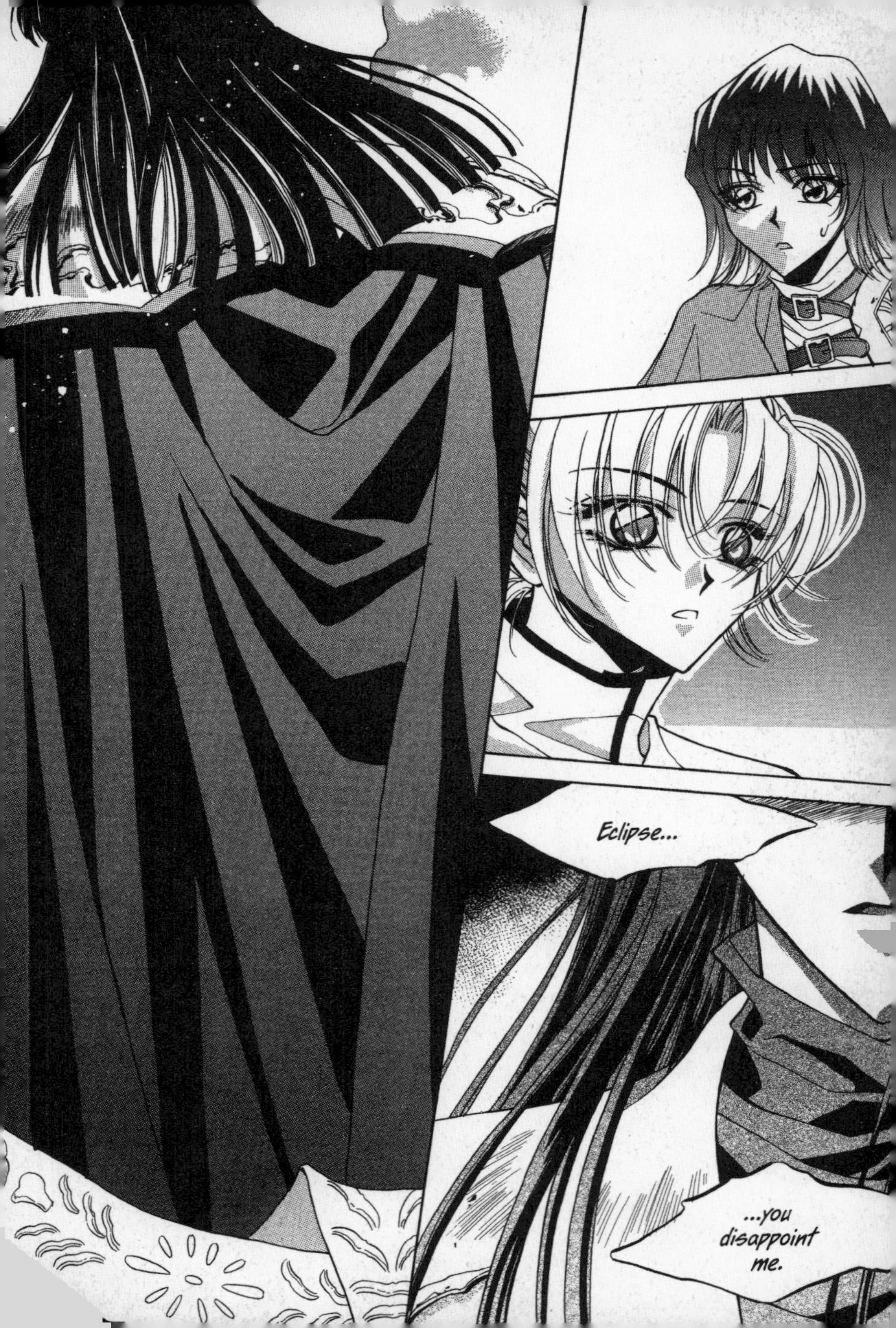
Eclipse...
...you disappoint me.

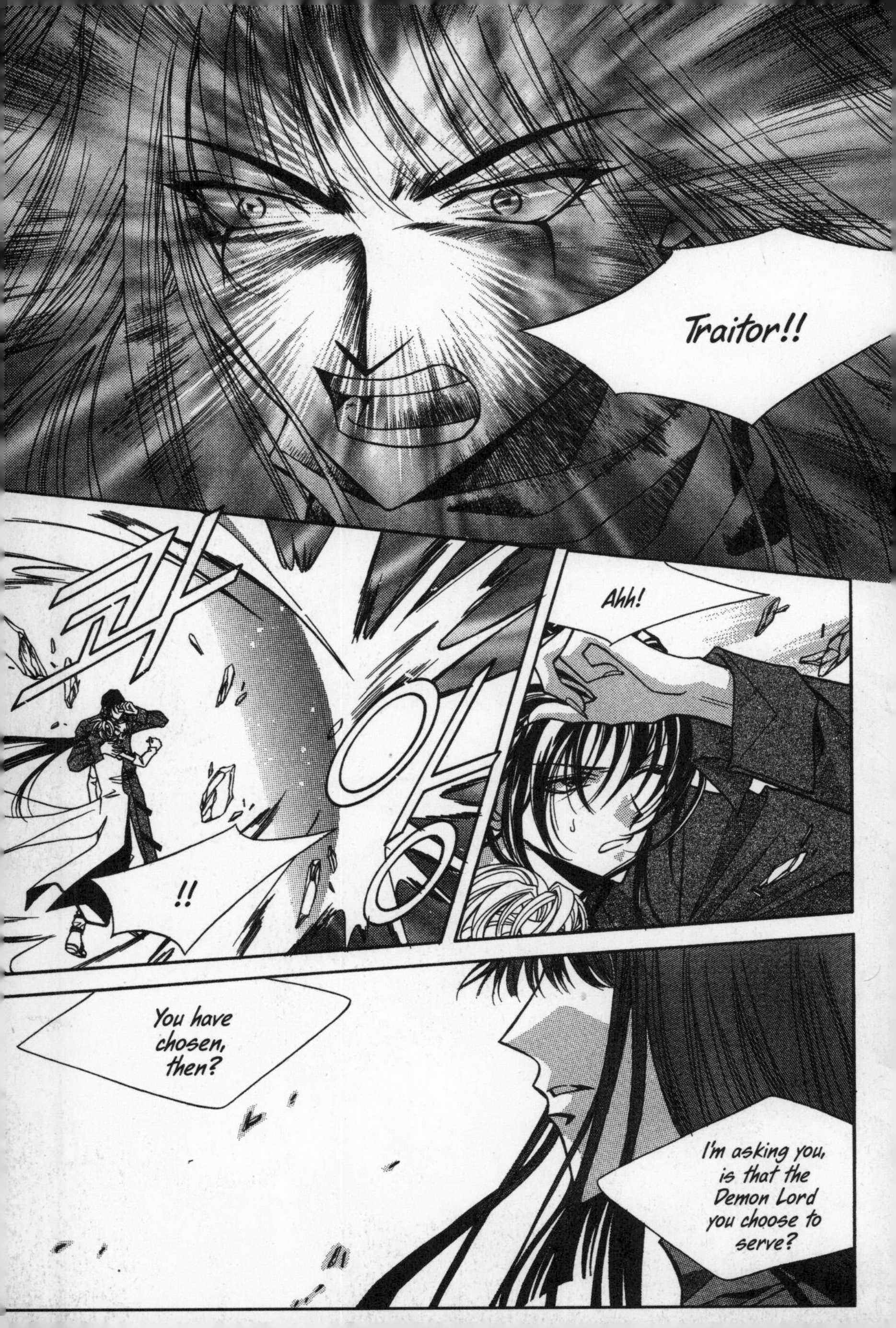
Traitor!!
!!
Ahh!
You have chosen, then?
I'm asking you, is that the Demon Lord you choose to serve?

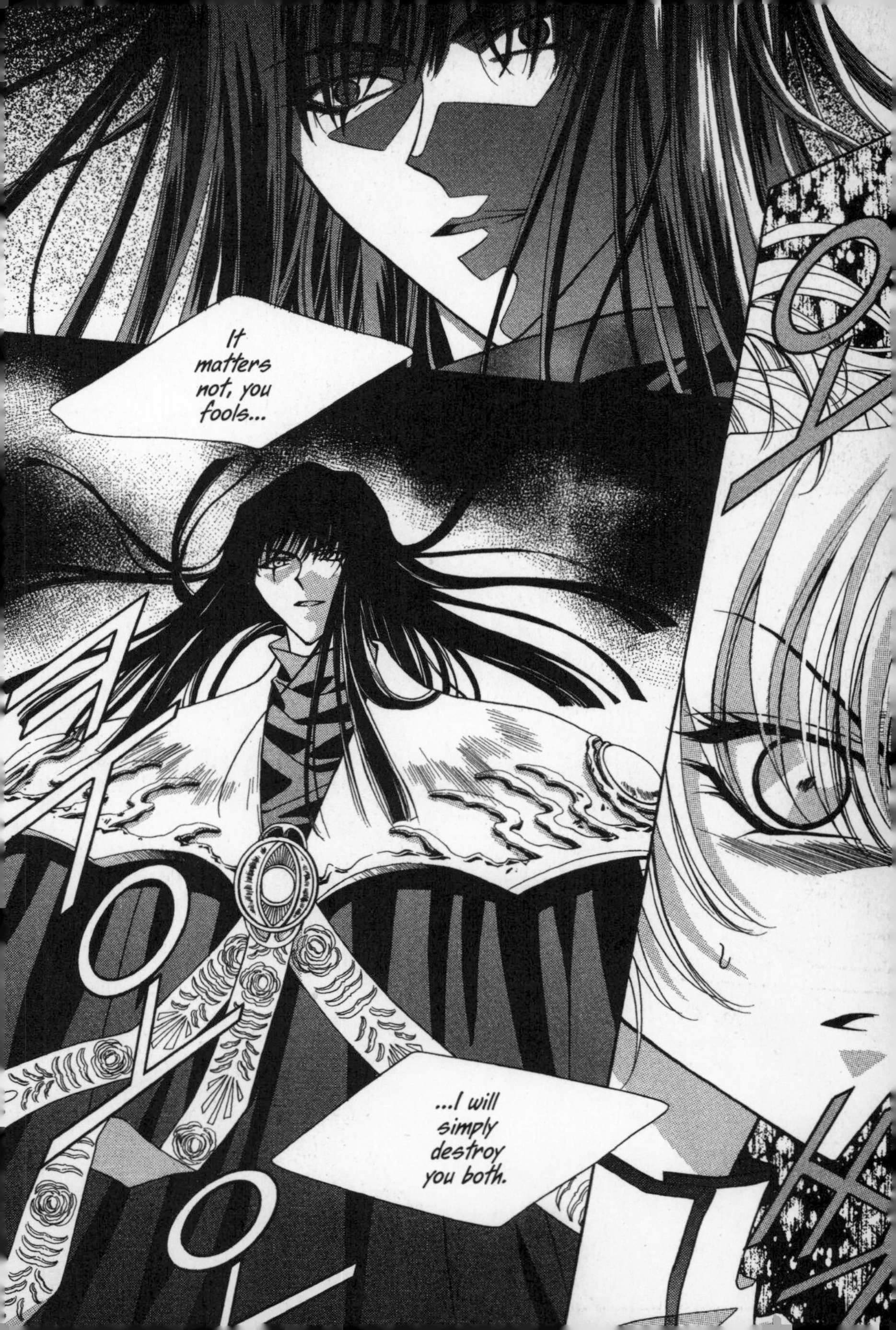
It matters not, you fools...
...I will simply destroy you both.

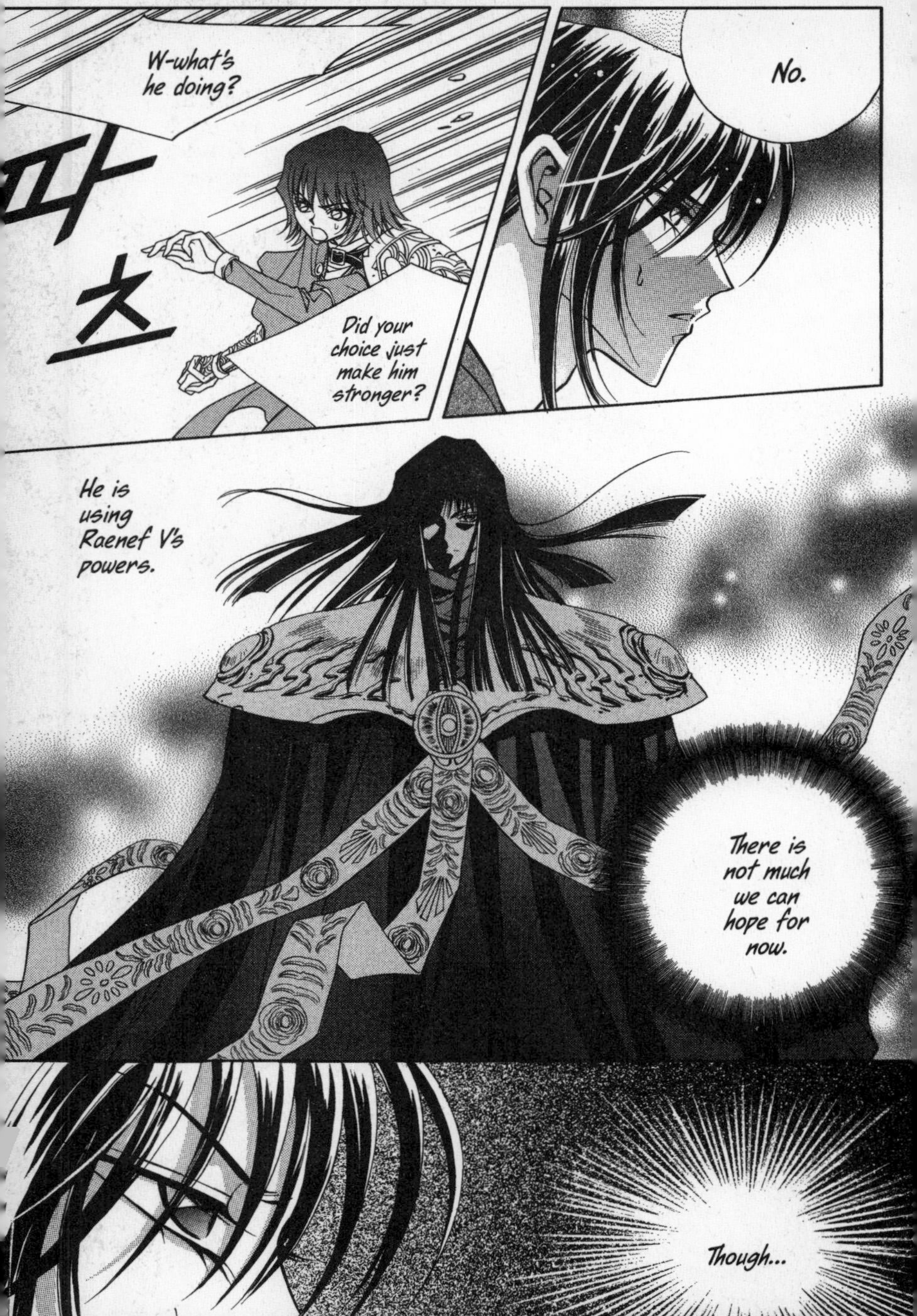
W-what's he doing?
파츠
Did your choice just make him stronger?
No.
He is using Raenef V's powers.
There is not much we can hope for now.
Though...

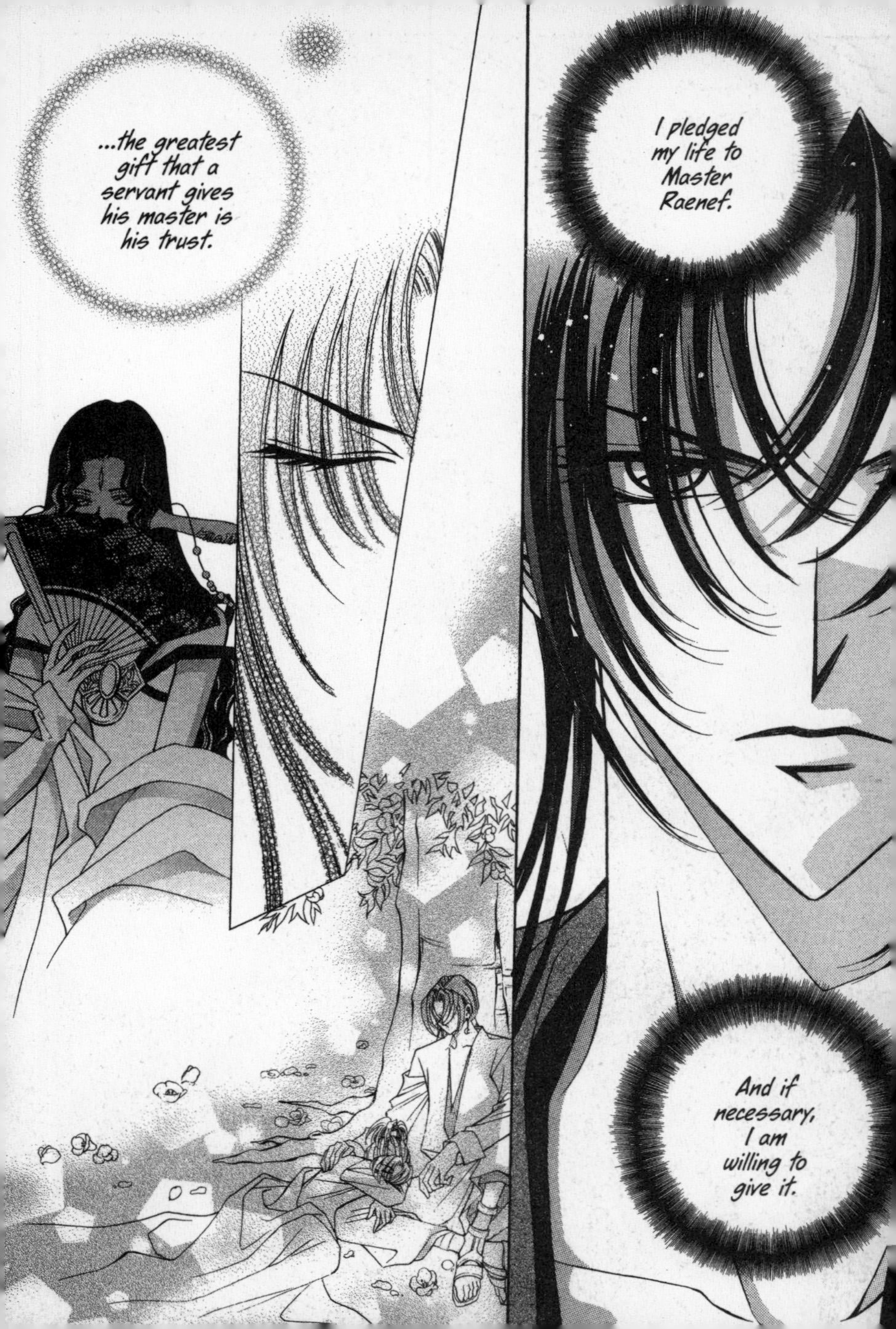
I pledged my life to Master Raenef.
And if necessary, I am willing to give it.
...the greatest gift that a servant gives his master is his trust.

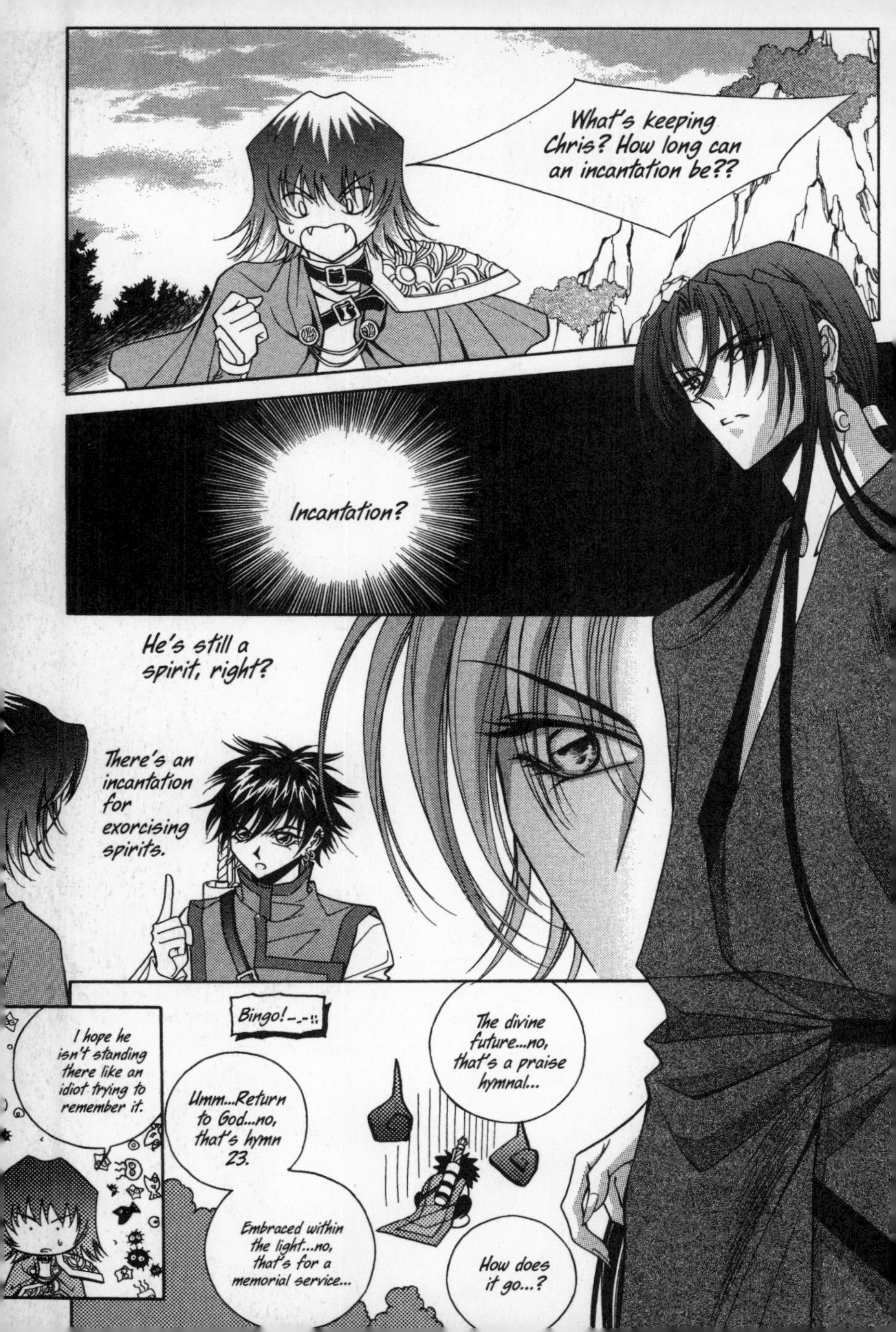

What's keeping Chris? How long can an incantation be??
Incantation?
He's still a spirit, right?
There's an incantation for exorcising spirits.
I hope he isn't standing there like an idiot trying to remember it.
Bingo! -_-;;
Umm...Return to God...no, that's hymn 23.
The divine future...no, that's a praise hymnal...
Embraced within the light...no, that's for a memorial service...
How does it go...?

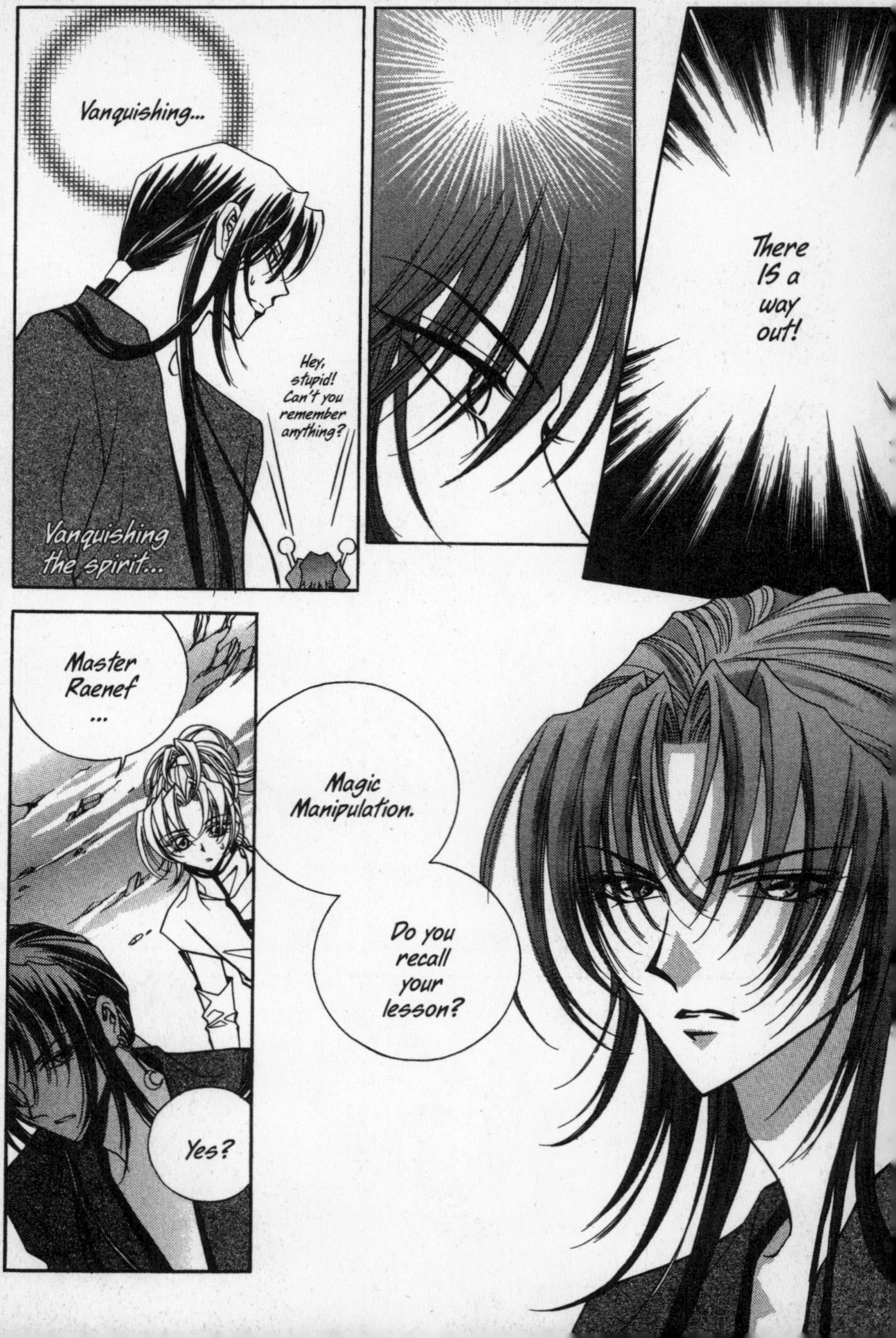
Vanquishing...
Hey, stupid! Can't you remember anything?
Vanquishing the spirit...
There IS a way out!
Master Raenef ...
Yes?
Magic Manipulation.
Do you recall your lesson?

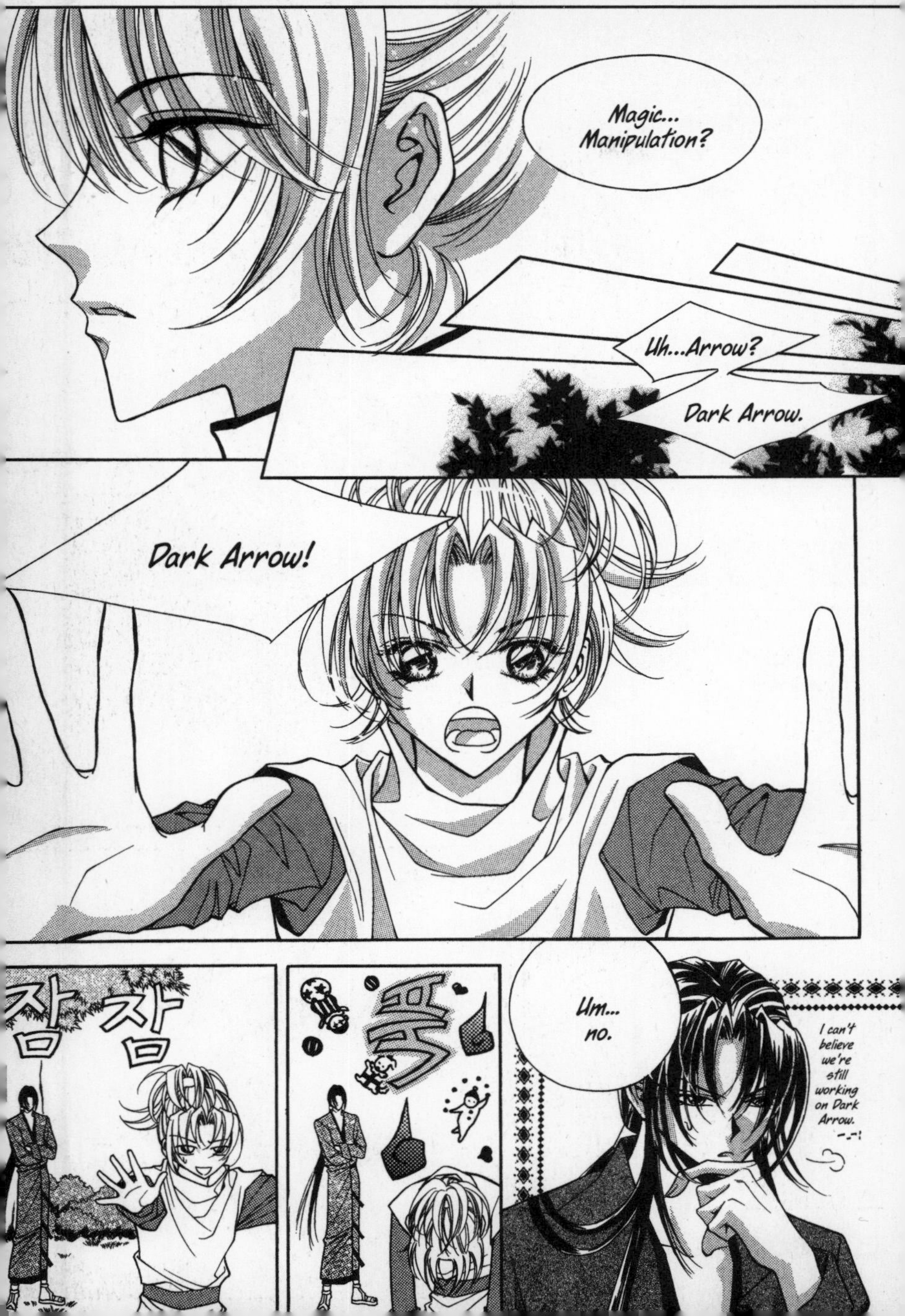
Magic... Manipulation?
Uh...Arrow?
Dark Arrow.
Dark Arrow!
잠 잠
Um... no.
I can't believe we're still working on Dark Arrow.

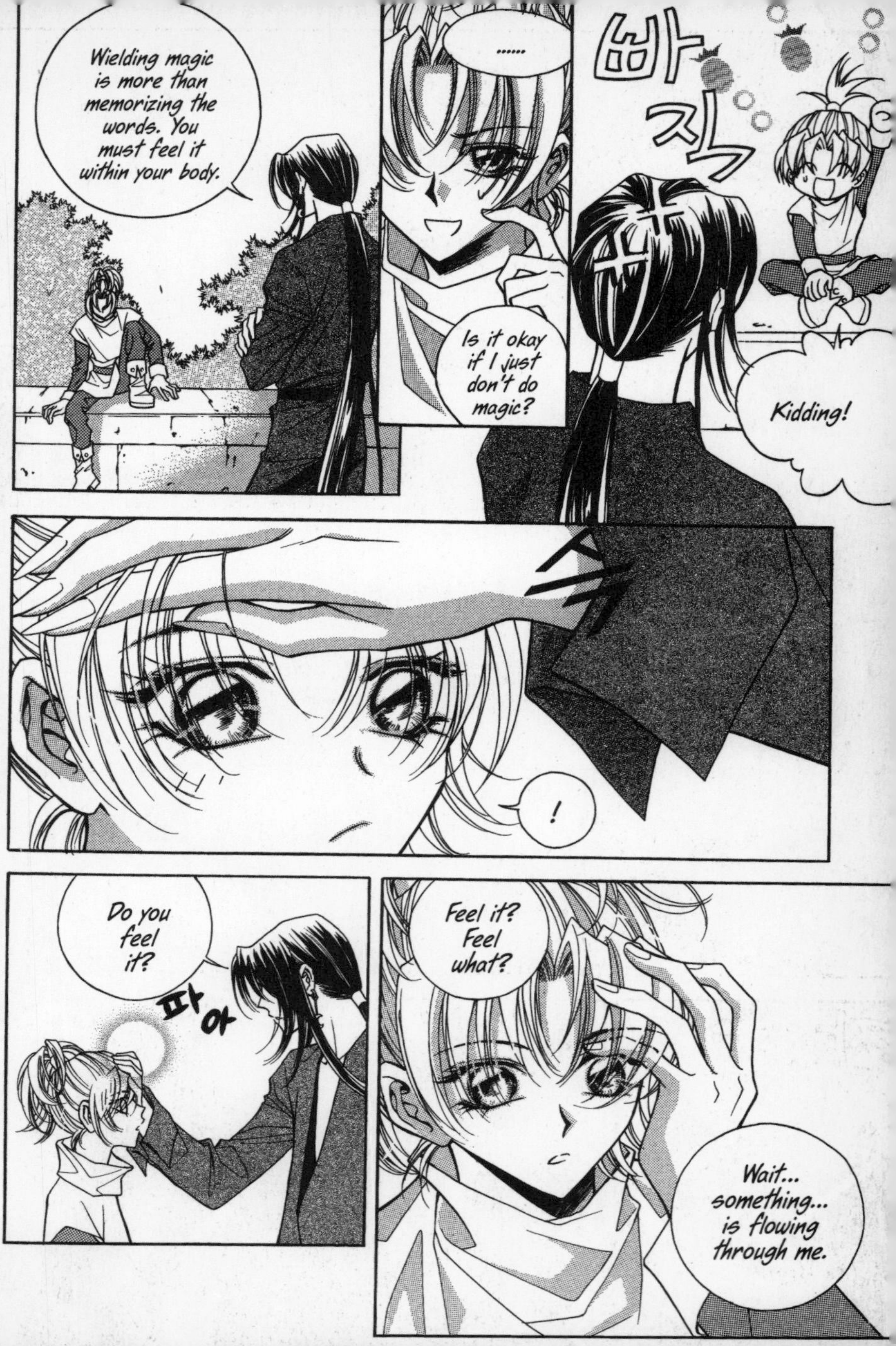
Wielding magic is more than memorizing the words. You must feel it within your body.
......
Is it okay if I just don't do magic?
빠직
Kidding!
!
Do you feel it?
파아
Feel it? Feel what?
Wait... something... is flowing through me.

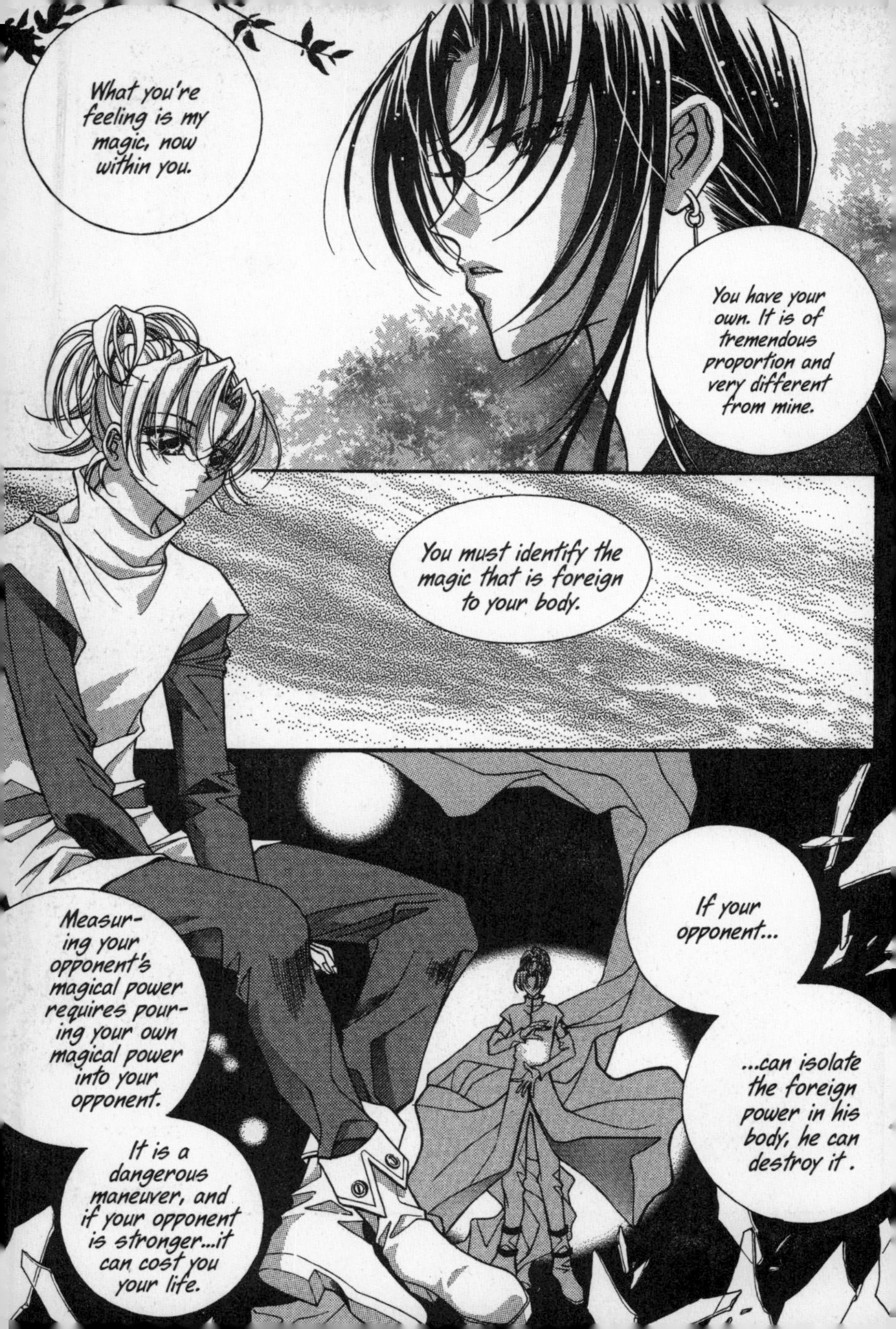
What you're feeling is my magic, now within you.
You have your own. It is of tremendous proportion and very different from mine.
You must identify the magic that is foreign to your body.
Measuring your opponent's magical power requires pouring your own magical power into your opponent.
It is a dangerous maneuver, and if your opponent is stronger...it can cost you your life.
If your opponent...
...can isolate the foreign power in his body, he can destroy it .

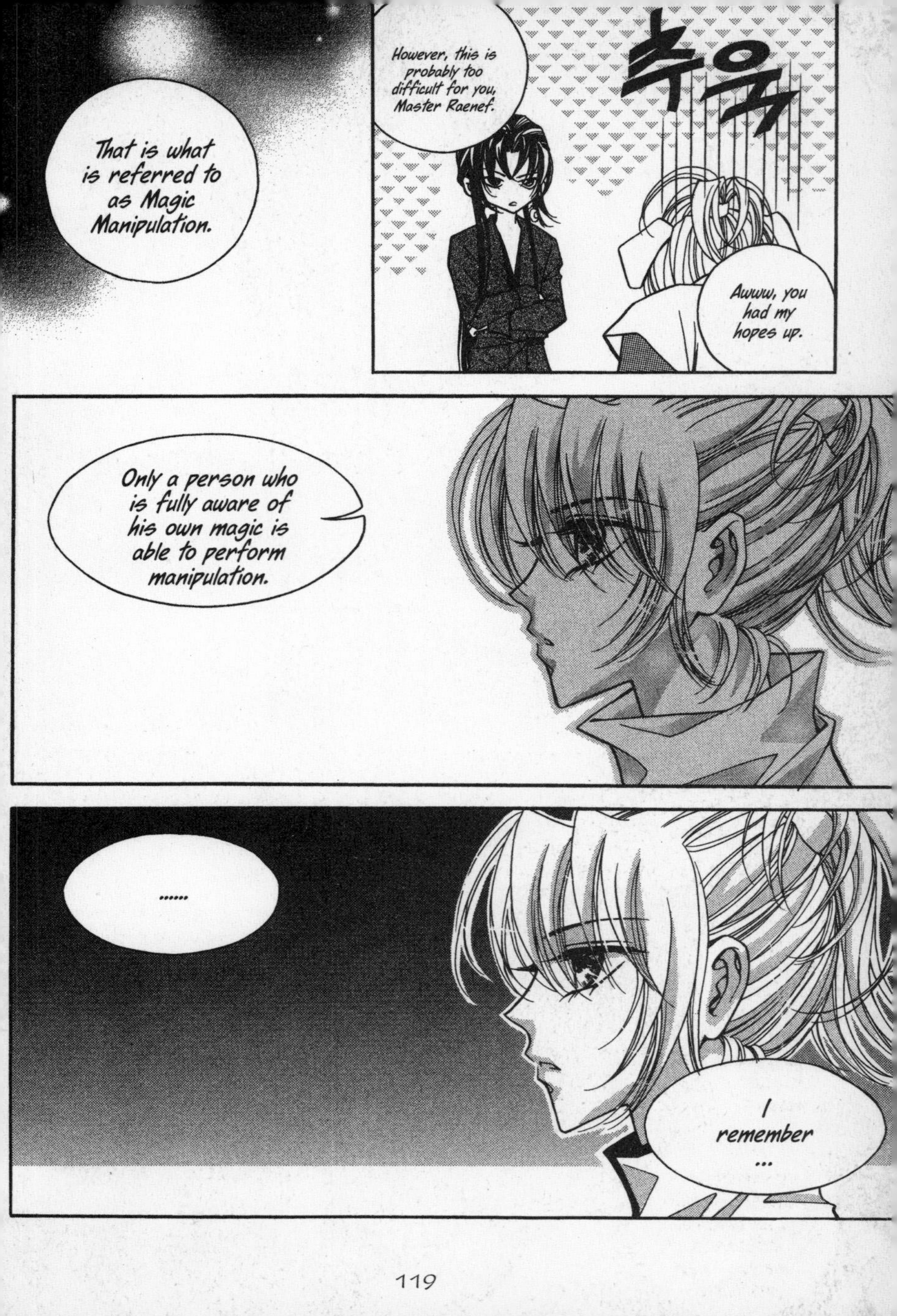
That is what is referred to as Magic Manipulation.
However, this is probably too difficult for you, Master Raenef.
추욱
Awww, you had my hopes up.
Only a person who is fully aware of his own magic is able to perform manipulation.
......
I remember ...

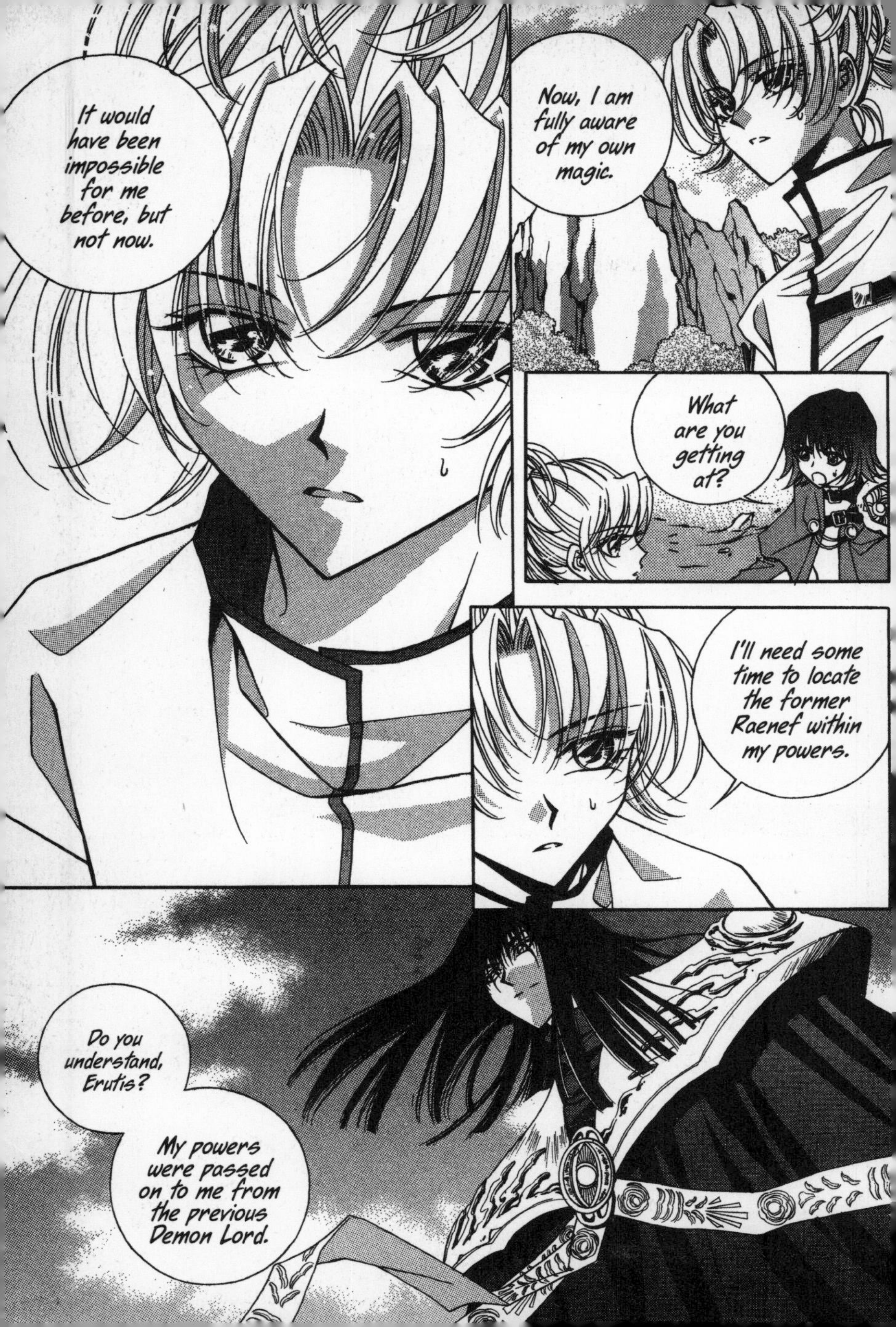
It would have been impossible for me before, but not now.
Now, I am fully aware of my own magic.
What are you getting at?
I'll need some time to locate the former Raenef within my powers.
Do you understand, Erutis?
My powers were passed on to me from the previous Demon Lord.

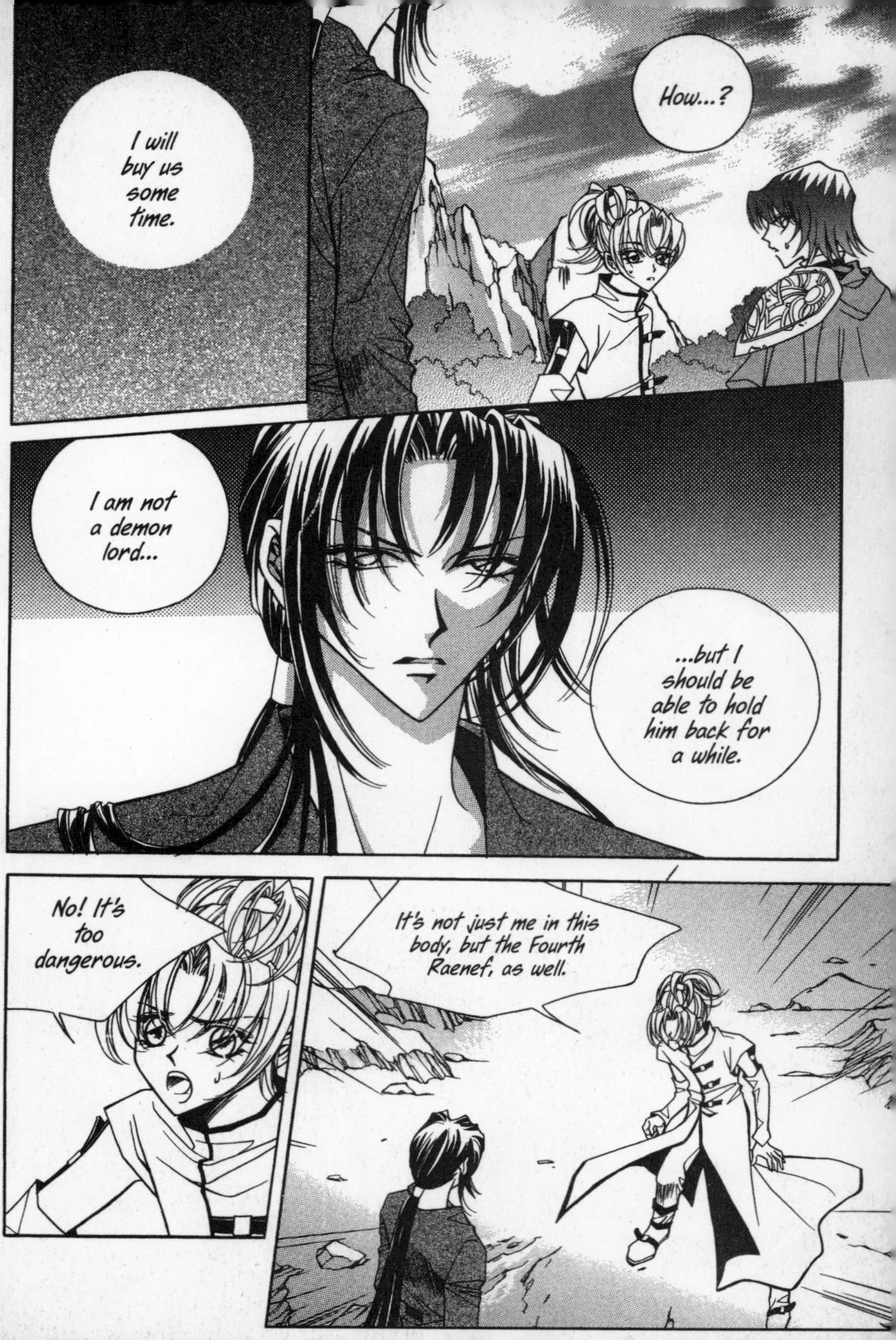
I will buy us some time.
How...?
I am not a demon lord...
...but I should be able to hold him back for a while.
No! It's too dangerous.
It's not just me in this body, but the Fourth Raenef, as well.

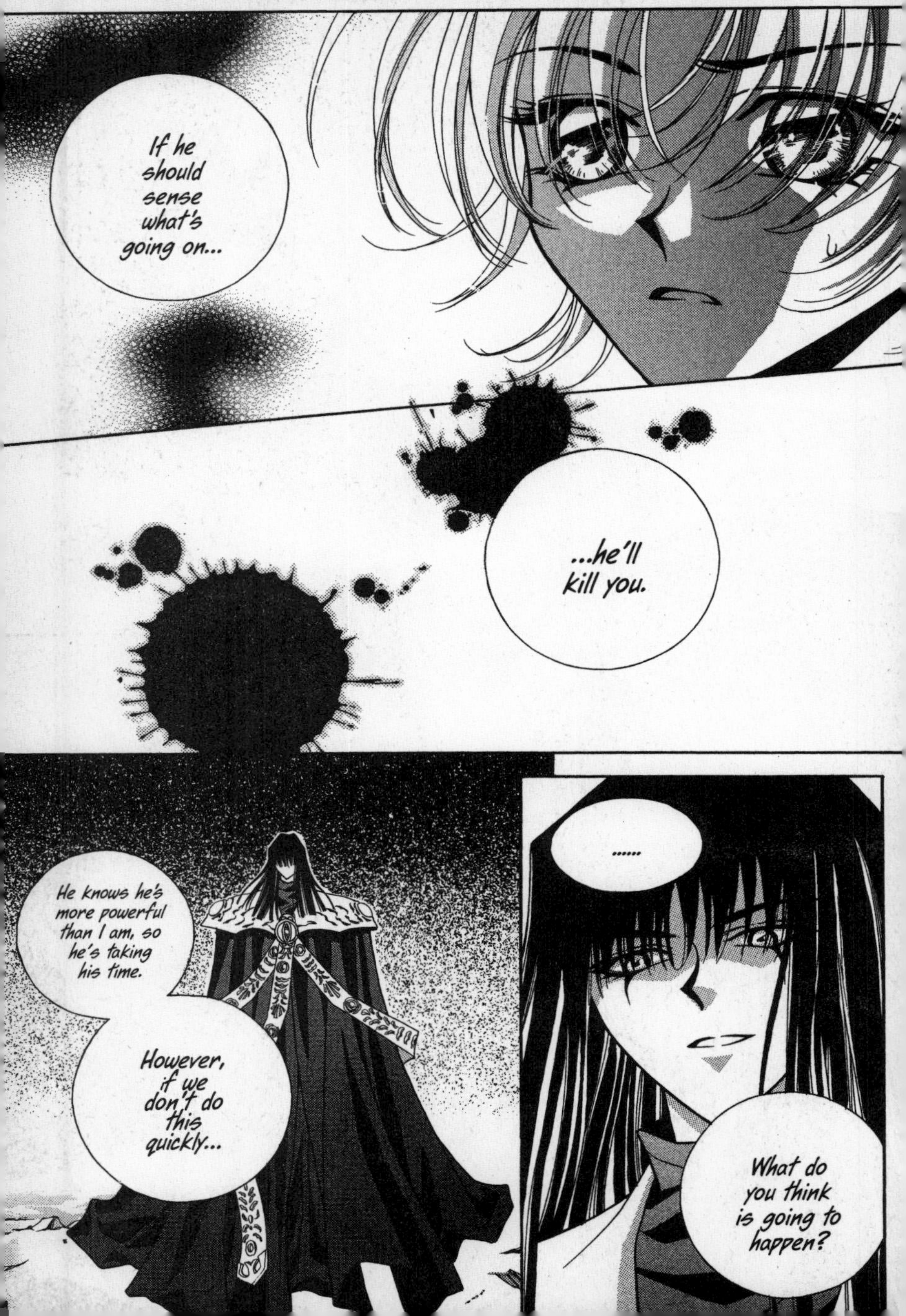
If he should sense what's going on...
...he'll kill you.
He knows he's more powerful than I am, so he's taking his time.
However, if we don't do this quickly...
......
What do you think is going to happen?

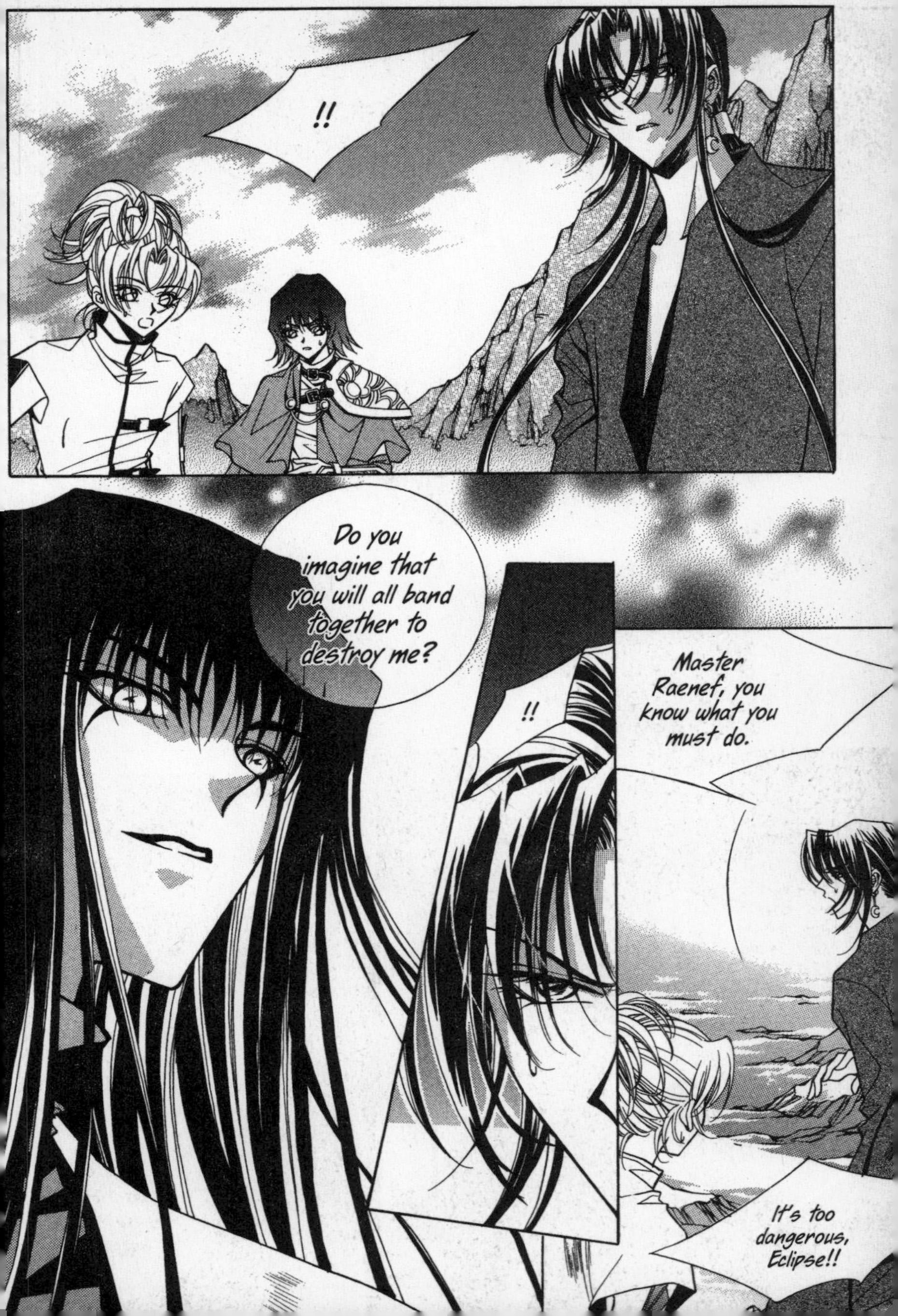
!!
Do you imagine that you will all band together to destroy me?
!!
Master Raenef, you know what you must do.
It's too dangerous, Eclipse!!

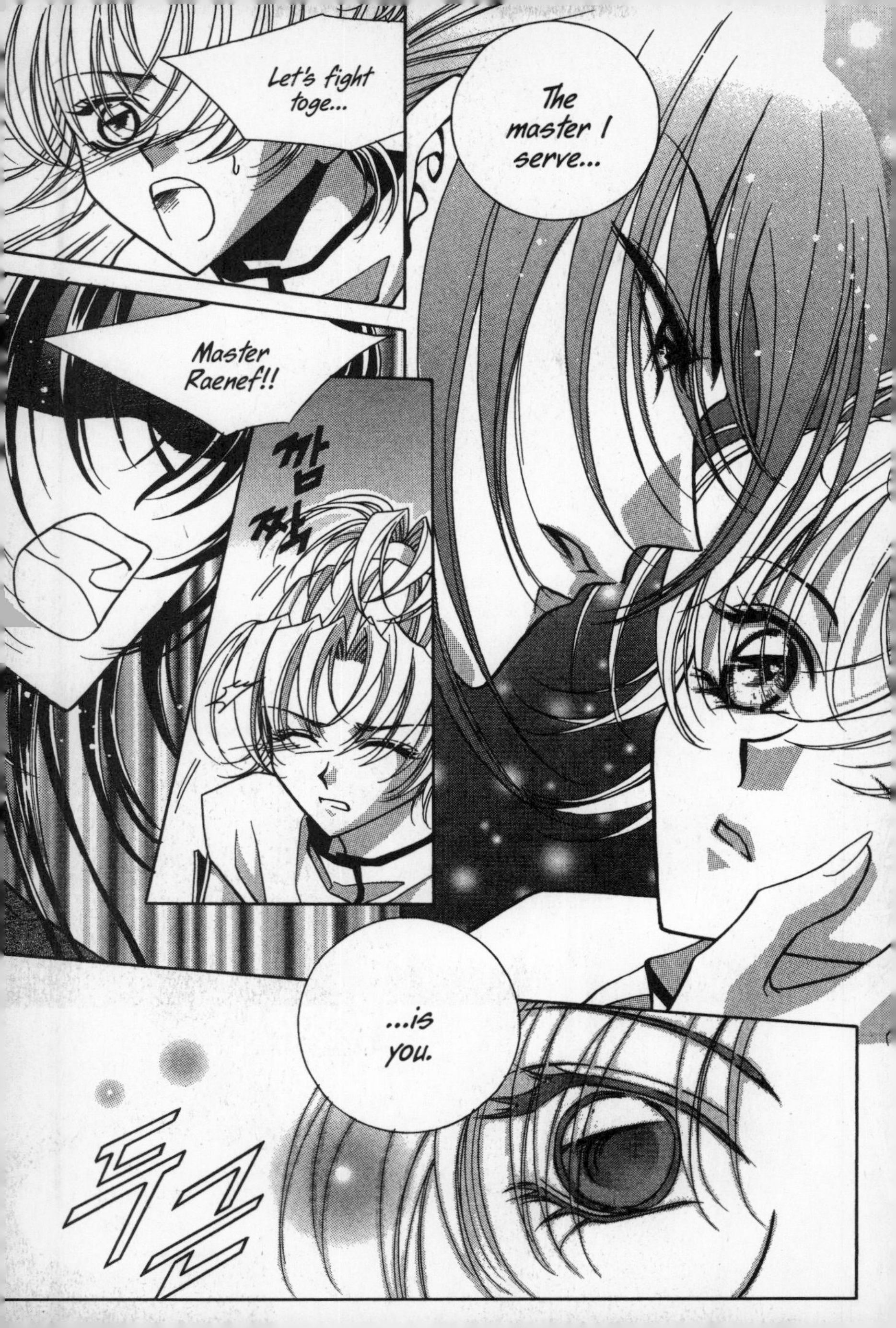
Let's fight toge...
The master I serve...
Master Raenef!!
깜짝
...is you.
두근

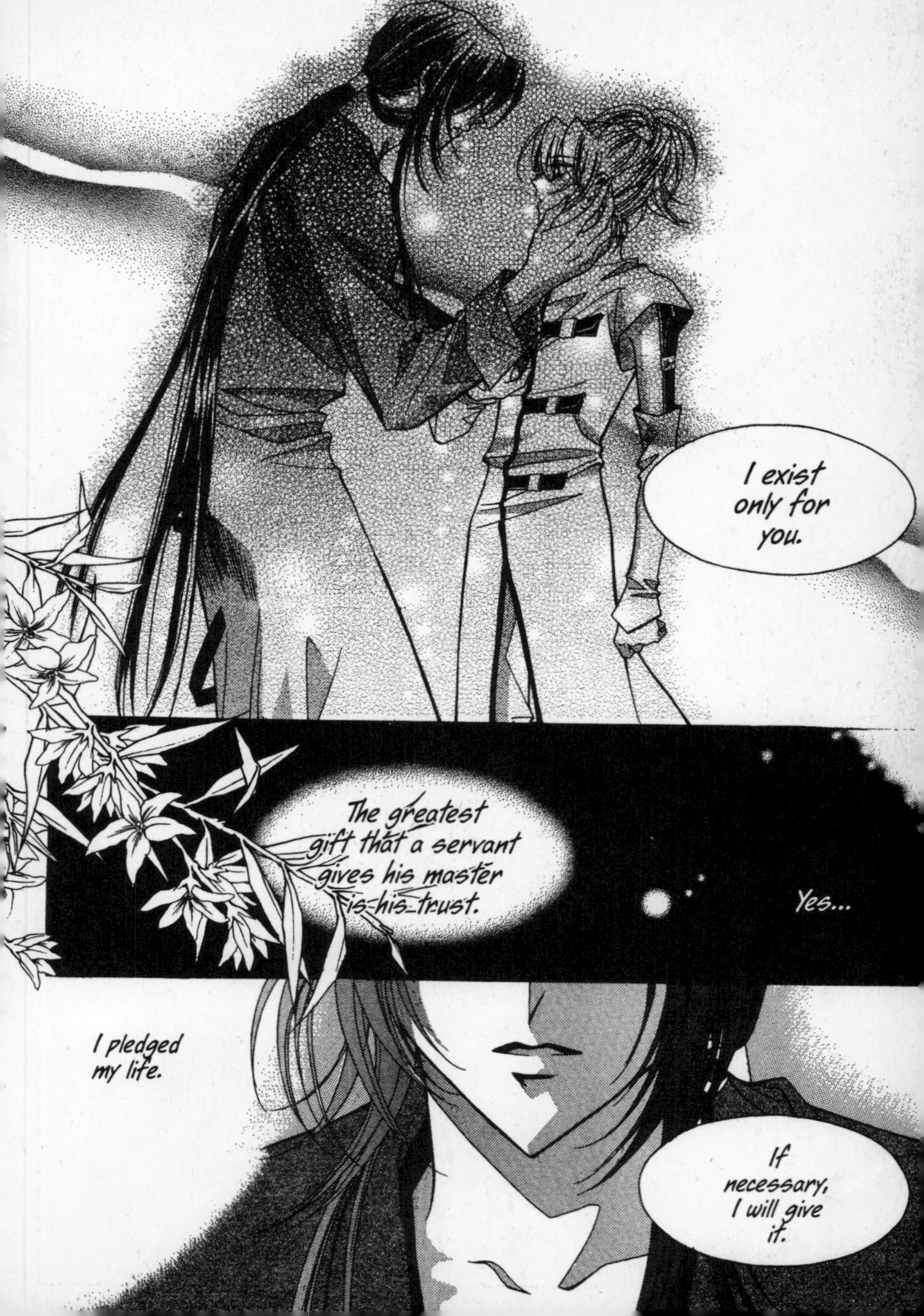
I exist only for you.
The greatest gift that a servant gives his master is his trust.
Yes...
I pledged my life.
If necessary, I will give it.

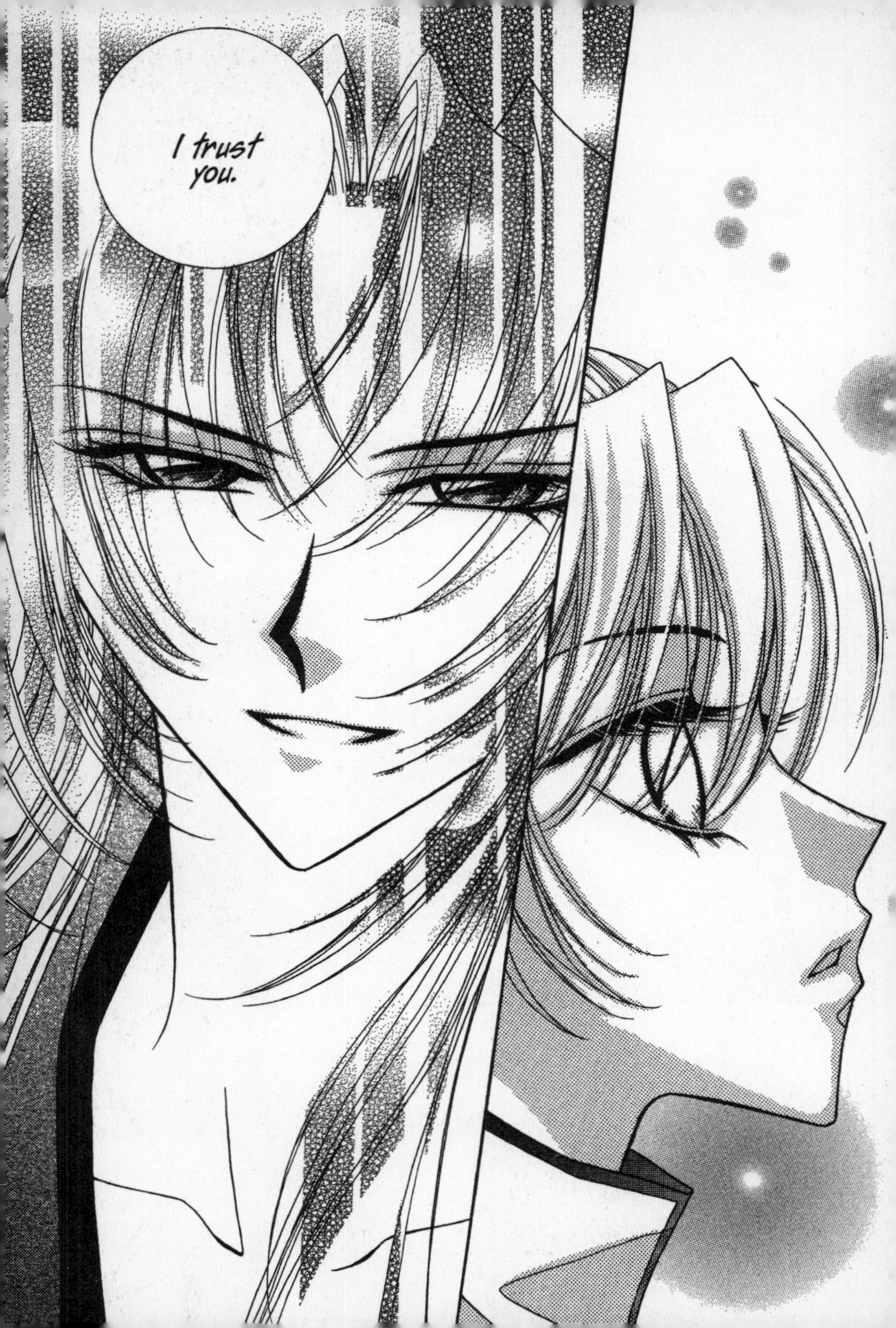
I trust you.

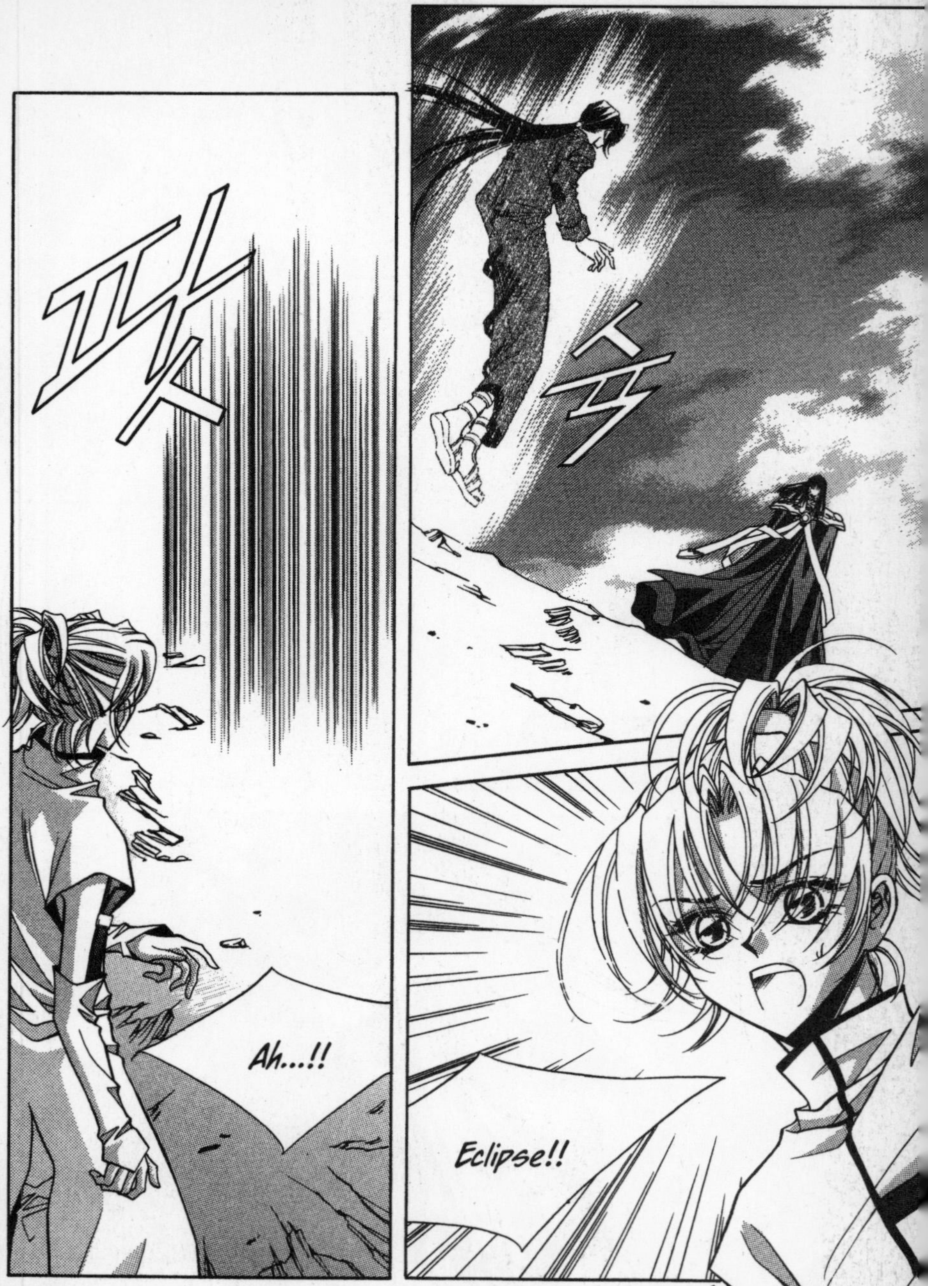
Ah...!!
Eclipse!!

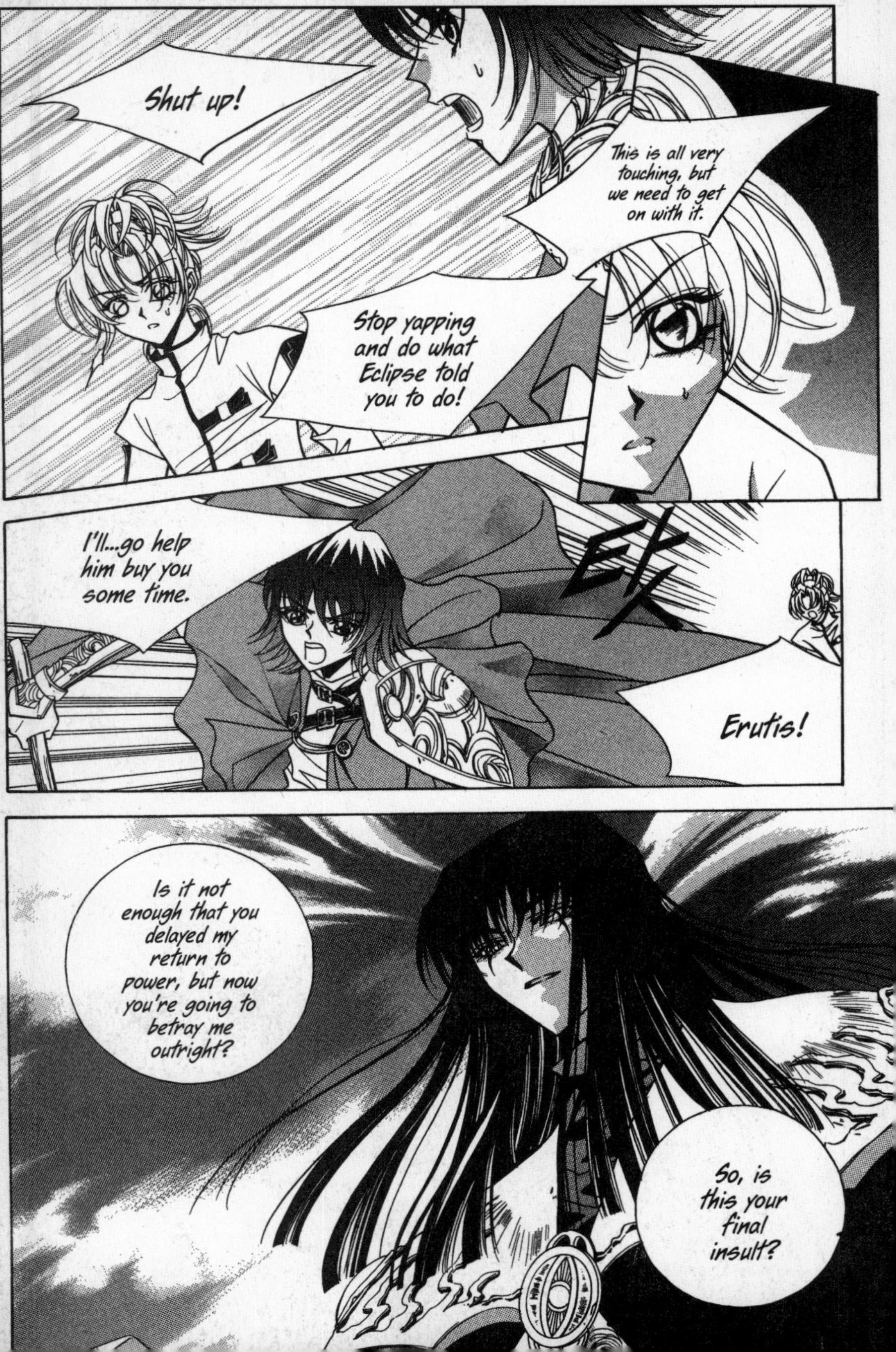
Shut up!
This is all very touching, but we need to get on with it.
Stop yapping and do what Eclipse told you to do!
I'll...go help him buy you some time.
Erutis!
Is it not enough that you delayed my return to power, but now you're going to betray me outright?
So, is this your final insult?

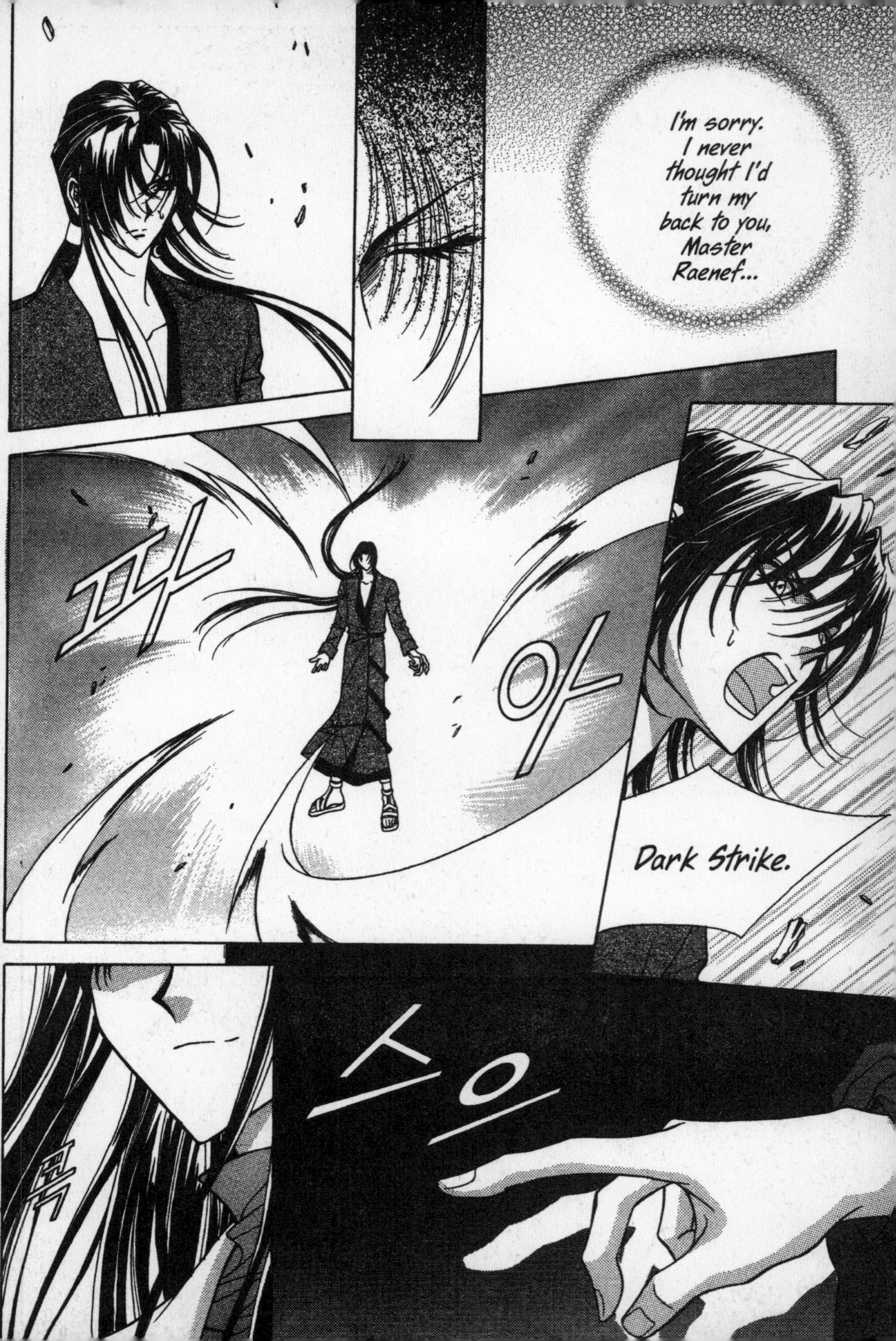
I'm sorry. I never thought I'd turn my back to you, Master Raenef...
Dark Strike.

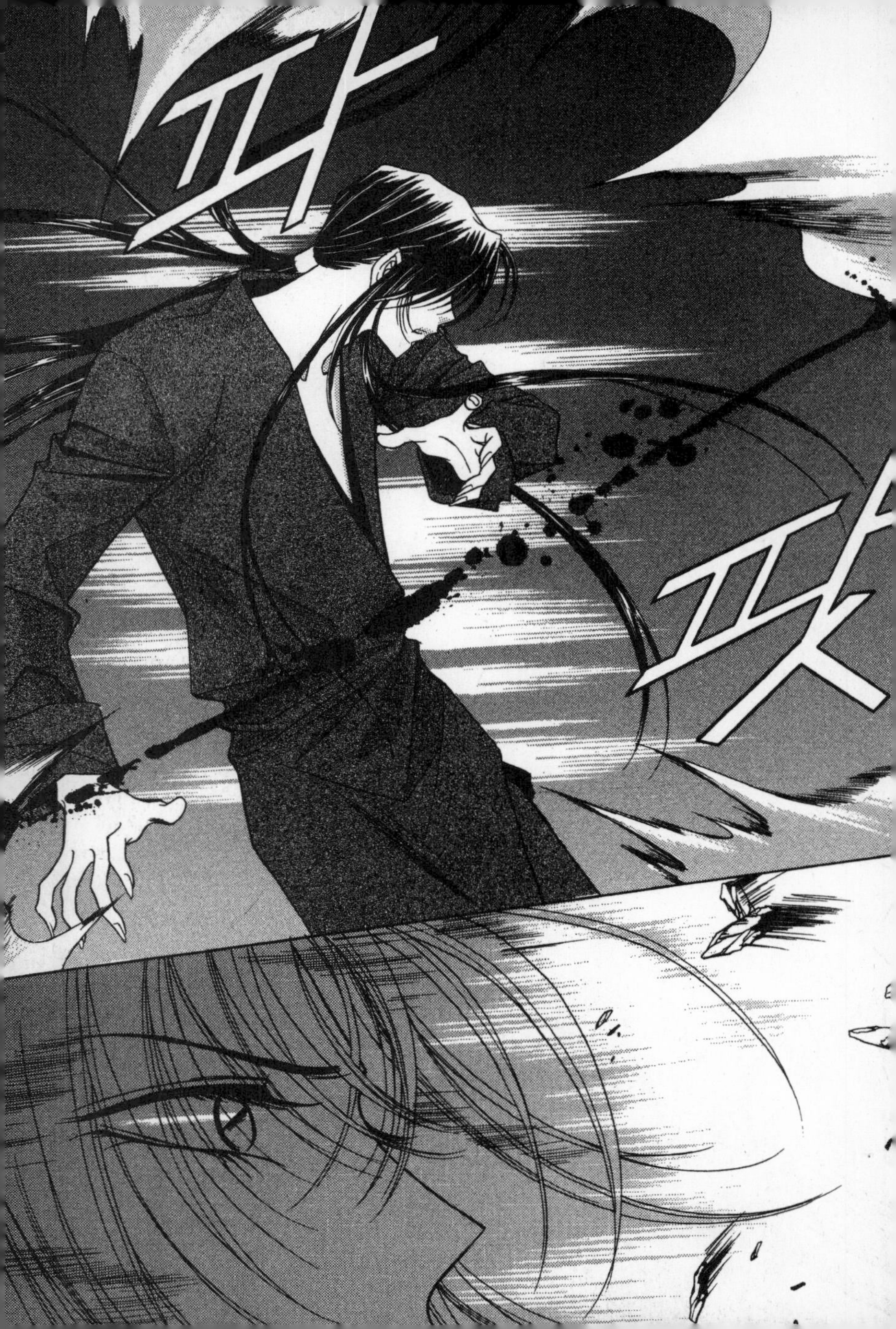

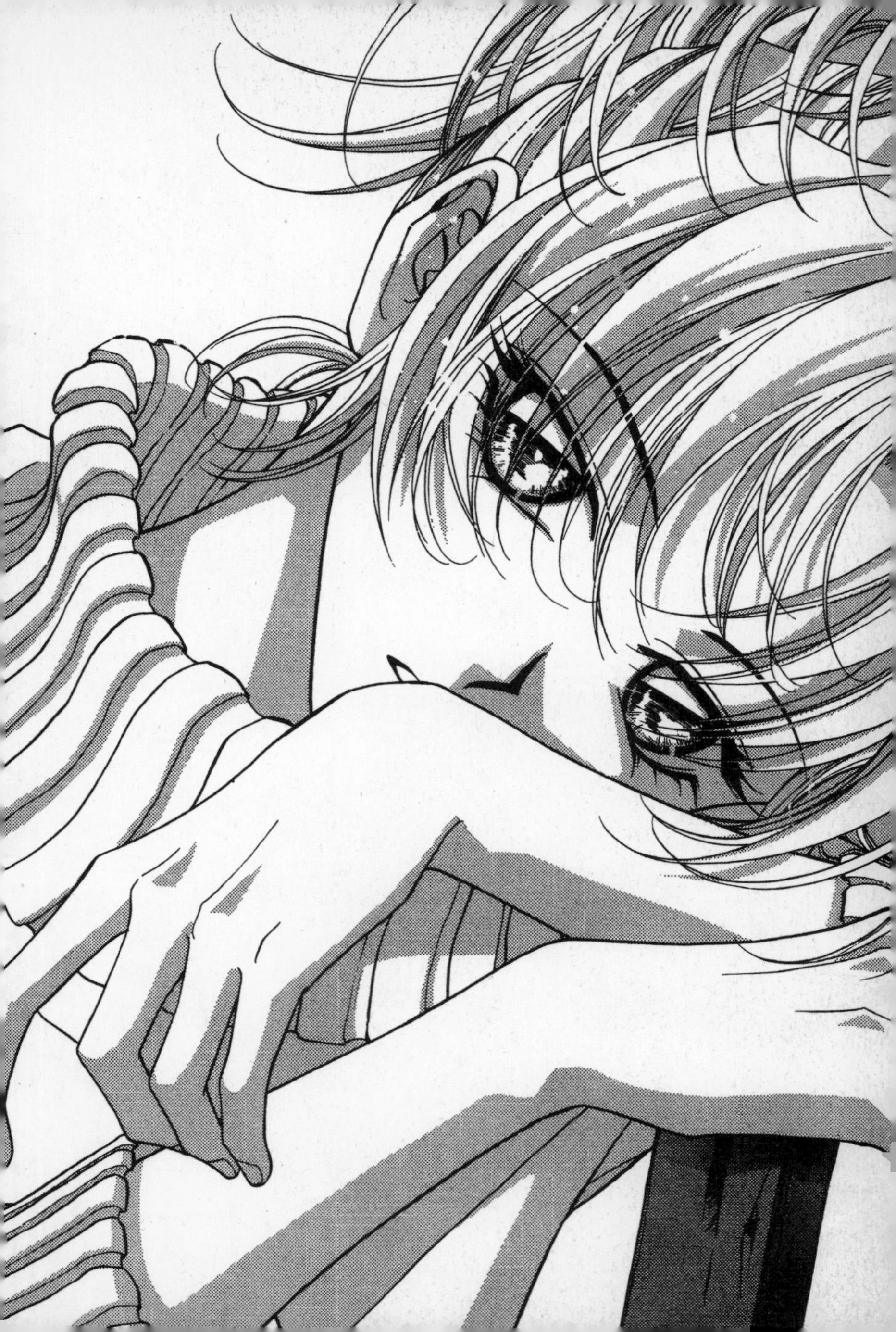

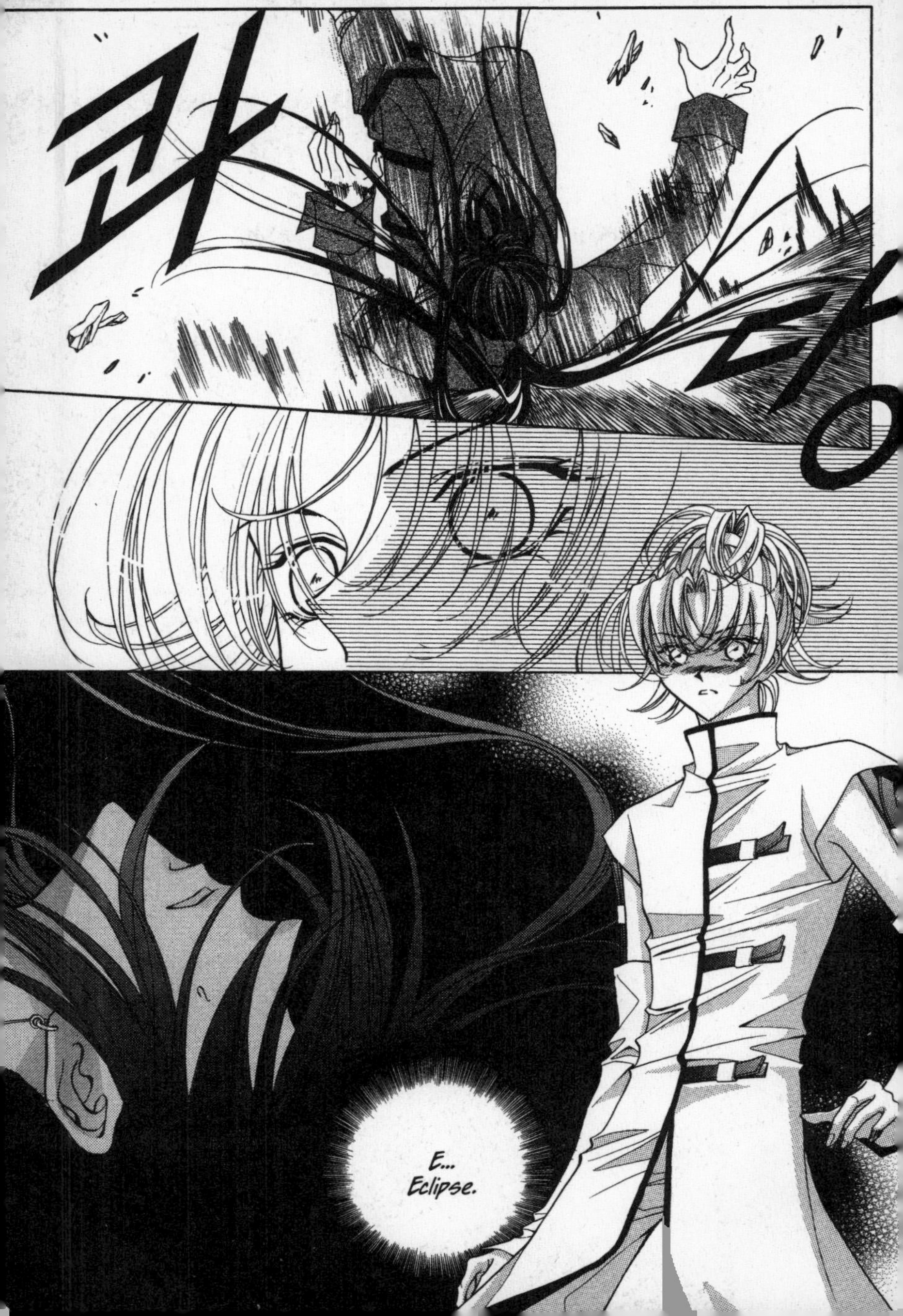

콰창
E...
Eclipse.

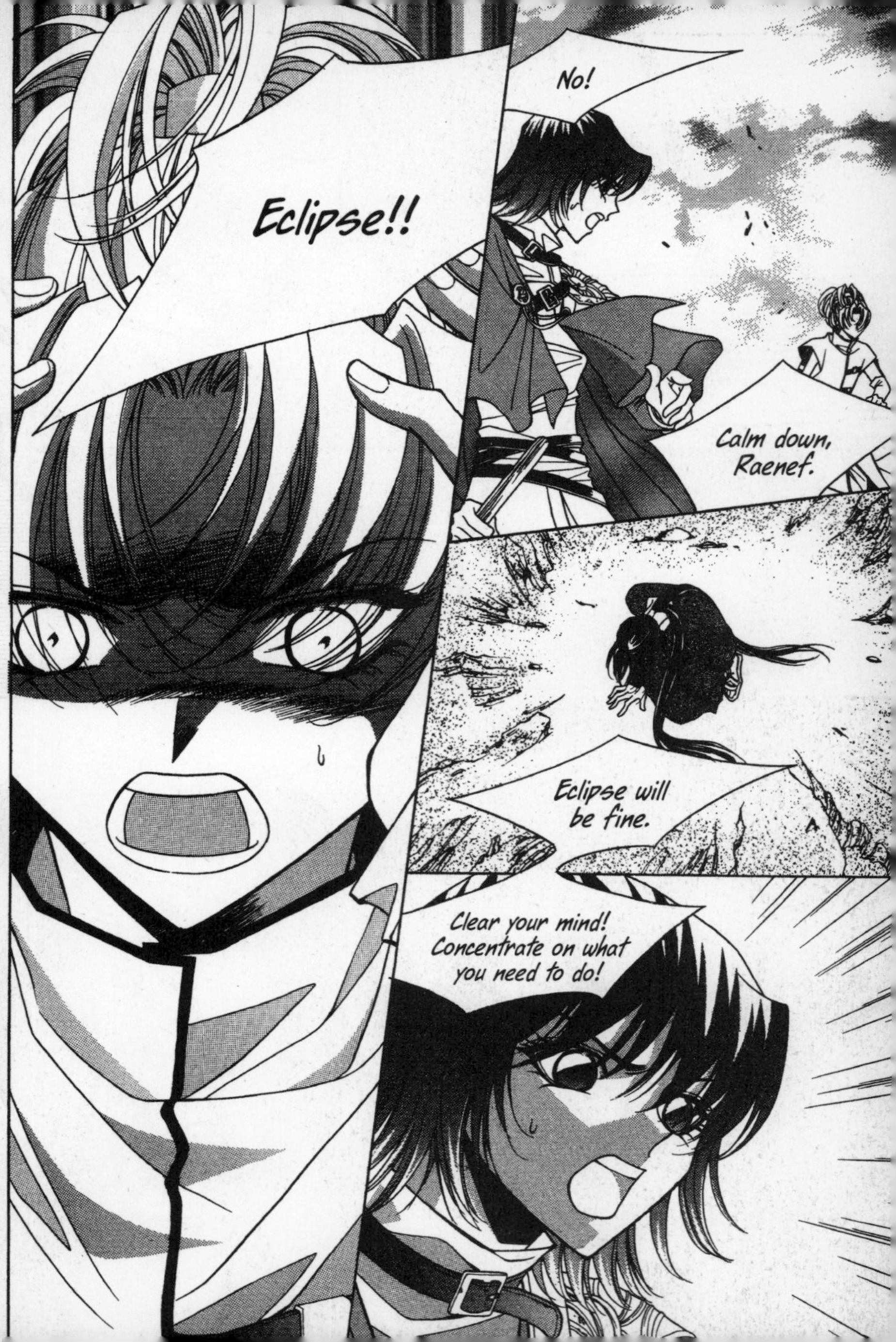
Eclipse!!
No!
Calm down, Raenef.
Eclipse will be fine.
Clear your mind! Concentrate on what you need to do!

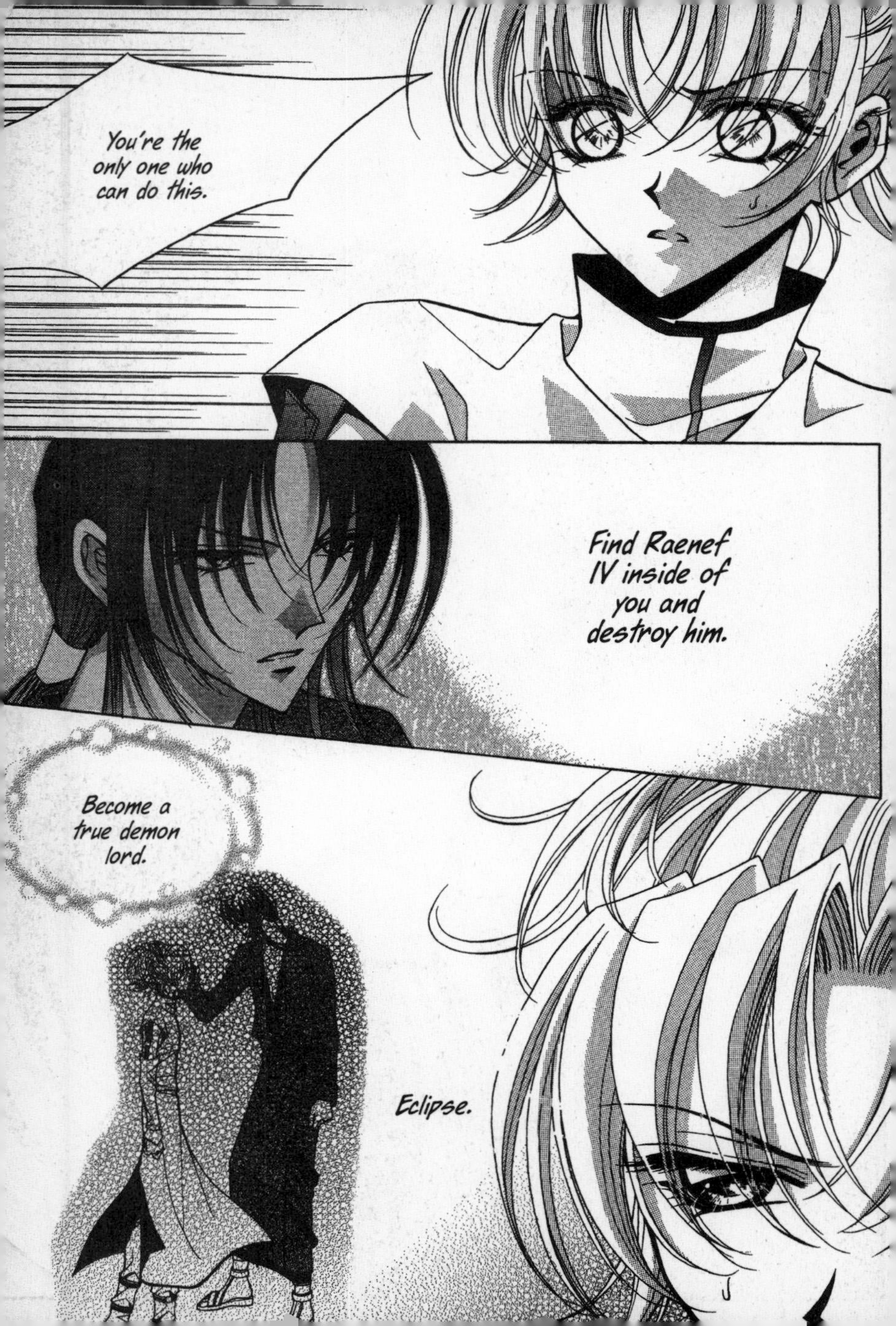
You're the only one who can do this.
Find Raenef IV inside of you and destroy him.
Become a true demon lord.
Eclipse.

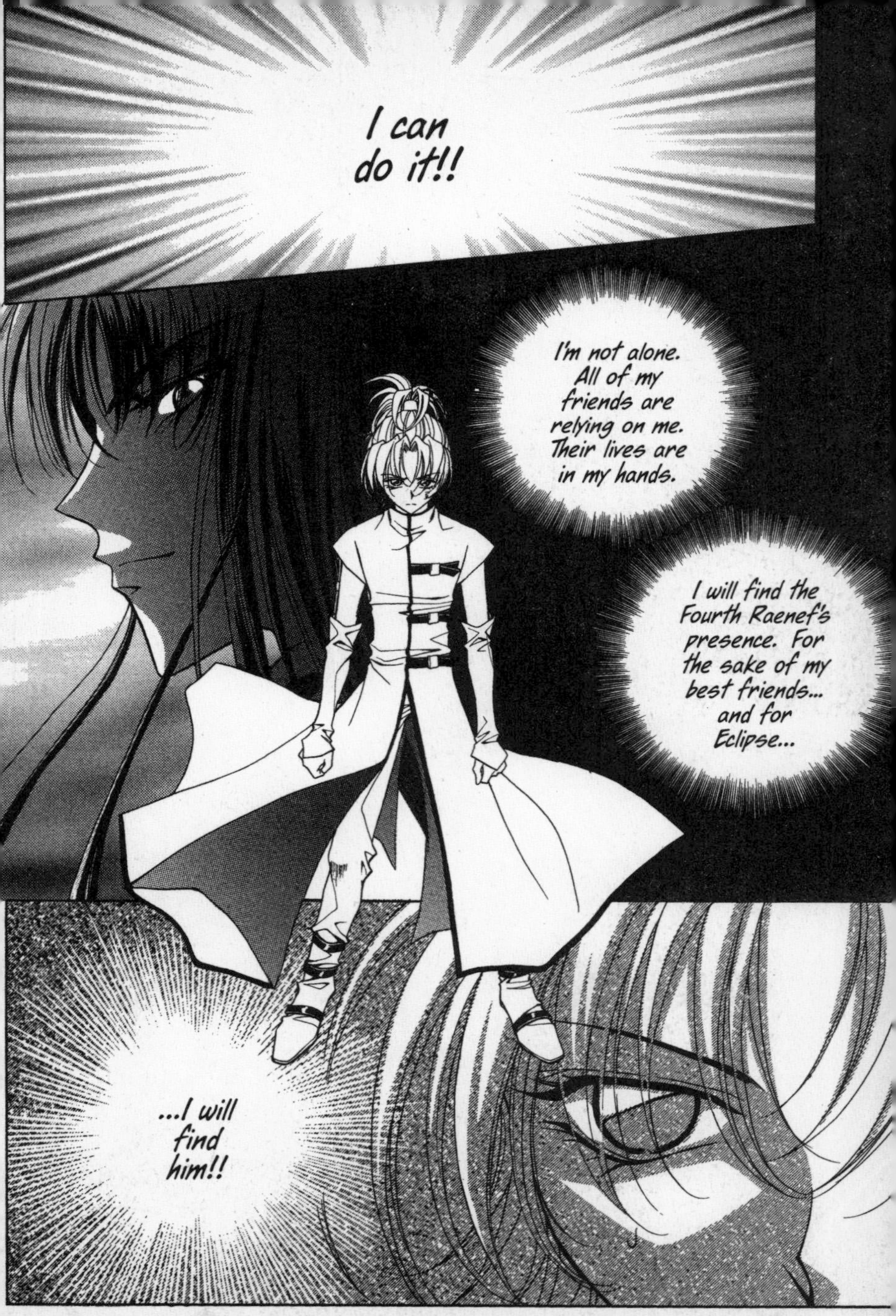
I can do it!!
I'm not alone. All of my friends are relying on me. Their lives are in my hands.
I will find the Fourth Raenef's presence. For the sake of my best friends... and for Eclipse...
...I will find him!!

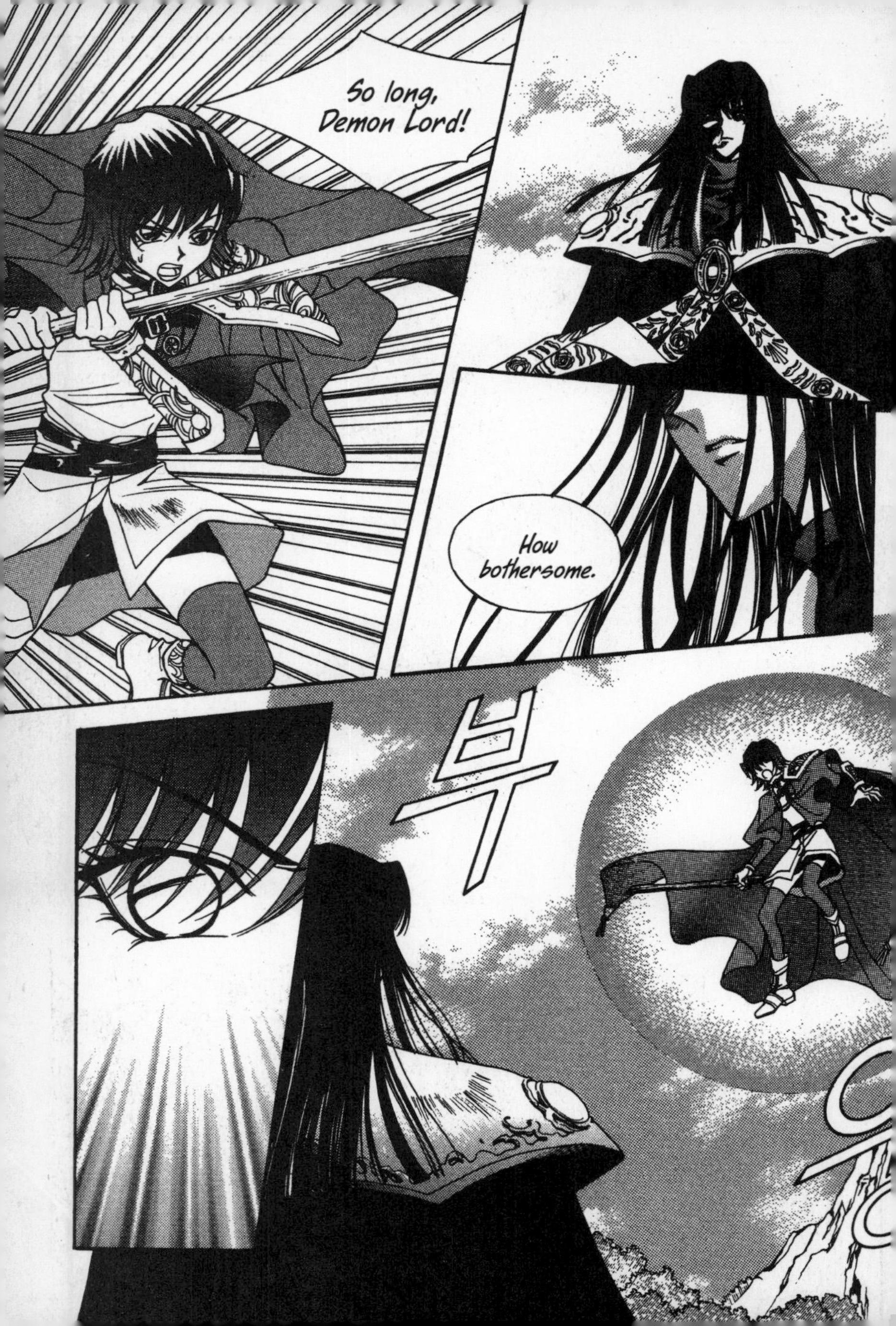
So long, Demon Lord!
How bothersome.

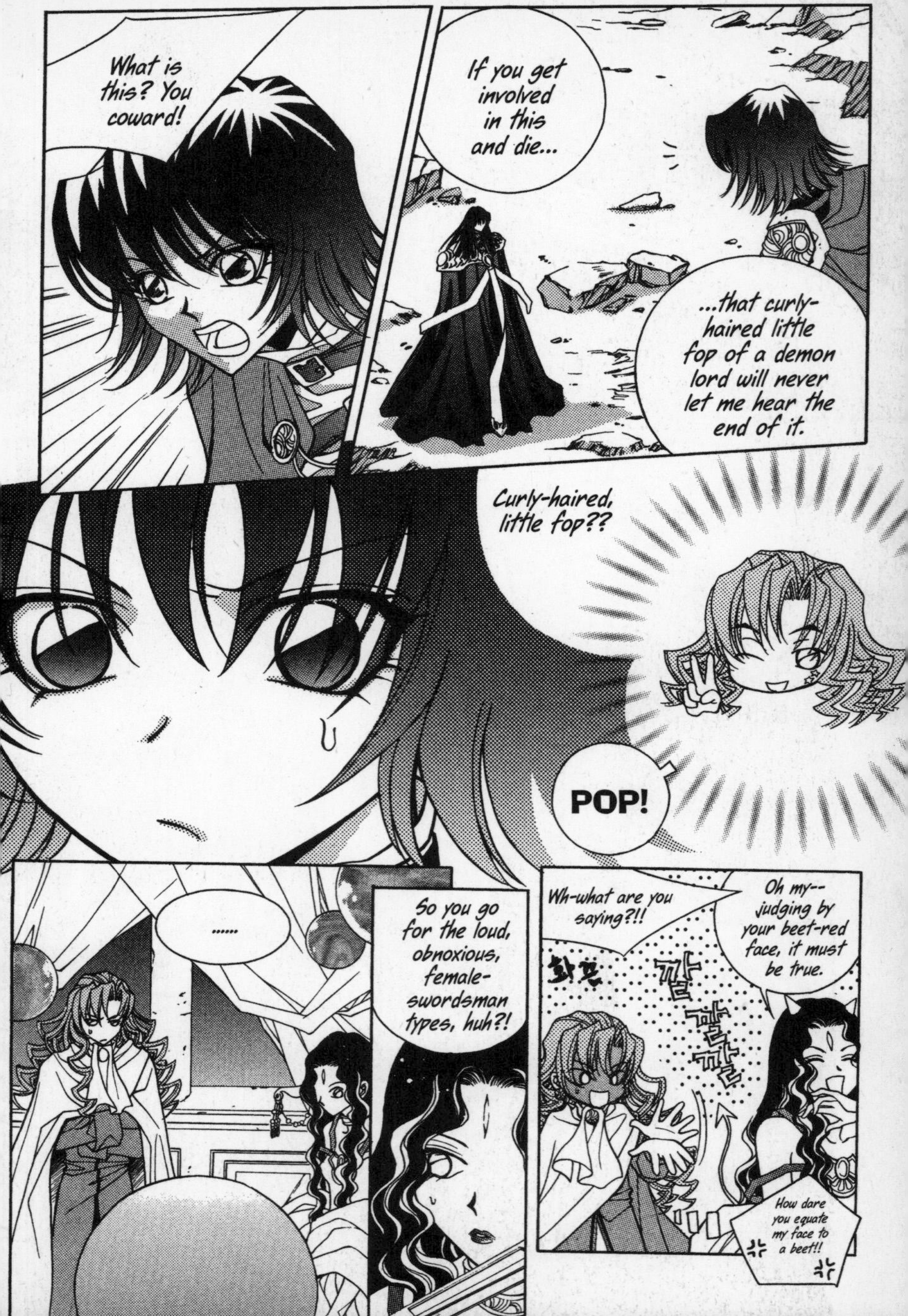
What is this? You coward!
If you get involved in this and die...
...that curly-haired little fop of a demon lord will never let me hear the end of it.
Curly-haired, little fop??
POP!
......
So you go for the loud, obnoxious, female-swordsman types, huh?!
Wh-what are you saying?!!
Oh my--judging by your beet-red face, it must be true.
How dare you equate my face to a beet!!

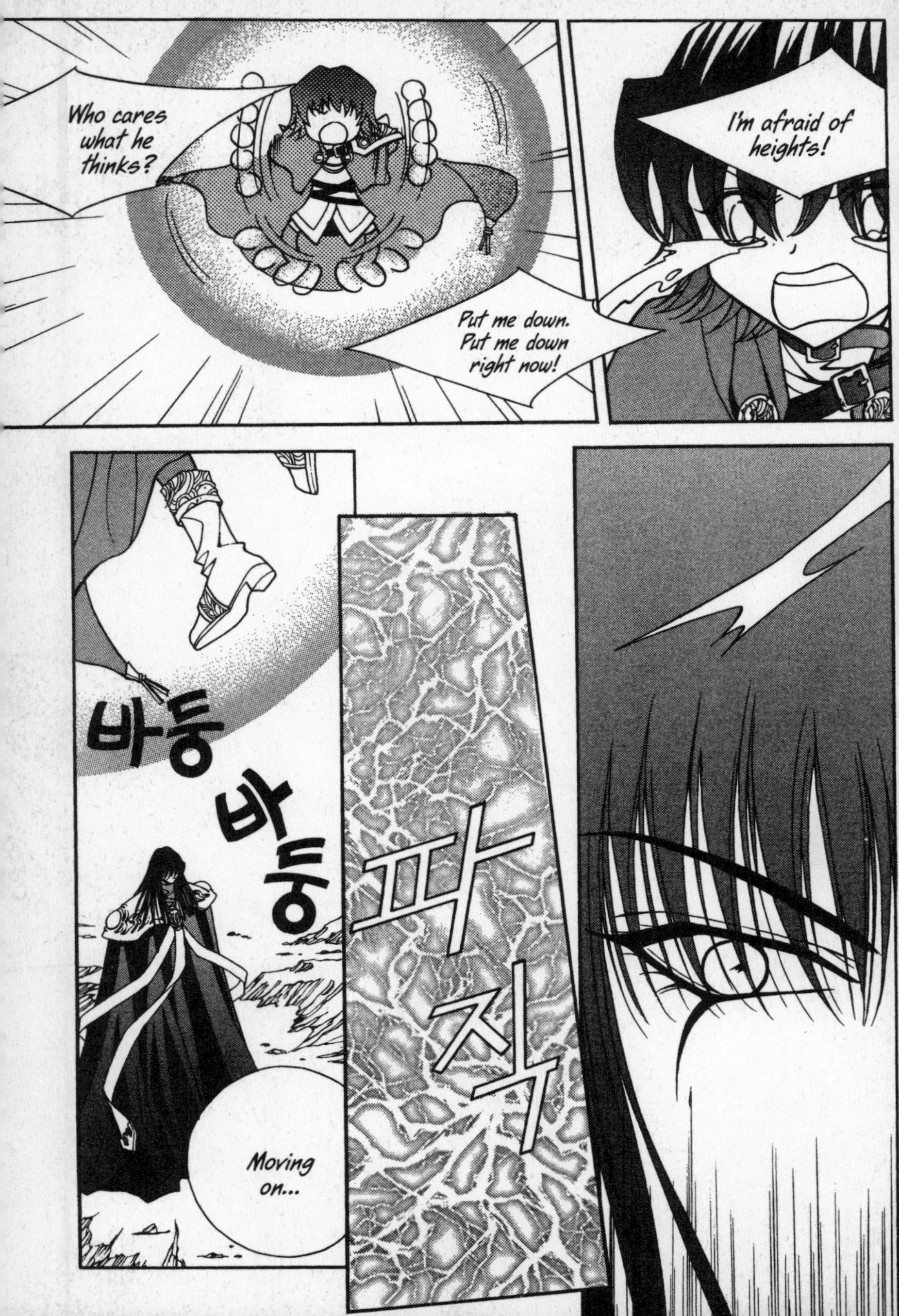
Who cares what he thinks?
Put me down. Put me down right now!
I'm afraid of heights!
바둥
바둥
Moving on...
파직

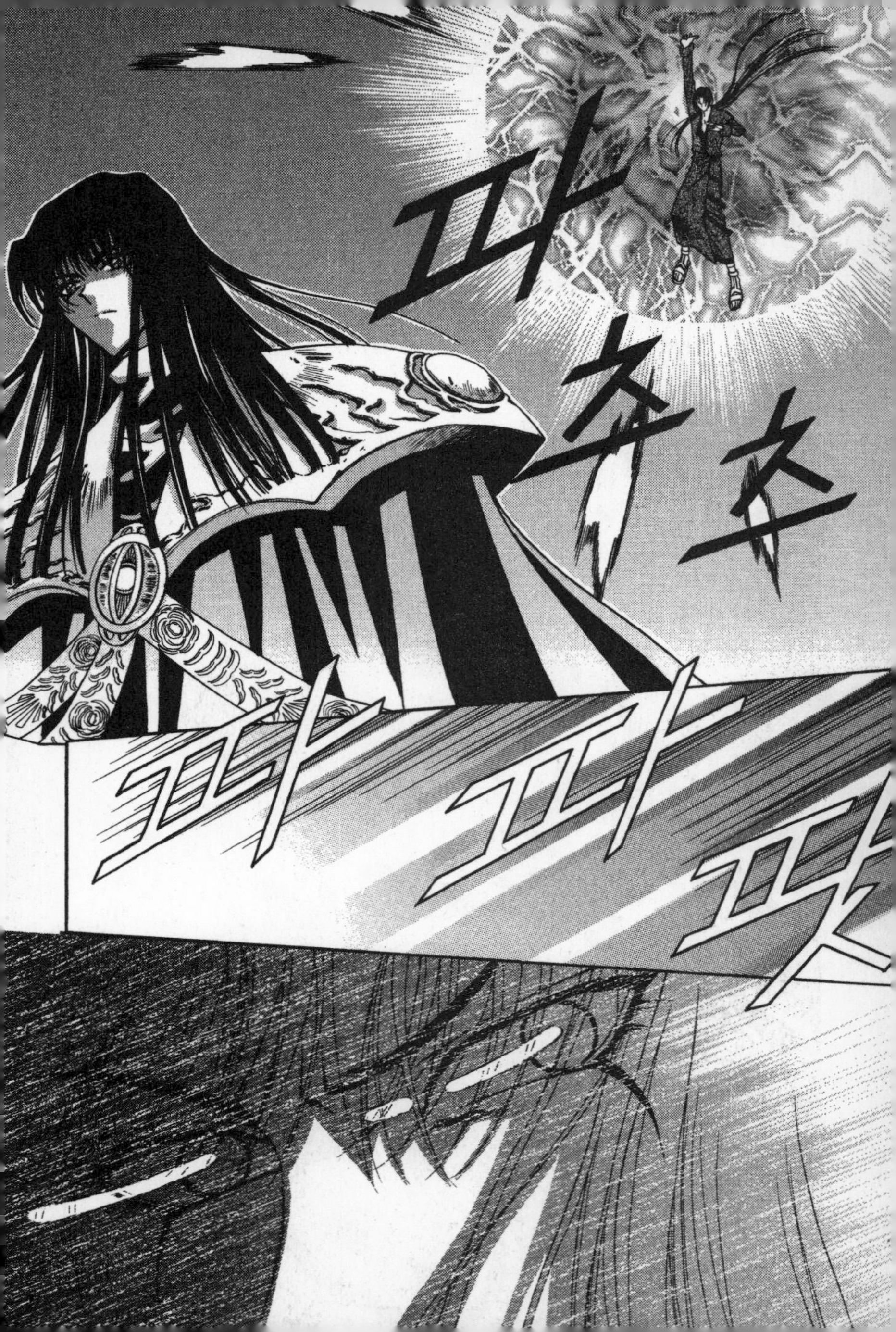

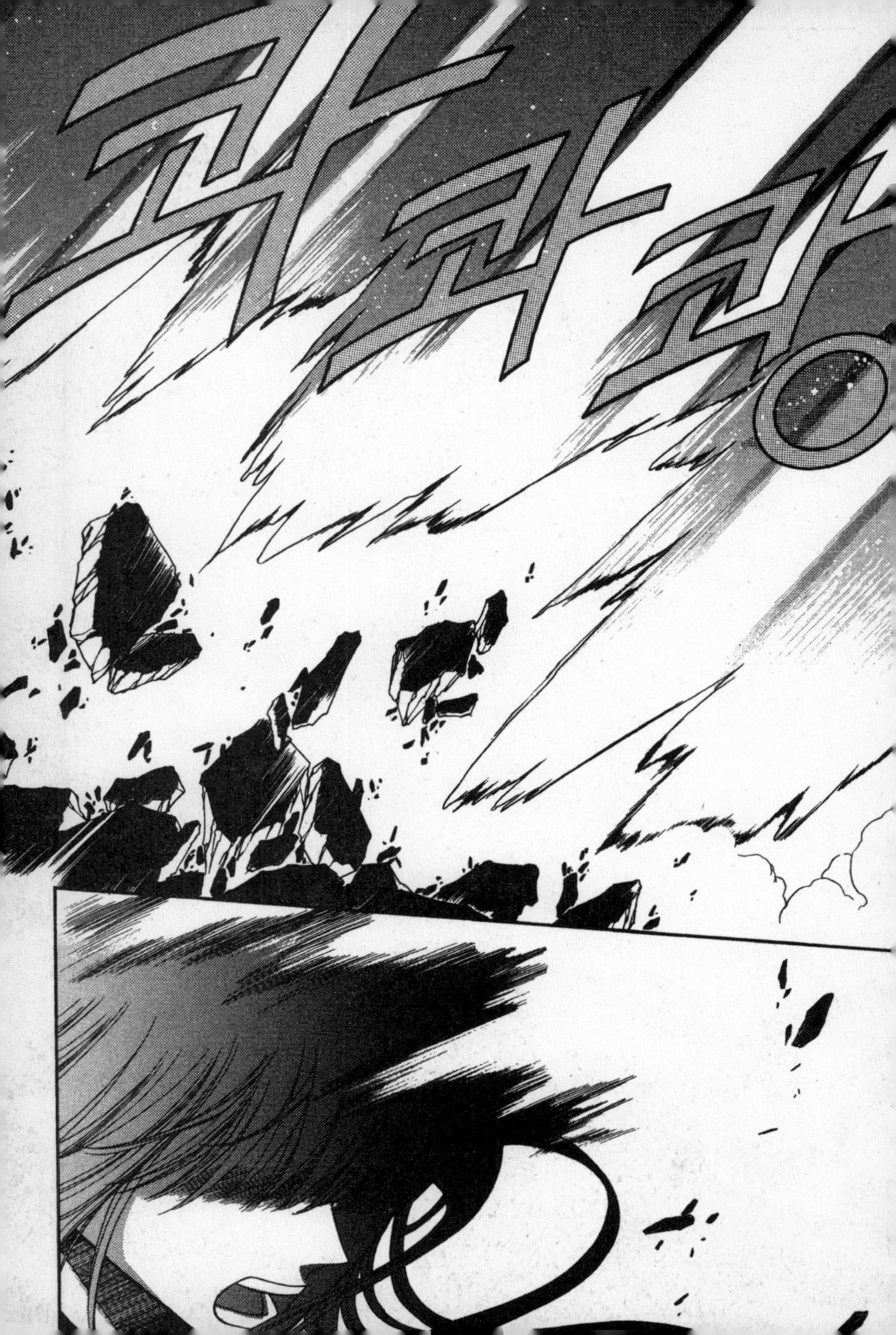
콰콰쾅

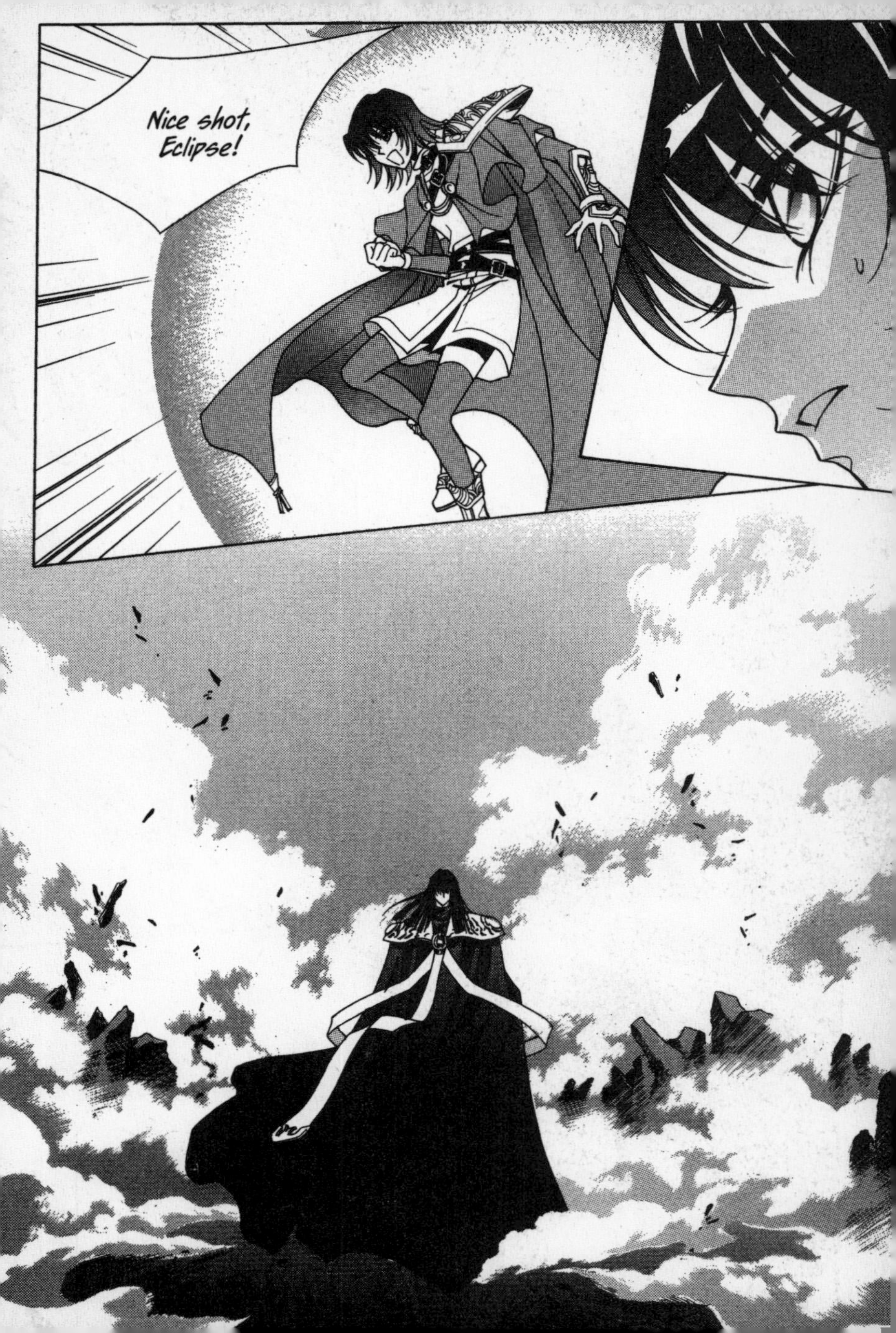
Nice shot, Eclipse!

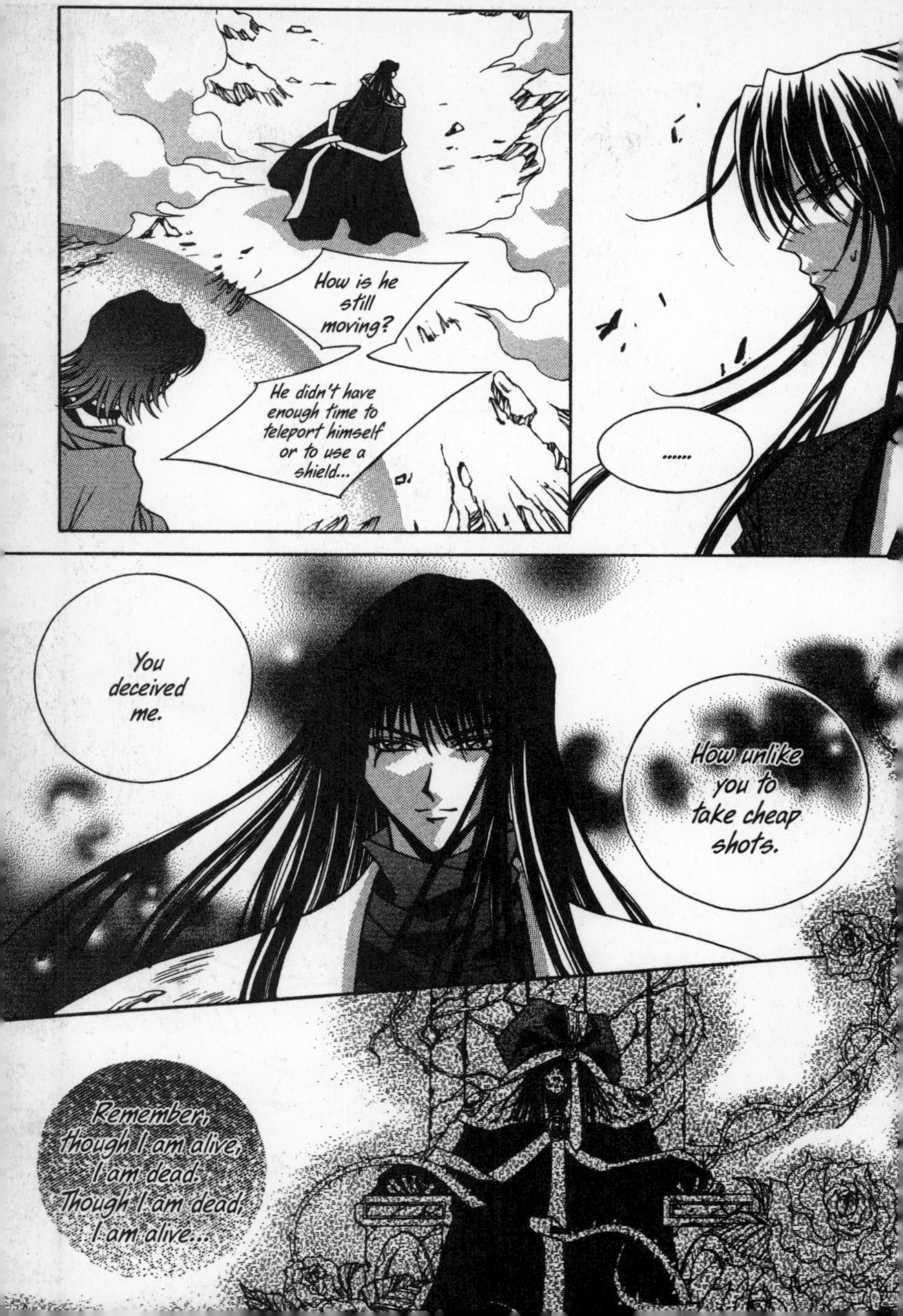
How is he still moving?
He didn't have enough time to teleport himself or to use a shield...
......
You deceived me.
How unlike you to take cheap shots.
Remember, though I am alive, I am dead. Though I am dead, I am alive...

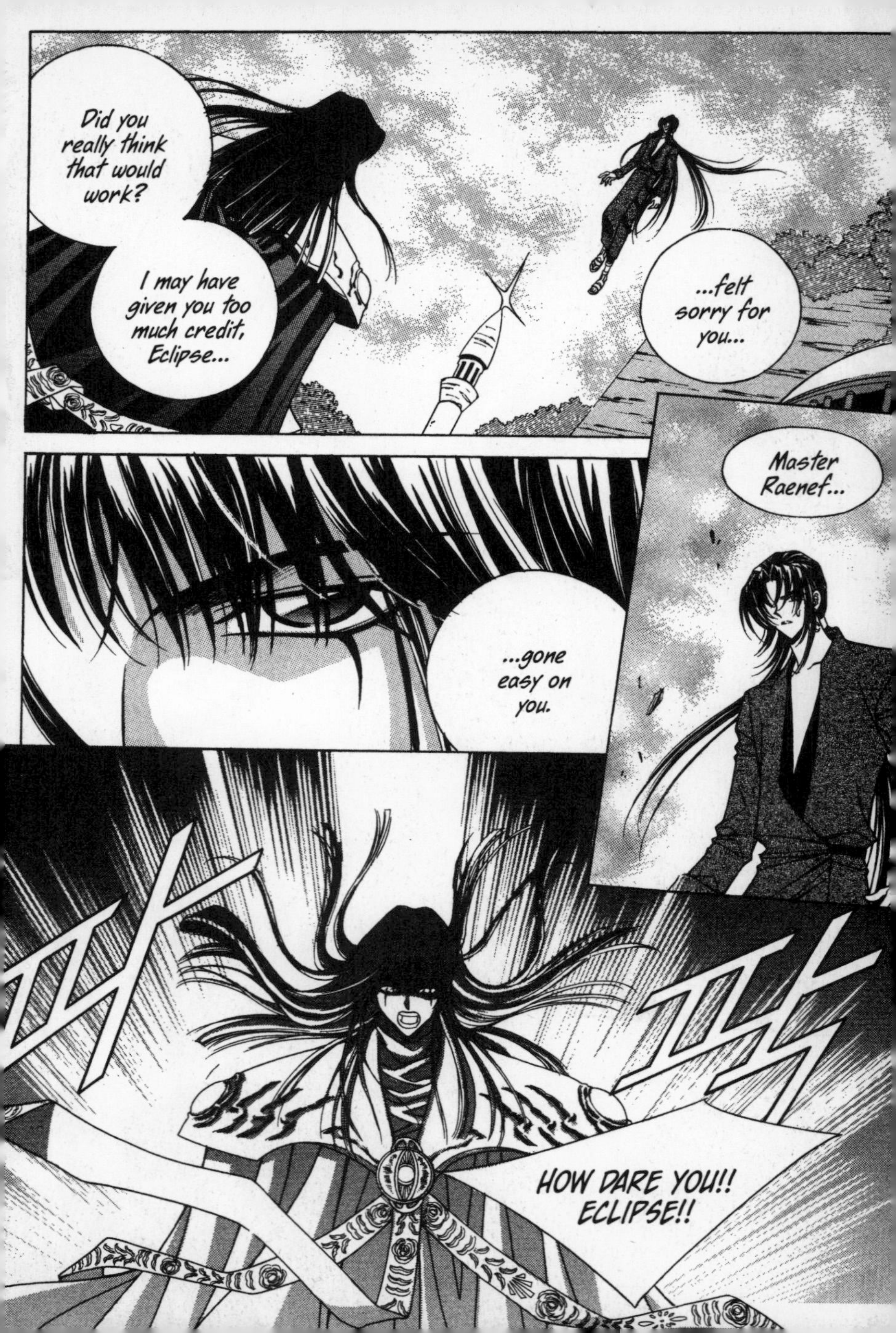
Did you really think that would work?
I may have given you too much credit, Eclipse...
...felt sorry for you...
...gone easy on you.
Master Raenef...
HOW DARE YOU!! ECLIPSE!!

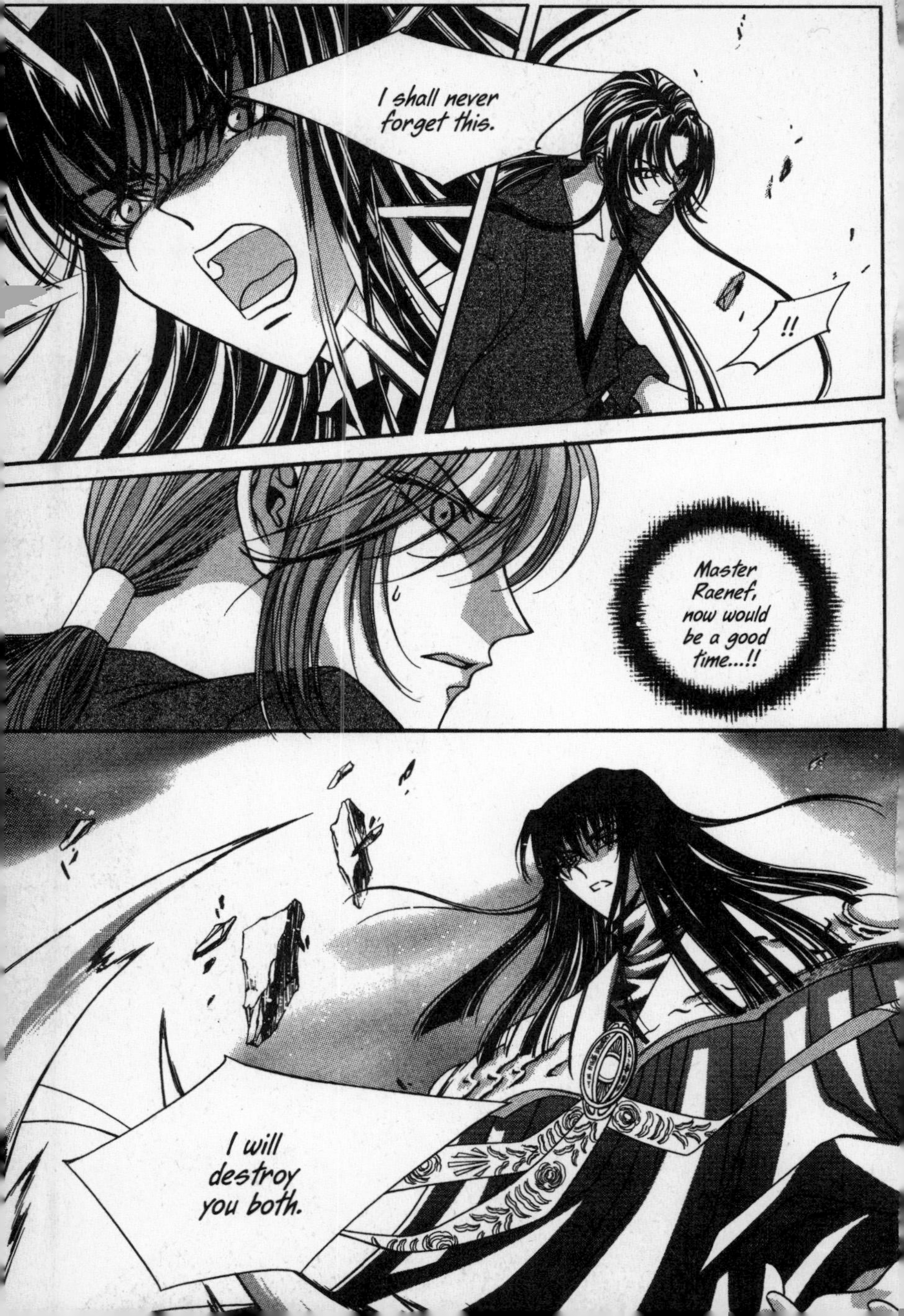
I shall never forget this.
!!
Master Raenef, now would be a good time...!!
I will destroy you both.

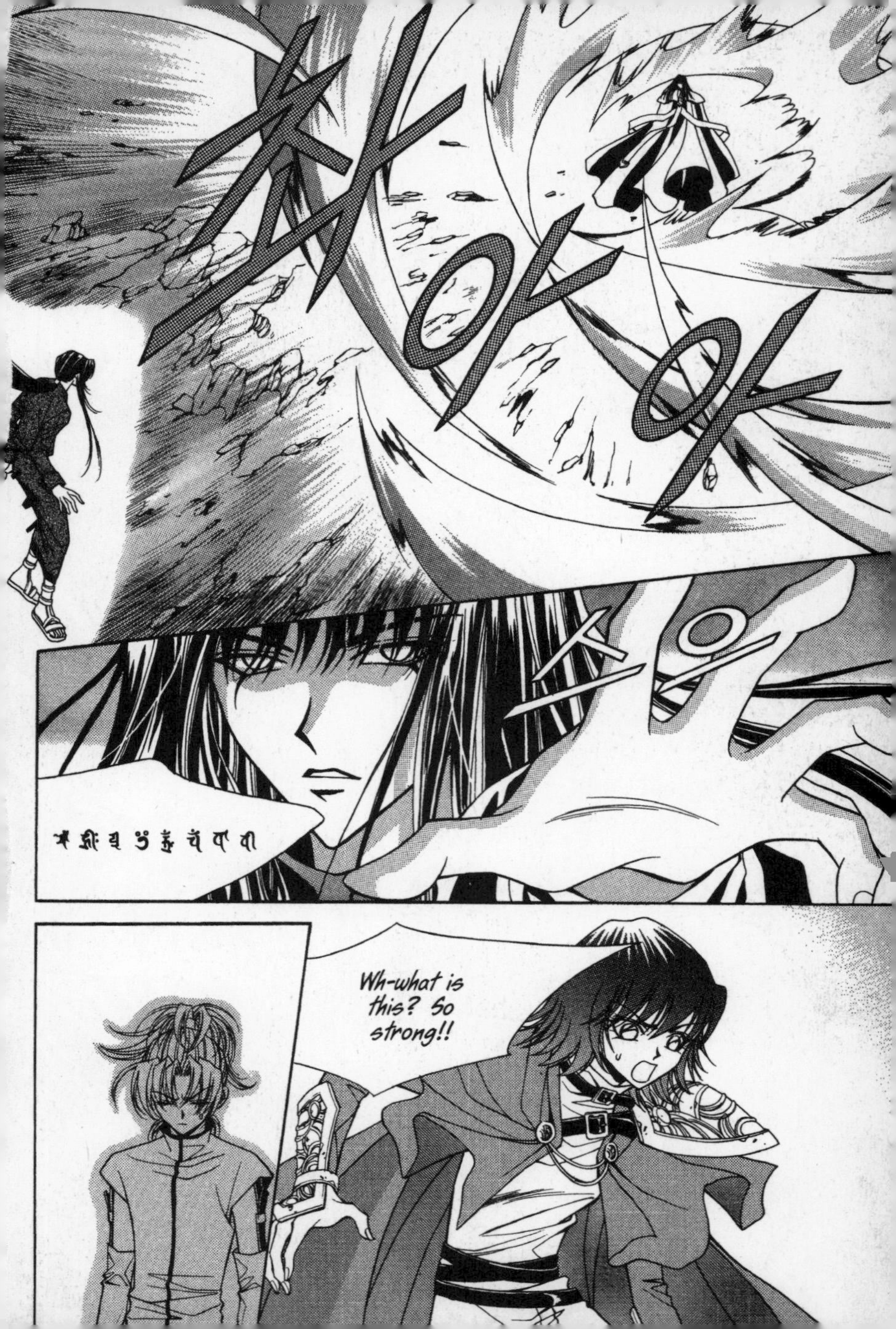
촤아아
Wh-what is this? So strong!!

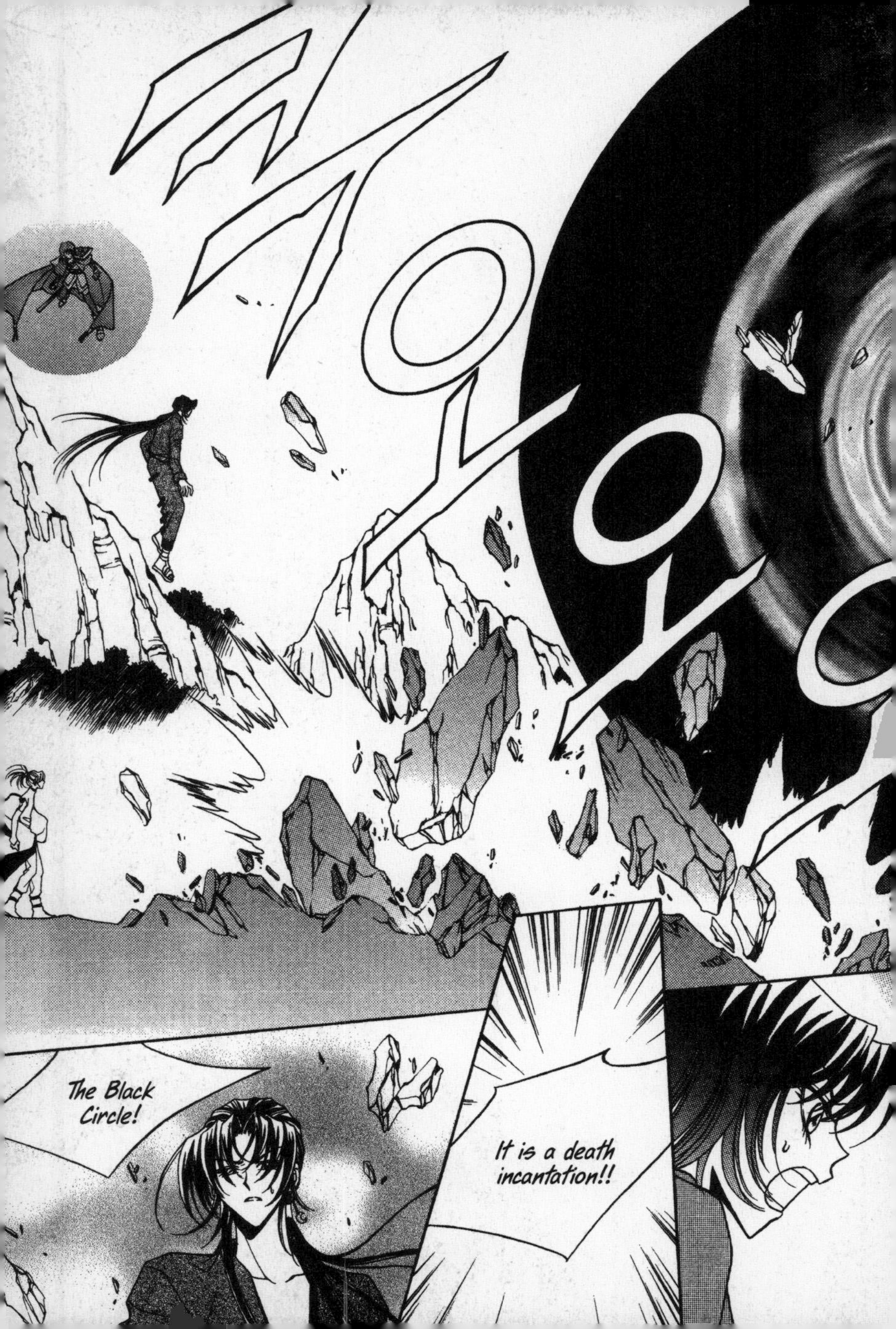
The Black Circle!
It is a death incantation!!

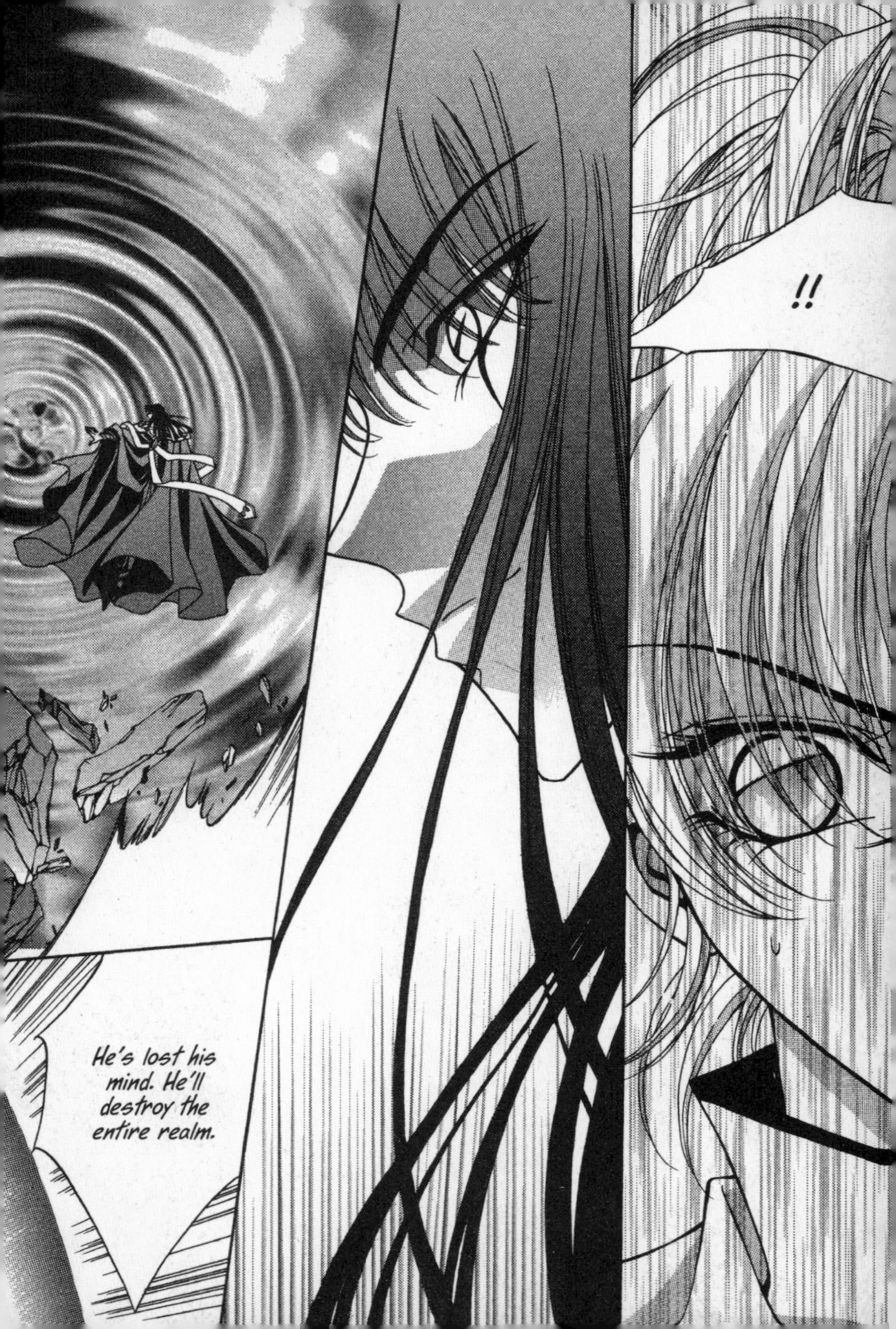
He's lost his mind. He'll destroy the entire realm.
!!

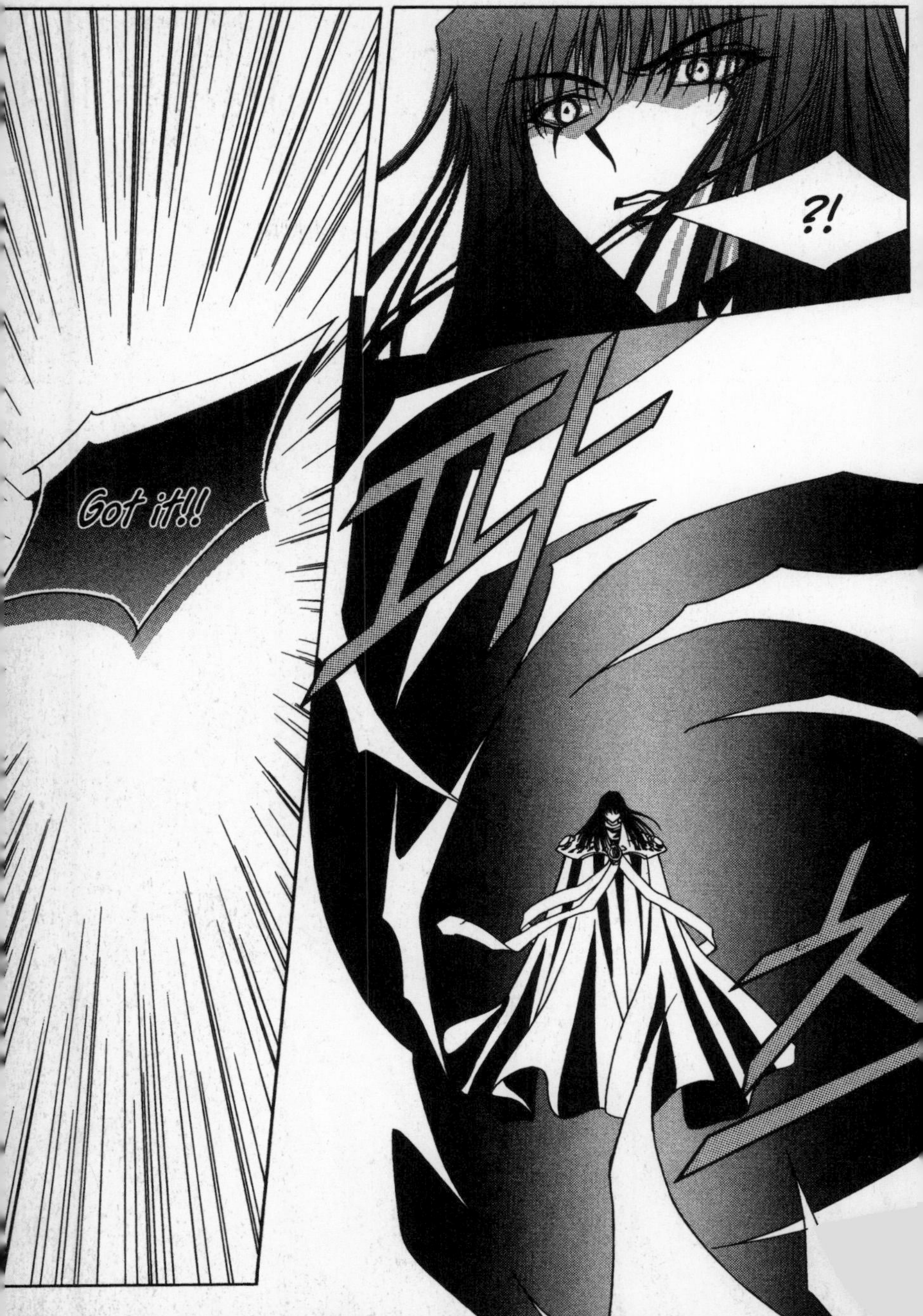
Got it!!
?!

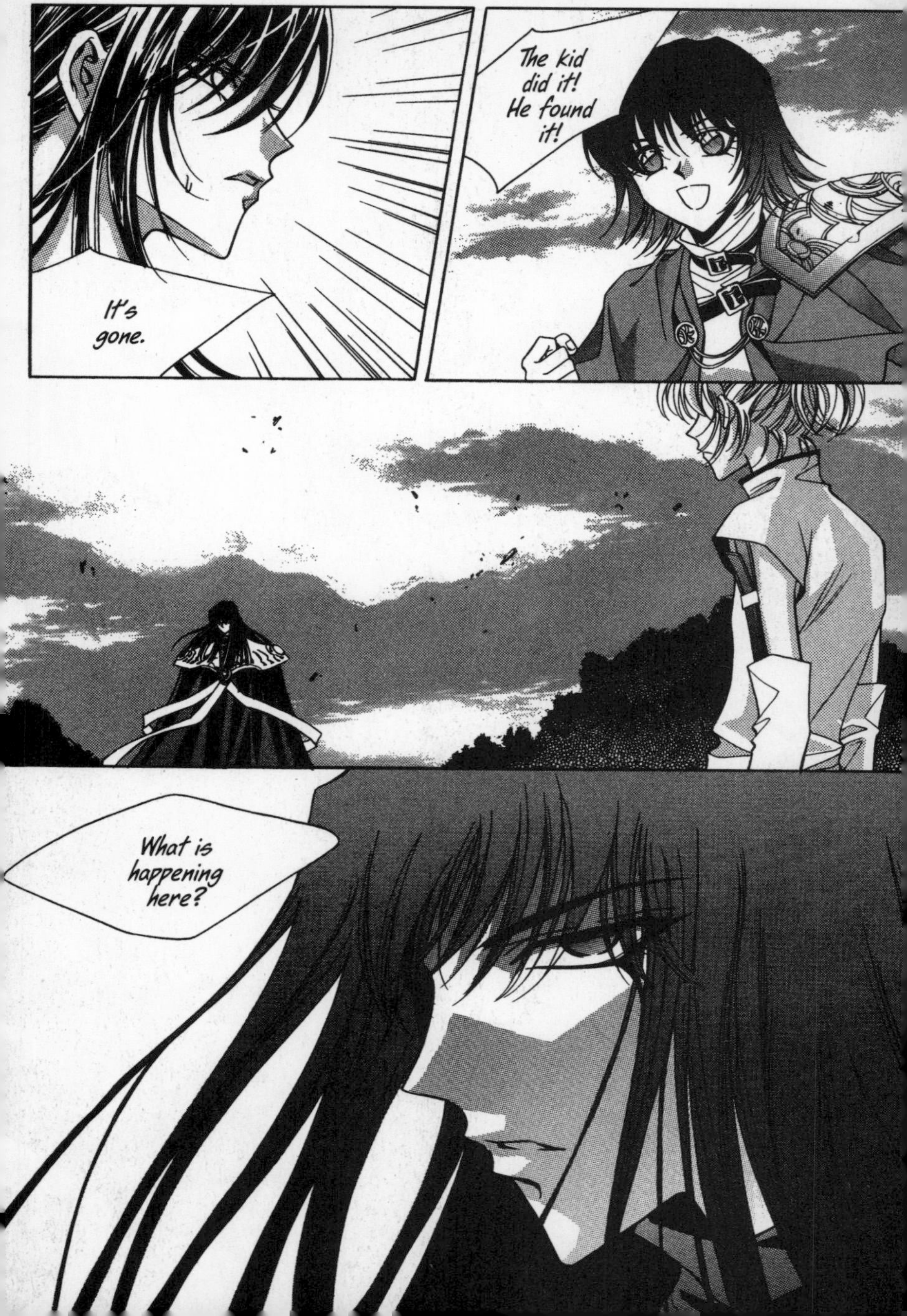
It's gone.
The kid did it! He found it!
What is happening here?

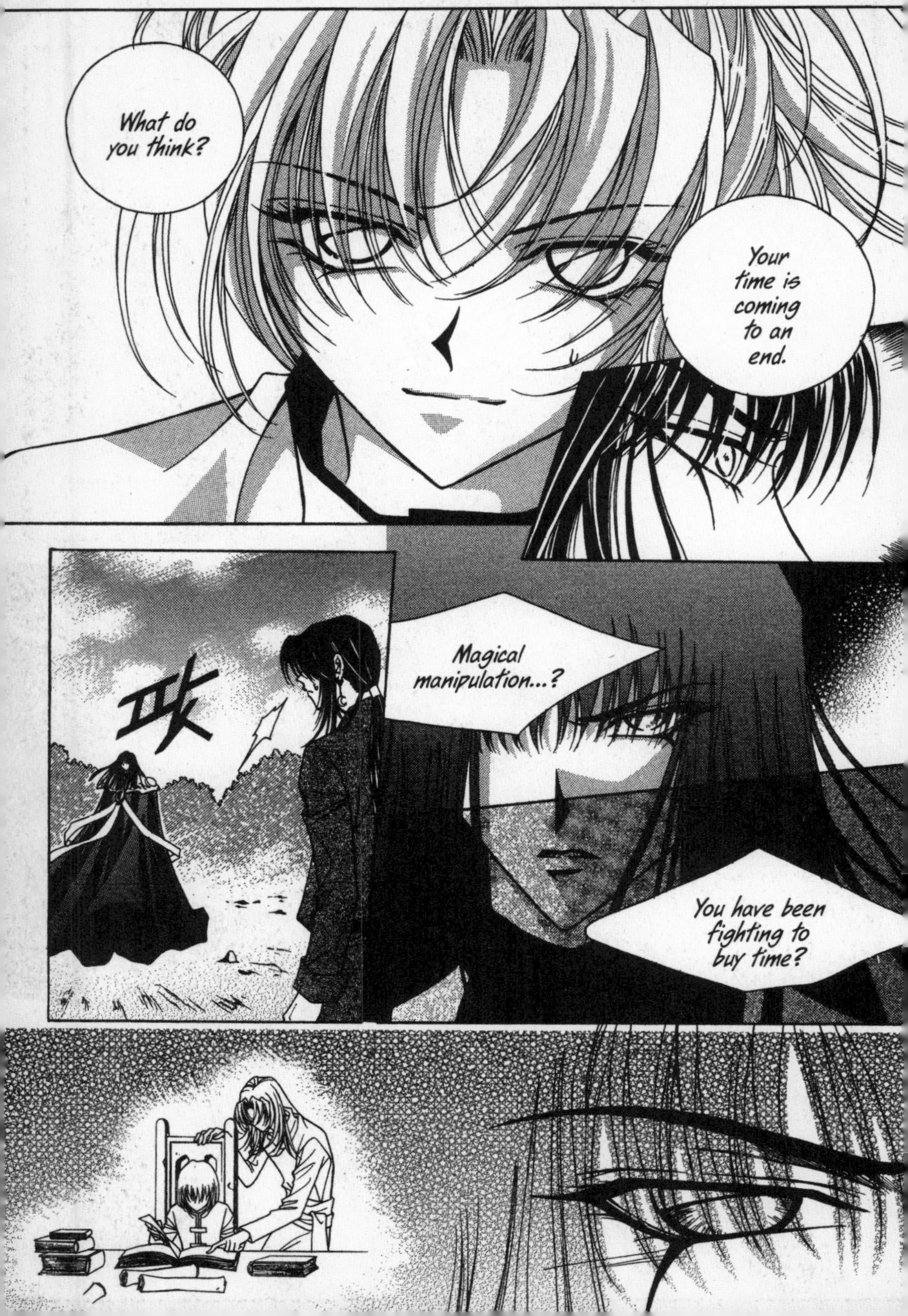
What do you think?
Your time is coming to an end.
Magical manipulation...?
You have been fighting to buy time?

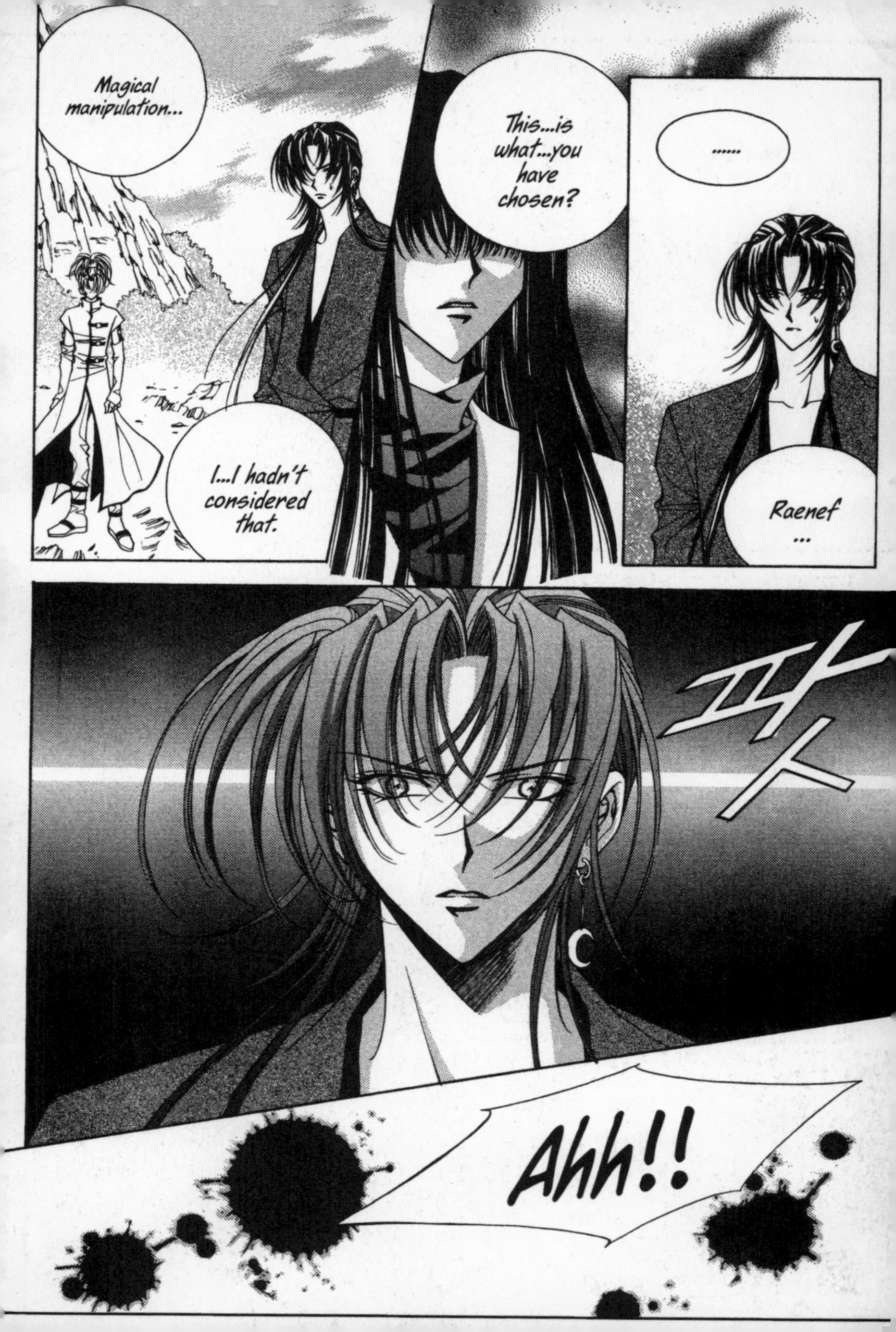
Magical manipulation...
I...I hadn't considered that.
This...is what...you have chosen?
......
Raenef ...
Ahh!!

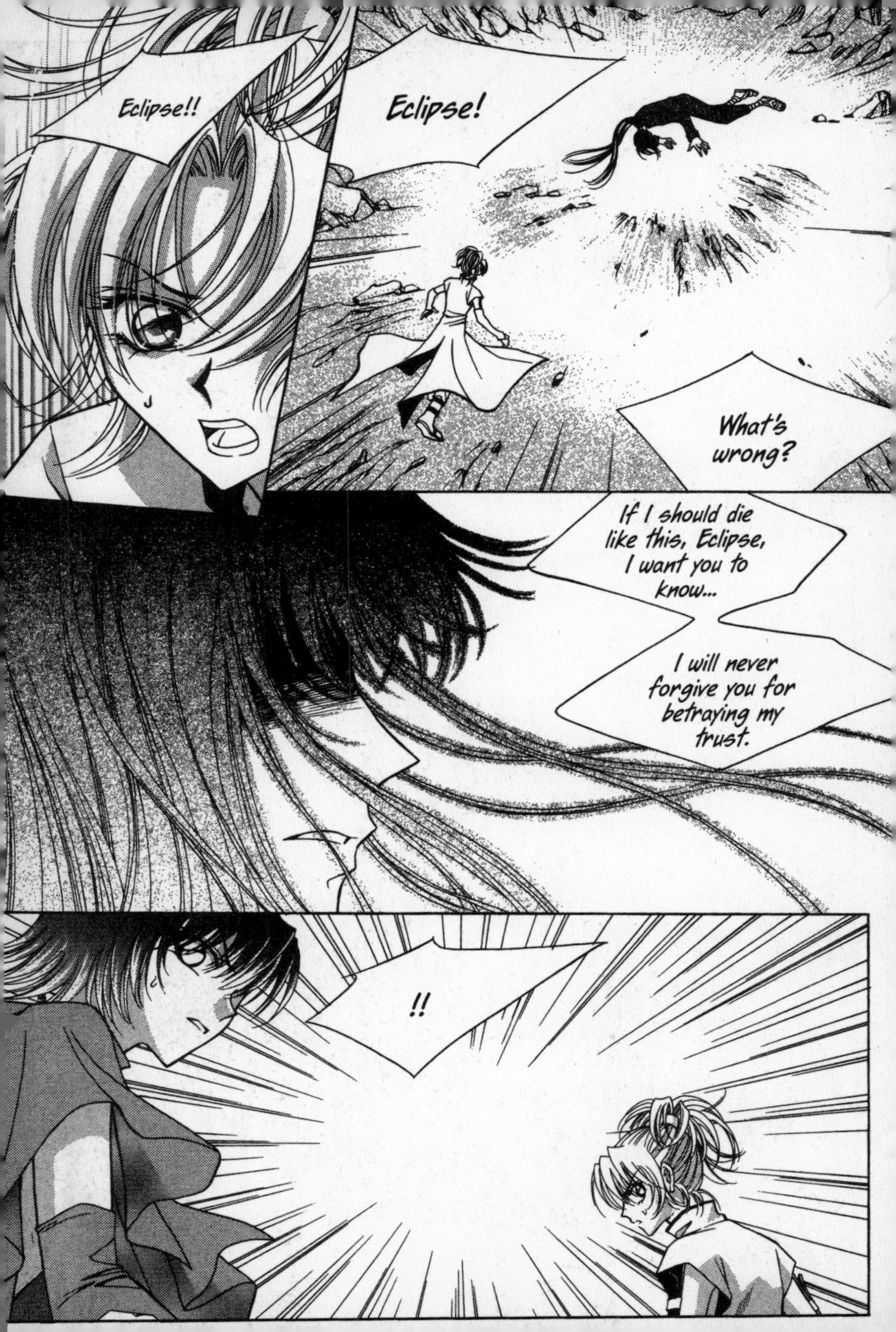
Eclipse!!
Eclipse!
What's wrong?
If I should die like this, Eclipse, I want you to know...
I will never forgive you for betraying my trust.
!!

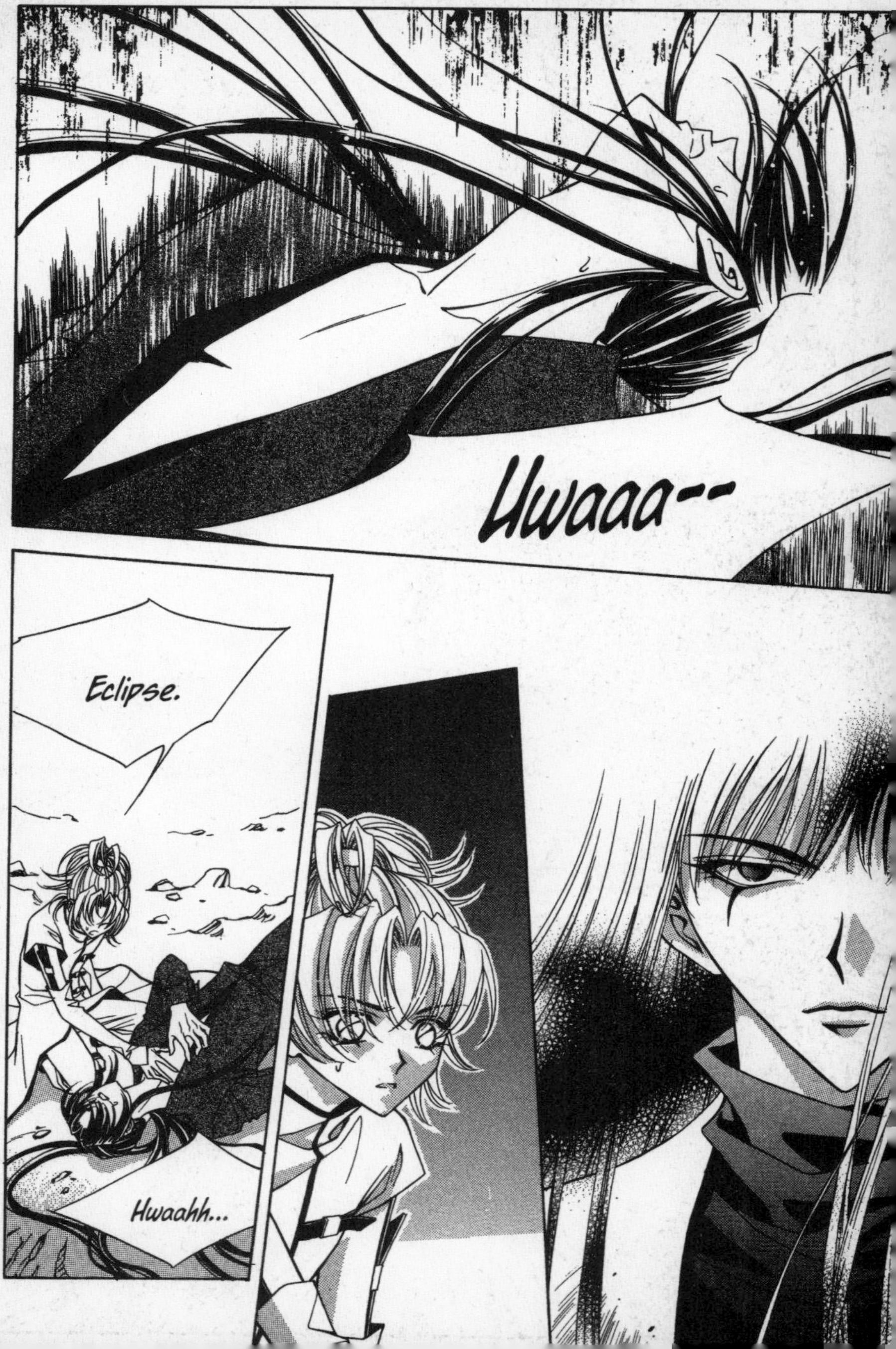
Uwaaa--
Eclipse.
Hwaahh...

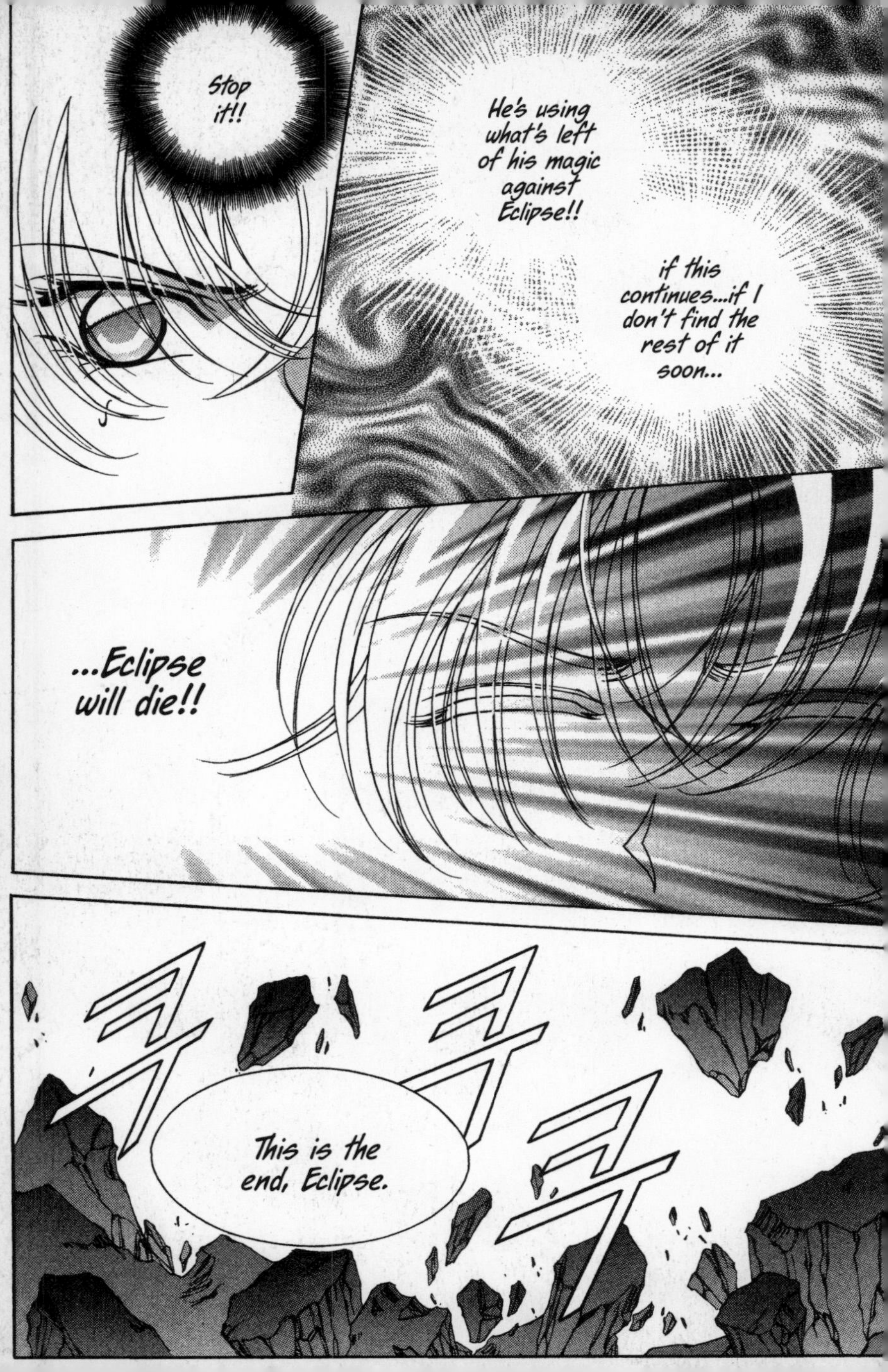
Stop it!!
He's using what's left of his magic against Eclipse!!
if this continues...if I don't find the rest of it soon...
...Eclipse will die!!
This is the end, Eclipse.

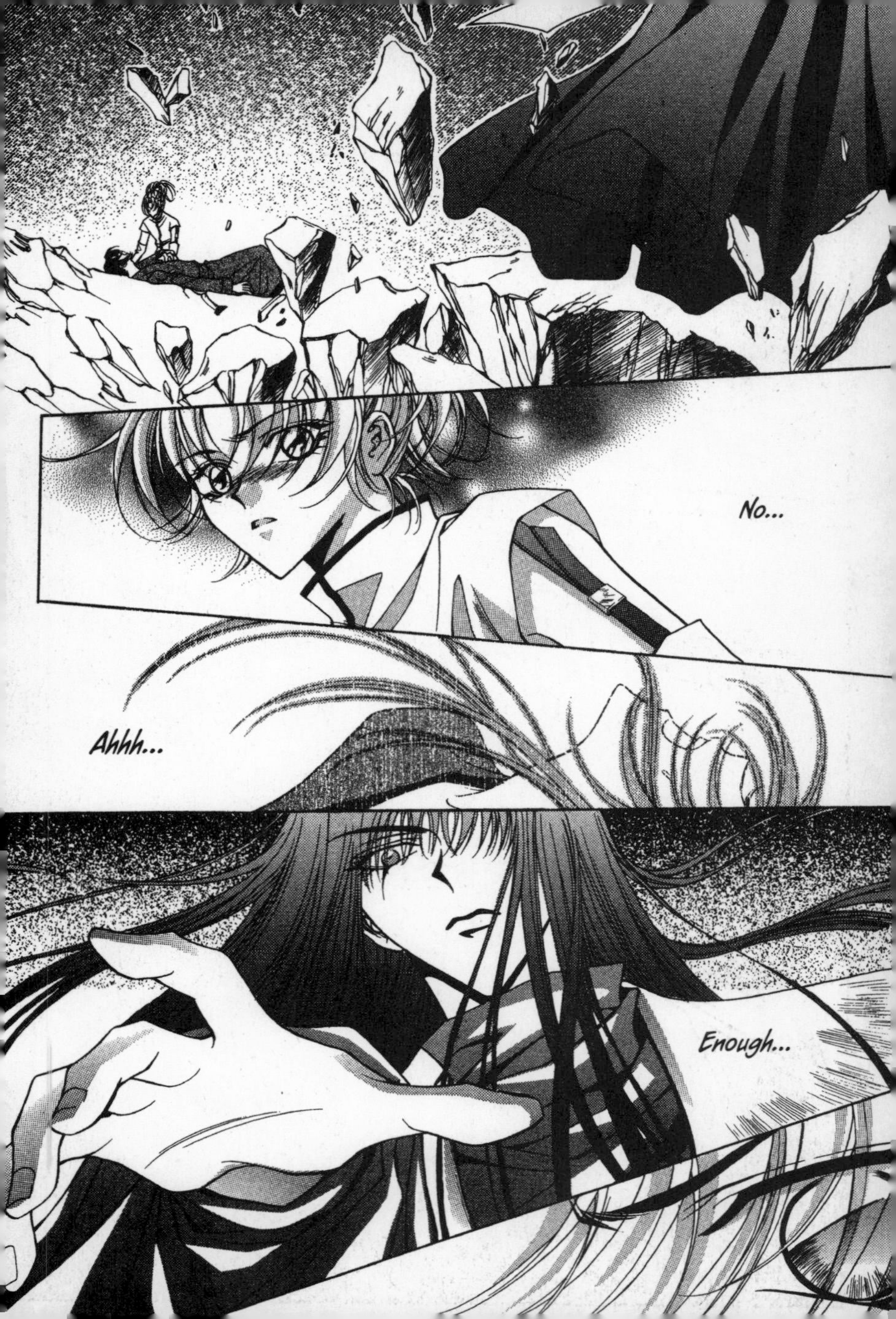
No...
Ahhh...
Enough...

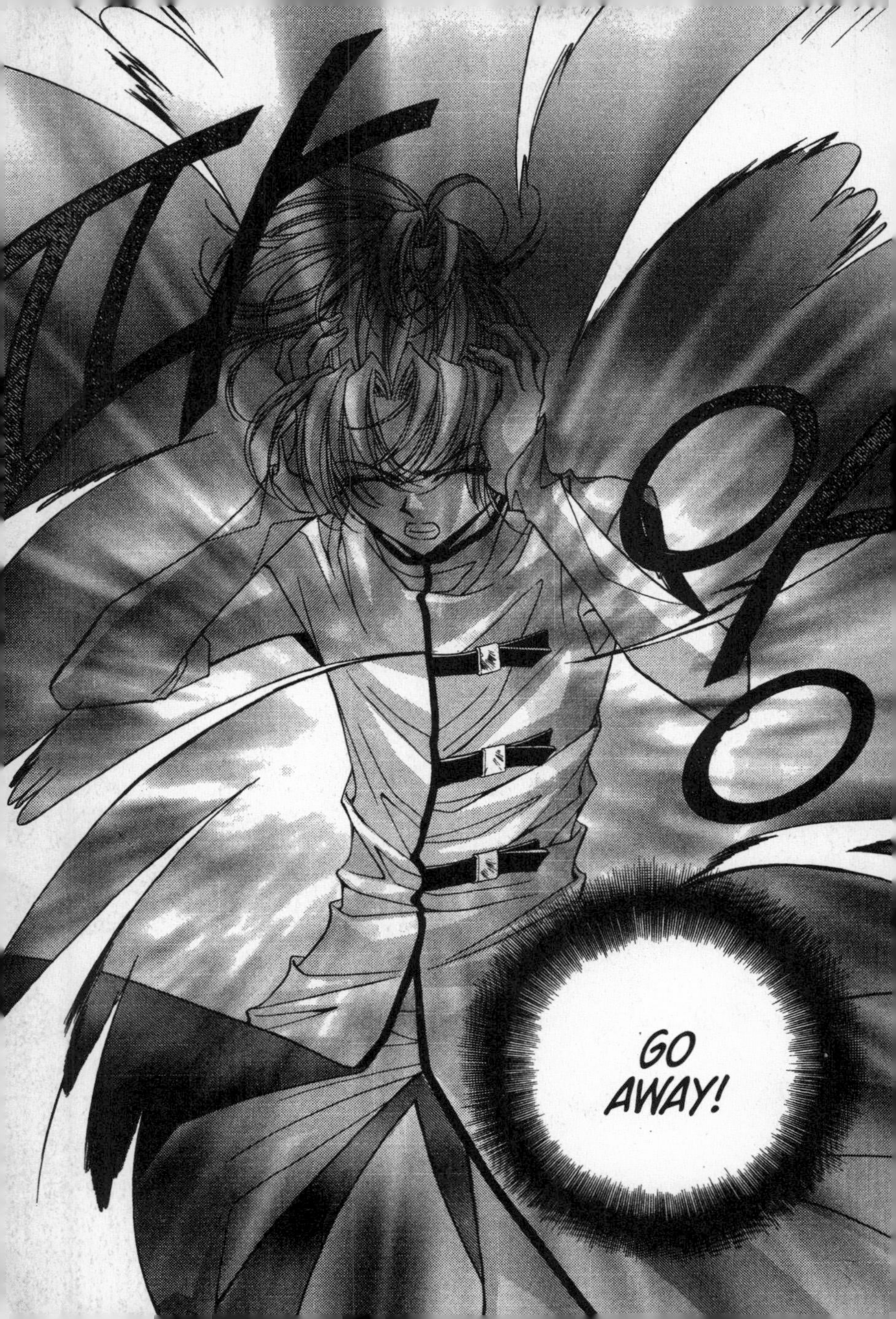
GO
AWAY!

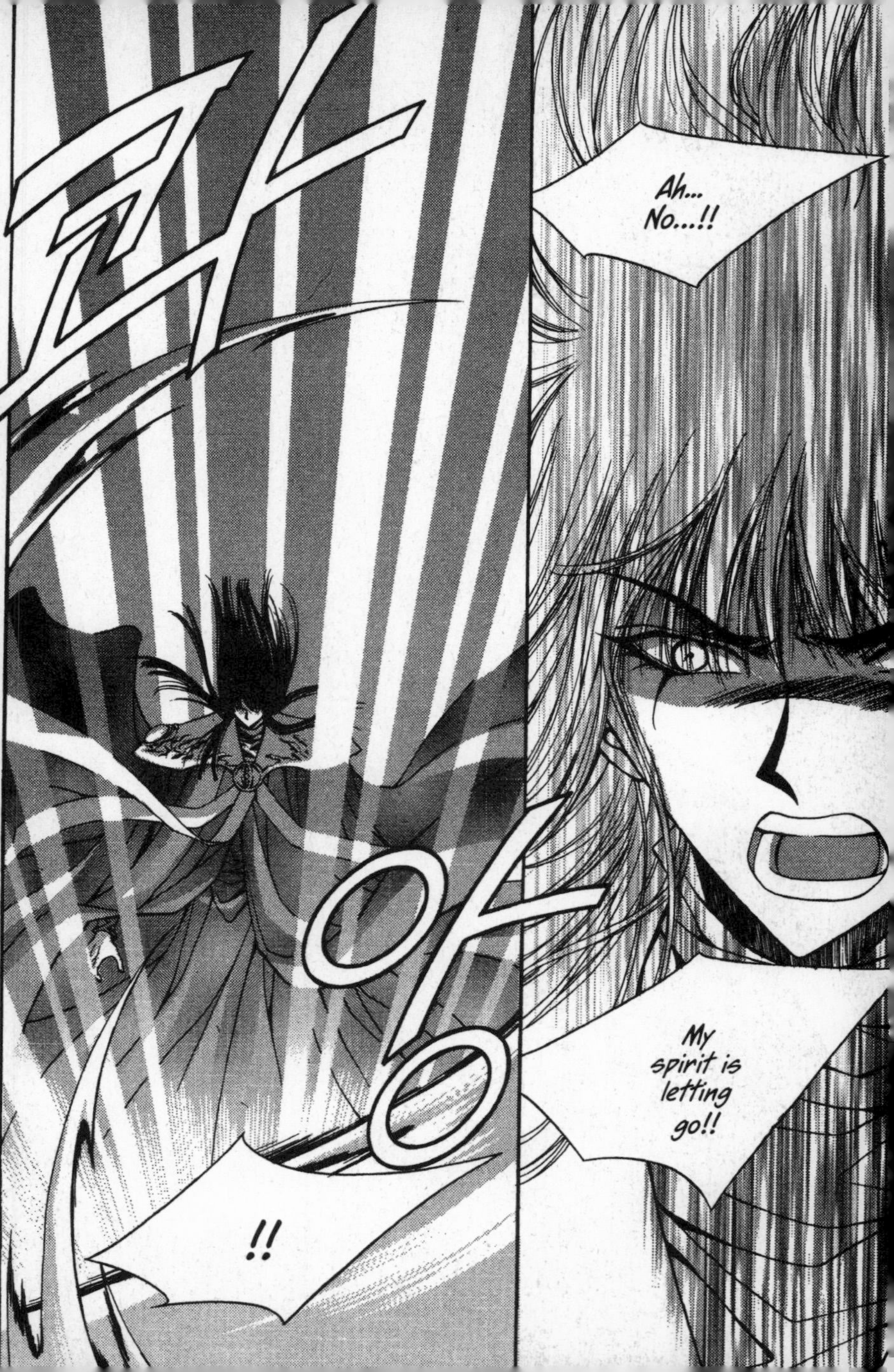
!!
Ah... No...!!
My spirit is letting go!!

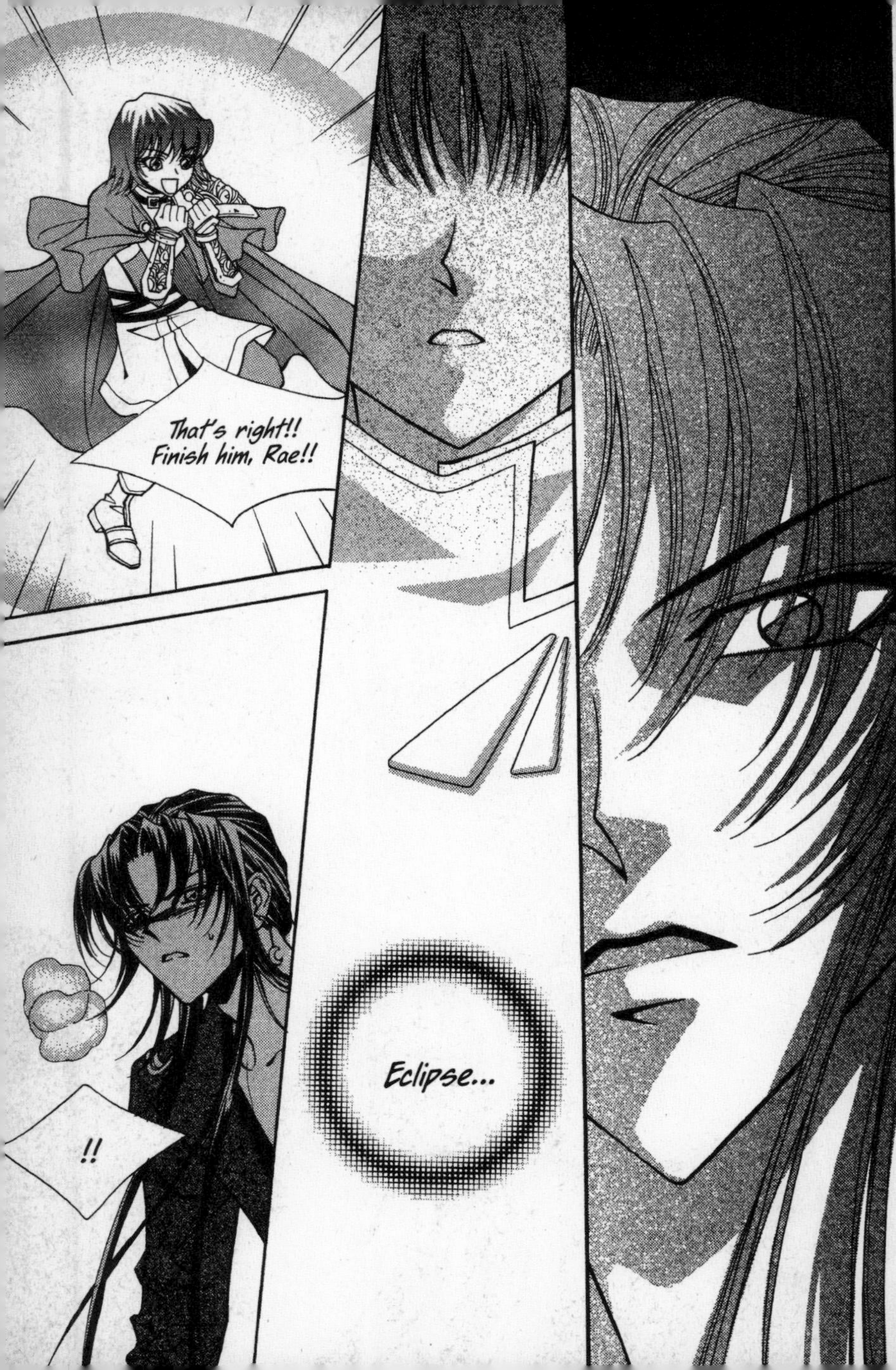
That's right!! Finish him, Rae!!
!!
Eclipse...

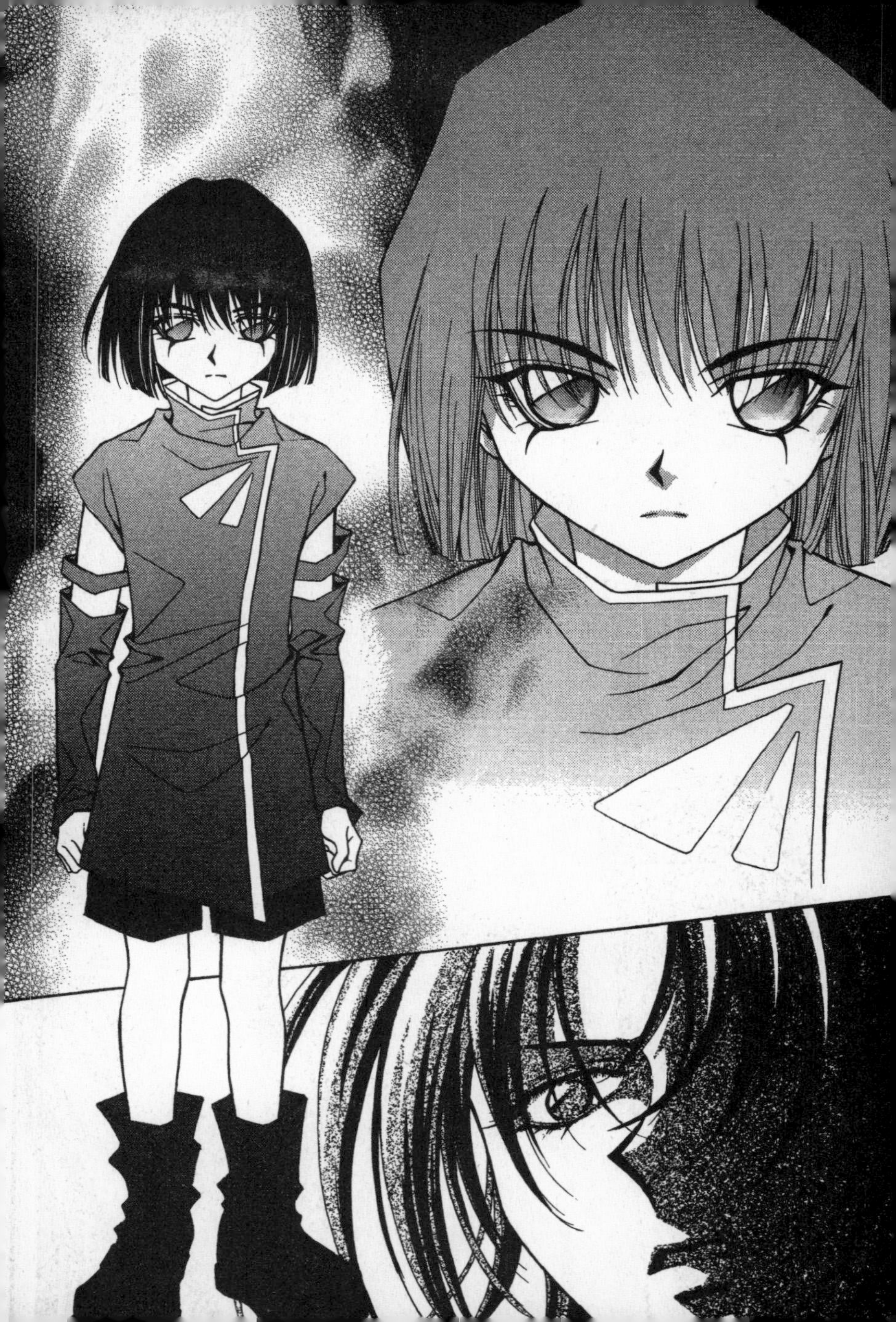

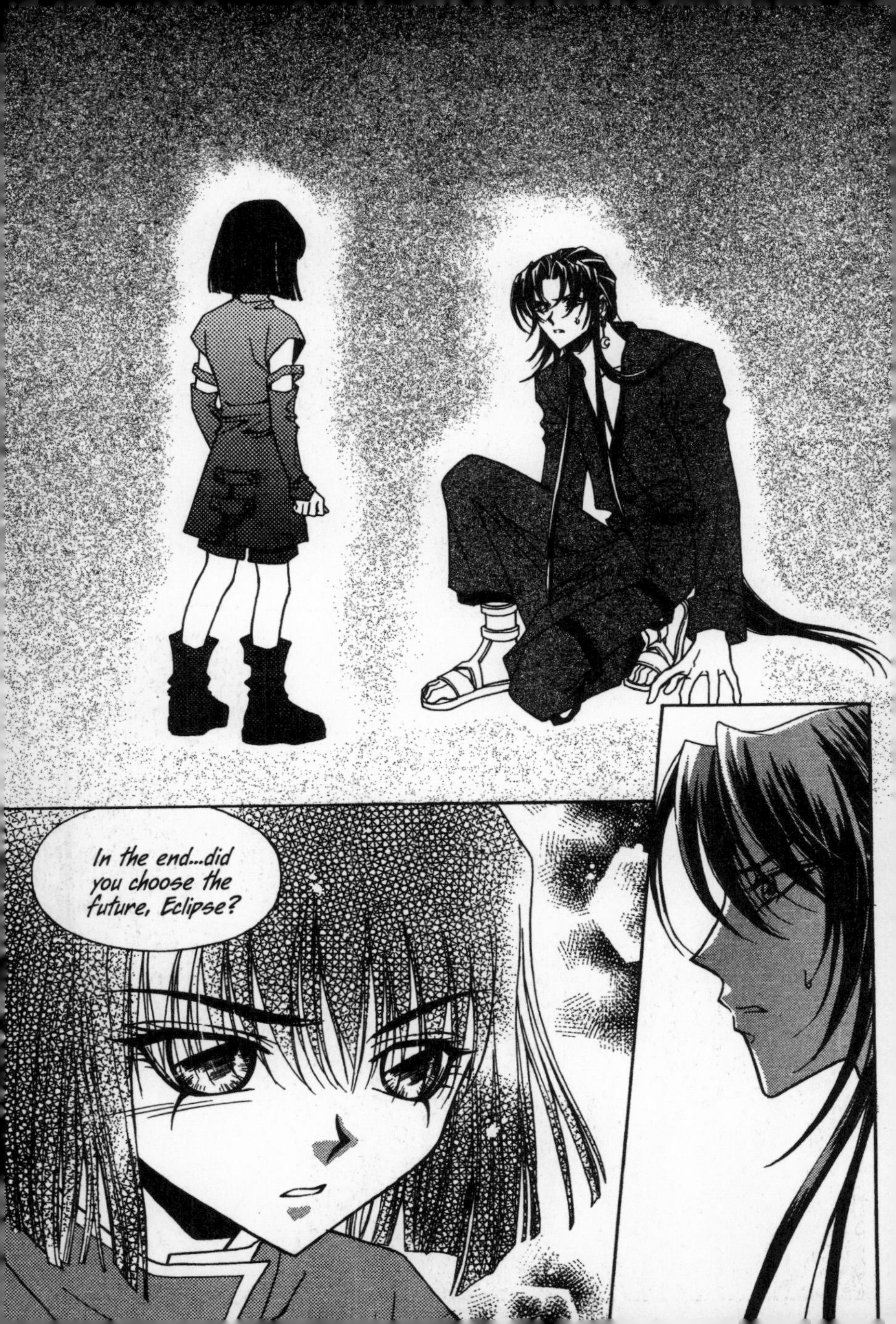
In the end...did you choose the future, Eclipse?

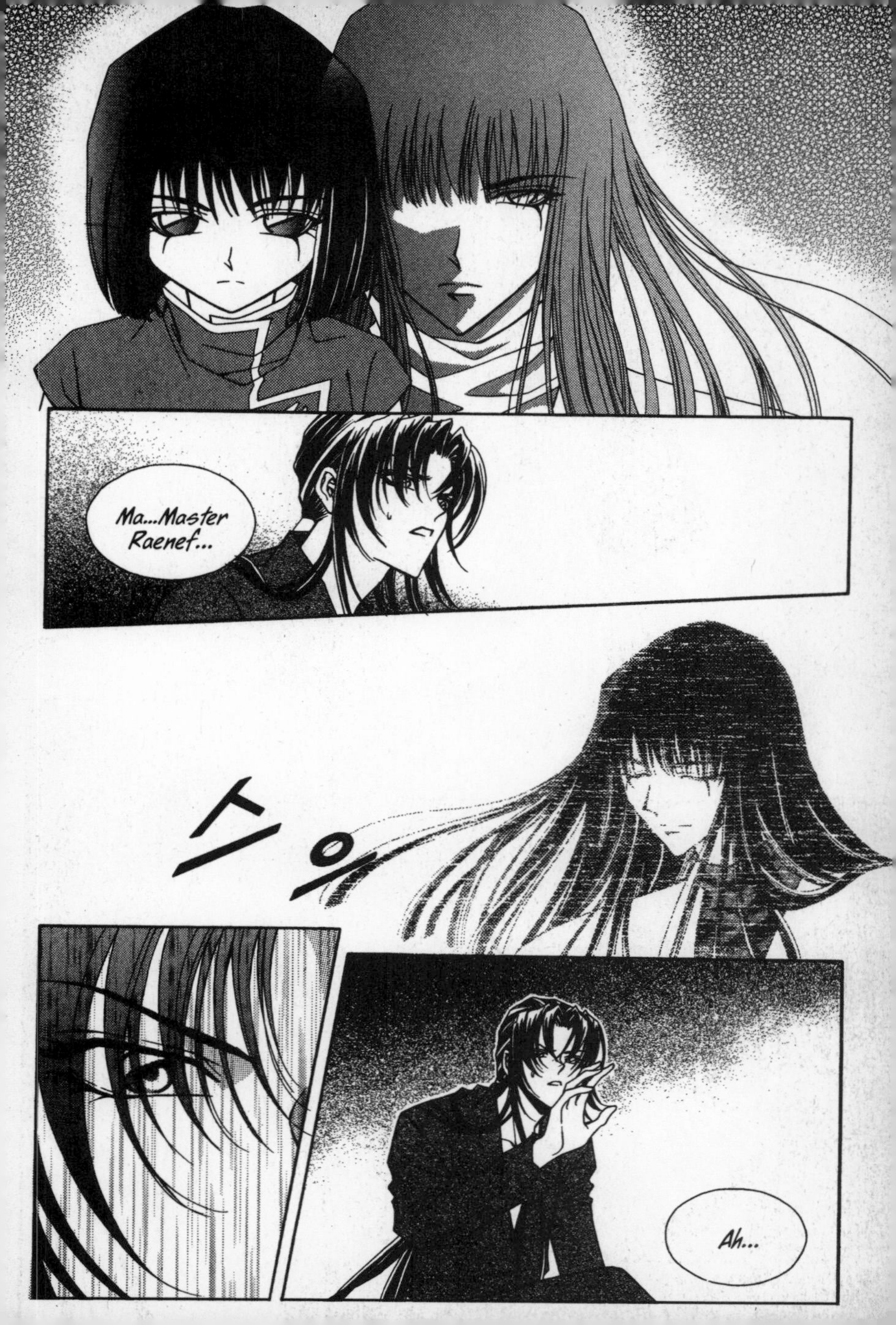
Ma...Master Raenef...
Ah...

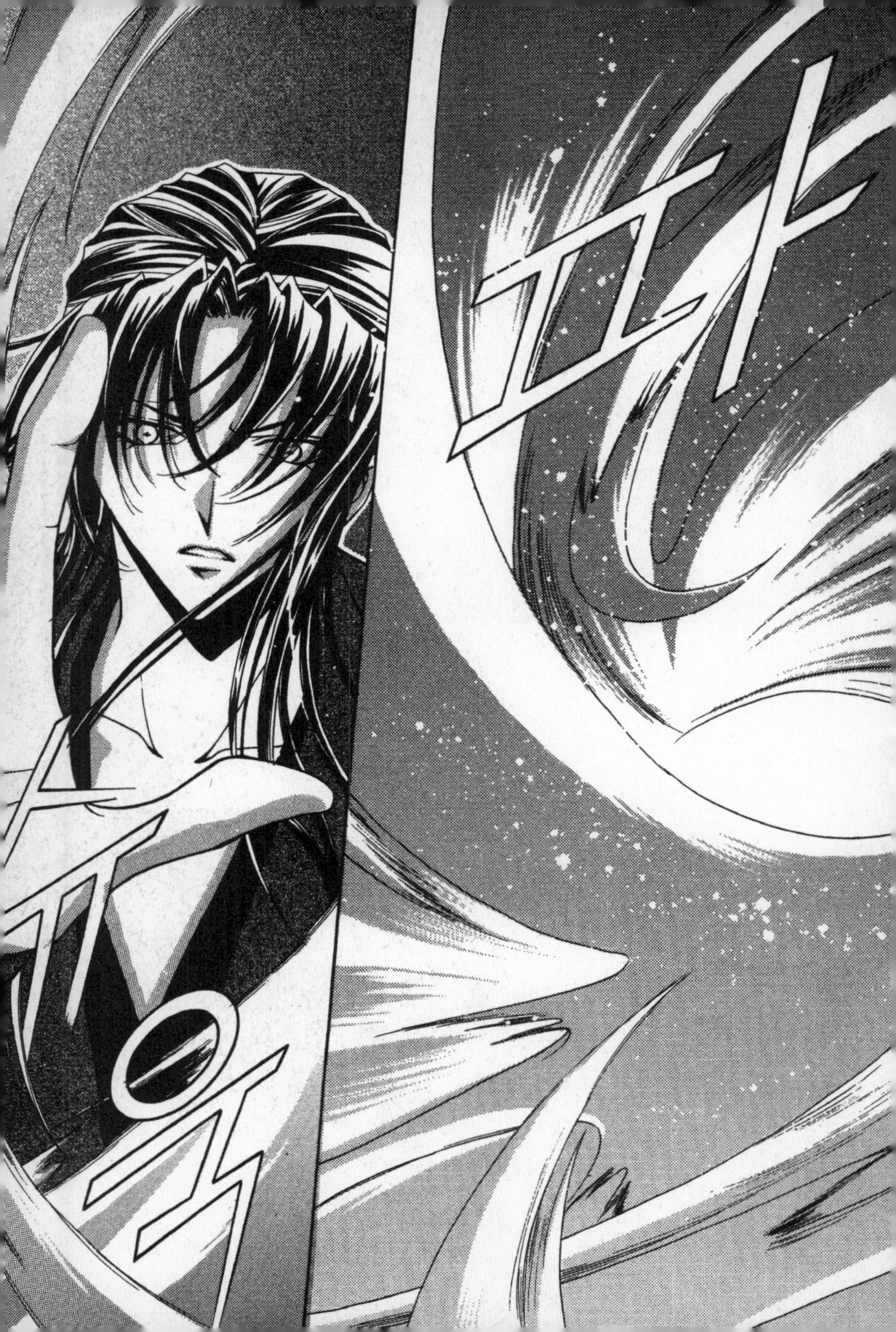

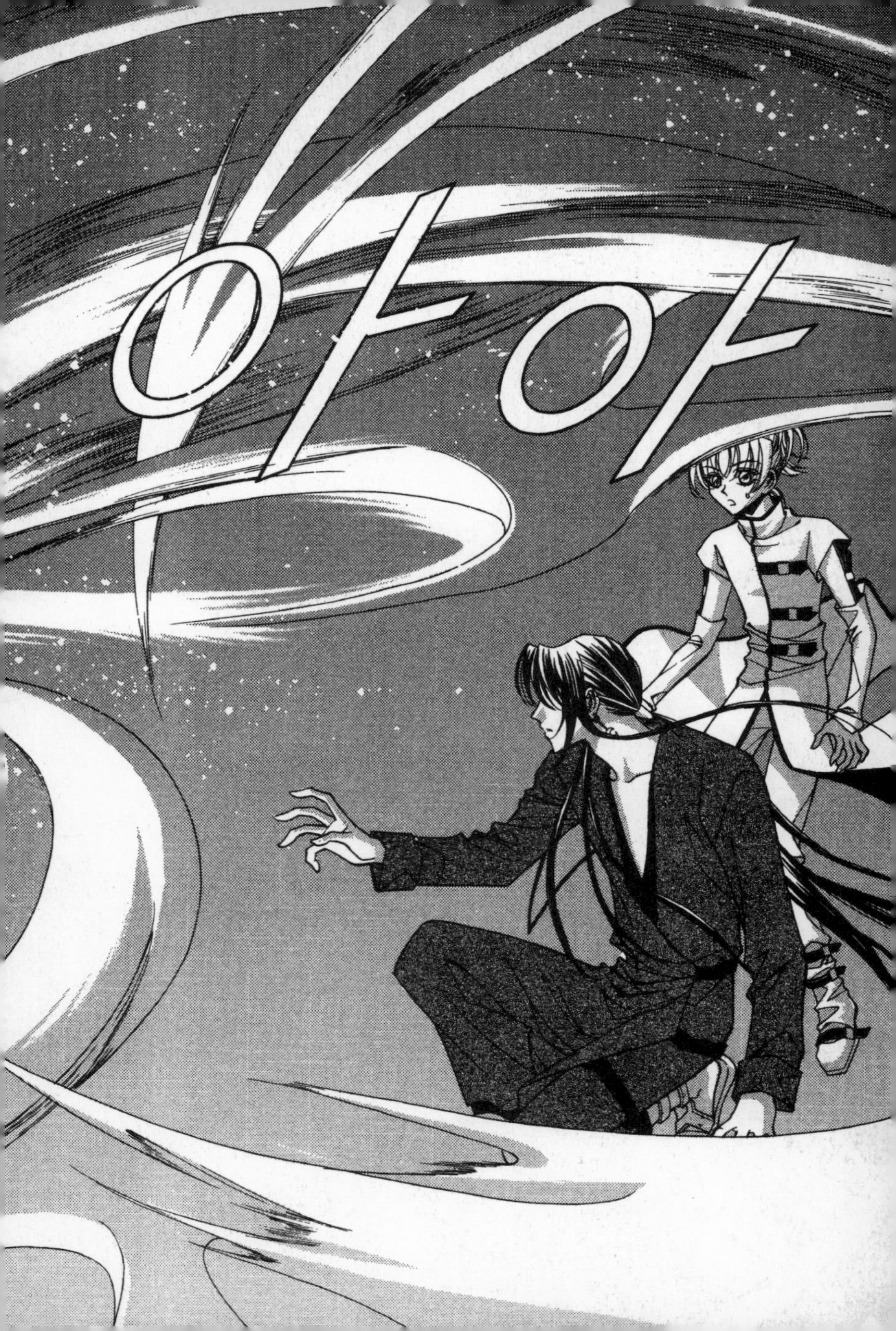
아아

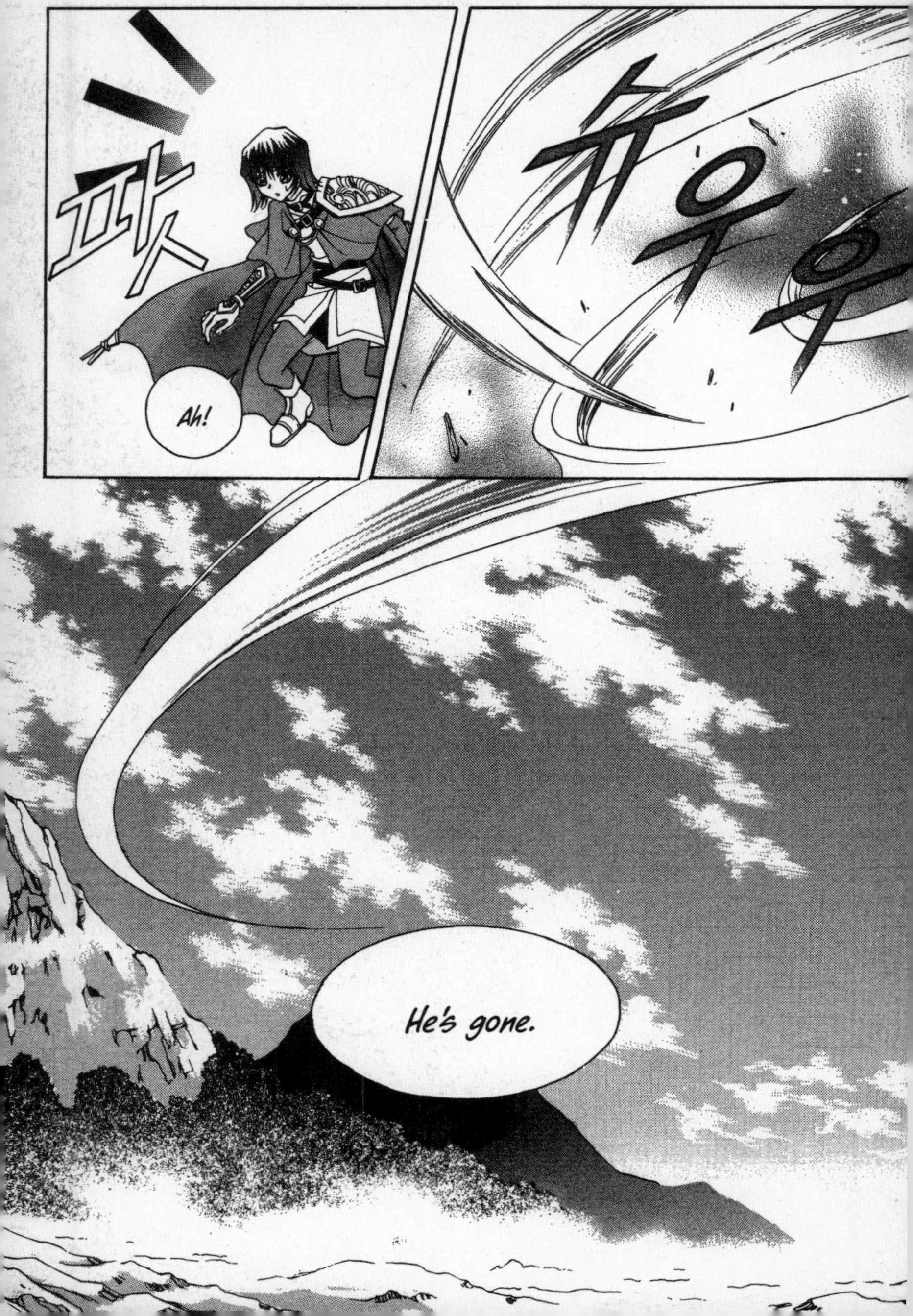
팟
Ah!
슈우웃
He's gone.

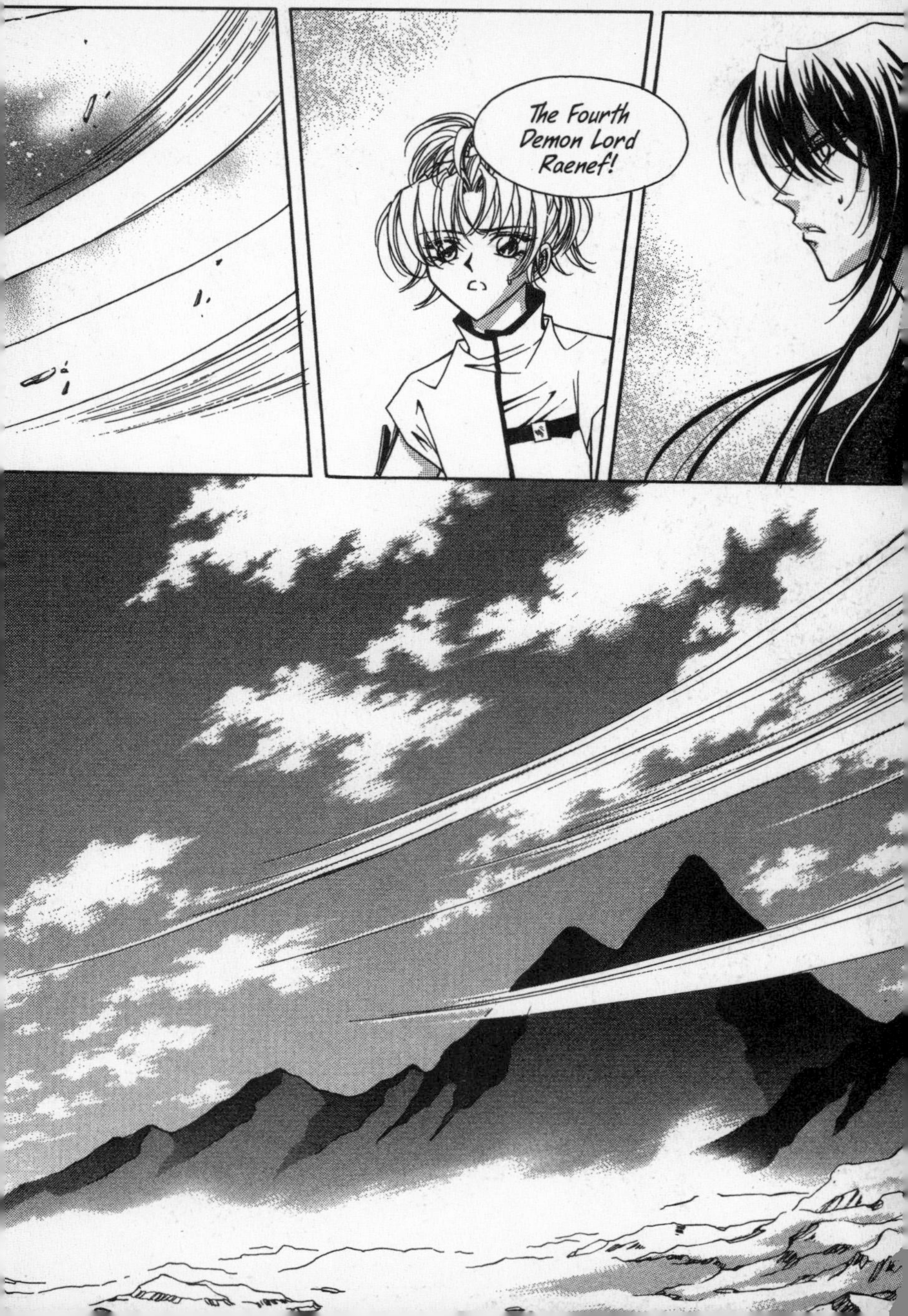
The Fourth Demon Lord Raenef!

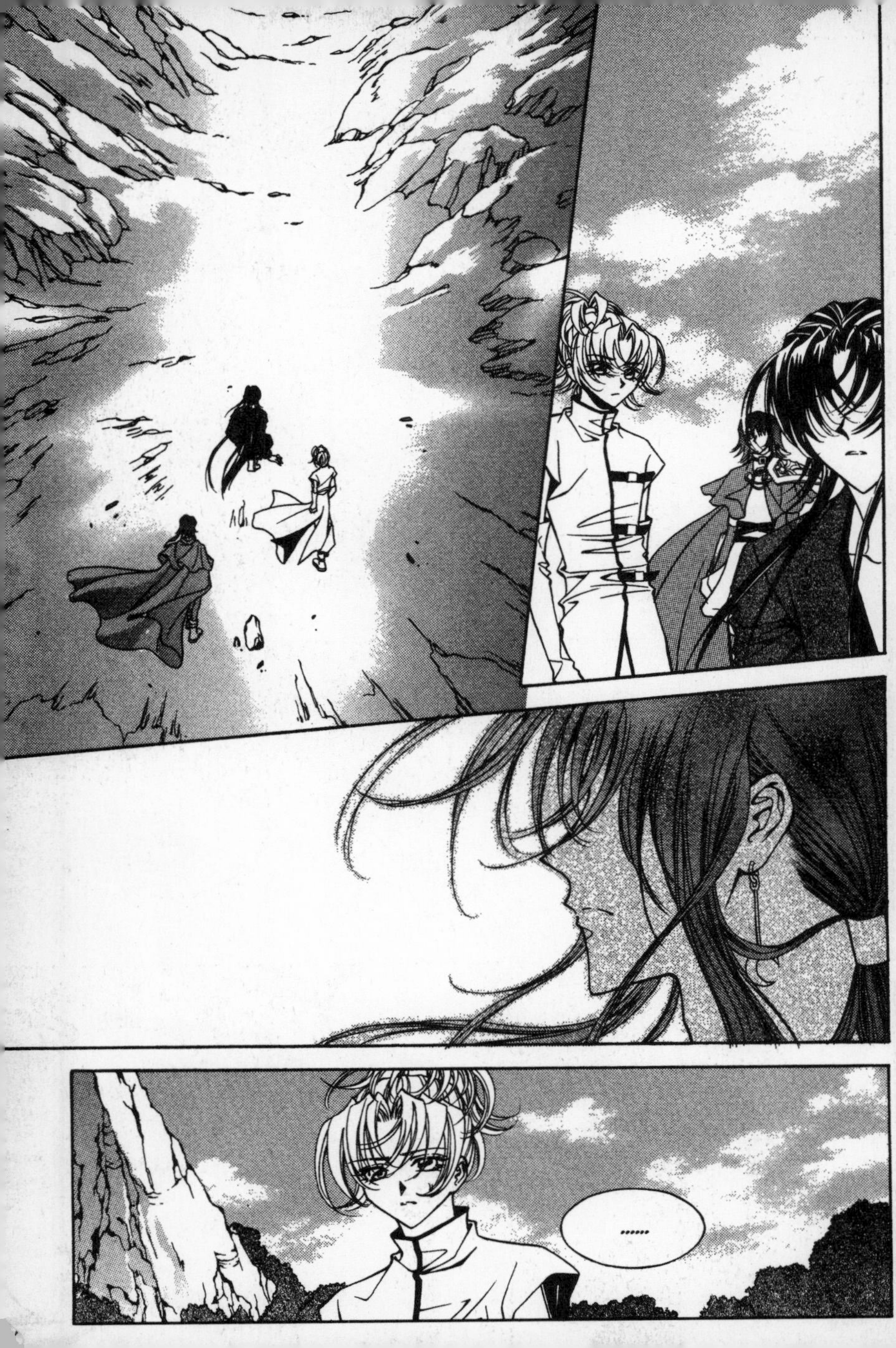
......

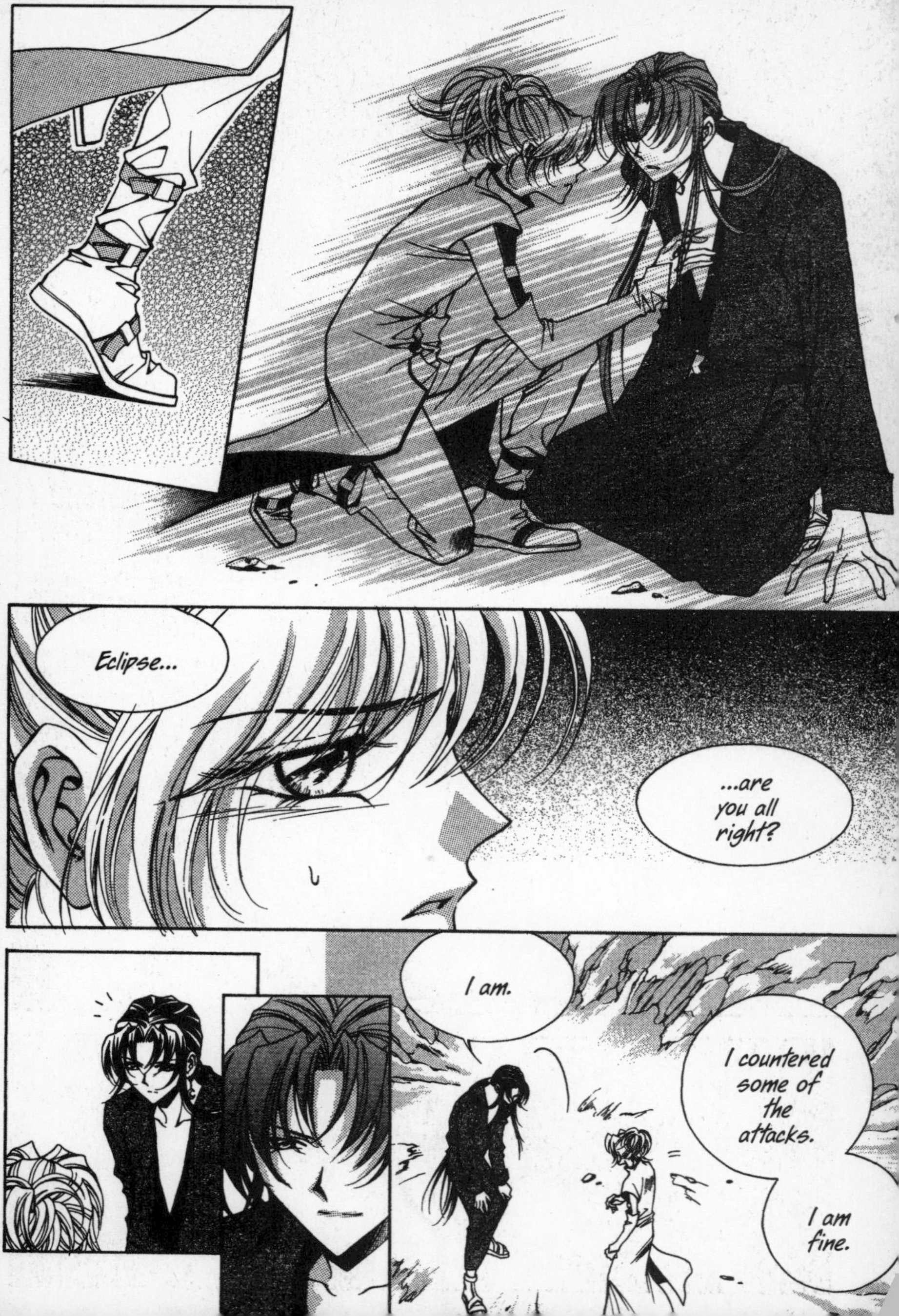
Eclipse...
...are you all right?
I am.
I countered some of the attacks.
I am fine.

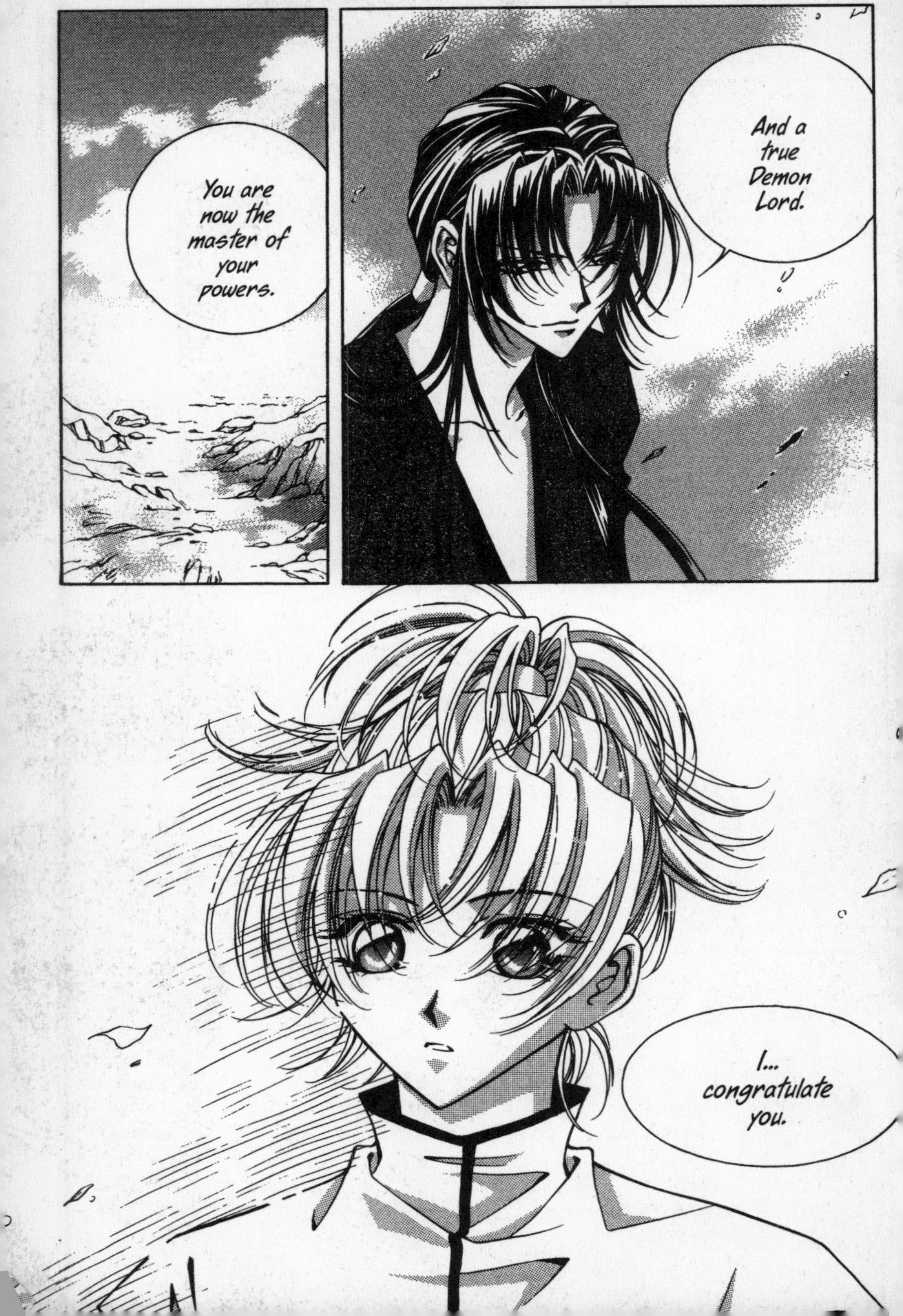
You are now the master of your powers.
And a true Demon Lord.
I... congratulate you.

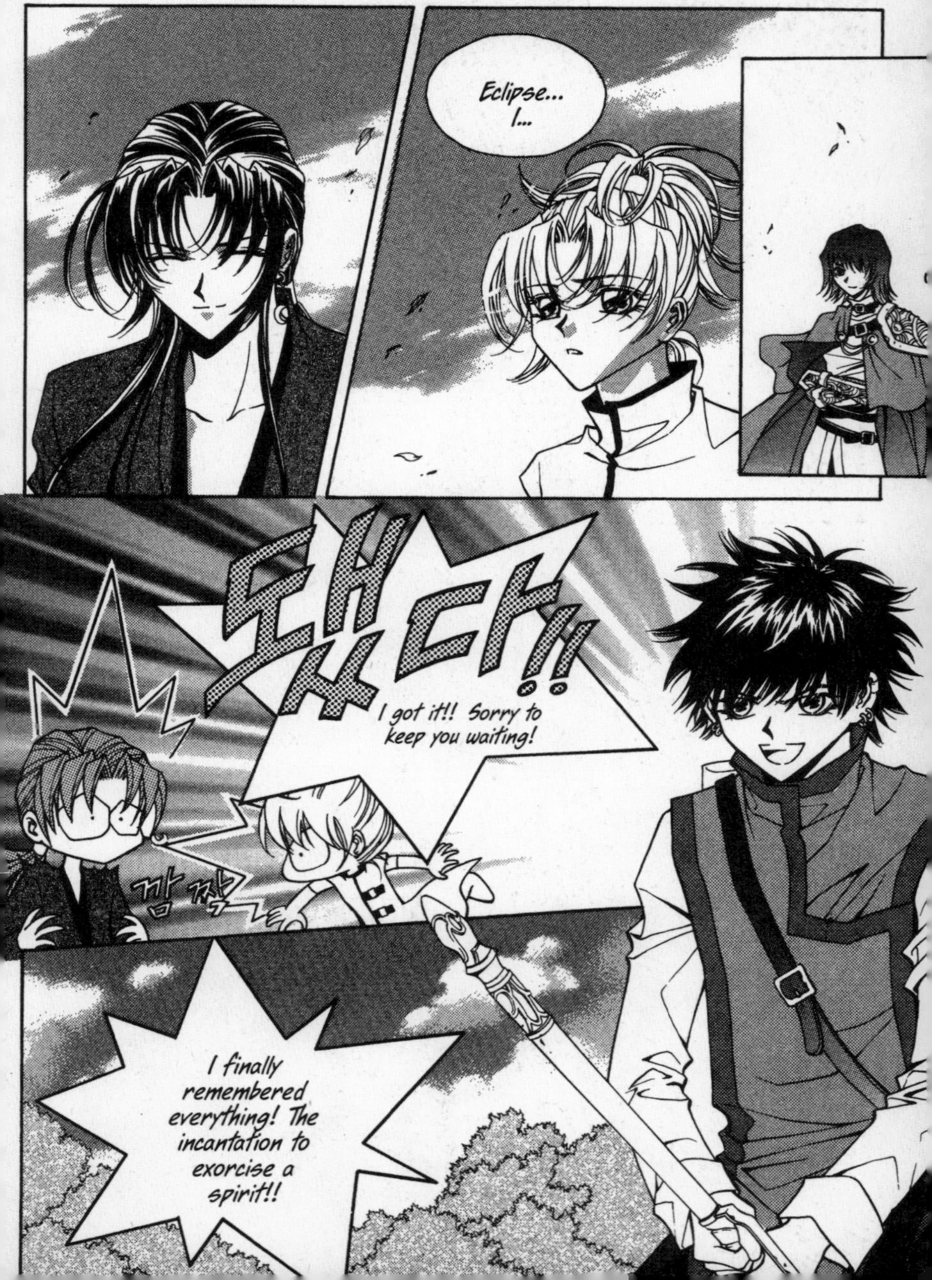
Eclipse... I...
I got it!! Sorry to keep you waiting!
깜 짝
I finally remembered everything! The incantation to exorcise a spirit!!

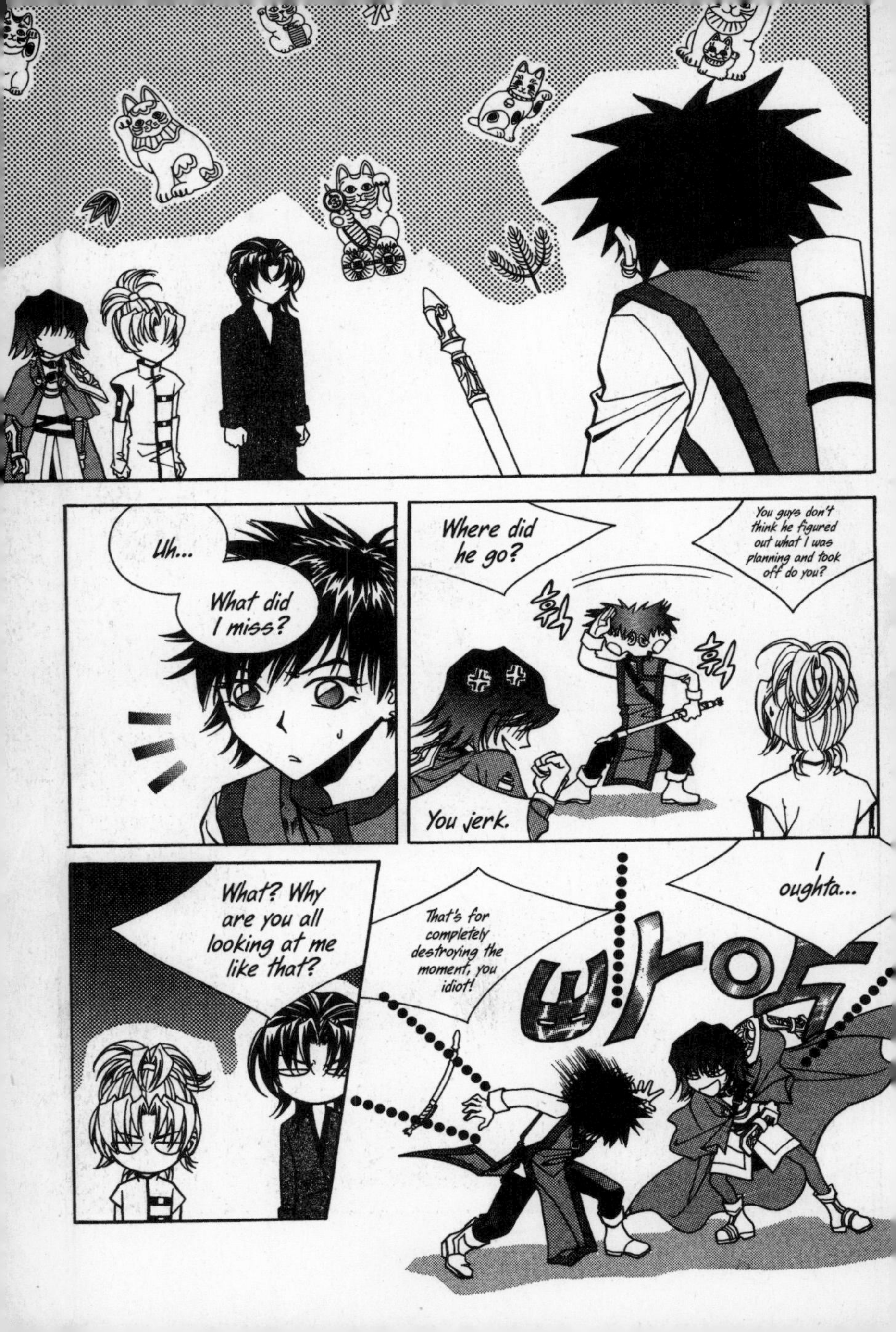
Uh...
What did I miss?
Where did he go?
You guys don't think he figured out what I was planning and took off do you?
You jerk.
What? Why are you all looking at me like that?
That's for completely destroying the moment, you idiot!
I oughta...

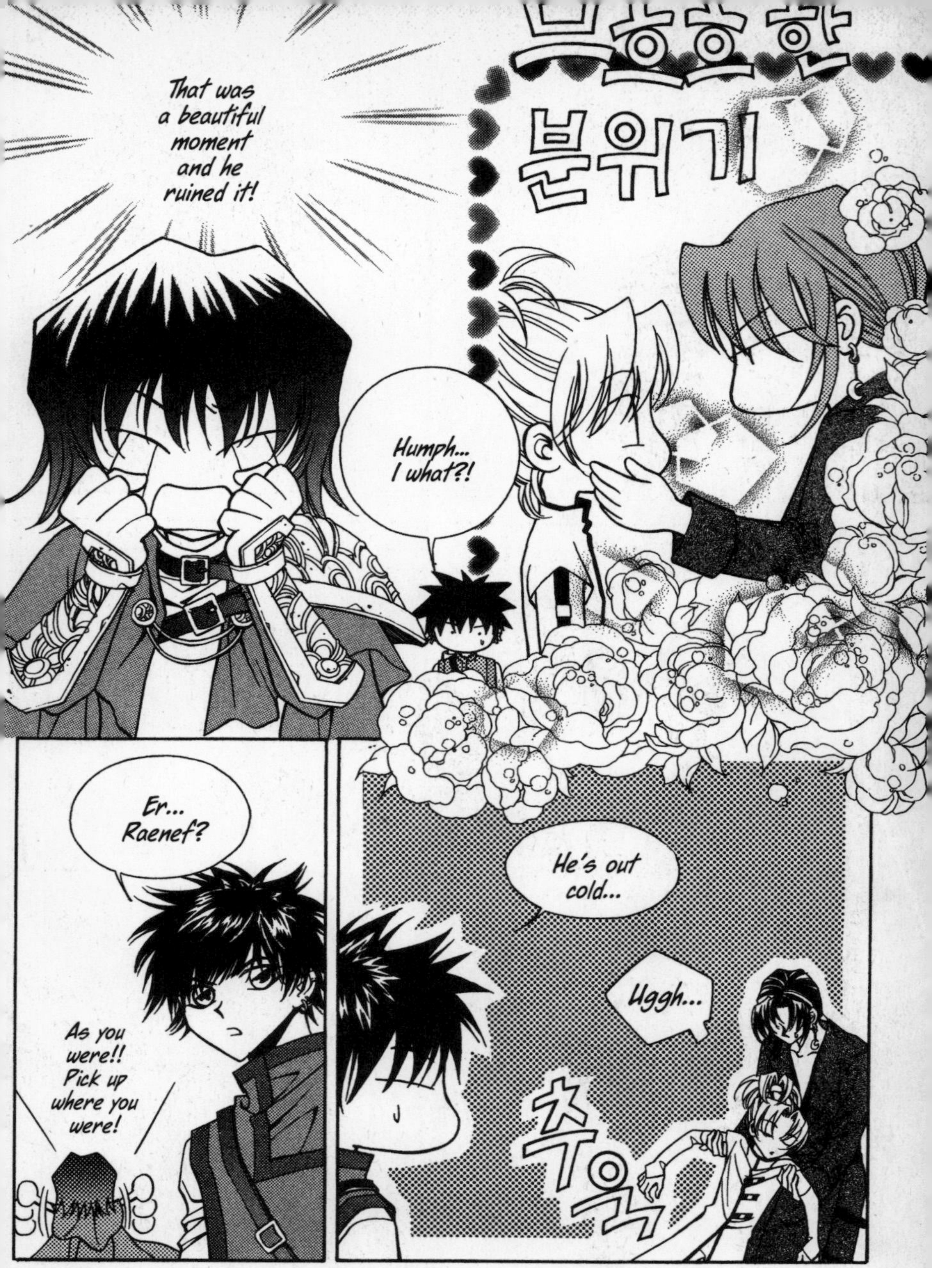
That was a beautiful moment and he ruined it!
므흐흐한 분위기
Humph... I what?!
Er... Raenef?
As you were!! Pick up where you were!
He's out cold...
Uggh...
추욱

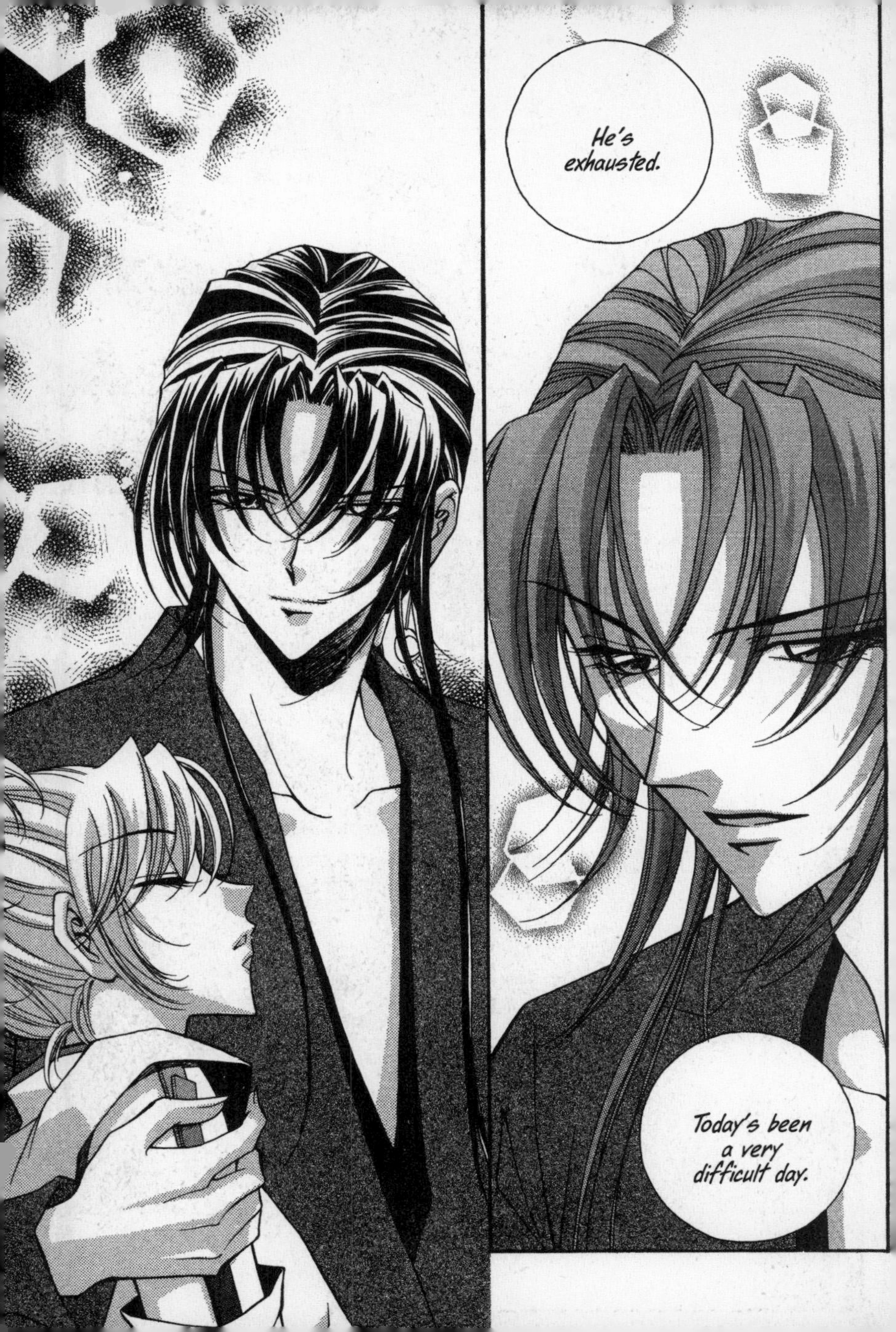
He's exhausted.
Today's been a very difficult day.

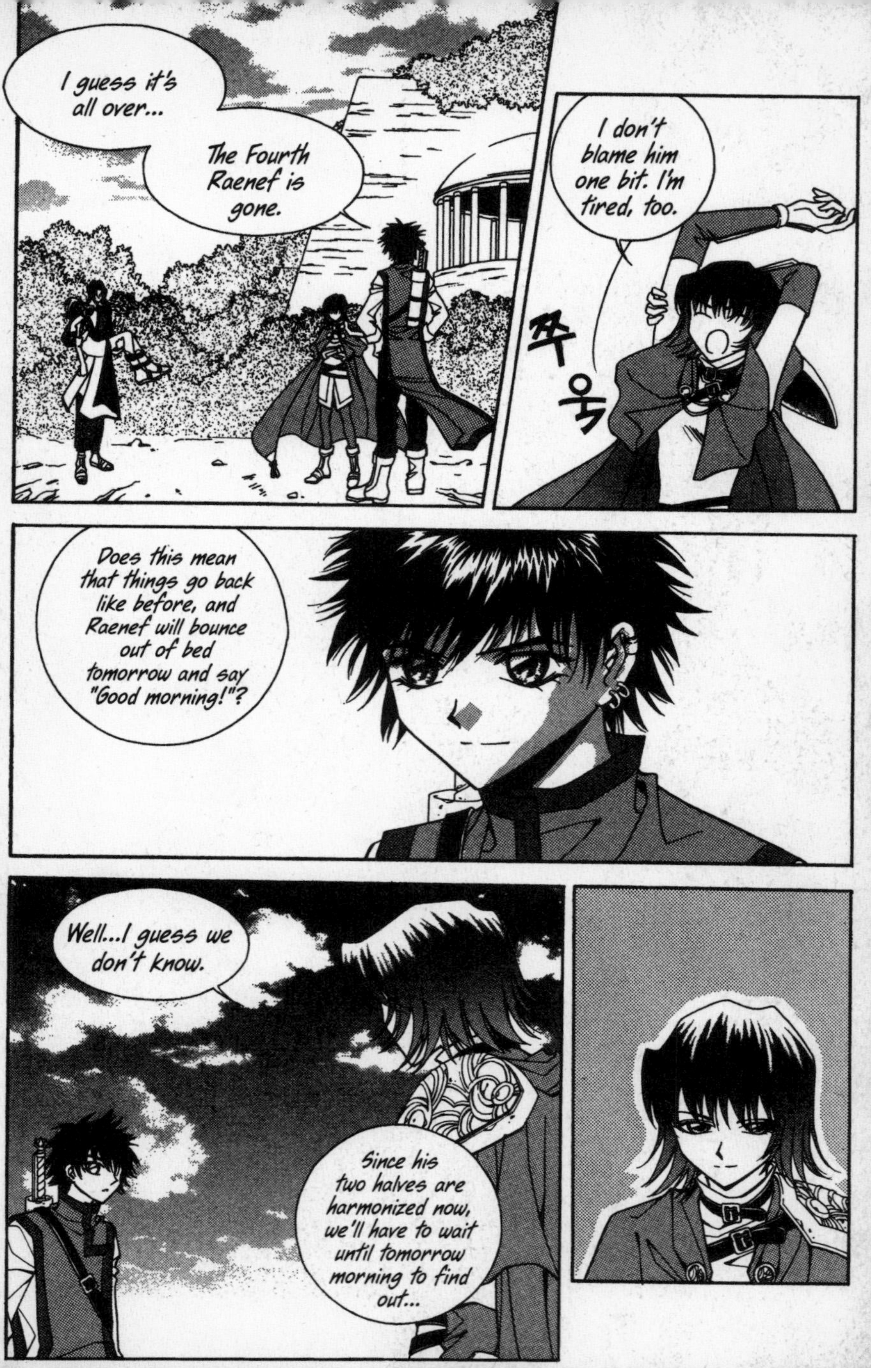
I guess it's all over...
The Fourth Raenef is gone.
I don't blame him one bit. I'm tired, too.
쭈욱
Does this mean that things go back like before, and Raenef will bounce out of bed tomorrow and say "Good morning!"?
Well...I guess we don't know.
Since his two halves are harmonized now, we'll have to wait until tomorrow morning to find out...

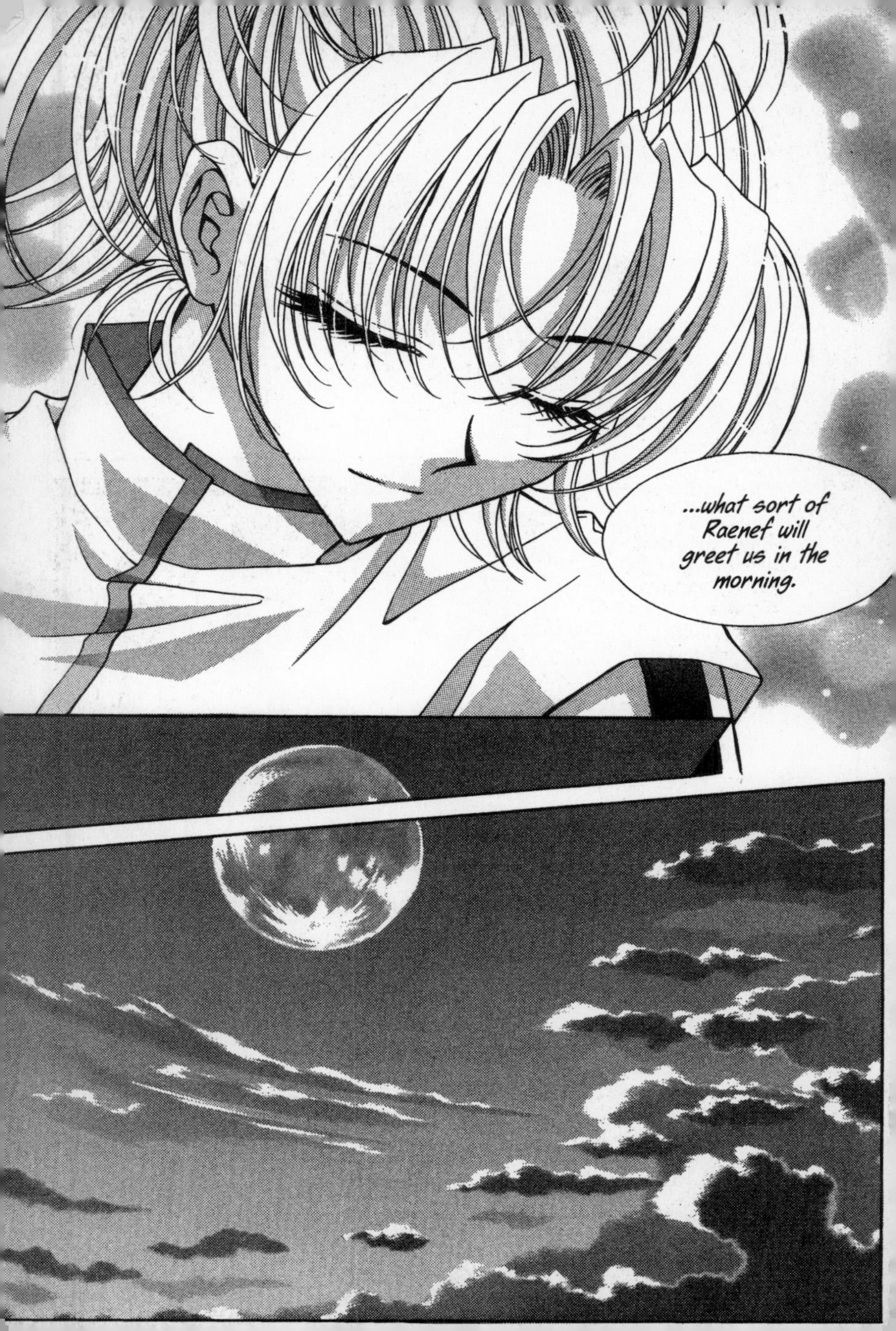
...what sort of Raenef will greet us in the morning.

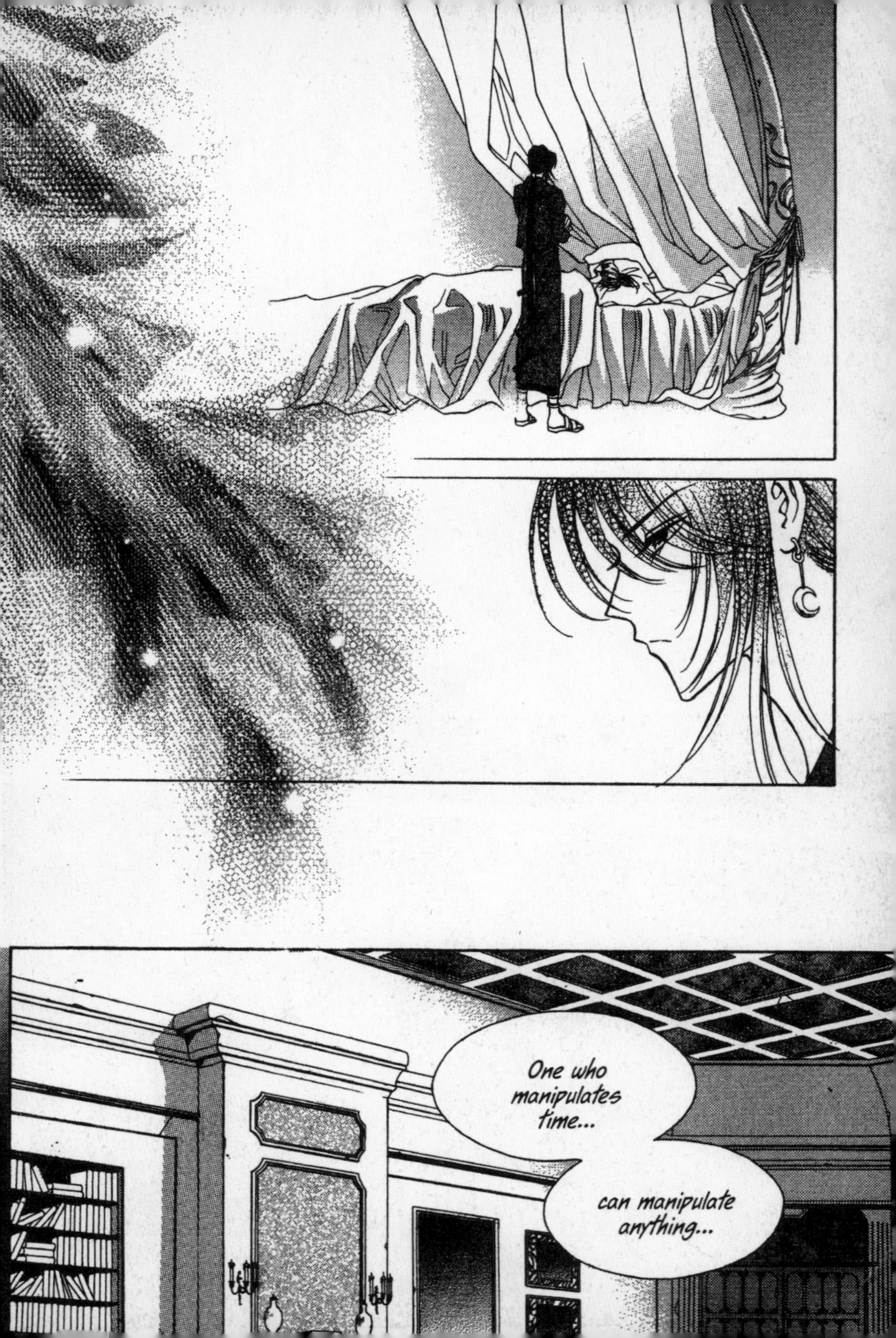
One who manipulates time...
can manipulate anything...

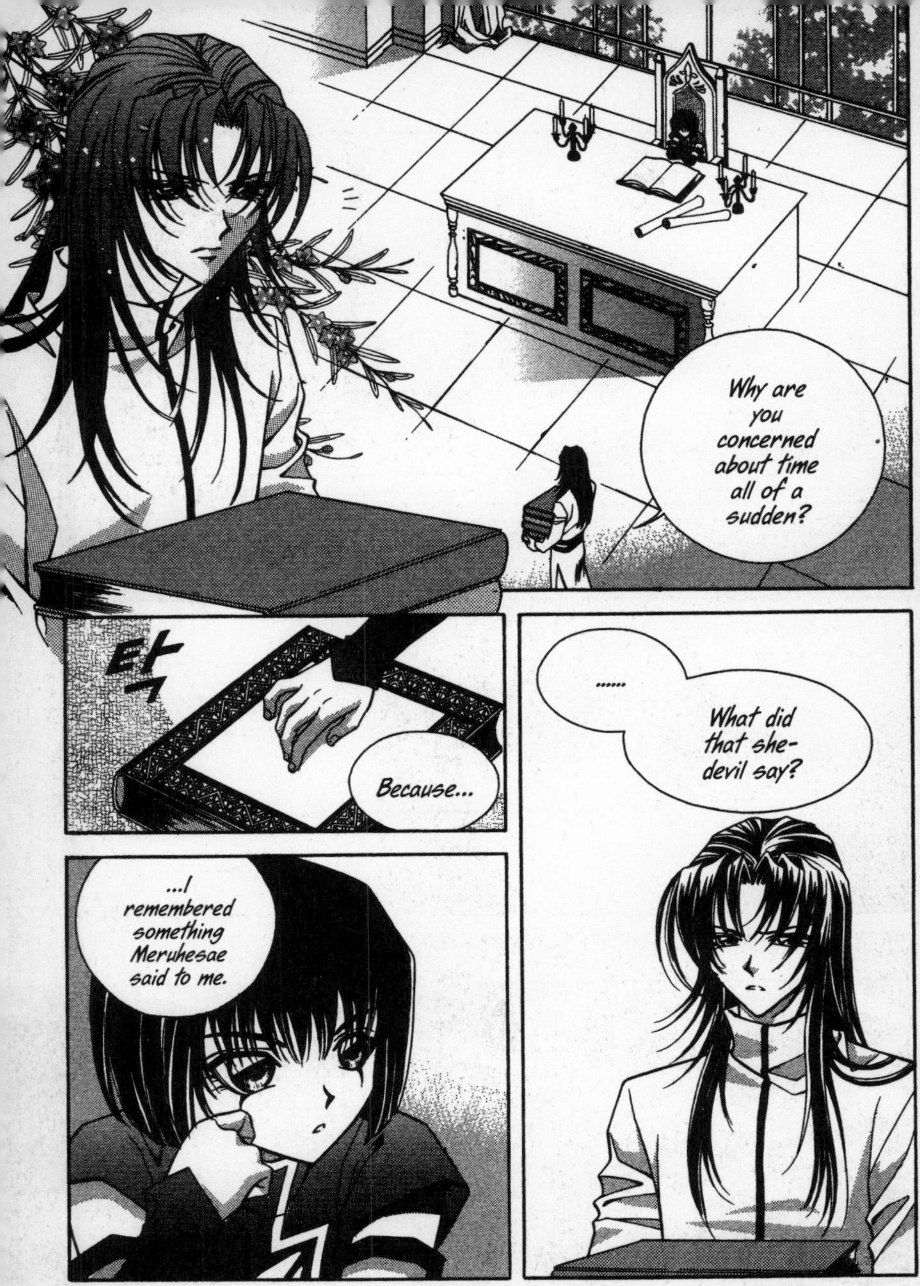
Why are you concerned about time all of a sudden?
Because...
...I remembered something Meruhesae said to me.
......
What did that she-devil say?

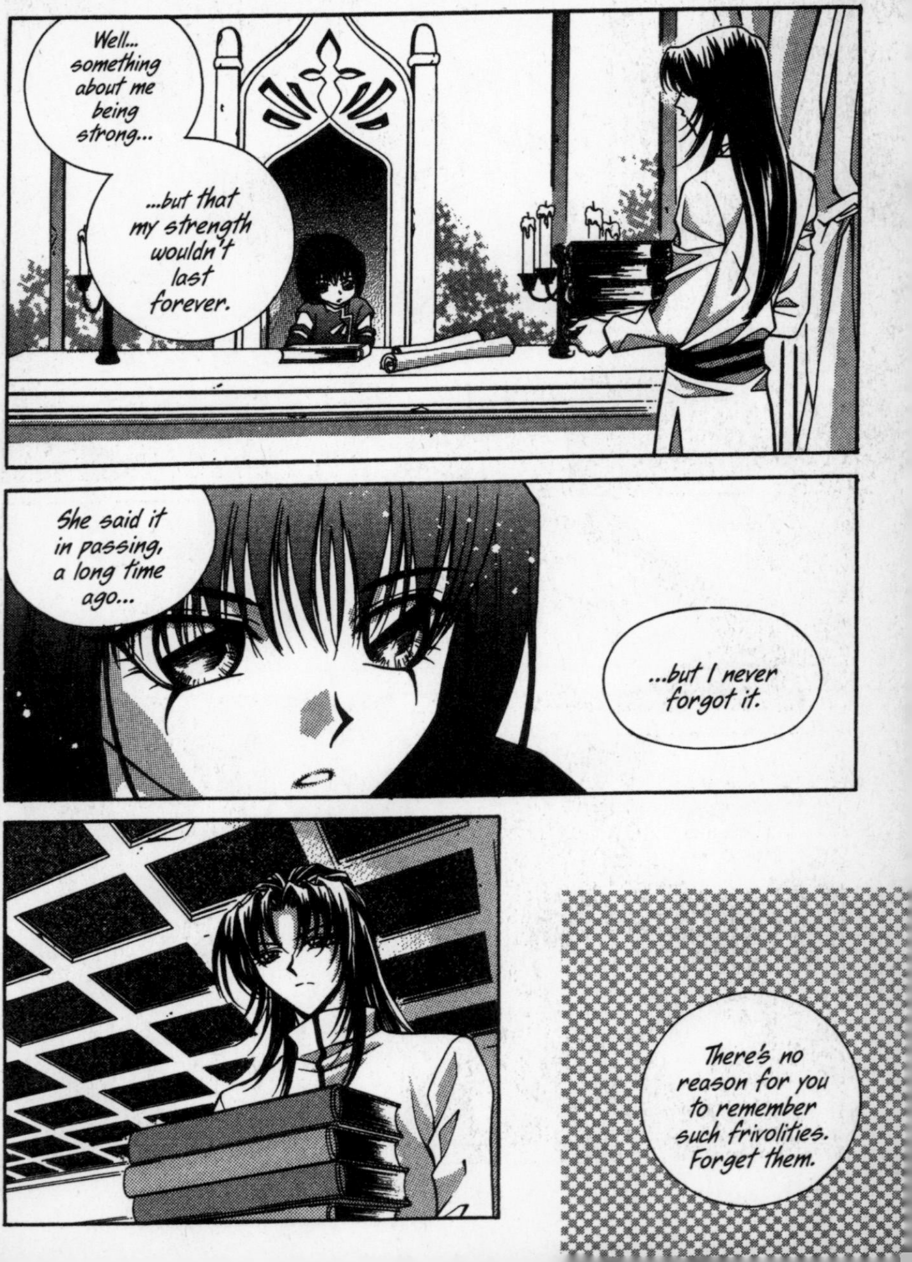
Well... something about me being strong...
...but that my strength wouldn't last forever.
She said it in passing, a long time ago...
...but I never forgot it.
There's no reason for you to remember such frivolities. Forget them.

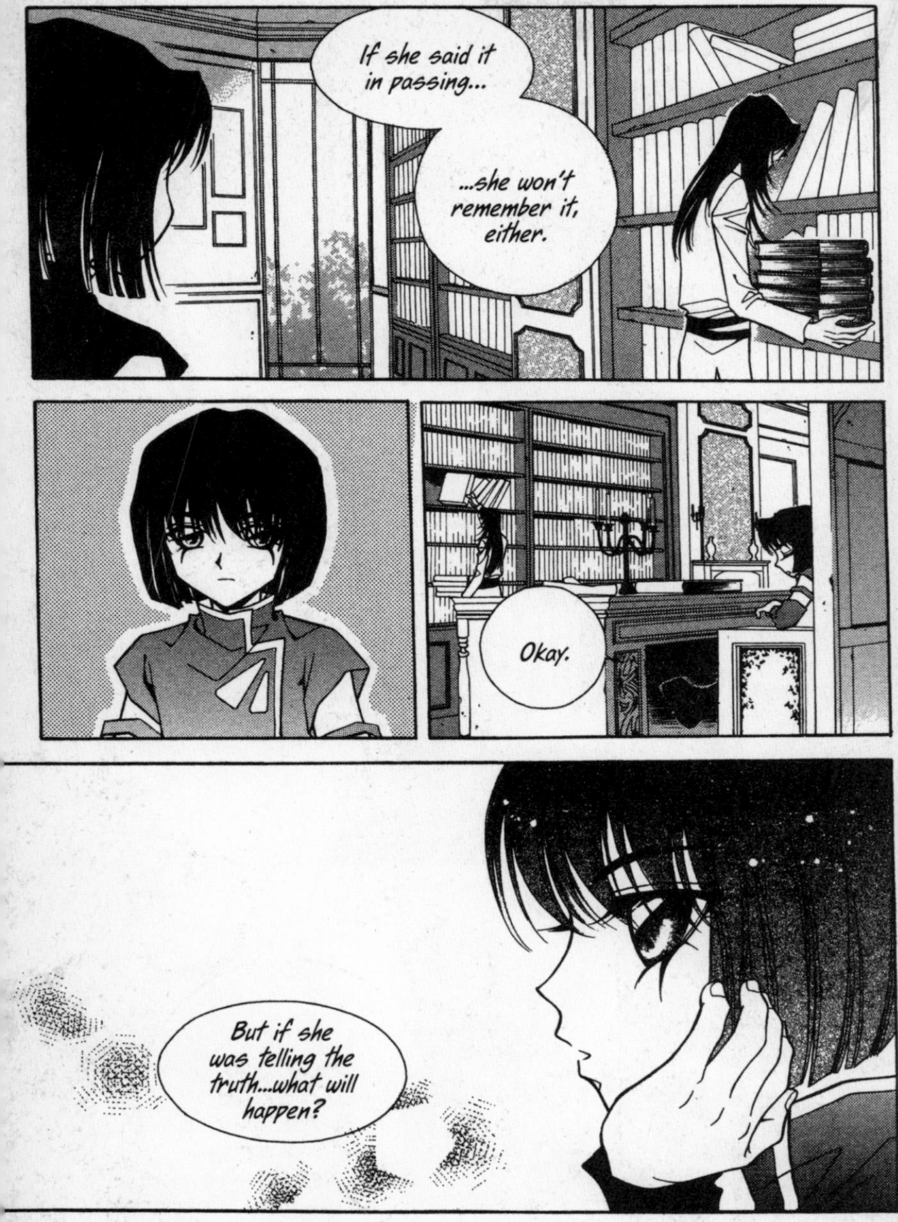
If she said it in passing...
...she won't remember it, either.
Okay.
But if she was telling the truth...what will happen?

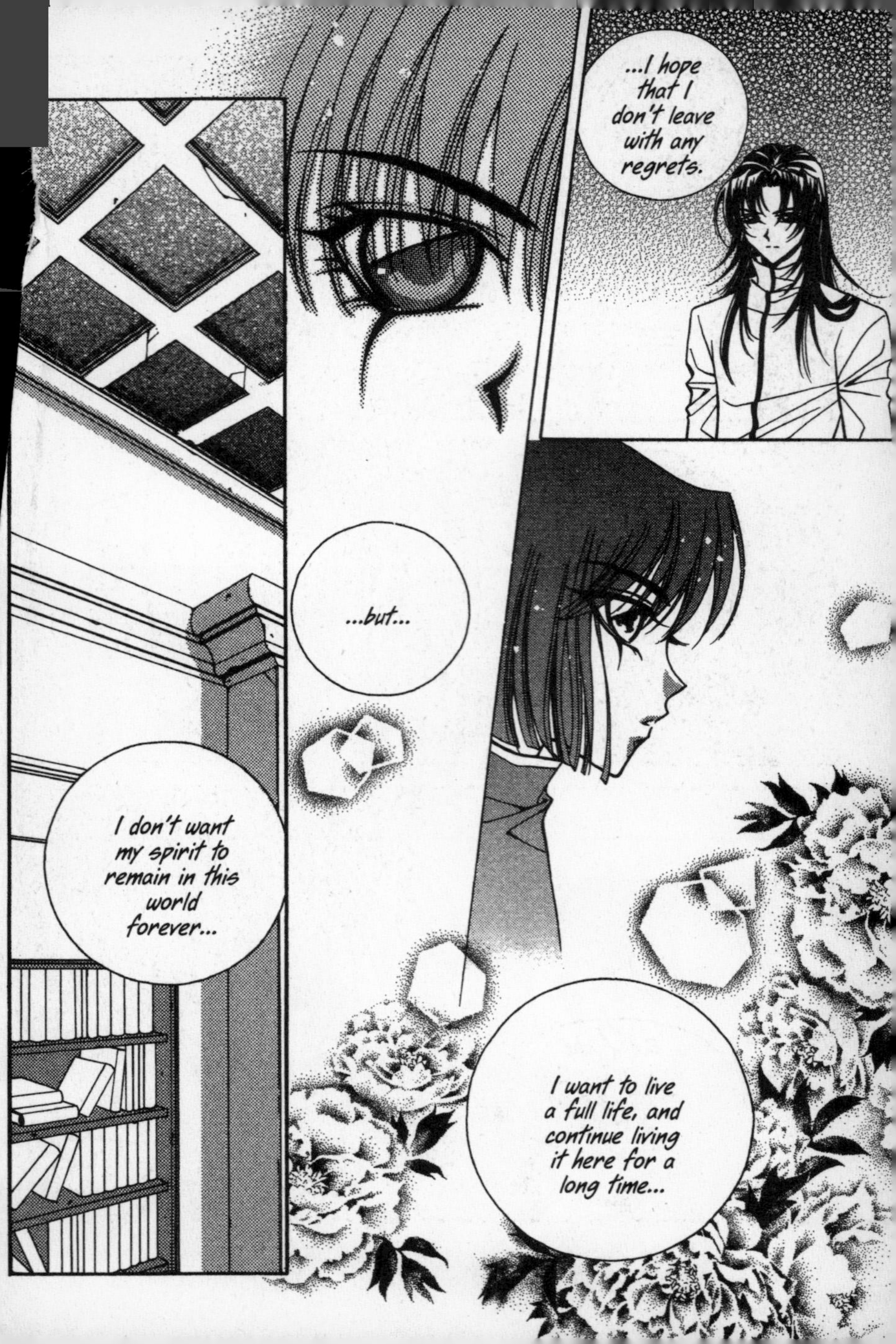
I don't want my spirit to remain in this world forever...
...but...
...I hope that I don't leave with any regrets.
I want to live a full life, and continue living it here for a long time...

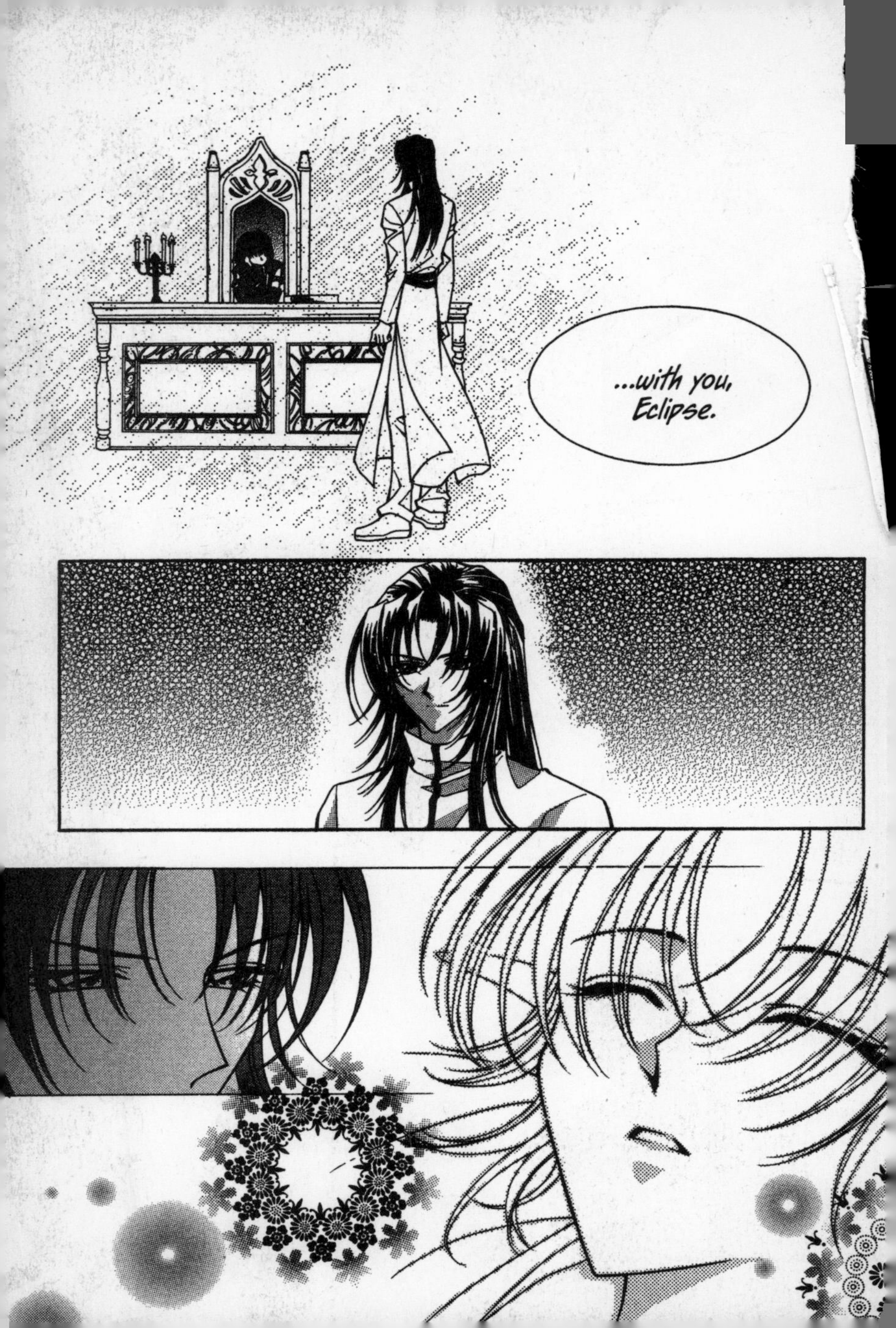
...with you, Eclipse.

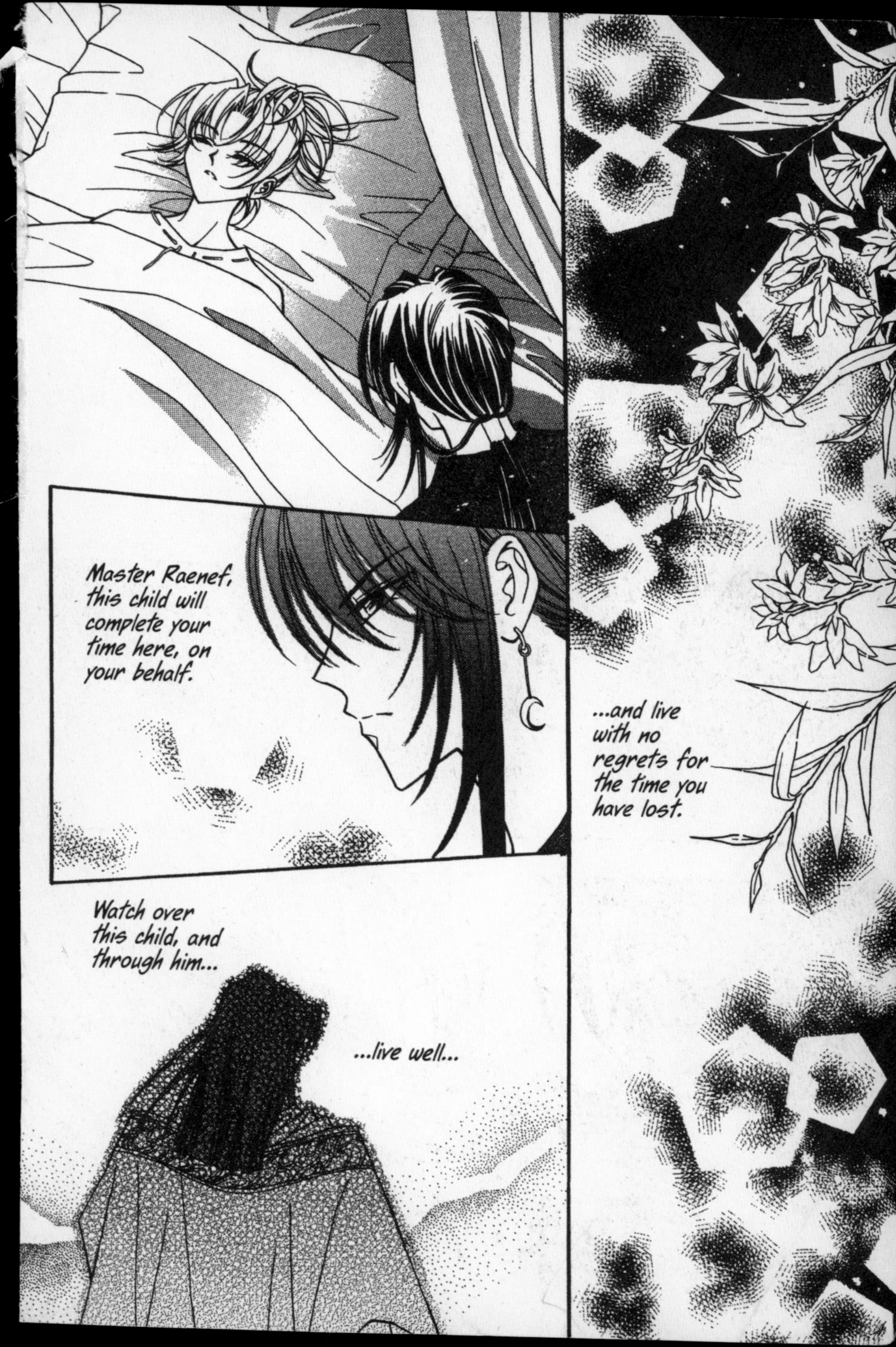
Master Raenef, this child will complete your time here, on your behalf.
Watch over this child, and through him...
...live well...
...and live with no regrets for the time you have lost.

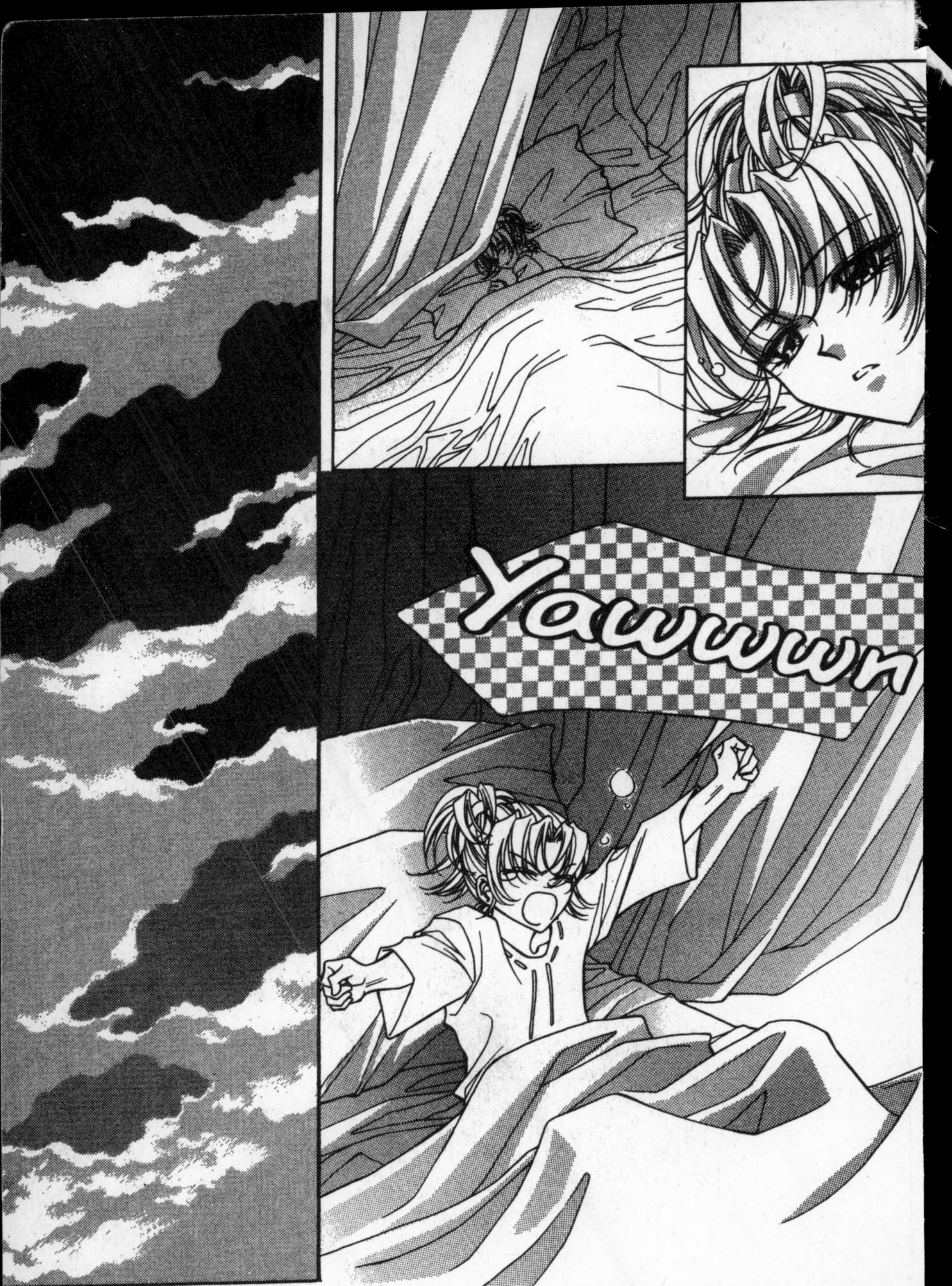
Yawwwn

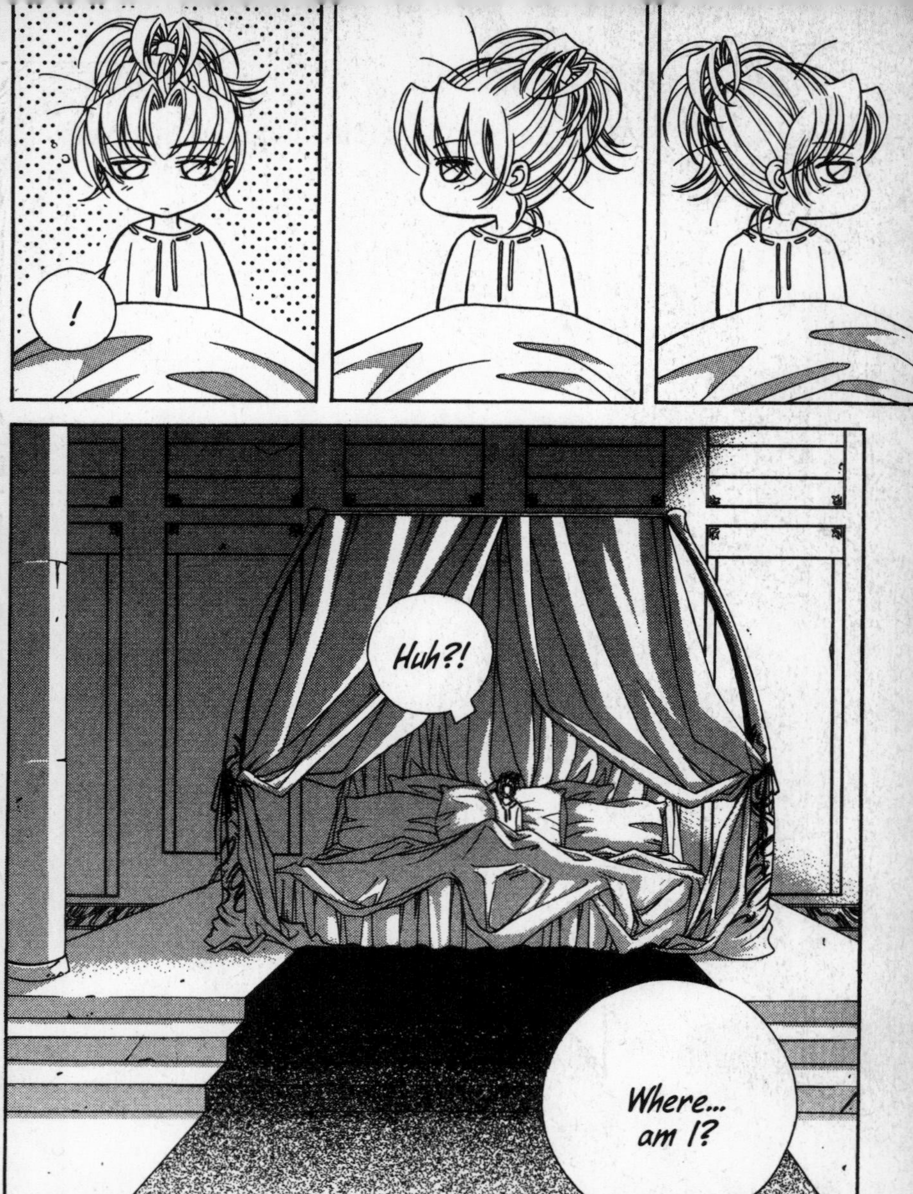
!
Huh?!
Where... am I?

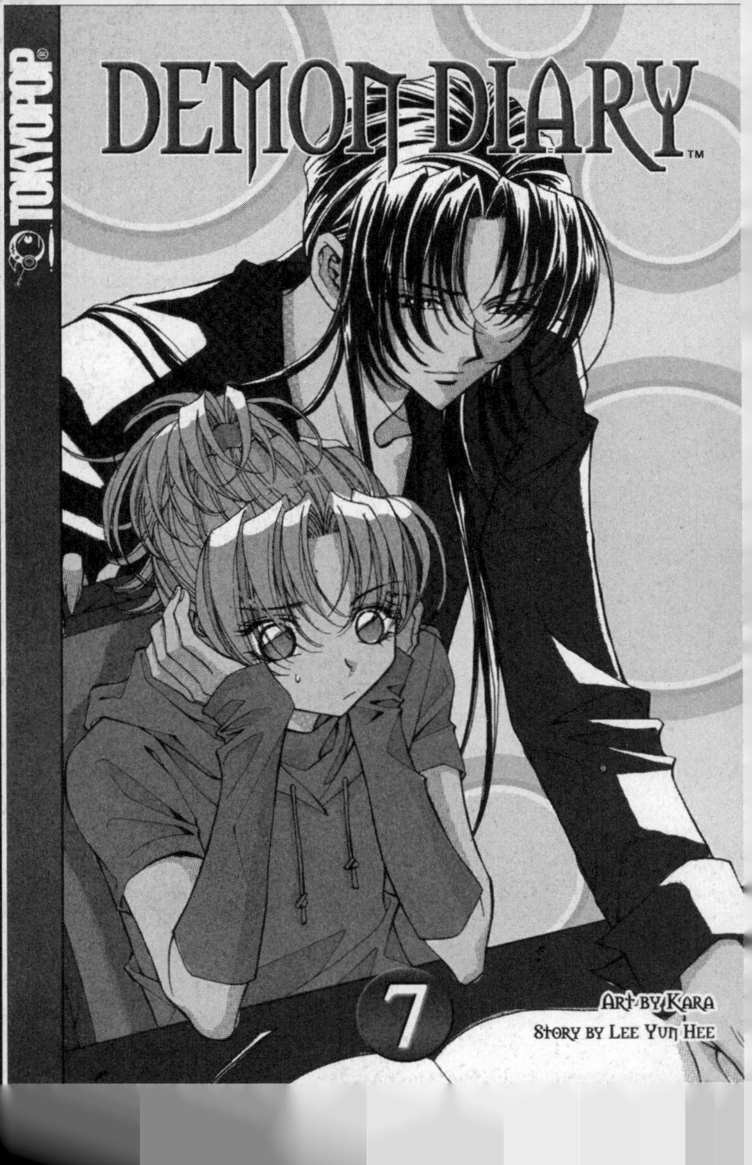
TOKYOPOP
DEMON DIARY™
7
Art by Kara
Story by Lee Yun Hee

PREVIEW FOR VOLUME 7

All Bad Things Must Come To An End...

As a Demon Lord-in-training, young Raenef has had many incredible experiences. He's fought knights, clerics, demon lords, and even his own evil self. He's made friends, cast spells, and developed a deep emotional bond with his tutor/servant Eclipse. Despite his ditzy nature, Raenef somehow managed to learn, mature, and change a great deal. Or did he?

In this, the final volume, Raenef finds himself back on the street with holes in his memory, his wallet, and his heart. Could this really be the final fate of the world's most lovable Demon Lord?!

DEMON DIARY

ALSO AVAILABLE FROM  TOKYOPOP®

For more information visit www.TOKYOPOP.com

01.09.04T

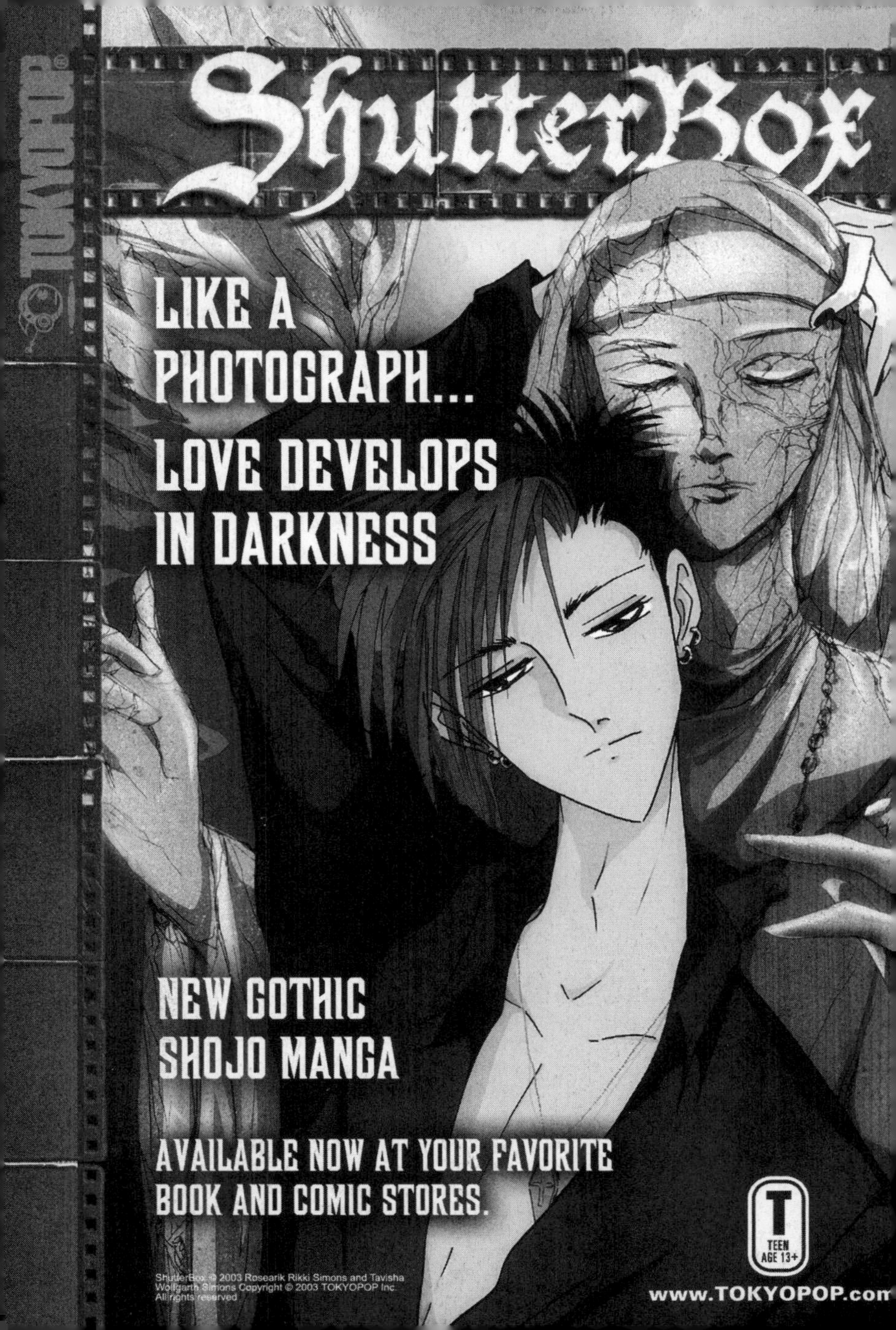

ShutterBox

LIKE A
PHOTOGRAPH...
LOVE DEVELOPS
IN DARKNESS

NEW GOTHIC
SHOJO MANGA

AVAILABLE NOW AT YOUR FAVORITE
BOOK AND COMIC STORES.

www.TOKYOPOP.com

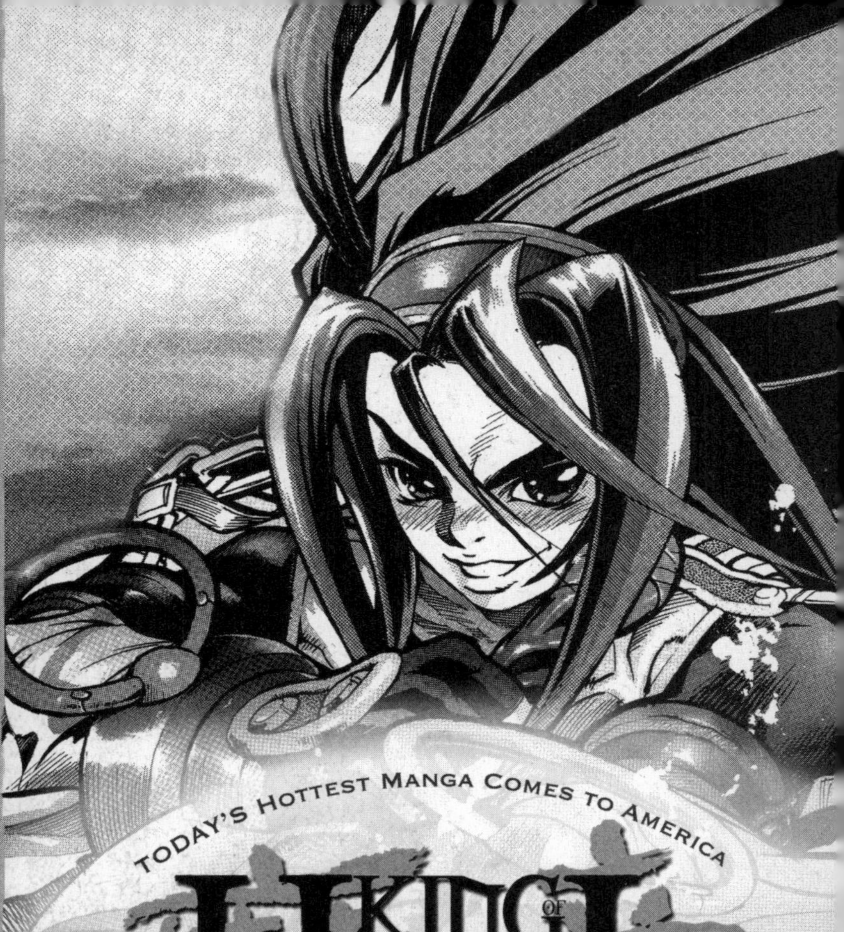

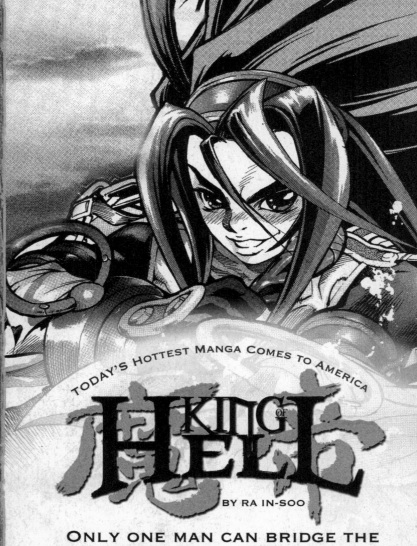

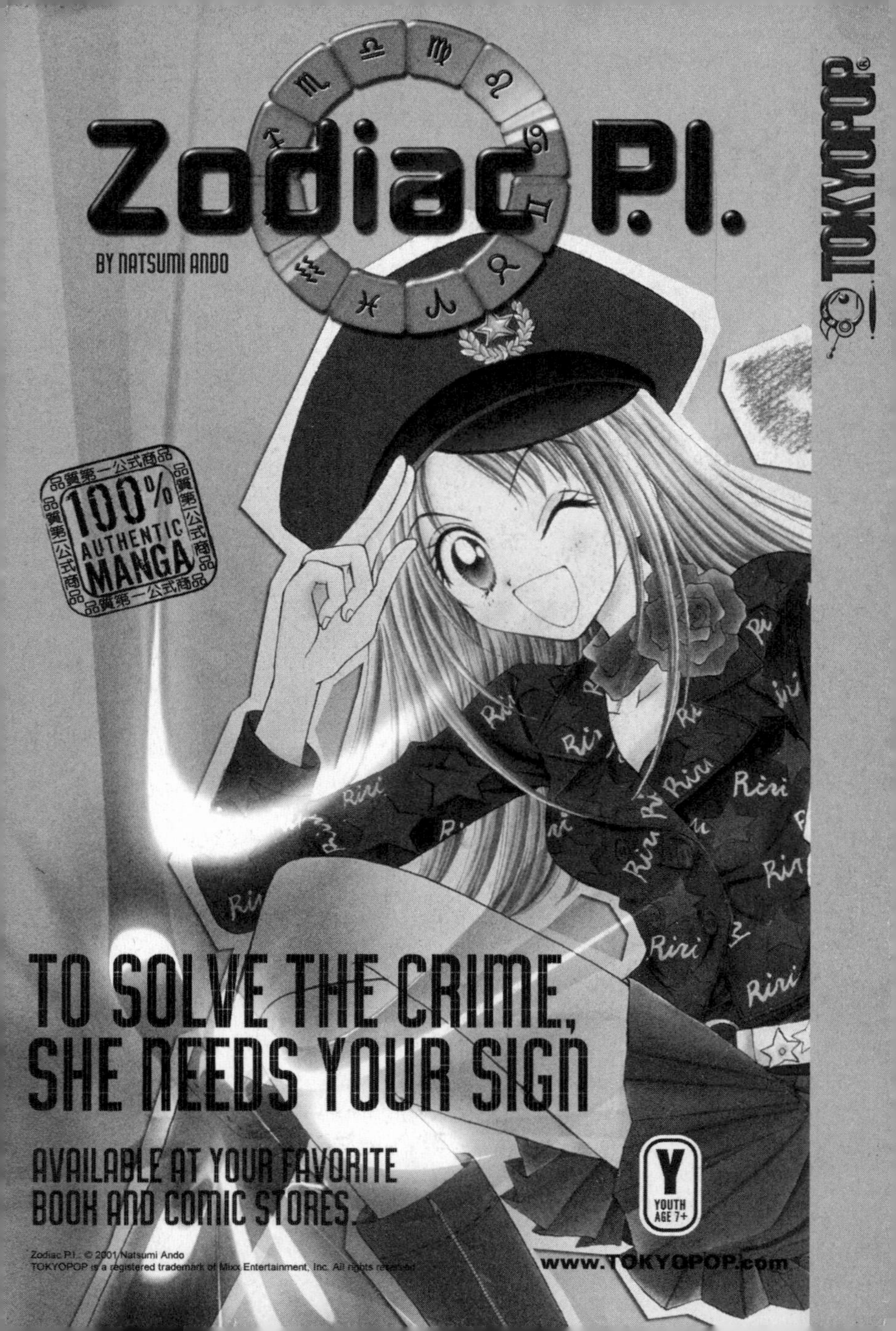

Zodiac P.I.
BY NATSUMI ANDO
TOKYOPOP
品質第一公式商品
100% AUTHENTIC MANGA
TO SOLVE THE CRIME, SHE NEEDS YOUR SIGN
AVAILABLE AT YOUR FAVORITE BOOK AND COMIC STORES.
Y YOUTH AGE 7+
Zodiac P.I. © 2001 Natsumi Ando
TOKYOPOP is a registered trademark of Mixx Entertainment, Inc. All rights reserved.
www.TOKYOPOP.com

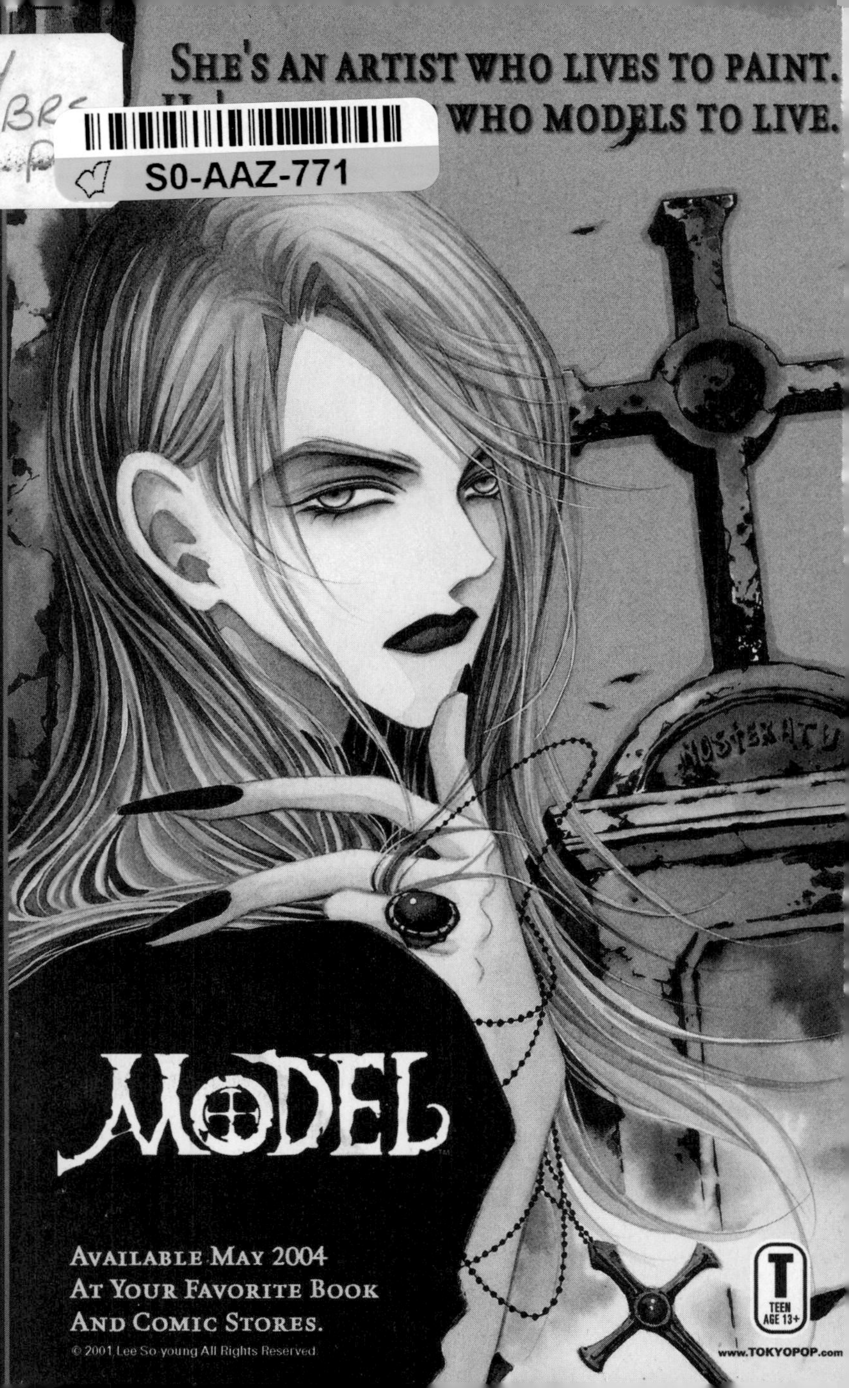

SHE'S AN ARTIST WHO LIVES TO PAINT.
WHO MODELS TO LIVE.
MODEL
AVAILABLE MAY 2004
AT YOUR FAVORITE BOOK
AND COMIC STORES.
© 2001 Lee So young All Rights Reserved.
TEEN AGE 13+
www.TOKYOPOP.com